MATHEMATICS FOR ELEMENTARY TEACHERS

MATHEMATICS FOR ELEMENTARY TEACHERS

ALICE J. KELLY and DAVID E. LOGOTHETTI

University of Santa Clara

WADSWORTH PUBLISHING COMPANY, INC.

Belmont, California

DESIGNER: Dare Porter

MATHEMATICS EDITOR: Don Dellen

COPY EDITOR: Diane Kravif

PRODUCTION EDITOR: Joanne Cuthbertson

TECHNICAL ILLUSTRATOR: Carleton Brown

CARTOONIST: Dave Logothetti

ISBN-0-534-00397-4

L. C. Cat. Card No. 75-11452

Printed in the United States of America

1 2 3 4 5 6 7 8 9 10—80 79 78 77 76

CONTENTS

CHAPTER   4   INTEGERS   167

PREFACE

THE TEXTBOOK
PROBLEM

When a textbook sales representative enters our of-
fices, already heaped with hundreds of sample texts,
we peer out from the stacks and ask, "What's different
about *your* company's book?" It usually develops that
there's "functional use of a second color," an "expanded set of exercises," and, depending on the latest
fad, either "complete rigor" or "an intuitive approach"
throughout. In other words, it's pretty much the same
as those already on our desks.

In the case of our book, the sales pitch is somewhat
different:

1. There's a consistent, corny sense of humor
throughout, often illustrated with cartoons. This
humor arises from our joy in doing mathematics, rather
than as a sort of sugar coating around a bitter pill.

2. The objectives of the book are specifically
noted, so neither student nor instructor will have to
guess at what's really going on. Objectives marked
with an asterisk are ones that we feel are less crucial
and might be omitted.

3. More than average attention is devoted to problem
solving in general and pattern recognition in particular.

4. The chapter on informal geometry is longer than
in most books, both to *introduce* geometric terms and to
use them in interesting problems.

5. Each chapter begins with a novel, interest-
arousing problem.

6. Each chapter ends with a list of important words
and concepts that are the keys to that chapter and a
list of the chapter's objectives, which may be used by
the student as a self-test.

Our book is oriented not so much to CUPM, SMSG,
UNICSM, UIAP, etc., as it is to the *Mathematics Frame-
work for California Public Schools* (the second "Strands
Report"*) and the textbooks currently adopted in elementary schools. Whether or not we agree with the
various states' Departments of Education, we feel that
we are best serving our students, the future teachers,
by preparing them for the present "party line." Hence
our selection of topics does not vary from the standard
list in such a text as much as we might like.

---

*The "Strands Report" is the report of the Advisory Committee on Mathe-
matics to the California State Curriculum Commission specifying what the
content in elementary school mathematics (K-8) should be. The members
of the committee were university mathematics professors, school district
supervisors, specialists in mathematics, and a representative of the
California State Department of Education.

All of the exercises are based either directly on the objectives or on manipulative skills auxiliary to these objectives (except those put in as jokes). Some of the exercises are sequential and build up to a discovery of one sort or another, with some of these discoveries involving introduction of ideas not found in the exposition. Thus it's a good idea to read the exercises carefully, as well as the main body of the text. Answers for all exercises are given in the back of the book.

We close the preface with a few words of thanks. We thank our Math 2 students at the University of Santa Clara for their warm responses to our course. We are also grateful to our department chairman, Gerald Alexanderson; our editor, Don Dellen; and an appreciated reviewer, James Schultz, for their encouragement. Finally, we must acknowledge the constant, well-intentioned prodding of our dear spouses, without whose encouragement we may not have sat down to write.

Alice Kelly

Dave Logothetti

The following broad chapter outline might be helpful in using this text and in selecting and combining topics for classroom use.

Chapter 1 is about sets and establishes terminology used in the rest of the book. Although it mostly consists of routine definitions, it does go into the question of how we can use sets and Venn diagrams to broaden our problem-solving powers. Students using the preliminary version of the text have generally been pleased with this approach, and we recommend concentration on The Big Problem (using Venn diagrams to count elements in sets systematically) and only a light treatment of the rest of the chapter.

Chapter 2, the longest, is about cardinal numbers and their numerals. (Most books separate these numbers and their numerals into two chapters.) In it we try to develop only enough theory so that teachers will see the rationale behind the exercises in the state-adopted elementary school textbooks. The topics of Chapter 2 are definition of cardinal numbers, numeration systems, operations with cardinals (including several alternative algorithms with which we may individualize instruction for those elementary school students who are having trouble or intrigue those students who are fast and bored); cardinals on the number line and their two-dimensional analogue, lattice points in the plane, factors and prime, order relations, Diophantine equations, and modular ("Clock") arithmetic.

Chapter 3 goes into the nonnegative rational, or "fractional," numbers. Again we treat (in less detail than in Chapter 2) definition of these numbers and their operations, as well as the idea of a group and why it pops up so frequently in mathematics. We also discuss decimals and percent. A special feature of this chapter is a grating method for adding fractions, devised by Logothetti (in *Bulletin of the California Mathematics Council*.

Chapter 4 is about integers, treated as analogues of nonnegative rationals (in the group-theoretic sense). We discuss definitions and various interpretations of integers, operations, solutions of more Diophantine equations (if possible), the ideas of an integral domain, and divisors of zero. Absolute value of an integer is also included here.

Chapter 5 deals with the rational numbers, their definition, operations, field properties, linear equations and congruences with rational coefficients, graphing on the number line, and density in the number line.

In Chapter 6 we sketch out extensions of the field of rationals: algebraic numbers, transcendental numbers, the real numbers, and complex numbers. Most of our attention is on decimal expansion as a criterion for telling the rational from the irrational. We also touch upon completeness of the real numbers.

Chapter 7 is about relations and functions and their graphs. Chapters 7, 8, and 9 are essentially independent of Chapters 2 through 6 and therefore needn't be studied in numerical order. Relations and functions are defined (and their inverses, although we don't really see why they need to be studied in elementary school) in terms of ordered pairs, and are graphed. The slightly unusual greatest integer or ("postage stamp") function is discussed because it has such an interesting graph. Graphs of polynomial functions are noted to have only four basically different shapes.

Chapter 8 is devoted to statistics and probability. We try to emphasize the concepts rather than realism, and thus most of our examples and exercises deal with data consisting of a few small scores. We discuss grouped and ungrouped frequency distributions; histograms; frequency polygons; and mean, mode, median, and standard deviation, with emphasis on the meaning and interpretation of these terms. We also dip into probability, with simple experiments in dropping thumbtacks, drawing cards, flipping coins, etc. Our aim is to develop the basic idea of mathematical probability rather than go into detailed calculations of complicated events. We discuss odds, then the statistics and probability together in considering normal distributions. We close the chapter by discussing the Birth Date Problem and the notion of computing probabilities by subtracting from 1.

Chapter 9 is perhaps the least standard chapter in the book. It deals with "intuitive" geometry and is a departure from so much arithmetic. (We recommend that it be taught in tandem with the chapters on number systems, to provide variety.) The approach to Chapter 9 is not just to name and define certain geometric figures, but to use these definitions in solving problems. Thus there is application to measurement, with most of the units metric rather than English (with an eye on imminent metrization in the U.S.). There is also a lot of work on gathering empirical data and recognizing patterns. These approaches are used with points, lines, and planes; rectangles, triangles, and other polygons; boxes and other polyhedra; and cylinders, cones, and spheres. Questions revolve around not only measure but also combinatorial topology (e.g., Euler's formula for convex polyhedra).

Some of the material is developed in the exercises so a careful selection can extend the section topics. Other sections rely almost entirely on exercises to develop the topics, giving the student a chance at a little discovery and semi-original thought. The answers to all discovery-type exercises are included.

Those of you who are not interested in explicitly using the objectives of this book for testing and grading should skip this section. However, even if you do not use the objectives as in the following description your students can use the list of objectives and words to know at the end of each chapter as a self test. The main content of the chapter is very briefly summarized on these two pages.

Now we will indicate how we ran our courses based on these objectives.

First of all, most of the objectives were made explicit, so that both instructor and student knew precisely what they were aiming for. Consider Objective 38, to solve given linear Diophantine equations for cardinal number solutions. This tells what the student (not the instructor) is supposed to be able to do at the end of the course. But there are other considerations: Open or closed book test? All given equations or only one? Unlimited time? We were interested not only in the task, but also the conditions under which it was done and the standards to be met in doing it. These conditions and standards will vary from instructor to instructor, and that's the reason we have listed only the tasks in our objectives in this book. The version of Objective 38 that we used in class was as follows: "Given five linear Diophantine equations, to solve, if possible, at least four for cardinal number solutions on a standard, closed book test in approximately 25 minutes. (Standard, closed test conditions were understood for all objectives unless otherwise stated.) As for standards, except with definitions we didn't demand perfection, but we did want students to show their stuff on more than one equation, and this with some expedition (i.e., in five minutes per equation). By stating a rough time limit, the instructor can inform the students as to "how cold" they must know the material; the shorter the time, the colder they must know it.

The students were then tested on these objectives and their final grades were determined by attainment of the objectives. There are all sorts of schemes for doing this, but we used those that emphasized what the student learned, not their speed of learning it. Thus, we gave students more than one chance to show what they knew. We accomplished this by giving weekly quizzes on the objectives, giving either total or no credit for each objective on the quiz (total credit for 4 out of 5 on Objective 38, for example, no credit for only 3 out of 5). Students who attained an objective did not have to try again for that objective until the final examination. Students who missed an objective could try for it again on a later quiz, receiving full credit whenever it was attained. Thus, on each quiz different students were trying for those objectives they had not already attained. At the end of the term, we graded as follows:

    50% - 64% of all objectives: D
    65% - 79% of all objectives: C
    80% - 89% of all objectives: potential B
    90% - 100% of all objectives: potential A

Potential Bs and As could be converted to actual Bs and As on the final examination. On our final exam, in addition to giving students a last try at unattained objectives, we chose ten starred objectives from the whole course. To show they had not forgotten all of the objectives after attaining them, students had to get nine or ten of these starred objectives to clinch an A, eight out of ten to clinch a B.

We found that with an objective based system, we were able to work together with the students more efficiently, and the students were more relaxed and able to concentrate on learning rather than surviving.

CHAPTER 1

SETS

A band of French pigs was sitting in a sidewalk cafe
one day, consuming petit fours and counting money. All
the while, a clumsy agent of the Big Bad Wolf, disguised as the Maitre D, spied on the pigs, spilling
Vichy water on several of them in his attempts. After
taking down data, the agent scampered back to his boss,
yelling "Here it is, B. B., the latest report on those
low-down pigs!" The report ran as follows:

Males	24
Damp pigs	14
Male money counters	12
Money counters	17
Damp money counters	9
Damp males	11
Damp males counting	7

"Dolt!" cried the wolf, "Imbecile! You've left out the
most important part: *How many doused sows were counting
their sous*?"

Inasmuch as the informant had not, unfortunately,
taken mathematics for elementary teachers, he couldn't
answer this question and so was eaten up by the petu-
lant wolf.

Challenge

Try to solve the Big Pig Problem, i.e., find out how
many doused sows are counting their sous. (Note:
You're not expected to be able to solve this exercise
yet. If you can, you're extra smart.)

The Big Pig Problem and similar problems are instances
in which ideas from set theory can provide a systematic
means of thinking out a solution. There are other reasons for studying sets—as a basis for concepts of
counting and as a unifying thread throughout the fabric
of mathematics, for example. In fact, these particular
reasons are the ones that are generally advanced as
justification for study of sets, but they don't always
strike students as convincing, perhaps because the students don't see any practicality in them. Perhaps the
most practical application of the topic of sets is as
an aid to sorting out our thoughts in an orderly way.
With this in mind, then, we start out on a brief review of set theory. *Many readers may want to skip this
review and proceed directly to page 14 and The Big Pig
Problem.*

● ●

Objective   1.   To explain and illustrate with *original* examples each
                    of the following terms: (a) "set,"   (b) "element."

● ●

Note: The objectives in this book are set for the students who use it. Thus, each objective is in the form of an infinitive, with the subject understood to be "you," the student. "Original" here means "other than what is presented here in the text or by your professor," so that you don't just parrot back phrases that may be meaningless to you. Also, "explain" means in terms of everyday language, without attempting a rigorous definition. There are two reasons for not emphasizing rigor: (a) so we can avoid getting bogged down in excessive mathematical hairsplitting, and (b) (more importantly) because we must accept some terms as theoretically, at least, undefined; in any logical structure it is necessary to start with some undefined terms because it is impossible to define *all* terms. Back in high school geometry, for example, the term "point" was taken as undefined, and D. Logothetti had the following conversation with a student: Student: Ha! I can define "point"! It's a geometrical figure with zero dimensions! D. L.: Ah, very good. Let's skip over the meanings of "geometrical," "figure," and "zero." I forgot what "dimension" means. . . . Student: That's easy—it's length. D. L.: Hm. I hadn't thought of that. But, excuse me, what's "length"? Student: Easy again: The distance between two points . . . (oops). Thus as you can see, our student had used "point" to define "point" and so was just running in circles. So for Objective 1 we will settle for informal comments, perhaps as follows:

Comments   1.   *A* set *is a collection, bunch, heap, class, conglomeration, etc. Thus, we might talk of the set of all students in this class, or the set of all chickens and cats, or a set consisting of a particular bunch of cats, or a set consisting of a cat, a mouse, and a fig. (Not all of the members of a set have to be the same sort of thing.)*

             2.   *An* element *is a member, unit, basic ingredient, etc. of a set. Thus a student is an element of a class; Puff the cat (of "Run, Puff, run!" fame) is an element of the set of all cats; Puff is also an element of the set consisting of a particular pig, a particular prune, and Puff.*

DEFINITIONS
AND
OPERATIONS

• •

Objective   2.   To define and illustrate with original examples each of the following expressions: (a) $\{a,b,c\}$,   (b) $\{x: x$ has a certain property$\}$,   (c) $a \in A$,   (d) $a \notin A$,   (e) U, (f) $\emptyset$ or $\{\ \}$,   (g) $A \subset B$,   (h) $A = B$,   (i) $A \cap B$,   (j) "A and B are disjoint,"   (k) $A \cup B$,   (l) $A \sim B$,   (m) $\sim A$,   (n) $A \otimes B$.

• •

Notice that in this objective it says "define" rather than "explain" as in Objective 1. By "define" we mean to give a rigorous, mathematically precise definition of the expression in terms of either previously admitted undefined words or previously officially defined terms.

Objective 2 is long and not typical of those to come. Since we intend only to review set theory, if you have difficulty with this objective we suggest you discuss it with your instructor.

Before we get too far into set theoretic definitions, a word about the *definition* of a term vs. *how it is read*. U, for example, is read "universe," but to say that U means "universe" is *not* a good definition, as it does not define U in terms of previously established concepts. Note carefully, then, in the following definitions both the definition of the term and how it is read.

═══

LIST OR
ROSTER
METHOD

───

Definition   "$\{a,b,c\}$" *means "the set consisting of elements a, b, and c and only those elements."*

This is the "list" or "roster" method of defining a set. All the elements in the set are listed and enclosed by braces. Only the elements listed are in the set.

───

Examples   1.   If a is you and b is Vincent's left hand and c is Professor Kelly's newest car, then $\{a,b,c\}$ is the set consisting precisely of you, the hand, and the car.

Note that $\{a,b,c\}$ can also be written $\{b,c,a\}$ or $\{c,b,a\}$, etc. The order is not important.

The roster method is often generalized to take the following form: $A = \{a,b,c, \ldots, r,s,t\}$. This set A is the set of all letters in our alphabet from the letter a to the letter t inclusive. The ellipses mean that the list is not complete and that all missing elements between the first three and the last three and of the same type as these specified elements are also in the set. The set ends with t; so m is in the set A, while u is not because u is not between c and r.

2. Let A be the set of classical Greek elements {earth, water, air, fire}. Then A is the set of the four elements named; cinder, neon, and mercury, for example, are *not* members of set A.

3. Let A be the set of all counting numbers which are multiples of 5; then $A = \{5,10,15,20,25, \ldots\}$. Here the ellipsis means "continue in this pattern forever." Is 105 an element of this set? Yes! What about 1068 and 1065?

4. Suppose $B = \{1,2,3, \ldots, 10,11,12\}$ is the set of all hours, in the sense of "on the hour," in the day. Thus 8 and 5 are in B but 2:30, 3:45, and 13:00 are not.

RULE METHOD

| Definition | "$\{x: x$ has a certain property$\}$" means "the set of all x such that x has a certain property." |

| Examples | 1. | $\{x: x$ is one of Professor Logothetti's sons$\}$ is the same set as {Vincent, Teddy, Jonathan}. |

2. $\{x: x$ is an even whole number less than 10$\}$ is the same set as $\{0,2,4,6,8\}$.
    This is called the "rule" method of defining a set. The elements in the set are all those objects that satisfy the rule, i.e., "x has a certain property."

3. Let $A = \{x: x$ is a son of President Richard Nixon or of President Lyndon Johnson$\}$. Then A has no elements, i.e., it is empty. (See the definition on p. 7.)

4. However, if $A = \{x: x$ is a daughter of President Lyndon Johnson$\}$, then A is the set {Lynda, Luci}.

5. Using the rule method, the set of all counting numbers that are multiples of 5 is written $\{x: x = 5n, n$ any counting number$\}$. (By "counting numbers" we mean those numbers that one counts with, i.e., $\{1,2,3,4,5,6,7,8,9, 10,11, \ldots\}$.)
    The standard notation for naming sets is to use capital letters, reserving small letters for elements of sets. We will abide by this convention.

Definition		*"a ∈ A" means "a is an element of set A." The expression "a ∈ A" is read "lowercase a is an element of (or 'is in') set A."*

Examples	1.	Let *A* be the set of all students currently studying mathematics for elementary teachers, and *a* be you; then *a ∈ A*.
	2.	Let *B* be the set of all mathematics books and *b* be this book; then *b ∈ B*.

Definition		*"a ∉ A" means "a is not an element of set A."*

Examples	1.	Let set *A* be the set of all green plants and *a* be a dog; then *a ∉ A*.
	2.	Or let *A* be the set of all United States Presidents and let *a* represent Goldilocks; then *a ∉ A*.
	3.	Let *X* be the set of all American citizens over the age of 65. Are you *∉ X*? Professor Logothetti *∉ X*. Jack Benny *∈ X*, but Raquel Welch *∉ X*. Is Princess Anne *∉ X*? What about Golda Meir?
	4.	Or if *Z* = {*x*: *x* is an American-made car}, then a Ford *∈ Z* and a Barracuda *∈ Z*, but a Volvo and a Mazda *∉ Z*. Is a Nader *∉ Z*?

NULL SET AND UNIVERSAL SET	The following two definitions are of interesting and important sets, the "everything" and "nothing" of the set world.

Definition		*"U" means "the set of all elements currently under discussion." U is called the "universe" or "universal set."*

Examples	1.	Maybe *U* = {*x*: *x* is a whole number} in one discussion of numbers.
	2.	*U* = {*x*: *x* is a weed} in another discussion.
	3.	If we wish to study green-eyed redheads, then we might decide to limit our universe to girls; thus our universal set *U* = {*x*: *x* is a green-eyed redheaded girl}.
	4.	If we wish to discuss Mickey, Donald, and Goofy, our universe could be all cartoon characters. Or, more restrictive, our universe could be all Walt Disney cartoon characters.

As you can see from the examples, the problem solver selects the universal set, choosing a broad universe or more restrictive one depending upon the problem or the extent to which the solver wishes to investigate it.

Definition	"∅" or "{ }" *means* "*the set with no elements.*" *This set is called the* "*empty set*" *or* "*null set.*"

Examples	1.	The set {x: x is a freshman and x has 48 toes} is an empty set.
	2.	The set {x: x is a 20-year-old United States president} is an empty set.
	3.	The set {x: x is a 30-month-old college freshman} is an empty set.
	4.	The set {x: $x^2 + 1 = 0$ and x is one of the following: ±1,±2,±3 . . .} has no elements.
	5.	The set of all 38-inch yards or 13-inch feet or 4-foot yards is also the null set.
	6.	Consider the set {∅}. Is this set the empty set? The answer is a loud clear emphatic *no*. This set has an element listed, and that element is the set ∅. Thus {∅} is not empty. ∅ = { } ≠ {∅}.

SUBSETS AND
SET EQUALITY

Definition	"$A \subset B$" *means* "*if* $a \in A$, *then* $a \in B$ *also*" *and is read* "A *is a subset of* B" *or* "*set* B *contains set* A." *In the latter case the symbols may be reversed:* $B \supset A$. *If* B *is not a subset of* A, *we write* $B \not\subset C$.

Examples	1.	Let A be {1,b,γ,?} and B be {1,#,b,*,γ,?}; then $A \subset B$.
	2.	Let A = {a,2,III} and B = {a,2,III}; then $A \subset B$ and $B \subset A$. Notice that this definition admits the possibility of A and B being identical.
	3.	Let A be the set of all United States presidents and B be the set {Truman, Eisenhower, Johnson}. Then $B \subset A$, or B is a subset of A.
	4.	If set B = {apple, grape, cherry}, then set C = {apple}, set D = {apple, grape}, and set E = {grape, cherry} are all subsets of B; i.e., $C \subset B$, $D \subset B$, and $E \subset B$. Note also that $C \subset D$. Is $D \subset E$? Consider the following sequence:

(a) $\{1,2\} \subset \{1,2,3,\dots\}$ (b) $\{1\} \subset \{1,2,3,\dots\}$
$\{1,2\} \subset \{1,2,3,\dots,8\}$ $\{1\} \subset \{1,2,3,\dots,8\}$
$\{1,2\} \subset \{1,2,3\}$ $\{1\} \subset \{1,2,3\}$
$\{1,2\} \subset \{1,2\}$ $\{1\} \subset \{1,2\}$
$\{1,2\} \not\subset \{1\}$ $\{1\} \subset \{1\}$
$\{1,2\} \not\subset \{2\}$. $\{1\} \not\subset \{2\}$.

(c) $\{\ \} \subset \{1,2,3,\dots\}$
$\{\ \} \subset \{1,2,3,\dots,8\}$
$\{\ \} \subset \{1,2,3\}$
$\{\ \} \subset \{1,2\}$
$\{\ \} \subset \{1\}$
$\{\ \} \subset \{2\}$
$\{\ \} \subset \{\ \}$.

That is, the fewer elements in set A, the more sets of which A is a subset. The null set is a subset of every set, and any set is a subset of the universal set.

Definition

"A = B" means "A $\subset$ B and B $\subset$ A," read "set A is equal to set B" or "A is identical to B."
  If we refer to the definition of subsets we see that A = B means every element in A is in B and every element in B is in A.

Examples

1. Let $A = \{x: x^2 - 1 = 0\}$ and let $B = \{1,-1\}$.

2. Or let $A = \{2,4,6,8, \dots\}$ and $B = \{x: x$ is an even counting number$\}$.

3. Now we can justify the earlier statement that the order in which elements are listed is unimportant. If $A = \{a,b,c\}$ and $B = \{b,a,c\}$, then $A = B$ since every element in A is also in B and every element in B is in A.

Exercises

1. Give at least three *original* examples of each of the concepts defined so far.

2. (a) If $A = \{a,b,c\}$, then in how many different ways can A be written? (Some of the ways are $\{a,c,b\}$, $\{b,a,c\}$, $\{b,c,a\}$. How many ways are there?) Note: $\{a,b,c,a\}$ is the same as $\{a,b,c\}$.

(b) If $A = \{t,i,g,s\}$, then in how many different ways can A be written?

(c) If $A = \{a_1,a_2,a_3,a_4,a_5\}$, then in how many different ways can A be written?

(d) If $A = \{a_1,a_2,a_3, \dots, a_n\}$, then in how many different ways can A be written?

3. Rewrite each of the following in the roster notation, when $U = \{x: x$ is a whole number$\} = \{0,1,2,3, \dots\}$.

(a) $\{x: x$ is a multiple of $3\}$,

(b) $\{x: x$ is a positive multiple of $3\}$,

(c) $\{x: x$ has a remainder of 2 upon division by $5\}$,

(d) $\{x: x$ is one of your three favorite professors$\}$,

(e) $\{x: x^2 + 2x = 8\}$.

4. Rewrite each of the following sets using the rule method.

(a) $\{2,4,6,8,10\}$,

(b) $\{2,4,6,8,10, \ . \ . \ .\}$,

(c) $\{2,4,6, \ . \ . \ . \ , \ 10\}$,

(d) $\{2,4,8,16,32, \ . \ . \ .\}$,

(e) $\{7,14,21,28, \ . \ . \ .\}$,

(f) $\{0,\pm7,\pm14,\pm21, \ . \ . \ .\}$,

(g) $\{$Washington, Adams, Jefferson, . . . , Kennedy, Johnson, Nixon, Ford$\}$,

(h) $\{$puppy, kitten, calf, lamb, fawn, platypuslet, . . .$\}$.

5. (a) If $A = \{a\}$, list all subsets of set A. (Set A is an example of a type of set called a *singleton set* —it has only one element.) How many subsets does A have?

(b) If $A = \{a,b\}$, list all subsets of set A. How many are there?

(c) If $A = \{a,b,c\}$, list all subsets of set A. How many are there?

(d) If $A = \{a,b,c,d\}$, list all subsets of set A. How many are there?

(e) If set $A = \{a_1,a_2,a_3, \ . \ . \ . \ , \ a_n\}$, how many subsets of A are there?

(The set of all subsets of a set A is called the *power set* of A.)

INTERSECTION, DISJOINTNESS, AND UNION

Now we continue on with our set theoretic definitions and examples. We remind you again that this material should be just a review. If you are finding it difficult, consult your instructor.

Definition

"$A \cap B$" means "$\{x: x \in A$ and $x \in B\}$." The expression "$A \cap B$" is read "set A intersected with set B" or simply "A intersect B" or "the intersection of A with B."

The set $A \cap B$ is defined to be the set of all elements in both sets A and B, that is, all elements common to both A and B.

1. Let $A = \{p,q,r,s\}$ and $B = \{p,i,g,s\}$. Then $A \cap B = \{p,s\}$.

2. Let $A = \{x\colon x$ is a four-legged animal$\}$ and $B = \{x\colon x$ is an animal which barks$\}$. Then $A \cap B = \{x\colon x$ is a four-legged animal which barks$\}$.

3. Let $A = \{m,a,n\}$ and $B = \{w,o,m,a,n\}$. Then $A \cap B = A$. This illustrates a general relation, i.e., if $A \subset B$, then $A \cap B = A$.

4. Let $A = \{x\colon x^2 + 1 = 0, x$ a counting number$\}$ and let $B = \{x\colon x^2 - 4 = 0, x$ a counting number$\}$. Then $A \cap B = \emptyset$. Why?

    Well, here $A = \emptyset$. Do we have another general principle? No, just a special case of the general principle in Example 3: If $A = \emptyset$ or $B = \emptyset$, then $A \cap B = \emptyset$. Is the reverse true?

Definition

"A and B are _disjoint_" means "$A \cap B = \emptyset$."

The answer to the last question in Example 4 is given in Example 1 immediately below:

Examples

1. Let $A = \{m,i,n,o,r\}$ and $B = \{a,d,u,l,t\}$. Then $A \cap B = \emptyset$ but neither A nor B is the null set.

2. Let $A = \{x\colon x^2 - 1 = 0\}$ and $B = \{x\colon x^2 = 0\}$. Then again, $A \cap B = \emptyset$.

3. Let $A = \{$apple, pear, cherry$\}$ and $B = \{$Delicious, Bartlett, Bing$\}$. Then again, $A \cap B = \emptyset$.

We saw in Example 4 of the definition of $A \cap B$ that $A \cap \emptyset = \emptyset$. What general statement can we make from this bit of information? Yes, the null set is disjoint from any other set. Even itself? Yes again.

Definition

"$A \cup B$" means "$\{x\colon x \in A$ or $x \in B\}$," read "_A union B_," or "_the union of A and B._"

Notice that word "or" (in contrast to the "and" in the definition of $A \cap B$); it means here either in A or in B or in both. We perform the operation of set union often in everyday life.

Examples

1. When Grades 7 and 8 join together in a classroom to view a movie, the people (students) watching the movie form a set which is the union of the two previous sets.

2. Let $A = \{x: x$ is an even counting number$\}$ and let $B = \{1,3,5,7, \ldots\}$. Then $A \cup B = \{1,2,3,4,5, \ldots\}$.

3. Let $C = \{x: x$ is an A student$\}$ and $D = \{x: x$ is a smart student$\}$. Then $C \cup D = \{x: x$ is either an A student or a smart student$\}$. Suppose John is an A student because he takes only very easy classes. Is John in $C \cup D$? Suppose Joe is smart but was sick fall quarter of his freshman year, flunked a final, and received only a B. Is Joe in $C \cup D$? The answer to both questions is yes.

4. Let $A = \{\#,*,@,+\}$ and $B = \{\#,*,@\}$. Then $A \cup B = A$. Do we have a general principle here? What?

COMPLEMENTATION

Definition

"$A \sim B$" means "$\{x: x \in A$ and $x \notin B\}$," read "$\underline{A \ not \ B}$," or "A minus B," or the "difference of A and B."

Examples

1. Let $A = \{x: x$ is a redhead studying this book$\}$ and $B = \{x: x$ is a boy studying this book$\}$. Then $A \sim B$ is the set of all redhead girls reading this book. On the other hand, $B \sim A$ is the set of all nonredheaded boys who are studying this book.

2. Or let $A = \{w,o,m,a,n\}$ and $B = \{m,a,n\}$. Then $A \sim B = \{w,o\}$ (no pun intended—you women's libbers!) and $B \sim A = \emptyset$. (Maybe, on second thought—all puns intended!)

3. Let $A = \{x: x$ is a house$\}$ and $B = \{x: x$ is a home$\}$. Then $A \sim B$ is the set of all houses which are not homes and $B \sim A$ is the set of all homes which are not houses.

4. Let $A = \{a,b,c,d,e\}$ and $B = \{b,d,f,g\}$. Then $A \sim B = \{a,c,e\}$ and $B \sim A = \{f,g\}$

This operation is one many students have trouble with. So we suggest you review again the definition and examples, especially Example 4. Note that $f \notin A \sim B$ since $f \notin A$, and that $e \notin B \sim A$ since $e \notin B$.

Definition

"$\sim A$" means "$U \sim A$."

Examples

1. If U is the set $\{1,2,3, \ldots\}$ of all counting numbers and A is the set $\{2,4,6, \ldots\}$ of all even counting numbers, then $\sim A$ is the set $\{1,3,5, \ldots\}$ of all odd counting numbers. Notice that $\sim A$ makes sense only if the universe U is specified. $\sim A$ is often called the *complement* of A or A *complement*.

2. If $U = \{x: x$ is a redheaded human$\}$ and A is the set of all redheaded children, then $\sim A$ is the set of all redheaded adults.

3. If $U = \{x: x$ is a letter in our alphabet$\}$ and $G = \{x: x$ is a consonant$\}$ then $\sim G = \{a,e,i,o,u\}$.

CARTESIAN PRODUCT AND ORDERED PAIRS	And finally:

Definition	*"A* $\otimes$ *B" means* "$\{(x,y): x \in A$ and $y \in B\}$," *read "A cross B" or "the Cartesian product of set A with set B."*

Examples

1. If $A = \{a,b\}$ and $B = \{1,2\}$, then $A \otimes B = \{(a,1), (a,2), (b,1), (b,2)\}$.

2. If A is $\{b,o,y\}$ and B is $\{g,i,r,l\}$, then $A \otimes B$ is $\{(b,g), (b,i), (b,r), (b,l), (o,g), \ldots , (y,l)\}$.
   Notice that $A \otimes B$ may be thought of as consisting of copies of B, each copy having each of B's elements preceded by some element of A. The elements in $A \otimes B$ are called *ordered pairs*, where $(x,y) = (u,v)$ means $x = u$ and $y = v$. The first element in the ordered pair must be from set A and the second element from set B. The name "ordered pair" is descriptive, since $(a,b) \neq (b,a)$, unless $a = b$; i.e., the order of the elements distinguishes the pair. (Not all pairs are ordered, e.g., $\{a,b\} = \{b,a\}$.)

3. Let $M = \{\#,?\}$ and $N = \{m,n,o\}$. Then $M \otimes N = \{(\#,m), (\#,n), (\#,o), (?,m), (?,n), (?,o)\}$ and $N \otimes M = \{(m,\#), (n,\#), (o,\#), (m,?), (n,?), (o,?)\}$.

Exercises

1. Give at least three original examples of each of the concepts defined above.

2. Guess (intelligently, please) simplifications if possible, for each of the following (give reasons for your guesses):

   (a) $A \cap U$, (b) $A \cup U$, (c) $A \sim U$, (d) $\sim U$, (e) $A \otimes U$, (f) $A \cap \emptyset$, (g) $A \cup \emptyset$, (h) $A \sim \emptyset$, (i) $\sim \emptyset$, (j) $A \otimes \emptyset$.

3. (a) If A has three elements and B has four elements, then $A \otimes B$ has how many elements? $B \otimes A$?

   (b) If A has 23 elements and B has five elements, then $A \otimes B$ has how many elements? $B \otimes A$?

   (c) If A has m elements and B has n elements, then $A \otimes B$ has how many? $B \otimes A$?

4. Let $A = \{2,4,6,8\}$, $B = \{1,2,3,4\}$, and $U = \{1,2,3,4,5,6,7,8,9,10\}$. Express each of the following sets using the roster method.

   (a) $A \cup B$, (b) $A \cap B$, (c) $A \sim B$, (d) $A \cap (\sim B)$, (e) $\sim (A \cap B)$, (f) $\sim A \cap \sim B$, (g) $\sim (A \cup B)$, (h) $\sim A \cup \sim B$, (i) $A \otimes B$, (j) $B \otimes A$.

5. Let $A = \{x: x \text{ is male}\}$, $B = \{x: x \text{ is a student}\}$, and $C = \{x: x \text{ is a beauty}\}$, where $U = \{x: x \text{ is an American}\}$. Find

   (a) $A \cup B$, (b) $(A \cap B) \cup C$, (c) $\sim (A \cup B)$, (d) $\sim A \cap \sim B$, (e) $\sim A \cup \sim B$, (f) $\sim (A \cap B)$, (g) $A \cap \sim C$, (h) $A \sim B$, (i) $C \sim B$, (j) What would Gertrude Stein's comment be upon $U \cap C$? (Answer: "A rose is a rose is a rose.")

VENN DIAGRAMS
Now, on to an interesting, and we hope challenging use of sets.

● ●

Objective 3. (a) To solve a given word problem like the Big Pig Problem. (b) To write an *original* word problem like the Big Pig Problem, including sufficient, noncontradictory information to solve it.

● ●

If you've already solved the problem at the beginning of the chapter, compare your solution with this one. If you haven't solved it, follow this solution closely to see how sets can help you think systematically.

To begin, we introduce the old idea of a *Venn diagram*, which exemplifies the old saying, "A picture is worth a thousand words."

One set A

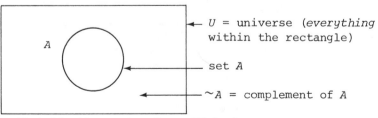

← U = universe (*everything* within the rectangle)

— set A

— $\sim A$ = complement of A

(Outside the rectangle: nothing)

Two sets A and B

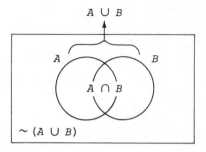

Three sets A, B, and C

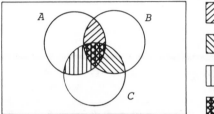

(Note: Set A is everything in the circle labeled A.

Set $A \cap B$ is everything in the ⬯-shaped region

(including that region labeled $A \cap B \cap C$).)

    The utility of such a diagram lies in any situation
in which a condition is either satisfied or is not satisfied, with no third possibility. (An illustration of
a situation for which this is *not* the case: Let A be
the set of all men who are shaved by Joe, the barber,
who shaves all those and only those who do not shave
themselves. If a = Joe, then is $a \in A$? Or is $a \notin A$?)

SOLUTION OF
THE BIG PIG
PROBLEM

Meanwhile back at the Big
Pig Problem, what condi-
tions are both pertinent
and either satisfied or
not satisfied? One is
that every pig in the universe U (the set of all
pigs under discussion) is
either in the set M of all
males or in $\sim M$ (set M is
shaded):

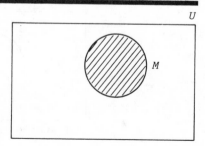

Another is that all pigs, both male and nonmale, are either in the set D of all damp pigs or in $\sim D$ (set D shaded):

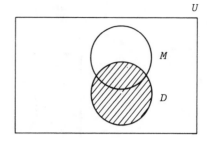

The third pertinent condition is that every pig is either in the set C of money counters or in $\sim C$ (set C shaded):

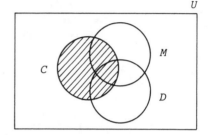

Now let us fill in the diagram with what information we know and hope that we can figure out what is wanted. Professor George Polya, one of the World's Leading Problem Solving Experts, suggests beginning with the piece of given information which involves the most conditions. In our problem, the first three pieces of information deal with only one condition: the next three deal with two conditions, and the last deals with all three conditions. So we will start with that and work backward through all of the given information. *Regardez*:

Step 1.

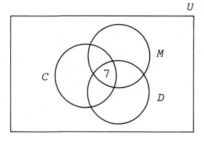

7 male damp pigs counting:

Step 2.

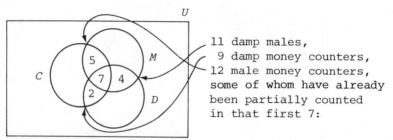

11 damp males,
 9 damp money counters,
12 male money counters,
some of whom have already
been partially counted
in that first 7:

(Note: We could stop at Step 2 if all we really wanted
was the number of doused sows counting their sous. But
in our unquenchable thirst for knowledge we press on!)

Step 3.

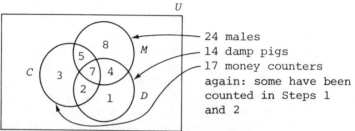

24 males
14 damp pigs
17 money counters
again: some have been
counted in Steps 1
and 2

(Another Note: We have no information whatever on the
number of pigs outside of $M \cup D \cup C$.)

   Finally, to get the answer we ask "What is the unknown?" Well, "doused" means "damp," "sows" means
"females = nonmales," and "counting their sous" means
"counting money." So we want the number of elements
in $(D \cap C) \sim M$, i.e., in D and simultaneously in C but
not in M. The answer is 2.

Some students reading this
text will murmur rebel-
liously, "Yeah, okay. But
what if I don't pick the
same categories as you do?
Suppose I think of the
setup as follows:

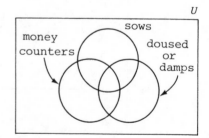

Then what?" Our answer is, "Don't worry and proceed as before":

Step 1.

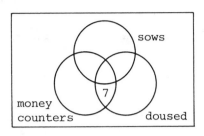

Step 2.

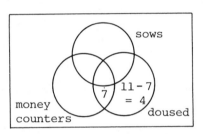

Step 3.

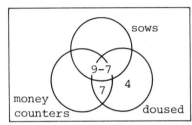

Step 4.

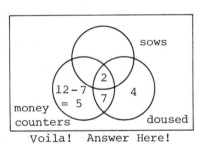

Voila! Answer Here!

Step 5.

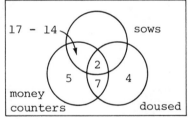

Step 6.

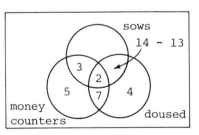

Step 7.

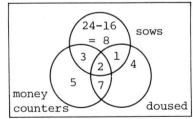

Exercise	Which piece of information was used in each step of this last solution?

THE BIG PIG
PROBLEM
REVISITED

(Cover the following Venn diagram, and try to figure this out on your own before peeking at the answer.)

Total number of pigs	51
Males	20
Money counters	29
Doused pigs	24
Sows counting sous	15
Doused sows	14
Doused pigs counting sous	11
Dry male money counters	8

The big question: How many dry sows are not counting money? (*Note:* "$n(U)$" means "the number of elements in U.")

Step 1.   Step 2.

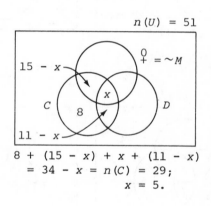

$n(U) = 51$

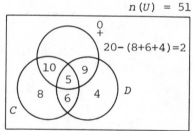

$n(U) = 51$

$8 + (15 - x) + x + (11 - x)$
$= 34 - x = n(C) = 29;$
$x = 5.$

So the terrifically big answer is 2. For completeness' sake, we note that $51 - (2 + 10 + 5 + 9 + 8 + 6 + 4)$ $= 7$, so

Step 3.

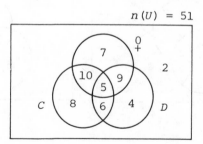

$n(U) = 51$

Exercises   1.   THE GREAT ROCK FESTIVAL PROBLEM.
A rock festival was attended by 50,000 young people,
24,000 boys, 20,000 barefooted, 27,000 listening to the
music. If there were 12,000 barefoot boys, 10,000
barefoot listeners, 11,000 boys listening, and 4000
barefoot boys listening, then how many barefoot girls
were there? How many shod boys not listening?

2.   THE GREAT ROCK FESTIVAL PROBLEM REVISITED.
Attendance: 60,000 total, 37,000 boys, 30,000 barefooted, 26,000 listeners, 16,000 barefoot boys, 7000
barefoot listeners, 17,000 boys listening, and 8000
barefoot girls not listening. How many shod girls not
listening?
   (Note: The setting of these word problems is probably not appropriate for elementary school kids. What
kind of a novel setting would be?)

3.   "DON'T PUT ALL OF YOUR BASQUES IN ONE EXIT"
Picture to yourself the end of a company picnic in the
West Pyrenees mountains. As the picnickers head out of
a valley through a narrow pass, 12 are still eating; 12
are kowtowing to their superiors, and 14 are females.
If seven females are eating, five females are kowtowing, four people are kowtowing while eating, four males
are neither eating nor kowtowing, and two females are
both eating and kowtowing, how many people are in the
pass?

4.   The Zooter Zoo of Zonkers received a shipment of ten
Gnus early one spring morning, bringing the Zoo gnu total to 22. The gnus were accompanied on their journey
by 32 assorted animals making their new home at Zooter
too. Their arrival at the zoo coincided with the dis-
closure of a particularly juicy piece of gossip involving Zooter's senior lion and his next-door neighbor, a
very comely tiger teen. By dawn the following day the
rumor had spread like lightening through the zoo, and
66 of the total Zooter population of 166 had heard it.
Even 20 of the previous day's arrivals had heard the
tale. In fact, only seven gnus were uninformed, two of
which were old-time Zooterites. So how many new gnus
knew? How many old gnus knew? How many old non-gnus
didn't know?

5.   For Big-Pig-type problems in general, how many pieces
of information do we need that involve only one condition? How many pieces that involve three conditions?
What else?

6.   Write at least three *original* word problems like the
Big Pig Problem, including sufficient, noncontradictory
information to solve them.

We saw in the Big Pig and related problems that Venn diagrams can serve as visual aids to systematic thinking. They also serve as concise descriptions of the various operations with sets defined in Objective 2. Dwell upon the following diagrams:

1.

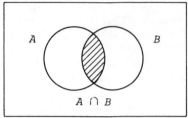

$A \cap B$

Everything in A and B

2.

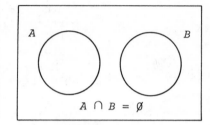

$A \cap B = \emptyset$

3.

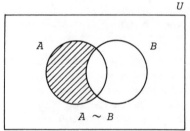

$A \sim B$

Everything in A which is not in B

4.

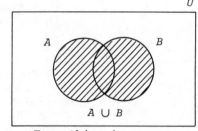

$A \cup B$

Everything in A or B

5.

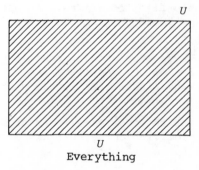

U

Everything

6.

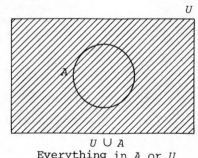

$U \cup A$

Everything in A or U

7.

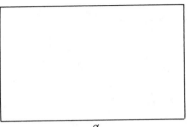

Ø

Nothing

8.

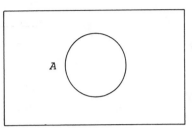

Ø ∩ A = Ø

Everything in Ø and in A
(everything in Ø which is
also in A)

9.

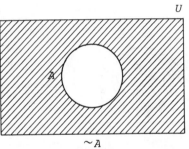

~A

Every element not in A

10.

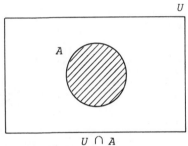

U ∩ A

Every element common to
A and U

11.

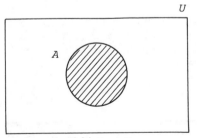

Ø ∪ A = A

Every element in Ø *or* in A

12.

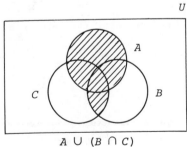

A ∪ (B ∩ C)

Every element in A *or* all
those in both B and C

13.   14.

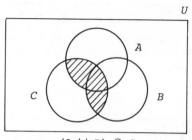

$(A \cup B) \cap C$
Every element in A or B
which is also in C

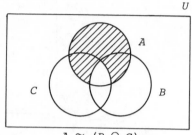

$A \sim (B \cap C)$
Every element in A which
is not also in B and C

15.

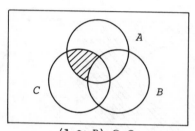

$(A \sim B) \cap C$
Every element in A but not
in B, which is also in C

Exercise

Illustrate the following with Venn diagrams.

(a) $A \cup (B \cup C)$,   (b) $(A \cap B) \cap C$,   (c) $A \cap (B \cup C)$,
(d) $(A \cap B) \cup C$,   (e) $(A \cap B) \cup (A \cap C)$ (what's the
message here?),   (f) $A \sim (B \cup C)$,   (g) $(A \sim B) \cup C$,
(h) $(\sim A) \cup (B \cap C)$,   (i) $\sim (A \cup (B \cap C))$,   (j)
$(A \sim B) \cup U$,   (k) $\sim (A \cup U)$,   (l) $A \sim (\emptyset \cup B)$,   (m)
$(A \sim \emptyset) \cup B$,   (n) $(A \cup B) \sim \emptyset$,   (o) $\sim ((A \cup B) \cap \emptyset)$.

THE CAD LAWS

As is generally the case with mathematical figures,
Venn diagrams can *suggest* or *illustrate* true relationships, although they *do not prove* these relationships.
They may constitute an intuitively plausible argument
that might or might not lead to a rigorous proof. Inasmuch as elementary school mathematics is far more
concerned with the intuitively plausible than with the
rigorous, we pose the next objective.

●●

*Objective 4. To illustrate with Venn diagrams or braces, if possi-
                 ble, the following properties of set union, intersec-
                 tion, and Cartesian product: commutativity, associa-
                 tivity, distributivity (the "CAD" laws).

●●

*The laws are listed below as they would appear if they
were all valid.*
        Commutative laws: $A \cap B = B \cap A$

                           $A \cup B = B \cup A$

                           $A \otimes B = B \otimes A.$

Exercise   Which, if any, of these laws is valid?

        Associative laws: $A \cap (B \cap C) = (A \cap B) \cap C$

                           $A \cup (B \cup C) = (A \cup B) \cup C$

                  $A \otimes (B \otimes C) = (A \otimes B) \otimes C.$

Exercise   Which, if any, of these laws is valid?

        Distributive laws:

           $A \cup (B \cap C) = (A \cup B) \cap (A \cup C)$
              "union over intersection"

           $A \cap (B \cup C) = (A \cap B) \cup (A \cap C)$
              "intersection over union"

           $A \otimes (B \cap C) = (A \otimes B) \cap (A \otimes C)$
         "Cartesian product over intersection"

           $A \cap (B \otimes C) = (A \cap B) \otimes (A \cap C)$
         "intersection over Cartesian product"

           $A \otimes (B \cup C) = (A \otimes B) \cup (A \otimes C)$
              "Cartesian product over union"

           $A \cup (B \otimes C) = (A \cup B) \otimes (A \cup C)$
              "union over Cartesian product."

Exercise   Which, if any, of these laws is valid?

        Let us look at the commutativity of union: If $A =$
        $\{b,o,y\}$ and $B = \{g,i,r,l\}$, then $A \cup B = \{b,o,y,g,i,r,l\}$

*Objectives marked with an asterisk are ones that we feel are less cru-
cial and might be omitted.

= $\{g,i,r,l,b,o,y\}$ = $B \cup A$. This illustrates the commutativity of union, using brackets. (Does it prove it?)

Now let's turn to distributivity of intersection over union:

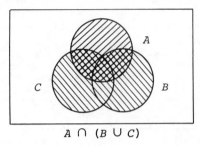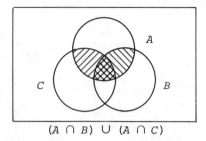

$$A \cap (B \cup C) \qquad\qquad (A \cap B) \cup (A \cap C)$$

Since the double-hatched region on the left is the same as the shaded (either single or double-hatched) region on the right, these Venn diagrams illustrate (but *don't prove*) the validity of this distributive law.

Finally, let's look at associativity of the Cartesian product. Let $A = \{1\}$, $B = \{2,3\}$, $C = \{1,3\}$. Then

$A \otimes (B \otimes C) = \{1\} \otimes (\{2,3\} \otimes \{1,3\})$

$\qquad\qquad = \{1\} \otimes \{(2,1),(2,3),(3,1),(3,3)\}$

$\qquad\qquad = \{(1,(2,1)),(1,(2,3)),(1,(3,1)),$
$\qquad\qquad\quad (1,(3,3))\}$.

(Note: We have *pairs within pairs* in this triple product.)

Meanwhile $(A \otimes B) \otimes C = (\{1\} \otimes \{2,3\}) \otimes \{1,3\}$

$\qquad\qquad\qquad = \{(1,2),(1,3)\} \otimes \{1,3\}$

$\qquad\qquad\qquad = \{((1,2),1),((1,2),3),$
$\qquad\qquad\qquad\quad ((1,3),1),((1,3),3)\}$,

which is not the same as $A \otimes (B \otimes C)$. See the discussion of ordered pairs, page 12. This not only *illustrates* that this law is not in general valid, it also *proves* it. That is, as a counterexample to the proposed law, it single-handedly destroys the validity of the law.

Exercises 1. How many ordered pairs can be made from elements of $\{a_1,a_2,a_3\}$?

2. How many from $\{a_1,a_2,a_3,a_4\}$?

3. How many from $\{a_1,a_2,a_3, \ldots , a_n\}$?

The following is a summary of the *valid* "CAD" laws. You can check your answers to the previous exercises now!

Commutative laws: $\qquad A \cup B = B \cup A$

$\qquad\qquad\qquad\qquad A \cap B = B \cap A.$

Associative laws: $\quad A \cap (B \cap C) = (A \cap B) \cap C$

$\qquad\qquad\quad A \cup (B \cup C) = (A \cup B) \cup C.$

Distributive laws: $A \cup (B \cap C) = (A \cup B) \cap (A \cup C)$

$\qquad\qquad\quad A \cap (B \cup C) = (A \cap B) \cup (A \cap C)$

$\qquad\quad A \otimes (B \cap C) = (A \otimes B) \cap (A \otimes C)$

$\qquad\quad A \otimes (B \cup C) = (A \otimes B) \cup (A \otimes C).$

An Ordered Pear

Definition   *Two sets A and B are <u>equivalent</u> (or matched or in <u>one-to-one correspondence</u>) if and only if there exists a set of ordered pairs (x,y), with x ∈ A, y ∈ B, such that (a) every x in A is used,   (b) every y in B is used,   (c) no y is used with more than one x,   (d) no x is used with more than one y.*

All of this discouraging detail is to say that each element of one set can be "matched up" with exactly one element of the other set.

Examples   1. $A = \{\alpha,\beta\}$; $B = \{\gamma,\delta\}$. Then one set of ordered pairs fulfilling the conditions in the definition is $\{(\alpha\ \gamma), (\beta,\delta)\}$. Another way of indicating these pairs, more common in elementary school work, is:

$$\begin{array}{cc} \alpha & \beta \\ \updownarrow & \updownarrow \\ \gamma & \delta \end{array}$$

2.   If $A = \{a,b,c\}$ and $B = \{@,\#,\$\}$, then one such set of ordered pairs is $\{(a,\$), (b,\#), (c,@)\}$; or

$$\begin{array}{ccc} a & b & c \\ \updownarrow & \updownarrow & \updownarrow \\ \$ & \# & @ \end{array}$$

● ●

*Objective   5.   Given two equivalent (finite) sets, to indicate all possible one-to-one correspondences between them.

● ●

Using A and B in Example 1, we can either draw a diagram:

$$\begin{array}{cccc} \alpha & \beta & \alpha & \beta \\ \updownarrow & \updownarrow & \updownarrow & \updownarrow \\ \gamma & \delta & \delta & \gamma \end{array}$$

or list the sets of ordered pairs:

$\{(\alpha,\gamma),(\beta,\delta)\}$, $\{(\alpha,\delta),(\beta,\gamma)\}$, $\{(\gamma,\alpha),(\delta,\beta)\}$, $\{(\gamma,\beta),(\delta,\alpha)\}$

If $A = \{$Mary, Kay, Joy$\}$ and $B = \{$Bob, David, Joe$\}$, how many ways can they pair off to dance? (Pairing off is the same as forming a one-to-one correspondence between sets A and B.)

1. {(Mary, Bob), (Kay, David), (Joy, Joe)}

2. {(Mary, Bob), (Kay, Joe), (Joy, David)}

3. {(Mary, David), (Kay, Bob), (Joy, Joe)}

4. {(Mary, David), (Kay, Joe), (Joy, Bob)}

5. {(Mary, Joe), (Kay, Bob), (Joy, David)}

6. {(Mary, Joe), (Kay, David), (Joy, Bob)}

Here, as in Examples 1 and 2, the pairs may all be reversed, matching set B to set A.

Let's look at all one-to-one correspondences between two sets with three elements again, this time graphically. Let $A = \{@,\#,\$\}$ and $B = \{a,b,c\}$.

1. @   # $ 2. @   # $
    ↕   ↕   ↕   ↕   ↕   ↕
    a   b   c   a   c   b

3. @   # $ 4. @   # $
    ↕   ↕   ↕   ↕   ↕   ↕
    b   a   c   b   c   a

5. @   # $ 6. @   # $
    ↕   ↕   ↕   ↕   ↕   ↕
    c   a   b   c   b   a

Exercises 1. What is the difference between writing $A \otimes B$ and listing all possible one-to-one correspondences between A and B? (Look at examples.)

2. Indicate all possible one-to-one correspondences between (a) $\{c,a,d\}$ and $\{f,u,n\}$, (b) $\{s,h,o,e\}$ and $\{s,o,c,k\}$.

3. How many one-to-one correspondences are there between two sets, each with (a) one element, (b) two elements, (c) three elements, (d) four elements, (e) five elements, (f) n elements?

4. Definition: $1! = 1$; $2! = 1 \cdot 2$; $3! = 1 \cdot 2 \cdot 3$; $4! = 1 \cdot 2 \cdot 3 \cdot 4$; and in general, $n! = 1 \cdot 2 \cdot 3 \cdot \ldots \cdot n$ ($n!$ is read "n factorial"). Compute (a) $6!$, (b) $6!/6$, (c) $6!/5!$, (d) $5! \cdot 6$, (e) $n!/(n-1)!$, (f) $n!(n+1)$.

5. Suppose $A = B$. Are they necessarily equivalent? Suppose A is equivalent to B. Are they necessarily equal?

6. Why is $0!$ defined to be $1!$? (*Hint*: look at Exercise 4(f).)

7. What has all of this factorial stuff to do with one-to-one correspondences between equivalent sets?

8. How many elements are there in A if the number of one-to-one correspondences between A and B is (a) 6, (b) 24, (c) 720, (d) 1000 (careful!), (e) 0?

9. List as many one-to-one correspondences as you can that occur naturally in ordinary life (such as cups with saucers at a table setting, or people with their positions in the box-office line for a movie).

With Objective 5 we finish a brief survey of the terminology of set theory. So far the only demonstrated usefulness of these set concepts has been as an aid to efficient thinking. In Chapter 2 we'll turn to the concept of the cardinal numbers (alias the "whole numbers"), where we'll find a new use for sets.

Exercise   List your own personal reasons for (a) liking, (b) disliking study of sets.

SUMMARY OF
OBJECTIVES

1. To explain and illustrate with *original* examples each of the following terms: (a) "set," (b) "element" (page 3).

2. To define and illustrate with original examples each of the following expressions: (a) $\{a,b,c\}$, (b) $\{x: x$ has a certain property$\}$, (c) $a \in A$, (d) $a \notin A$, (e) U, (f) $\emptyset$ or $\{\ \}$, (g) $A \subset B$, (h) $A = B$, (i) $A \cap B$, (j) "A and B are disjoint," (k) $A \cup B$, (l) $A \sim B$, (m) $\sim A$, (n) $A \otimes B$ (page 4).

3. (a) To solve a given word problem like the Big Pig Problem. (b) To write an *original* word problem like the big pig problem, including sufficient noncontradictory information to solve it (page 13).

*4. To illustrate with Venn diagrams or braces, if possible, the following properties of set union, intersection, and Cartesian product: commutativity, associativity, distributivity (the "CAD" laws) (page 23).

*5. Given two equivalent (finite) sets, to indicate all possible one-to-one correspondences between them (page 26).

WORDS TO KNOW

set   (page 3)
element   (page 3)
list method   (page 4)
roster method   (page 4)
rule method   (page 5)
universe (universal set)
    (page 6)
null set (empty set)
    (page 7)
subset   (page 7)
equal sets   (page 8)
singleton set   (page 9)
power set   (page 9)
intersection   (page 9)
disjoint   (page 10)
union   (page 10)

complement   (page 11)
Cartesian product
    (page 12)
ordered pairs   (page 12)
Venn diagram   (page 13)
noncontradictory
    (page 13)
commutative   (page 23)
associative   (page 23)
distributive   (page 23)
CAD laws   (page 25)
matched   (page 26)
equivalent sets
    (page 26)
one-to-one cor-
    respondence   (page 26)

CHAPTER 2

CARDINAL NUMBERS

31

THE COCONUT PROBLEM	Five sailors found themselves washed up on a deserted island, along with their pet monkey. Immediately they set about finding food and were lucky enough to find a grove of coconut trees, from which they harvested for the rest of the day. However, after piling the coconuts up in a heap, they were too tired even to eat, and so they all fell asleep. After the first couple of hours of deep sleep, the first sailor woke up, skulked over to the heap, and divided it up into five equal shares, with one left over. Waking the monkey, he fed it the extra coconut, buried his share, then replaced the rest of the coconuts, hoping that the resulting heap would look undisturbed to his mates. He then went back to sleep. About a half hour later, the second sailor repeated this performance: He divided the heap into five equal shares, one left over again, jammed it down the gullet of the pet monkey, buried his share, then replaced the remaining shares into a heap. Naturally, just after he returned to sleep the third sailor again repeated the performance, with one left over and stuffed it into the monkey, etc., and after him the fourth and fifth sailors did the same. *Now*, the question is, "What is the minimum number of coconuts in the original pile that would have allowed this process to take place?"

Challenges	1.	Try to solve the Coconut Problem with only three sailors and a monkey.
	2.	Try to solve the Coconut Problem with four sailors and a monkey.
	3.	Try to solve the Coconut Problem with the five sailors and a monkey.
	4.	Six sailors and a monkey?

CARDINALITY	The well-known Coconut Problem involves counting the number of elements in a certain set (the heap of coconuts), or, in more technical language, finding the *cardinal number* of that set. (Note: this is merely an informal explanation of cardinality, *not* an official definition, which will follow later.) Thus, cardinal numbers are the numbers invented for the purpose of answering the following question about a set: "*How many* elements are there in that set?"

Examples	1.	The cardinal number of $\{t,i,g\}$ is 3, which is the same as the cardinal number of $\{*,\$,\#\}$, which is the same as the cardinal number of $\{-,=,\neq\}$, which is the same as the cardinal number of $\{1,2,3\}$, etc.
	2.	The cardinal number of $\{x\colon x$ is a letter of the English alphabet$\}$ is 26.
	3.	The cardinal number of $\{x\colon x$ is an English word composed of all the letters of "smile" with no repeated letters$\}$ is 4, since the letters of "smile" can be left alone, or permuted to spell "limes," "miles," or "slime."

Exercises	1.	What are the cardinal numbers of the following sets? (a) $\{a,l,i,c,e\}$, (b) $\{w,a,r,t\}$, (c) $\{1,2,3\}$, (d) $\{\#,@\}$, (e) $\{\$\}$, (f) $\{\ \}$, (g) $\{\emptyset\}$, (h) $\{x\colon x$ is a letter of the Greek alphabet$\}$, (i) $\{x\colon x$ is an author of this book$\}$, (j) $\{x\colon x$ is a day of the week$\}$, (k) $\{x\colon x$ is an English word composed of all of the letters of "dog" with no repeated letters$\}$, (l) $\{x\colon x$ is an English word composed of *any* of the letters of "dog" with no repeated letters$\}$.
	2.	Try to define *cardinal number*.

DEFINITIONS

Possiby you smirk at that second exercise. Define cardinal number? Tut! Tut! *Everybody* knows what that is: It's a number that counts the number of elements in a set.

Well, that would be okay, if we knew what a "number" is. But we don't (yet). So before we start running in semantic circles, let's set an objective.

● ●

Objective 6. To define the *cardinal number* of a set and illustrate this definition for *zero* and for several other cardinal numbers.

● ●

Before getting to the abstract definition, we continue with intuitive discussion. What do we mean by "the number three"? One fairly predictable response is "This many things," holding up fingers as in the sketch at the right.

But this is just the same as saying, "Three is the property common to all sets in one-to-one correspondence with these upheld fingers of my left hand." Consider, moreover, the class (i.e., group or collection) of all sets in one-to-one correspondence with this set of extended fingers. Every set in that class has the property described by "three," and conversely, every set that has the property described by "three" is in that class. Therefore, since classes are easier to handle than properties, *we might think of "three" as being the class of sets* rather than the property that determines the class. This leads to the following definition, due in essence to the philosopher-mathematician, Bertrand Russell.

Definition	*The <u>cardinal number</u> of a Set A is the class of all sets in one-to-one correspondence with A (i.e., the class of all sets equivalent to A).*

Examples	1.	The cardinal number of the set of extended fingers may be illustrated as in the diagram below.

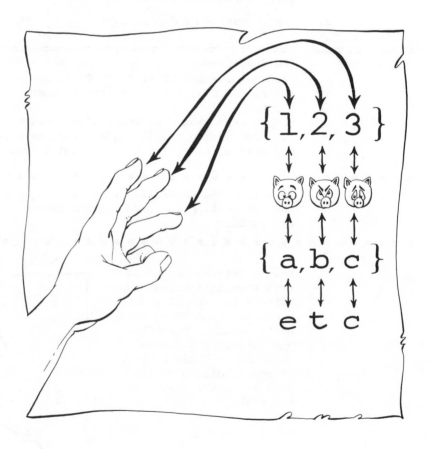

(In this case, the *finite* number "three" is represented by an infinite class of finite sets. There are also *infinite* cardinal numbers, represented by infinite classes of infinite sets.)

2.   The cardinal number "one" may be illustrated as follows:

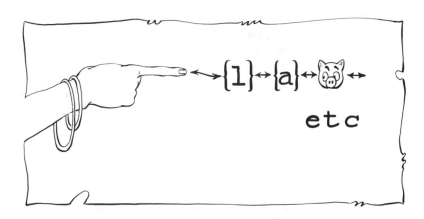

Exercises   1.   Illustrate the definition of the cardinal number "seven." (Hint: "Look, Ma! Two hands!")

2.   Illustrate the definition of the cardinal number "twelve." (Hint: Take off your shoe.)

3.   Try to illustrate the definition of the cardinal number "zero" (without looking at the next paragraph).

THE CARDINAL NUMBER ZERO

So in general a cardinal number is a class of all equivalent sets. Then in particular, zero must be such a class. Take a turn at programmed instruction and try to fill in the following blanks:

Exercise

Zero is the class of all sets in one-to-one correspondence with _____ . (Or, in other words, *zero* is the cardinal number of _____ .)

ORDERED SETS

Now that you're all expert on the definition of "cardinal number," the question arises, how much of this expertise should you pass on to your elementary students? That probably depends on the particular students and what questions they ask, but in general all that is asked of these students is that they recognize equivalent sets when they see them (hence, lots of exercises in "matching") and later on identify matched sets with correct "numerals" (to be defined a little later). This latter activity is usually called "counting." The students learn that some sets can be matched and some sets cannot, and that those that can are all associated with the same symbol. This is merely a concrete manifestation of the abstract, set-theoretical development as presented in the previous pages, a development intended only to give you future teachers an awareness of the overall picture. Hopefully, armed with this overall view, you will realize that once a child has attained the *end* of knowing how to count a set (i.e., how to find its cardinal number), he no longer need concern himself with the *means* of explicitly matching sets. (Unfortunately, this realization has not occurred to some teachers who think they are correctly presenting "The New Math.")

Once we realize that some sets are equivalent and some are not, we need a convenient way to communicate the notions of specific cardinal numbers. Life would be just too awkward if we went through it saying "I'm as old in years as the number of freckles on Suzie's left leg," or "The price of that kumquat is in pennies the same as the number of notches on this little brown stick," the problem being one of alluding to nonstandardized reference sets.

The obvious remedy for this problem is to establish standardized sets, to which all other sets are matched. One way to get such sets is to consider certain subsets of a universally recognized *ordered* set of symbols—a set for which, contrary to the case with ordinary sets, it makes a difference which symbol is written first, which is written second, etc.

To differentiate between an ordinary set and an ordered set, we'll extend the notation of ordered pairs. Remember that $\{x,y\} = \{y,x\}$, but $(x,y) \neq (y,x)$. Similarly, the *ordered* set consisting of 1, 2, 3 taken in that sequence will be denoted $(1,2,3)$, as opposed to the usual, unordered $\{1,2,3\}$. Thus, $(1,2,3) \neq (1,3,2) \neq (3,2,1)$, etc., but $\{1,2,3\} = \{1,3,2\} = \{3,2,1\} = \{3,1,2\}$, etc. Note, also, that the ordered set $(1,2,3) \neq ((1,2)3) \neq (1,(2,3))$; the latter two are ordered pairs where one element of each is itself an ordered pair.

Here are some examples of such sets, some that have actually been used (the civilization that used them is listed in parentheses) and some that have not:

$A = (1,2,3,4,5,6,7,8,9,10,11,12, \ . \ . \ .)$ (Arabic, base ten—ours)

$B = (1,2,3,4,5,6,7,10,11,12, \ . \ . \ . \ , 17,20,21, \ . \ . \ . \ , 27,30,31, \ . \ . \ .)$ (Arabic, base eight)

$C = (-,=,\neq,\#,-.,--,-=,-\neq,-\#,=.,=-,==, \ldots)$

$D = (/,//,///,////,/////,//////,///////,////////,$
$/////////,\cap,\cap/,\cap//,\cap///, \ldots ,\cap/////////,$
$\cap\cap,\cap\cap/,\cap\cap//,\cap\cap///, \ldots)$ (Egyptian)

$E = (+,+-,++,+--,+-+,++-,+++,+---,+--+,+-+-, \ldots)$

$F = (*,**,***,****,\underline{\quad},\underline{\,*\,},\underline{\,**\,},\underline{\,***\,}, \underline{\,****\,},\underline{\underline{\quad}},\underline{\underline{\,*\,}},$
$\ldots)$ (Mayan)

$G = (I,II,III,IV,V,VI,VII,VIII,IX,X,XI,XII, \ldots)$
(Roman).

Exercises

1. Write in order the next three elements of each of sets A through G.

2. Write the indicated element of each of sets A through G: (a) hundredth, (b) sixty-fourth, (c) twenty-fifth, (d) fourth, (e) thousandth, (f) five hundred twelfth, (g) one hundred twenty-fifth, (h) eighth.

3. How many different symbols are needed in each of sets A through G if each set goes on forever? (For example, in set C only five symbols are needed: $-$, $=$, $\neq$, $\#$ and $.$; in set B only eight symbols: 1, 2, 3, 4, 5, 6, 7, 0.)

4. Invent your own ordered sets of symbols such that: (a) only a finite number of symbols is needed, (b) an infinite number of symbols is needed.

NUMERALS AND NUMERATION SYSTEMS

Once we establish a standard, ordered set of symbols, we can give each of the symbols a name. For example, 1 is "one," 2 is "two," 3 is "three," etc. And having given these symbols names, we can use those same names for numbers as follows (even though it may lead to occasional confusion between a number and its symbol). We assign "one" to the cardinal number represented by (1), that is, the class of all sets in one-to-one correspondence with the set {1}. We assign "two" to the cardinal number represented by (1,2). We assign "three" to the cardinal number represented by (1,2,3). . . . We assign "seventeen" to the cardinal number represented by (1,2,3,4,5,6,7,8,9,10,11,12,13,14,15,16, 17), etc. In each case, a cardinal number is given the same name as the last symbol in the representative ordered set of the form (1,2,3, . . . , n). (Thus, the cardinal number n is named after and represented by (1,2,3, . . . , n).)

All of this brings us to the next objective.

Objective   7.   To explain what a *numeration system* is, as well as the
                 relationship between a cardinal number and its *numeral*.

● ●

A *numeration system* is a standardized, ordered set of
symbols used to name numbers. Each element of such a
set is called a *numeral*. Whereas a number is a certain
abstract concept (in fact, a class), its numeral is the
symbol that denotes it. Thus, in that first example
concerning the upheld fingers, the number "three" is
the class of all sets in one-to-one correspondence to
the set of fingers, while the (most common) numeral for
"three" is the symbol 3.

Officially armed, now, with names and symbols for the
cardinal numbers, we can attack the next objective:

● ●
Objective   8.   To explain the following types of numbers: *counting,
                 natural, whole, ordinal.*

● ●

The *counting numbers* and the *natural numbers* are the
same. They are the numbers 1, 2, 3, 4, 5, ... , .
The *whole numbers*, on the other hand, are the same as
the cardinal numbers: 0, 1, 2, 3, 4, 5, ... , . The
only difference between counting or natural numbers and
cardinal or whole numbers is the number zero. This may
be illustrated by the following Venn diagram:

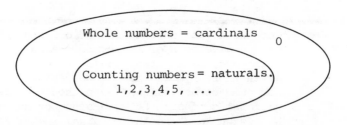

The term *ordinal number* is also used. If we think of
1, 2, 3, . . . , as "first, second, third, . . . ,"
then we are using them in their ordinal sense, whereas
if we think of them as standing for 1, 2, 3, . . . ,
elements in a set, then we are using them in their
cardinal sense.

ADDITION	The phrase "to put two and two together" is supposed to epitomize any elementary application of common sense.

Challenge	Try to *prove* that 2 + 2 = 4.

In regarding the preceding challenge you may have been baffled by the realization that you don't really know what it means to add. Hint: Think about unions of sets.

Challenge	Again try to prove that 2 + 2 = 4.

Paradox: Let {1,2} represent the cardinal number 2. Then 2 + 2 would be represented by {1,2} ∪ {1,2} = {1,2}!! 2 + 2 = 2? Remember, folks, you saw it here first!

Exercise	Explain what's wrong in the preceding "paradox."

● ●

Objective   9.   To define the *sum* of two cardinal numbers.

● ●

Definition	*For cardinal numbers a and b, let set A represent a, set B represent b, and A and B be disjoint. Then the sum a + b of a and b is the cardinal number represented by the set A ∪ B.*

(Note: If by any chance you are wondering if it makes any difference *which* sets we pick to represent *a* and *b*, you are to be congratulated for a particularly keen mathematical instinct and referred to Exercise 6 below.)

● ●

Objective   10.   To use the foregoing definition to show, for example, that 3 + 4 = 7.

● ●

Examples   1.   {1, 2, 3}   (This correspondence shows that
                 ↕ ↕ ↕   {a,b,c} really represents 3.)
                 {a, b, c}

$\{1, 2, 3, 4\}$ (Note that these two sets are
↕ ↕ ↕ ↕ disjoint.)
$\{d, e, f, g\}$

$\{a, b, c\} \cup \{d, e, f, g\} = \{a, b, c, d, e, f, g\}$
                          ↕ ↕ ↕ ↕ ↕ ↕ ↕
                        $\{1, 2, 3, 4, 5, 6, 7\}$

This shows that 3 + 4 does indeed equal 7.

2. Here is a concise demonstration that 3 + 3 = 6:

$\{1, 2, 3\}$ $\{1, 2, 3\}$
↕ ↕ ↕   ↕ ↕ ↕
$\{a, b, c\} \cup \{d, e, f\} = \{a, b, c, d, e, f\}$
                   ↕ ↕ ↕ ↕ ↕ ↕
                   $\{1, 2, 3, 4, 5, 6\}$

3. This demonstration that 3 + 3 = 6 is more appropriate for use in the elementary school classroom:

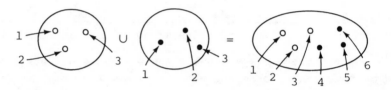

4. These two ways show that 2 + 3 = 5:

(a) $\{1, 2\}$ $\{1, 2, 3\}$
    ↕ ↕   ↕ ↕ ↕
    $\{a, b\} \cup \{c, d, e\} = \{a, b, c, d, e\}$
                  ↕ ↕ ↕ ↕ ↕
                  $\{1, 2, 3, 4, 5\}$

(b)

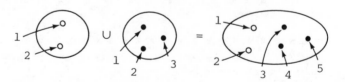

Exercises 1. Show that 2 + 2 = 4, two ways.

2. Show that 1 + 1 = 2, two ways.

3. Show that 2 + 1 = 3, two ways.

4. Show that 1 + 2 = 3. How does your demonstration differ from that in Exercise 3?

5. Pick your favorite sum of two cardinal numbers and show that it is what you think it is.

6. If our only aim is to represent 3 alone, why does it make no difference whether we represent it by $\{a,b,c\}$ or $\{d,e,f\}$?

● ●

*Objective 11. To prove rigorously that $n + 0 = n$ for any cardinal number n.

● ●

(Note: we do not recommend passing this kind of objective with an "obvious" result on to your own students. We include it as a brief illustration of the abstract axiomatic reasoning that is a crucial, but by no means sole aspect of modern mathematics.) Proof: Let N be any set representing n. Meanwhile, $\emptyset$ is the only set representing 0. N and $\emptyset$ are disjoint: $N \cap \emptyset = \emptyset$. Then $n + 0$ is the cardinal number (class of sets in one-to-one correspondence) represented by $N \cup \emptyset = N$. But n is the cardinal number represented by N. So $n + 0 = n$, QED. (QED stands for *quod erat demonstrandum*: "which was to be proved," i.e., a high-toned way of signaling the end of a proof.)

Exercises   1. Prove, using bracket set notation, that $3 + 0 = 3$.

2. Prove that $0 + 3 = 3$.

3. Prove that $0 + n = n$ for any cardinal number n.

===

ASSOCIATIVE
LAW

● ●

Objective 12. (a) To illustrate with sets the *associative law* for addition of cardinal numbers; (b) to give examples other than those in the text illustrating the *usefulness* of this law.

● ●

(Note: In teaching little kids it's probably a good idea to establish the usefulness first, then worry about the technical language and illustration with sets. As it is, too many teachers never get around to showing that the associative, commutative, and distributive laws are really good for anything.)

Definition *The associative law for addition of cardinal numbers says that $a + (b + c) = (a + b) + c$; i.e., we may* *associate b with either a or c, perform the addition between them, then add in the remaining part, and still obtain the same answer.*

Examples
1. Illustrating $1 + (2 + 3) = (1 + 2) + 3$ with braces:
Right-hand side:

$\{1\} \qquad \{1,2\} \qquad \{1,2,3\}$
$\updownarrow \qquad \updownarrow\updownarrow \qquad \updownarrow\updownarrow\updownarrow$
$\{a\} \cup (\{b,c\} \cup \{d,e,f\}) = \{a\} \cup \{b,c,d,e,f\}$
$= \{a,b,c,d,e,f\}$

Left-hand side: same

$(\{a\} \cup \{b,c\}) \cup \{d,e,f\} = \{a,b,c\} \cup \{d,e,f\}$
$\updownarrow \qquad \updownarrow\updownarrow \qquad \updownarrow\updownarrow\updownarrow \quad = \{a,b,c,d,e,f\}$
$\{1\} \qquad \{1,2\} \qquad \{1,2,3\}$

2. An alternative way to illustrate that $1 + (2 + 3) = (1 + 2) + 3$ more appropriate for primary children:

3. Illustrating the usefulness of the associative law: $25 + (75 + 57)$ is hard, but $(25 + 75) + 57$ is easy.

4. More usefulness: Joey wished to buy a popsicle for 12¢, a pencil for 8¢, and a comic book for 25¢. 12¢ + (8¢ + 25¢) is hard, but (12¢ + 8¢) + 25¢ is easy.

Exercises
1. Illustrate with sets that $(1 + 2) + 2 = 1 + (2 + 2)$
(a) with braces, (b) with dots.

2. Illustrate with sets that $3 + (1 + 1) = (3 + 1) + 1$
(a) with braces, (b) with dots.

3. Give at least three examples different from those in the text of the usefulness of the associative law for addition.

● ●

Objective 13.   (a) To illustrate with sets the *commutative law* for addition of cardinal numbers; (b) to give examples other than those in the text of the *usefulness* of this law.

● ●

Definition   *The commutative law for addition of cardinal numbers says that a + b = b + a.*

Examples follow illustrating the commutative law (in conjunction with the associative law, Examples 3 and 4).

Examples 1. $2 + 1 = 1 + 2$, with braces:

$\{1,2\}$ $\{1\}$ $\{1\}$ $\{1,2\}$

$\{a,b\} \cup \{c\} = \{a,b,c\} = \{a\} \cup \{b,c\}$

2. $2 + 1 = 1 + 2$, with dots:

3. $(25 + 57) + 75$ is hard, but

$(57 + 25) + 75 = 57 + (25 + 75)$ is easy.

4. $137 + 496 + 863$ is hard, but

$137 + 863 + 496$ is easier.

Exercises 1.   Illustrate with sets that $2 + 3 = 3 + 2$ (a) with braces,   (b) with dots.

2.   Illustrate with sets that $3 + 1 = 1 + 3$ (a) with braces,   (b) with dots.

3.   Give at least three examples different from those in the text of the usefulness of the commutative law for addition.

EXPANDED   So addition of cardinal numbers has been established
FORM   and some of its properties recognized. But going
               through life pulling out pairs of disjoint sets to

form unions every time we wanted to add could be one big pain. To get around this, people have invented *algorithms*—computational routines that call for a minimum of creative or foundational thought and a maximum of robot-like memorization; algorithms make life easier, not more glorious. Moreover, these algorithms for the most part exploit the particularities of the system of numeration, which means we must return for another look at such systems.

What, after all, does 1069 mean? (Aside from the fact that it's the weight in pounds of the heaviest man on record, who was buried in a piano case, according to the *Guinness Book of World Records**.) The answer is one thousand plus zero hundreds plus six tens plus nine ones:

$$1 \cdot (1000) + 0 \cdot (100) + 6 \cdot (10) + 9 \cdot (1),$$

or, for any exponent addicts in the crowd,

$$1 \cdot (10^3) + 0 \cdot (10^2) + 6 \cdot (10^1) + 9 \cdot (10^0).$$

(Note: $x^0 = 1$ by definition, except when $x = 0$, in which case 0^0 is not defined.)

As another example, let's look at 1.98 (the weight in pounds of an Indonesian fruit bat that holds the record for the longest wing span):

$$1 \cdot (10^0) + 9 \cdot (10^{-1}) + 8 \cdot (10^{-2}).$$

(Note: 10^{-1} means $1/10$; 10^{-2} means $1/10^2$; 10^{-3} means $1/10^3$, etc.)

When a numeral is written out in powers of 10, as in the examples, it is said to be written in *expanded form*.

Examples
1. $3792 = 3(10^3) + 7(10^2) + 9(10^1) + 2(10^0).$

2. $10,001 = 1(10^4) + 0(10^3) + 0(10^2) + 0(10^1) + 1(10^0).$

3. $23.45 = 2(10^1) + 3(10^0) + 4(10^{-1}) + 5(10^{-2}).$

4. $.0012 = 0(10^{-1}) + 0(10^{-2}) + 1(10^{-3}) + 2(10^{-4}).$

Exercises
1. Write the following numerals in expanded form: (a) 36, (b) 752, (c) 8406, (d) 3100, (e) 2.71, (f) 26.58, (g) 2.005, (h) .006302.

2. Guess what world records the entries in Exercise 1 stand for.

OTHER BASES
Why are our numerals all written as powers of ten, i.e., in base ten? The reason probably is anatomical:

*N. and R. McWirter, New York: Bantam Books, 1971.

Early people had ten fingers upon which to count and were either too nearsighted to see their toes clearly or considered their use too cumbersome. At any rate, we have ended up with powers of ten, the *decimal system* of numeration. Theoretically, at least, all of those tens could just as well have been threes, sevens, or twelves (that is, in base three, base seven or base twelve).

Examples

1. Consider one hundred fifty-one. How is this number written in base seven? First, we need to look at powers of seven: $7^0 = 1$, $7^1 = 7$, $7^2 = 49$, $7^3 = 343$, ... The largest of those that will go into 151 is 49, and it will go 3 times: $3 \cdot (49) = 147$. So 151 $= 3 \cdot (7^2)$ with 4 left over. How many times will $7^1 = 7$ go into 4? Zero (0), with 4 again left over. Finally, $7^0 = 1$ goes into 4 exactly 4 times. Thus

$$151 = 3 \cdot (7^2) + 0 \cdot (7^1) + 4 \cdot (7^0),$$

or one hundred fifty-one is written 304 in base seven (sometimes written 304_{seven}).

2. Similarly, looking at $3^0 = 1$, $3^1 = 3$, $3^2 = 9$, $3^3 = 27$, $3^4 = 81$, we can figure as follows to get this same number in base three: 81 goes into 151 once, with 70 left over; 27 goes into 70 twice, with 16 left over; 9 goes into 16 once, with 7 left over; 3 goes into 7 twice, with one left over. Thus

$$151 = 1 \cdot (3^4) + 2 \cdot (3^3) + 1 \cdot (3^2) + 2 \cdot (3^1) + 1 \cdot (3^0),$$

or one hundred fifty-one is written 12,121 in base three ($12,121_{three}$).

3. In looking at base twelve (*duodecimal*) we must invent two new symbols. We can't use 10 for ten, because in base twelve 10 means $1 \cdot (12^1) + 0 \cdot (12^0)$, which is twelve, not ten. (For this same reason, *10 will always be the numeral for the base*, whether the base is ten or two or twelve or whatever.) So let's take *T* as the symbol for ten. Likewise, we can't use 11 for eleven (since 11 in base twelve really stands for thirteen), so let's take *E* as the symbol for eleven. Thus, counting in base twelve looks like this:

1, 2, 3, 4, 5, 6, 7, 8, 9, *T, E*, 10, 11, 12, 13, 14, 15, 16, 17, 18, 19, 1*T*, 1*E*, 20, 21, . . . , 29, 2*T*, 2*E*, 30, 31, . . . , *T*0, *T*1, *T*2, *T*3, . . . , *T*9, *TT*, *TE*, *E*0, *E*1, *E*2, . . . , *E*9, *ET*, *EE*, 100, 101, 102, ...

If we want to write 151 in base twelve, we may proceed as follows:

$$\begin{aligned}151\\\underline{-144} &= 1\,(12^2)\\7\\\underline{-\quad 0} &= 0\,(12^1)\\7\\\underline{-\quad 7} &= 1\,(12^0)\\0\end{aligned}\Bigg\} \quad \text{So } 151 = (107)_{\text{twelve}}.$$

4. Another example, base eleven:

$$\begin{aligned}151\\\underline{-121} &= 1\,(11^2)\\30\\\underline{-\;22} &= 2\,(11^1)\\8\\\underline{-\quad 8} &= 8\,(11^0)\\0\end{aligned}\Bigg\} \quad \text{So } 151 = (128)_{\text{eleven}}.$$

Exercises

1. Count up to thirty in each of the following bases: (a) two, (b) three, (c) five, (d) eight, (e) twelve.

2. Count up to thirty in base one. What's special about this base?

3. Write the given numeral and the next three numerals in the indicated base: (a) 14, base five (Answer: 14, 20, 21, 22), (b) 21, base three (Answer: 21, 22, 100, 101), (c) 101, base two, (d) 1111, base two, (e) 23, base five, (f) 444, base five, (g) 565, base seven, (h) 2066, base seven, (i) 39, base twelve, (j) 100T, base twelve, (k) TTT, base twelve, (l) $EEEE$, base twelve.

4. Write the symbols (digits) 1, 2, 3, . . . , etc. that are used in each of the following bases: (a) four (Answer: 0, 1, 2, 3), (b) two, (c) three, (d) five, (e) eight, (f) twelve, (g) thirteen (careful!).

5. What is the message behind the answers in Exercise 4?

6. Translate the following to base ten (Example: $(344)_{\text{five}}$ $= 3\,(5^2) + 4\,(5^1) + 4\,(5^0) = 3\,(25) + 4\,(5) + 4\,(1) = 75 + 20 + 4 = 99$.): (a) $(1101)_{\text{two}}$, (b) $(1101)_{\text{three}}$, (c) $(1101)_{\text{twelve}}$, (d) $(123)_{\text{five}}$, (e) $(123)_{\text{eight}}$, (f) $(123)_{\text{twelve}}$, (g) $(456)_{\text{five}}$ (careful!), (h) $(456)_{\text{six}}$ (careful!), (i) $(456)_{\text{seven}}$.

7. What number does 23 (the record number of hours for nonstop Charleston dancing) stand for in: (a) base twelve, (b) base nine, (c) base seven, (d) base four, (e) base three (careful!), (f) base two (still careful!)?

8. What number does 2121 stand for in: (a) base twelve, (b) base nine, (c) base seven, (d) base four, (e) base three, (f) base two (careful!)?

9. What number does 110,101 stand for in: (a) base twelve, (b) base nine, (c) base seven, (d) base four, (e) base three, (f) base two?

10. Write one hundred thirty-nine (the women's record in feet for throwing a two-pound rolling pin) in each of the following bases: (a) twelve, (b) eight, (c) five, (d) three, (e) two.

11. What do we call a dance at which the guests discuss numeration? (Answer: a base ball.)

12. What do we call a writer who asks a question like Exercise 11? (Answer: a base author.)

13. What do we call a coarse cry in reaction to question 12? (Answer: a base bawl.)

14. What do we call an error in indicating the correct base in one of the computations? (Answer: a basin. Credit for this pun goes to Professor James E. Schultz, an appreciated reviewer.)

BASE EIGHT ("MICKEY DUCK")

Why should we study numeration systems other than base ten? Although some systems (notably the *binary*—base two—and the *octonary*—base eight) do have practical applications in specialized fields (those in which digital computers are extensively used), the principal reason for elementary teachers and students is as *means* rather than as *ends in themselves*. That is, the rationale is that students will have a better grasp of our everyday decimal system for having compared and contrasted it to similar systems with different bases. And for elementary teachers there is further reason: "Sesame Street" to the contrary notwithstanding, we must assume that many elementary students, especially in kindergarten through second or third grade, are unfamiliar with either the concept of numbers or the numerals used to denote them. If a prospective elementary teacher has struggled with an unfamiliar numeration system, that teacher may gain valuable empathetic insights in helping future students.

To begin this struggle, let us reconstruct mathematical history, this time assuming that, like certain cartoon characters, we were born with only four digits on each hand, a total of eight altogether.

Let us also construct original, reasonable symbols for the numbers zero through seven. (Why not eight?)

Mickey Duck and his four-fingered hands

Exercise   Invent at least two different original sets of symbols that might have evolved from an octonary numeration system.

You have taken your turn at numeral invention in the last exercise; let us have our turn:

zero: •   one: −   two: =   three: ≠   four: #   five: ⊕
six: ⊕̲   seven: ⊕̿

(Note the number of strokes in each numeral.)
In this "Mickey Duck" system, we count as follows:

−, =, ≠, #, ⊕, ⊕̲, ⊕̿, −•, −−, −=, −≠, −#, −⊕, −⊕̲,
−⊕̿, =•, =−, ==, =≠, =#, =⊕, =⊕̲, =⊕̿, ≠•, ≠−, etc.

And we get such numerals as

thirteen: −⊕ (one eight and five left over)
twenty-six: ≠= (three eights and two left over)
thirty-nine: #⊕̿ (four eights and seven left over)
seventy-eight: −−⊕ (one sixty-four, one eight and six left over)
one hundred sixty: =#• (two sixty-fours, four eights, and nothing left over).

Exercises   1.   Write Mickey Duck numerals for the following numbers: (a) three, (b) nine, (c) twenty-seven, (d) eighty-one, (e) two hundred forty-three, (f) seven hundred twenty-nine.

      2.   For what numbers do the following Mickey Duck numerals stand: (a) ≠⊕, (b) #⊕̲, (c) ⊕−−, (d) #••=, (e) ⊕̿⊕̿, (f) −−≠−, (g) −•••?

CHANGING BASES   As mentioned before, there are nondecimal numeration systems that have practical value. The binary (base two) system is used in work with electronic digital computers because it has the admirable virtue of requiring only two digits, 0 and 1, which fits in nicely with an electrical circuit, in which current is either off (0) or on (1) (and also makes for easy mutliplication tables!). Thus, the electrical message "on-off-off-on-on-off" stands for the binary numeral

$$100,110 = 1 \cdot (2^5) + 0 \cdot (2^4) + 0 \cdot (2^3) + 1 \cdot (2^2)$$
$$+ 1 \cdot (2^1) + 0 \cdot (2^0) = 38.$$

This example also points out a drawback of the binary system: it takes a six-digit number to represent a mere squirt like thirty-eight. You can imagine the kind of electronic mental breakdown that would be occasioned by such current numbers as found in annual government budgets, political payoffs, etc. To alleviate this difficulty, the octonary (base eight) system is brought in. Because $8 = 2^3$, it is easy to change from base eight to base two and back again. And because eight is almost equal to ten, octonary numerals are not too much more bulky than decimal numerals.

Examples   1.   Changing from base ten to base eight:

$$126 = 1(10^2) + 2(10^1) + 6(10^0) =$$
$$= 1(64) + 7(8) + 6 = 1(8^2) + 7(8^1) + 6(8^0)$$
$$= 176_{eight}.$$

Let's try a second method which might help in the next example.

$$126 = 1(10^2) + 2(10^1) + 6(10^0)$$
$$= 1(8 + 2)^2 + 2(8 + 2) + 6$$
$$= 1(8^2) + 2(2(8^1)) + 2^2 + 2(8^1) + 4 + 6$$
$$= 1(8^2) + 6(8^1) + 4 + 4 + 6$$
$$= 1(8^2) + 7(8^1) + 6(8^0) = 176_{eight}.$$

2.   Changing from base eight to base two:

$$27_{eight} = 2(8^1) + 7(8^0) = 2(2^3) + 7$$
$$= 1(2^4) + 1(2^2) + 1(2^1) + 1(2^0) = 10,111_{two}.$$

3.   Or $235_{eight} = 2(8^2) + 3(8^1) + 5(8^0)$

$$= 2(2^3)^2 + 3(2^3) + 5$$
$$= 1(2^7) + (2 + 1)(2^3) + 2(2^1) + 1$$
$$= 1(2^7) + 1(2^4) + 1(2^3) + 1(2^2) + 1(2^0)$$
$$= 10,011,101_{two}.$$

4. Changing from base two to base eight:

$$1010 = 1(2^3) + 1(2^1) = 1(8^1) + 2 = 1(8^1) + 2(8^0)$$
$$= 12_{eight}.$$
$$1101 = 1(2^3) + 1(2^2) + 1(2^0) = 1(8^1) + 5$$
$$= 1(8^1) + 5(8^0) = 15_{eight}.$$

Exercises
1. Change the following numbers from base ten to base eight: (a) 562,   (b) 46,   (c) 8092,   (d) 9873.

2. Change the following numbers from base eight to base two: (a) 73,   (b) 246,   (c) 4586 (careful!),   (d) 345.

3. Change the following numbers from base two to base eight: (a) 110,110,   (b) 110,   (c) 111,010,   (d) 10,101.

4. Change the following numbers from base eight to base ten: (a) 74,   (b) 743,   (c) 7432,   (d) 1625.

5. Change the following numbers from base two to base ten: (a) 110,   (b) 1101,   (c) 101,101,   (d) 1,101,101.

6. Change the following numbers from base ten to base two: (a) 65,   (b) 658,   (c) 232,   (d) 1026.

THE "YES-NO-MAYBE" TRICK

Some knowledge of the binary system will help us with the next objective.

● ●

*Objective 14.   To explain *how* and *why* the "yes-no-maybe" trick works.

● ●

A standard gambit in mathematical reasoning is: When nonplussed, try something similar and simpler. In line with this gambit, let's look at the "yes-no" trick (and we don't mean maybe).

MATHEMATICAL CON-ARTIST: UNSUSPECTING   Think of a cardinal number from 1 VICTIM: (11).   to 31, but don't tell it to me.

CON-ARTIST: Look at each of the following cards and say "Yes" if your Mystery Number is on the card,"No" if it isn't.

1 3 5 7
9 11 13 15
17 19 21 23
25 27 29 31

Exercises 1. Figure out *how* the "yes-no" trick works. In particular, when does the con artist add nonzero numbers and
when does he add zero? *What* are the nonzero numbers
that he adds?

2. Buzz off to your roommate or someone else with whom you
live, and try the "yes-no" trick yourself, casting
yourself as the con artist.

3. How many *consecutive* numbers appear on the first card? The second card? The third card? The fourth card? The fifth card?

4. What do the answers to questions in Exercise 3 have in common?

5. What base numeration system is involved in this trick?

6. Rewrite the numbers on the cards in the base chosen in Exercise 5.

7. Examine your answers to Exercise 6 and explain *why* the "yes-no" trick works. Then compare your answer with the next paragraph. (No preliminary peeking!)

In the "yes-no" trick we are seeking a mystery number. We would know the mystery number if we knew its base-two numeral. So we must trick the victim into revealing that information, and this we do, using the code yes = 1, no = 0. That is, we list on the first card (in base-ten numerals) all of those numbers from one to thirty-one, inclusive, which in *binary* numeration have a digit 1 in the ones column. Thus, a reply of yes to that card means that the binary notation for the mystery number ends in a 1, while a no means it ends in a 0. Then, on the second card, we cleverly list all numbers which in base-two notation have a 1 in the "twos" or second column, on the third card all of those with a 1 in the third (or "fours") column, etc. Hence, to identify the mystery number, we need only translate from, in the case of eleven, no-yes-no-yes-yes to $01011_{two} = 0(2^4) + 1(2^3) + 0(2^2) + 1(2^1) + 1(2^0)$ (base ten) $= 0 + 8 + 0 + 2 + 1 = 11$. The translation is facilitated by the convenient fact that the upper left-hand entry on each card is the power of two represented by the column which is associated with the card. Hence if the victim replies yes to a particular card, the con artist adds in the upper left number on that card, and if he replies no the con artist adds nothing.

Exercises
1. Why should the fact that the con artist asks for only two responses (yes or no) tip us off to the binary system?

2. Why, in the 1 through 31 trick, did we need five cards?

3. Why did we stop with 31?

4. If we extended the range of the trick to from 1 through a number greater than 31, how high could we go using six cards? Seven cards?

5. In a *three*-response trick ("yes-no-maybe"), what numeration system would we use?

6. Write the numbers one through twenty-six in the numeration system named in Exercise 5.

7. Why "twenty-six" in Exercise 6?

8. How many cards do we need for the "yes-no-maybe" trick for 1 through 26?

9. Make a set of "yes-no-maybe" cards, putting parentheses around those numerals representing numbers whose base notation of Exercise 5 is nonzero and non-one in the given column.

10. Try the "yes-no-maybe" trick on a friend—or enemy, if you want to make a little side wager.

11. Explain how to work the "yes-no-maybe" trick.

12. Explain why the "yes-no-maybe" trick works.

13. Invent a "yes-no-maybe-ha!" trick, perhaps printing numerals in different colors on each card. (How many different colors?)

ADDITION IN
NONDECIMAL
SYSTEMS

After that digression into the nature of some nondecimal numeration systems, let us investigate addition computations with these systems.

● ●

Objective 15.   To complete the computations of given indicated sums in bases other than ten (including the "eight finger" or "Mickey Duck" system).

● ●

(Note: Carrying out the computation of an addition exercise is also referred to as "naming the sum"—that is, substituting the numeral 13, for example, for the expression 2 + 4 + 7.)
   Throwing caution to the winds, we immediately leap into an example.

Examples   1.   Add, base nine: 237
                                    514
                                    860

This example will be carried out simultaneously on three fronts: (a) by manipulating the numerals, (b) by interpreting on an abacus-like diagram, (c) verbally (i.e., in words). The point of this three-pronged attack is to communicate as clearly and thoroughly as possible addition in "strange" bases. In actual computations, you will probably write only the numerals, although you may be thinking about the diagrams and accompanying words in your head.

Step 0. Numerals	Diagram	Words

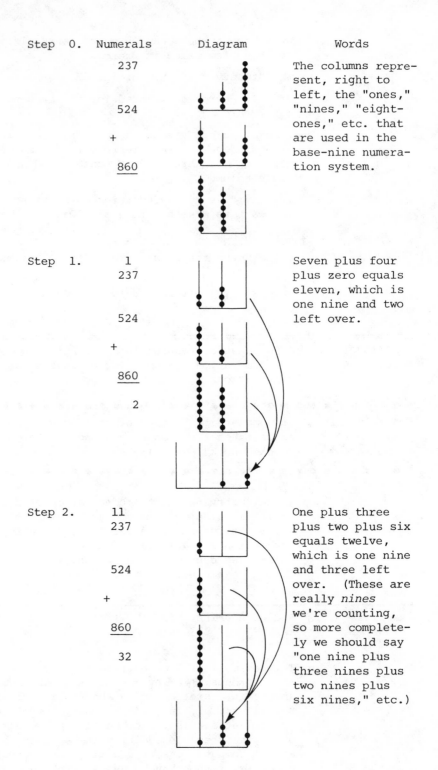

Step 0.

237

524

+

860

The columns represent, right to left, the "ones," "nines," "eight-ones," etc. that are used in the base-nine numeration system.

Step 1.

1
237

524

+

860

2

Seven plus four plus zero equals eleven, which is one nine and two left over.

Step 2.

11
237

524

+

860

32

One plus three plus two plus six equals twelve, which is one nine and three left over. (These are really *nines* we're counting, so more completely we should say "one nine plus three nines plus two nines plus six nines," etc.)

Step 3.	Numerals	Diagram	Words

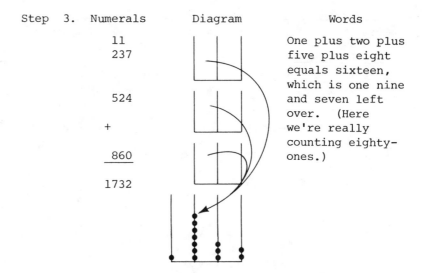

One plus two plus
five plus eight
equals sixteen,
which is one nine
and seven left
over. (Here
we're really
counting eighty-
ones.)

So the answer is 1732, base nine. Notice that this is
exactly the same *procedure* as ordinary addition with
our base-ten system, except that we are replacing ones,
tens, hundreds, etc. with ones, nines, eighty-ones,
etc. It is for this reason that nondecimal systems are
studied in elementary school—to increase the under-
standing of the structure of our place-value, base-ten
numeration system.

2. Another example, this time base three (*ternary*):

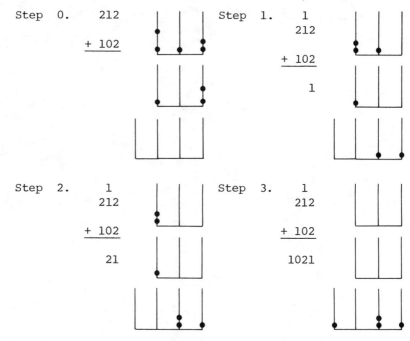

Exercise   Supply the words for the last example.

Example   An example in base twelve, with *T* for ten and *E* for eleven:

Step 0.   3*T*7   Step 1. $\overset{2}{3T7}$

296   296

+ 1*EE*   + 1*EE*

                         0

Step 2. $\overset{22}{3T7}$ Step 3. $\overset{22}{3T7}$

296   296

+ 1*EE*   + 1*EE*

80   880

Exercise   Supply abacus-type diagrams and words for the last example.

Examples   1.   Two more examples, in the base-eight "Mickey Duck" system:

Step 0.   # = ⊕   Step 1.   # $\overset{=}{=}$ ⊕
+ ⊖ • ≠   + ⊖ • ≠
                        −

Step 2.   # $\overset{=}{=}$ ⊕   Step 3.   # $\overset{=}{=}$ ⊕
+ ⊖ • ≠   + ⊖ • ≠
≠ −   − ≠ ≠ −

2.   Step 0.   ⊕ ≠ •   Step 1.   ⊕ $\overset{=}{\ne}$ •
⊖ ⊕ #   ⊖ ⊕ #
+   ⊕ #   +   ⊕ #
                        •

Step 2.   ⊖ $\overset{=}{\ne}$ •   Step 3.   ⊖ $\overset{=}{\ne}$ •
⊖ ⊕ #   ⊖ ⊕ #
+   ⊕ #   +   ⊕ #
⊖ •   − ⊕ ⊖ •

Complete the following additions:

1. Base two:

    (a) 1011   (b) 1101   (c) 1111   (d)   101
        101   111   1   1101
                                                   111

2. Base five:

    (a) 3142   (b) 3213   (c) 4444   (d) 1423
        201   442   1   234
                                               113

3. Base nine:

    (a) 8157   (b) 8438   (c) 8888   (d) 2814
        608   675   1   765
                                             438

4. Base twelve:

    (a) $T259$ (b) $E47T$ (c) $EEEE$ (d) $3ET4$
        $3E1$ $5T9$ 1 $4T9$
                                               867

5. Base eight ("Mickey Duck")

    (a) ⊕ • = ≠   (b)   # ≠ ⊕ –
        ⊕̄ – #   ⊕ • ⊕

    (c) ⊕̄ ⊕̄ ⊕̄ ⊕   (d) ⊕ • – #
             –   ≠ – ⊕
                                              ⊕ ⊕ ⊕

6. Determine in what base(s), if any, the following additions were calculated:

    (a)   121   (b)   146   (c)   345   (d) 1101
        101   352   231   1011
        222   520   576   2112

    (e)   127   (f)   127   (g) 1101   (h)   234
        653   653   1010   122
        245   245   111   323
     1003 $T14$ 21110   1012

7. Complete the following patterns:

    (a)

+	1	2	3	4	5	10	11
5	10	11					

    (b)

+	3	6	9	10	13	16	19
5	8	E	12				

(c)

+	4	7	11	14	17	21	24
x	10	13	16				

(Solve for x first)

(d)

3	7	12
5	4	
7	1	
11	7	
30		

(How can you check your work?)

(e)

4	1	5
10	3	
15	5	
20	7	
26	9	
74		

(f)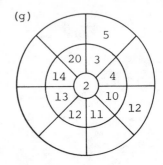

(g)

8. A *magic square* is a square array of numbers that have the same sum along any row, column or main diagonal. Thus, the figure at the right is a magic square, where the numerals are base ten. Complete the following magic squares, using the given bases:

```
              15
  ┌───┬───┬───┐
  │ 8 │ 1 │ 6 │ → 15
  ├───┼───┼───┤
  │ 3 │ 5 │ 7 │ → 15
  ├───┼───┼───┤
  │ 4 │ 9 │ 2 │ → 15
  └───┴───┴───┘
    ↓   ↓   ↓
   15  15  15  15
```

(a) Three:

		22
	12	1
		20

(b) Eight:

20	1		6
		4	16
	17		14
11		16	

(c) Twelve:

		1	8	13
	5	7	12	14
4	6	11		
T	10			3
E			2	9

SUBTRACTION

How do we define subtraction? Well, there are a number of alternatives, but they all amount, essentially, to performing addition backward (or at least sideways). Subtraction is the process of finding a difference, which brings us to the next objective.

Objective 16. To define the *difference* of two cardinal numbers and illustrate this definition with an example other than in the text.

• •

Definition   *For cardinal numbers a, b, c, the <u>difference</u> <u>a - b</u> is defined as follows: a - b = c means a = b + c.*

Examples   1. 5 - 2 = 3 means 5 = 2 + 3, which we always knew! Or did we?

2. 11 - 7 = 4 means 11 = 7 + 4.

3. Or 324 - 85 = 239 means 324 = 85 + 239.

Notice that this definition does not guarantee the existence of every difference *a - b*. It just says that *if* there are cardinal numbers *a, b, c* such that *a = b + c*, then another way of expressing this same fact is to write *a - b = c*. By way of illustration, 5 - 2 = 3, means $5 = 2 + 3$, or $13 - 7 = 6$ means $13 = 7 + 6$. Meanwhile, neither $2 - 5$ nor $7 - 13$ has any meaning within the universe of cardinal numbers. (Later, in Chapter 4, the negative integers will be introduced, and only as of that time will $2 - 5$ or $7 - 13$ have meaning.)

Exercises   1. Rewrite the following sums as differences: (a) $1 + 1 = 2$, (b) $1 + 2 = 3$, (c) $2 + 3 = 5$, (d) $3 + 5 = 8$, (e) $5 + 0 = 5$.

2. Rewrite the following differences as sums: (a) $4 - 1 = 3$, (b) $9 - 4 = 5$, (c) $16 - 9 = 7$, (d) $25 - 16 = 9$, (e) $9 - 0 = 9$.

3. Illustrate the definition of *difference* of two cardinal numbers with at least three examples other than those in the text.

4. What equation *should* have come after (d) in Exercise 1, if the pattern were to remain consistent?

5. What equation *should* have come after (d) in Exercise 2, if the pattern were to remain consistent? What *is* the pattern in Exercise 2?

ALGORITHMS

● ●

Objective 17. To perform a given subtraction via (a) "regrouping," (b) "equal additions," (c) "complement."

● ●

Well, it's algorithm time again. We have defined subtraction, but computation directly from this definition would be cumbersome, and we therefore turn to algorithms. The variety of algorithms offered in this objective, remember, is *not* part of the "new math"; instead it is different versions of the "old math," presented so that you can provide some variety for those of your future students who are nonplussed by subtraction.

Examples   1. "Regrouping." (Some people call this method "borrowing," which is not really correct, since we don't return what we "borrow"; perhaps "stealing" is more appropriate.)

(a)   423   We can't take 7 from 3 ($3 - 7$ is not
     -157 defined yet), so we "steal" one 10 from
                   the 20 and think of it as ten 1's.

(b)   4 $\overset{1}{2}$ $^{1}3$ We now subtract 7 from 13 and get six
     -1 5 7   1's left.
          6

(c) $4\ \overset{1}{2}\ {}^{1}3$ We can't take five 10s from one 10, so
     $-1\ \ 5\ \ 7$ we "steal" one hundred from the four
            6   hundred and think of it as ten 10s.

(d) $\overset{3}{4}\ \overset{11}{2}\ {}^{1}3$ We now take five 10s from eleven 10s and
     $-1\ \ 5\ \ 7$ one hundred from three hundred.
     $\ \ 2\ \ 6\ \ 6$ Finished!

2.   Another example of "regrouping" (alias "stealing"):

   $\overset{8}{9}\ \overset{9}{0}\ \overset{10}{1}\ {}^{1}3$
   $-2\ \ 8\ \ 7\ \ 5$
   $\ \ 6\ \ 1\ \ 3\ \ 8$

3.   "Equal additions":

   (a) $4\ \ 2\ \ 3$ Here we add ten 1's to 423 and make up
       $-1\ \ 5\ \ 7$ for it by adding one 10 to 157; this is
               legal because $(423 + 10) - (157 + 10) =$
               $266 = 423 - 157.$

   (b) $4\ \ 2\ \ {}^{1}3$ Next we add ten 10s to the upper number
          6   and make up for it by adding one 100 to
      $-1\ \ \overset{6}{5}\ \ 7$ the lower number.
          6

   (c) $4\ \ {}^{1}2\ \ {}^{1}3$ We now finish the computation.
        2   6
      $-\overset{2}{1}\ \ \overset{6}{5}\ \ 7$
         6

   (d) $4\ \ {}^{1}2\ \ {}^{1}3$ (This algorithm is the one currently
        2   6   used in many European countries, espe-
      $-\overset{2}{1}\ \ \overset{6}{5}\ \ 7$ cially France.)
      $\ \ 2\ \ 6\ \ 6$

4.   Second example of "equal additions":

   $9\ \ {}^{1}0\ \ {}^{1}1\ \ {}^{1}3$ (Note that here we do not have the
     $\overset{3}{\ }\ \ \overset{9}{\ }\ \ 8$ problem of stealing from the 0 in 90.)
   $-\overset{3}{2}\ \ \overset{9}{8}\ \ \overset{8}{7}\ \ 5$
   $\ \ 6\ \ 1\ \ 3\ \ 8$

5.   "Complements":

The complement of 7 is 3
The complement of 69 is 31
The complement of 438 is 562
The complement of 2501 is 7499

As you can see, complements are pairs of numbers whose sum is the nearest power of ten greater than either number.

Subtraction via "complement":

   (a) $4\ \ 2\ \ 3$ Here we substitute the addition of the
       $-1\ \ 5\ \ 7$ complement of 157 for the subtraction
               of 157.

(b)   4   2   3   Next we just add.
            8   4   3
      - 1̶--5̶--7̶

(c)   4   2   3   Finally, we cross off the 1 at the left
            8   4   3   of the sum.
      - 1̶--5̶--7̶
      1   2   6   6

(d)   4   2   3   You might object that the "complement"
            8   4   3   algorithm substitutes a subtraction and
      - 1̶--5̶--7̶   an addition for the original subtrac-
      1̶   2   6   6   tion. This is true, but the substi-
                       tuted subtraction is a special one,
                       easily done (see Exercise 1 below), and
                       most people seem to prefer addition to
                       subtraction.

6.   Another "complement" example:

      9   0   1   3
        7   1   2   5
      - 2̶--8̶--7̶--5̶
      1̶   6   1   3   8   Answer: 6138.

Exercises   1.   Find the complements of the following numbers: (a) 37,
                 (b) 198, (c) 998, (d) 2698, (e) 3876, (f) 3891.

            2.   Complete each of the following subtractions via
                 (i) "regrouping," (ii) "equal additions,"
                 (iii) "complement":

                 (a)   91   (b)   823   (c)   1875   (d)   4885
                     -37   -198   - 998   -2698

                 (e)   5002   (f)   6020
                    -3876   -3891

            3.   Complete each of the following subtractions in the given
                 base via (i) "regrouping," (ii) "equal additions,"
                 (iii) "complement":

                 (a) Two,   1101   (b) Five,   4201
                         -111   -3222

                 (c) Mickey Duck,   ⊕   -   =   -   (d) Twelve, T542
                          - ≠   ≠   =   =   -3E53

            4.   Give an algebraic proof that "equal additions" always
                 works.

            5.   Give an algebraic proof that the "complement" algorithm
                 always works. (Hint: Consider $a - b$ and 10^n, where
                 10^{n-1} is less than b while 10^n is greater than b; for
                 example, if a is 341 and b is 295, then $10^2 = 100$ is
                 less than b, while $10^3 = 1000$ is greater than b.)

6. State (i) advantages, (ii) disadvantages of: (a) "regrouping," (b) "equal additions," (c) "complement."

7. Try to invent your own, original algorithm for subtraction.

MULTIPLICATION

Before we can multiply we must chat about what we mean by "multiply" so that we can come up with a definition which both has our intended meaning and also is suitably precise. To begin with, we can check the Latin roots: "Multi" means "many," and "ply" means "layer," as in two- or four-ply tires, radial-ply tires, plywood, etc. Okay, the next question is, "Many layers of *what*?" To get at this, let's consider a specific example: 3 × 5. We will want this to represent 3 layers of 5 objects each:

· · · · · ⎫
· · · · · ⎬ (Fifteen dots in all, which is as we
· · · · · ⎭   want it to be.)

This array of dots is interesting, but anonymous. To introduce more individuality, let's give the rows names and do the same for the dots in each row, thus:

Row: Dots:
Flopsy: Rabbit, Bunny, Hare, Pika, Moran
Mopsy: Rabbit, Bunny, Hare, Pika, Moran
Bugs: Rabbit, Bunny, Hare, Pika, Moran.

or, using only initials:

F: *R, B, H, P, M*
M: *R, B, H, P, M*
B: *R, B, H, P, M.*

Finally, we may put the first and second initials together, forming a bunch of *ordered pairs*:

(F,R), (F,B), (F,H), (F,P), (F,M),
(M,R), (M,B), (M,H), (M,P), (M,M),
(B,R), (B,B), (B,H), (B,P), (B,M).

And what is this last set of ordered pairs? Merely the Cartesian product $\{F,M,B\} \otimes \{R,B,H,P,M\}$. So in considering 3 × 5 first as three layers of five dots each, then associating the layers and dots with initials, we came up with 3 × 5 represented by a Cartesian product of two sets, the first with three elements, the second with five elements. Another way of thinking of this is as three copies of the five-element set $\{R,B,H,P,M\}$. Each element of the first copy is decorated with an *F*, each element of the second copy with an *M*, and each

element of the third with a *B*. This brings us to the
next objective.

● ●

Objective 18. To define the *product* of two cardinal numbers and illustrate this definition with a result of the type
$3 \times 5 = 15$.

● ●

Definition | *For cardinal numbers a and b, let set A represent a and
set B represent b. Then the <u>product</u> <u>a × b</u> (or a • b,
or just ab) of a and b is the <u>cardinal number</u> represented by A ⊗ B.*

It turns out, as was the case in addition, that it
does not matter *which* sets we pick to represent *a* and *b*
(see the following exercises). And in contrast to the
case for addition, here *A* and *B need not be distinct.*

Examples   1.   Consider the product 2×3: $\{1,2\} \otimes \{1,2,3\} =$

$\{ (1,1), (1,2), (1,3), (2,1), (2,2), (2,3) \}$
$\updownarrow$ $\updownarrow$ $\updownarrow$ $\updownarrow$ $\updownarrow$ $\updownarrow$
$\{ \ \ 1, \quad 2, \quad 3, \quad 4, \quad 5, \quad 6 \ \}$

Thus we see that $2 \times 3 = 6$.

2.   Or let's look at $3 \times 5 = 15$ again, this time without
going through the heuristic discussion of why consideration of Cartesian products is appropriate.

$\{1,2,3\} \otimes \{1,2,3,4,5\}$

$= \{ (1,1), (1,2), (1,3), (1,4), (1,5), (2,1), (2,2), (2,3),$
$\updownarrow$ $\updownarrow$ $\updownarrow$ $\updownarrow$ $\updownarrow$ $\updownarrow$ $\updownarrow$ $\updownarrow$
$\{ \ \ 1, \quad 2, \quad 3, \quad 4, \quad 5, \quad 6, \quad 7, \quad 8,$

$(2,4), (2,5), (3,1), (3,2), (3,3), (3,4), (3,5)\}$
$\updownarrow$ $\updownarrow$ $\updownarrow$ $\updownarrow$ $\updownarrow$ $\updownarrow$ $\updownarrow$
$9, \quad 10, \quad 11, \quad 12, \quad 13, \quad 14, \quad 15 \ \}$

3.   Let's look at a simple product such as $3 \times 1 = 3$ and illustrate it with sets of elements that are not numbers.
Let $A = \{@,\#,\$\}$ and $B = \{\%\}$, so that A represents 3
(i.e., has cardinal number 3) and B has cardinal number
1.

$A \otimes B = \{ (@,\%), (\#,\%), (\$,\%) \}$
$\updownarrow$ $\updownarrow$ $\updownarrow$
$\{ \ \ 1, \quad 2, \quad 3 \ \}$

Exercises 1. Explain why sets A and B above need not be distinct, while in the definition of addition they must be.

2. Suppose we want to compute 3×5 and we're set on using $\{r,b,h,p,m\}$ to represent 5, but we can't make up our minds as to whether to choose $\{f,m,b\}$ or $\{t,i,g\}$ to represent 3. Why does it make no difference which we choose to represent 3?

3. Why does it make no difference which set we use to represent 5, $\{r,b,h,p,m\}$ or $\{a,b,c,d,e\}$ or $\{*,\#,\$,\cent,\&\}$ or . . . ?

4. Illustrate the definition of product by computing each of the following products using Cartesian products: (a) $2 \times 4 = 8$, (b) $1 \times 3 = 3$, (c) $4 \times 2 = 8$, (d) $0 \times 3 = 0$.

5. Illustrate the definition with $2 \times (2 \times 2) = 8$.

6. (a) Explain why, in the $3 \times 5 = 15$ example, it is unnecessary to write $\{1,2,3\} \otimes \{1,2,3,4,5\}$
$$\updownarrow\updownarrow\updownarrow \qquad \updownarrow\updownarrow\updownarrow\updownarrow\updownarrow$$
$$\{a,b,c\} \otimes \{d,e,f,g,h\}$$
$= \{\,(a,d),(a,e),(a,f),(a,g),(a,h),(b,d),(b,e),(b,f),$
$\qquad \uparrow \qquad \uparrow \qquad \uparrow \qquad \uparrow \qquad \uparrow \qquad \uparrow \qquad \uparrow \qquad \uparrow$
$\{\;\; 1, \qquad 2, \qquad 3, \qquad 4, \qquad 5, \qquad 6, \qquad 7, \qquad 8,$

$\qquad (b,g),(b,h),(c,d),(c,e),(c,f),(c,g),(c,h)\}$
$\qquad \updownarrow \qquad \updownarrow \qquad \updownarrow \qquad \updownarrow \qquad \updownarrow \qquad \updownarrow \qquad \updownarrow$
$\qquad 9, \quad 10, \quad 11, \quad 12, \quad 13, \quad 14, \quad 15 \;\}$

(b) Is it incorrect to illustrate the example this way? Why?

COMMUTATIVITY
AND
ASSOCIATIVITY

• •

Objective 19. To illustrate with sets the following multiplicative properties of cardinal numbers: (a) commutativity, (b) associativity, (c) $n \times 1 = n$ for any cardinal number n.

• •

Illustration of commutativity, $2 \times 3 = 3 \times 2$:

$\{1,2\} \otimes \{1,2,3\} = \{\,(1,1),(1,2),(1,3),(2,1),(2,2),(2,3)\}$
$\qquad\qquad\qquad\qquad\quad \updownarrow \qquad \updownarrow \qquad \updownarrow \qquad \updownarrow \qquad \updownarrow \qquad \updownarrow$
$\qquad\qquad\qquad\qquad\quad \{\,(1,1),(1,2),(2,1),(2,2),(3,1),(3,2)\}$
$= \{1,2,3\} \otimes \{1,2\}$

Illustration of associativity, $2 \times (2 \times 3)$
$= (2 \times 2) \times 3$:

$\{1,2\} \otimes (\{1,2\} \otimes \{1,2,3\})$

$= \{1,2\} \otimes \{(1,1),(1,2),(1,3),(2,1),(2,2),(2,3)\}$

$= \{(1,(1,1)),(1,(1,2)),(1,(1,3)),(1,(2,1)),(1,(2,2)),$

$(1,(2,3)),(2,(1,1)),(2,(1,2)),(2,(1,3)),(2,(2,1)),$

$(2,(2,2)),(2,(2,3))\}$

which is in one-to-one correspondence with

$\{((1,1),1),((1,1),2),((1,1),3),((1,2),1),((1,2),2),$

$((1,2),3),((2,1),1),((2,1),2),((2,1),3),((2,2),1),$

$((2,2),2),((2,2),3)\}$

$= \{(1,1),(1,2),(2,1),(2,2)\} \otimes \{1,2,3\}$

$= (\{1,2\} \otimes \{1,2\}) \otimes \{1,2,3\}$

Illustration of *multiplicative identity*, $3 \times 1 = 3$:

$\{1,2,3\} \otimes \{1\} = \{(1,1),(2,1),(3,1)\}$
$$\qquad\qquad\qquad\quad \updownarrow \qquad \updownarrow \qquad \updownarrow$$
$$\qquad\qquad\qquad \{ \quad 1, \qquad 2, \qquad 3 \quad \}$$

Note: the somewhat tedious writing out of these illustrations could have been circumvented by introducing
the abstract one-to-one correspondences $(x,y) \leftrightarrow (y,x)$,
$(x,(y,z)) \leftrightarrow ((x,y),z)$, and $x \leftrightarrow (1,x)$, respectively.
Of course, the efficiency introduced through the ab-
straction is paid for by a decrease in concreteness;
that is, the abstract formulation does not give us as
much to visualize.

Even more visualizable is the dot representation of
Cartesian products:

```
. . . . .
. . . . .
. . . . .
```

Examples   1. $2 \times 3 = 3 \times 2$:

2×3 3×2.

2. $2 \times (2 \times 3) = (2 \times 2) \times 3$:

$2 \times (2 \times 3)$

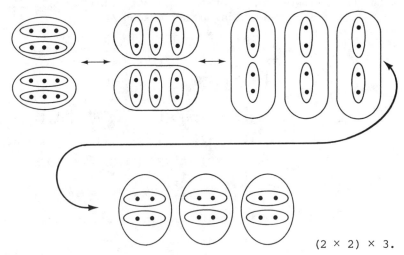

$(2 \times 2) \times 3.$

3. $3 \times 1 = 3$:

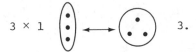

3×1 3.

Exercises

1. Illustrate multiplicative commutativity of cardinal numbers with at least two examples of your own, different from those in the text (a) with braces, (b) with dots.

2. Illustrate multiplicative associativity of cardinal numbers with at least two examples of your own, different from those in the text (a) with braces, (b) with dots.

3. Illustrate the multiplicative identity of cardinal numbers with at least two of your own examples, different from those in the text (a) with braces, (b) with dots.

DISTRIBUTIVITY

● ●

*Objective 20.   (a) To illustrate with sets that multiplication is distributive over addition; (b) to state and prove whether or not addition is distributive over multiplication.

● ●

The general statement of distributivity of multiplication over addition is: If $a, b,$ and c are cardinal numbers then $a \times (b + c) = (a \times b) + (a \times c)$.

Examples   1.   Illustration of distributivity of multiplication over addition, using braces:

$2 \times (1 + 3) = (2 \times 1) + (2 \times 3)$

{1,2} {1} {1,2,3}
↕↕   ↕ ↕↕↕

$\{1,2\} \otimes (\{a\} \cup \{b,c,d\}) = \{1,2\} \otimes \{a,b,c,d\}$

$= \{(1,a),(1,b),(1,c),(1,d),(2,a),(2,b),(2,c),(2,d)\}$

$= \{(1,a),(2,a)\} \cup \{(1,b),(1,c),(1,d),(2,b),(2,c),(2,d)\}$

$= (\{1,2\} \otimes \{a\}) \cup (\{1,2\} \otimes \{b,c,d\})$

↕↕ ↕ ↕↕ ↕↕↕

{1,2} {1} {1,2} {1,2,3} .

2.   Same example illustrated with dots:

$2 \times (1 \times 3)$:

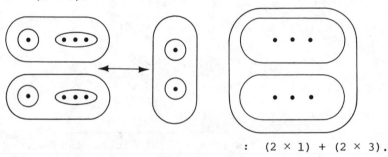

: $(2 \times 1) + (2 \times 3)$.

Exercises   1.   What's wrong with beginning Example 1 with {1,2} ⊗ ({1} ∪ {1,2,3})?

2.   Use sets to illustrate the following instance of the distributive law: $3 \times (2 + 2) = (3 \times 2) + (3 \times 2)$, (a) with braces,   (b) with dots.

3.   Illustrate distributivity of multiplication over addition for cardinal numbers with at least two examples of your own, different from those in the text.

4.   Write out a *proof* of the distributive law for cardinal numbers, using previously established set theoretic distributivity of Cartesian product over union.

Is addition distributive over multiplication?   That is, for cardinal numbers *a*, *b*, *c*, is $a + (b \times c) = (a + b) \times (a + c)$?

Exercises   1.   Look at several specific examples and guess whether or not addition is distributive over multiplication.

2.   What does it take to *prove* your assertion in Exercise 1?

3. If we take $a = 1$, $b = 0$, $c = 0$, then $a + (b \times c) = 1 + (0 \times 0) = 1 + 0 = 1 \times 1 = (1 + 0) \times (1 + 0) = (a + b) \times (a + c)$. Find *all* possible values of a, b, c such that $a + (b \times c) = (a + b) \times (a + c)$.

4. If we (Professors Kelly and Logothetti) say "Theorem: for all cardinal numbers a and b, $(a + b)^2 = a^2 + b^2$," you naturally ask "Is that really true?" and then try some numbers, say $a = 1$, $b = 2$: $(a + b)^2 = (1 + 2)^2 = 3^2 = 3 \times 3 = 9 \neq 5 = 1 + 4 = (1 \times 1) + (2 \times 2) = 1^2 + 2^2 = a^2 + b^2$. "Ha!" you say, "the authors have goofed again because we have found a *counterexample* to their theorem!" And you would be quite right, too. Now in general, what kinds of statements can be proved by exhibiting counterexamples?

Well, now you know the CAD (commutative, associative, distributive) properties. It turns out that these are all the rage in current textbooks, both for elementary school students and their teachers. But there's still the question, "What are they *good* for?" That's a natural question—so natural that in teaching your own students you may want to attend to it first, before you go into the official nomenclature. One way to sell the CAD properties is to introduce examples in which their application is really useful. Once these useful properties are recognized by the students *then* you can present the technical language.

● ●

Objective 21. To cite examples other than those in the text illustrating the usefulness of the three multiplicative CAD properties.

● ●

Examples   1. Multiplicative associativity:

      Hard: $25 \times (4 \times 73)$ Easy: $(25 \times 4) \times 73$.

    2. Multiplicative commutativity:

      Hard: $25 \times 375 \times 4$ Easy: $25 \times 4 \times 375$ (Associativity is also used here.)

    3. Distributivity:

      Hard: $(17 \times 3) + (17 \times 2) + (17 \times 5)$ Easy: $17 \times (3 + 2 + 5) = 17 \times 10$.

      Hard: $35 \times 22 = 35 \times (20 + 2)$ Easy: $(35 \times 20) + (35 \times 2)$.

Exercises 1. Make up at least two examples other than those in the text illustrating the usefulness of the following properties of cardinal numbers: (a) additive associativity, (b) additive commutativity, (c) multiplicative associativity, (d) multiplicative commutativity, (e) distributivity.

2. How was associativity used together with commutativity in the text's examples of multiplicative commutativity? (Explain in detail.)

3. Make up an example altogether different from those given in the text illustrating the usefulness of the CAD laws.

4. Why is it really unnecessary to complete the addition and multiplication tables below? Which law's usefulness is revealed here?

+	0	1	2	3	4	5	6	7	8	9
0	0	1	2	3	4	5	6	7	8	9
1		2	3	4	5	6	7	8	9	10
2			4	5	6	7	8	9	10	11
3				6	7	8	9	10	11	12
4					8	9	10	11	12	13
5						10	11	12	13	14
6							12	13	14	15
7								14	15	16
8									16	17
9										18

×	0	1	2	3	4	5	6	7	8	9	10
0	0										
1	0	1									
2	0	2	4								
3	0	3	6	9							
4	0	4	8	12	16						
5	0	5	10	15	20	25					
6	0	6	12	18	24	30	36				
7	0	7	14	21	28	35	42	49			
8	0	8	16	24	32	40	48	56	64		
9	0	9	18	27	36	45	54	63	72	81	
10	0	10	20	30	40	50	60	70	80	90	100

5. Here's another shortcut for computing, called "collect-ing tens":

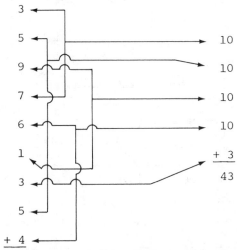

Which of the CAD laws are used here? (Explain in de-tail.)

6. Find another example of an addition and/or multiplica-tion computational shortcut and explain in detail which of the CAD properties are used in it.

7. Here's an old saw from beginning algebra: $(a + b)^2 = a^2 + 2ab + b^2$. Explain in detail which CAD laws are used to derive this result.

EXPANDED FORM

Let's pretend that we don't know anything more than the addition and multiplication tables given in Exercise 4 and the CAD properties, and consider multiplying 73 by 5. Then, according to our "let's pretend":

$73 \times 5 = (7(10) + 3) \times 5$, by expanded notation,
$= 5 \times (7(10) + 3)$, by multiplicative commutativ-ity,
$= (5 \times (7 \times 10)) + (5 \times 3)$, by distributivity,
$= ((5 \times 7) \times 10) + (5 \times 3)$, by multiplicative associativity,
$= (35 \times 10) + 15$, from multiplication tables,
$= ((3 \times 10 + 5) \times 10) + (1 \times 10 + 5)$, expanded notation,
$= (10 \times (3 \times 10 + 5)) + (1 \times 10 + 5)$, multipli-cative commutativity,
$= (3 \times 10^2 + 5 \times 10) + (1 \times 10 + 5)$, distribu-tivity and multiplicative commutativity,
$= 3 \times 10^2 + (5 \times 10 + (1 \times 10 + 5))$, additive associativity,

$$= 3 \times 10^2 + ((5 \times 10 + 1 \times 10) + 5), \text{ distribu-}$$

tivity and additive asso-

ciativity,

$$= 3 \times 10^2 + (10(5 + 1) + 5), \text{ distributivity and}$$

multiplicative commutativ-

ity,

$$= 3 \times 10^2 + (10 \times 6 + 5), \text{ addition table,}$$

$$= 3 \times 10^2 + (6 \times 10 + 5), \text{ multiplicative commu-}$$

tativity,

$$= 365, \text{ by base-ten notation.}$$

The result, 365, is the number of days in a year, which when one considers the tedium of the example seems appropriate.

Exercises   1.   Multiply 7 × 21, justifying each step as in the example.

2.   Do the same for 49 × 3.

3.   List ten things more fun to do than Exercises 1 and 2.

ALGORITHMS   Now that last example was unquestionably one of the big pains of the entire universe, and if that were the only way to multiply, none of us would do it. What has rescued us from such a fate worse than death? The answer is *algorithms*, those noble mechanistic procedures for cranking out answers. Thus, by the usual algorithm for multiplication of cardinal numbers, the computations of that last example would consist of merely

```
   73                      73
 ×  5  which is short for ×  5   which in turn is short
  365                       15
                            35
                           365
```

```
            73
for      ×   5   which again in turn is short for all of that
            15
           350
           365
```

manipulation on the preceding pages.

   This algorithm, however, is not the only one that has been (or is) used for multiplication. And even historical interest aside, there are good pedagogical reasons for returning to the "old math." Consider the plight of a student who is in the sixth grade and has flunked multiplication in the third, fourth, and fifth grades. We could teach the standard algorithm, just as we did in the previous grades, and the student would probably again flunk, just as in the previous grades. But perhaps if we dipped back into another time or another place and tried alternative algorithms we could trick the student into learning to multiply before he realized that this is what he's famous for not being able to do.

Exercises 1. Here is Mexican "cup multiplication" used in the 1500s:

(a) Start with
```
  45
× 73
```
(b) Think 4 × 7 = 28; write
```
  45
× 73
  28
```

(c) Think 4 × 3 = 12; write
```
  45
× 73
 282
   1
```
(d) Think 5 × 7 = 35;

write
```
  45
× 73
 282
  15
   3
```
(e) Think 3 × 5 = 15; write
```
  45
× 73
2825  Here's the
  15   "cup."
  31
```

(f) Add:
```
  45
× 73
2825
  15
  31
3285, Answer.
```

Multiply each of the following by the Mexican cup algorithm. (a) 268 × 73, (b) 8 × 735, (c) 29 × 86.

2. Explain the similarities and differences of the Mexican cup and our own standard multiplication algorithm.

3. Multiply 73 × 5 by the Mexican cup and explain which CAD laws are used and where.

● ●

Objective 22. To perform a given indicated multiplication (or "name the product") according to the following algorithms; explaining each step: (a) grating, (b) Napier's bones, (c) duplication, (d) "mental lightning."

● ●

Grating (or "lattice" or "galley," used in the 12th through 16th centuries in Europe and the Middle East):

Examples 1. 45 × 73

(a)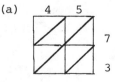

(b)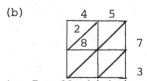

4 × 7 = 28 which is placed in the box below 4 opposite 7

(c)

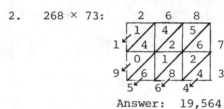

Continuing in the
same manner . . .

(d)

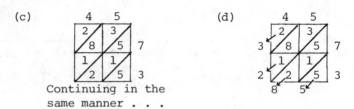

(The 1, 8, 3 diagonal adds to 12, but only the 2
is written down; the 1 is carried to the next
diagonal, going from bottom to top: 1 + 2 = 3.
The answer is 3285.)

2.   268 × 73:

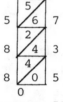

Answer: 19,564

3.   8 × 735:

```
        8
      ┌───┐
    5 │ 5╱│ 7
      │╱6 │
      ├───┤
    8 │ 2╱│ 3
      │╱4 │
      ├───┤
    8 │ 4╱│ 5
      │╱0 │
      └───┘
        0
```

Answer: 5880

Exercises   1.   Multiply the following, using the grating algorithm:
                 (a) 29 × 86,   (b) 317 × 54,   (c) 298 × 3.

            2.   Using the example 8 × 735 = 5880, explain why the
                 grating algorithm works.

            3.   State advantages and disadvantages of the grating al-
                 gorithm.

            4.   Show how the grating algorithm may be used to multiply
                 the algebraic expressions: (a) $(3x + 2) \cdot (2x + 1)$,
                 (b) $(3x^2 + 2x + 4) \cdot (2x + 1)$,   (c) $(3x^2 + 2x + 4) \cdot$
                 $(2x^2 + x + 5)$.

Napier's bones or "rods" were invented in 1617 by John
Napier, an Englishman, and used in Europe and the Far
East. The following rods were originally carved out of
ivory (hence the appellation "bones"):

Examples 1. 45 × 73:

(a) "Four-bone"
    "Five-bone"
    "One-bone"

(b)

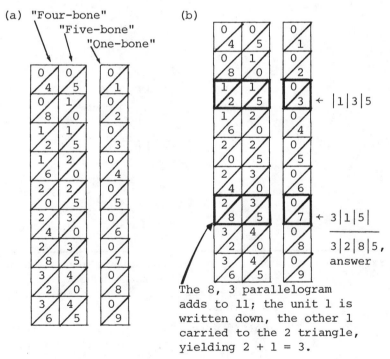

← |1|3|5

← 3|1|5|
_____
3|2|8|5,
answer

The 8, 3 parallelogram
adds to 11; the unit 1 is
written down, the other 1
carried to the 2 triangle,
yielding 2 + 1 = 3.

Note carefully the use of the "one-bone" and the column position of the products.

2. 268 × 73:

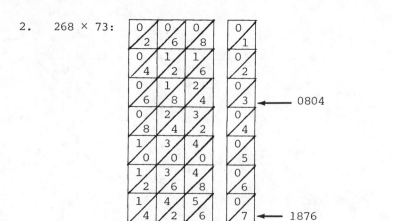

0804

1876

19564, answer

3. 8 × 735:

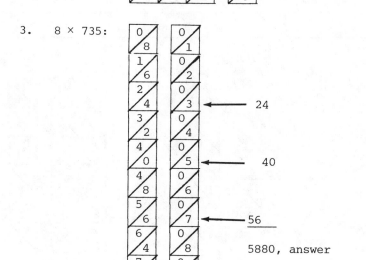

24

40

56

5880, answer

Exercises   1. Make a set of 27 Napier's bones (three one-bones, three two-bones, three three-bones, etc.) out of heavy cardboard strips (bright colors would be nice), 1 inch by 9 inches.

2. Multiply the following, using Napier's bones: (a) 29 × 86,   (b) 317 × 54,   (c) 298 × 3,   (d) 707 × 5, (e) 707 × 551.

3. Using the example 8 × 735 = 5880, explain how the Napier's bones method is related to the grating algorithm.

4. State advantages and disadvantages of Napier's bones in carrying out multiplication computations.

Duplication (sometimes called "duplation" and widely used by ancient Egyptians and by Europeans on up into the Renaissance, still used by Russian peasants in this century) relies on a sound knowledge of how to multiply by 2.

Examples   1.   45 × 73:

(a)   1 × 73 =   73   (b) Pick out the   1 × 73 =   73
       2 × 73 = 146   powers of 2 that   ~~2 × 73 = 146~~
       4 × 73 = 292   add up to 45 and   4 × 73 = 292
       8 × 73 = 584   cross out the oth-   8 × 73 = 584
   16 × 73 = 1168   ers; then add: ~~16 × 73 = 1168~~
   32 × 73 = 2336   32 × 73 = 2336

45 × 73 = 3285, Answer

2.   268 × 73:

268 × 1 =   268
~~268 × 2 =   536~~
~~268 × 4 =   1072~~
268 × 8 =   2144
~~268 × 16 =   4288~~
~~268 × 32 =   8576~~
268 × 64 = 17152
268 × 73 = 19564

3.   8 × 735:

~~1 × 735 =   735~~
~~2 × 735 =   1470~~
~~4 × 735 =   2940~~
8 × 735 =   5880

Exercises   1.   Multiply the following, using the duplication algorithm: (a) 29 × 86,   (b) 317 × 54,   (c) 298 × 3,   (d) 707 × 5,   (e) 707 × 551.

2.   Using the example 45 × 73 = 3285, explain why the duplication algorithm works.   (Which of the CAD laws is the most crucial one here?)

3.   With which number do we begin the doubling (= "duplication")?   Why?   Does it really matter?   Why?

4.   State advantages and disadvantages of the duplication algorithm.

5.   Here's a variation of duplication used by the ancient Egyptians, which requires no more than doubling three times and multiplying by some tens:

45×73:

$$
\begin{array}{rcr}
1 \times 73 &=& 73 \\
\sout{2 \times 73} &=& \sout{146} \\
4 \times 73 &=& 292 \\
\sout{8 \times 73} &=& \sout{584} \\
\sout{10 \times 73} &=& \sout{730} \\
\sout{20 \times 73} &=& \sout{1460} \\
\hline
40 \times 73 &=& 2920 \\
\hline
45 \times 73 &=& 3285, \text{ Answer}
\end{array}
$$

Use this variation to multiply   (a) 29×86,
(b) 317×54,   (c) 298×3,   (d) 707×5,
(e) 707×551.

6.   Why does the algorithm in Exercise 5 work?

7.   The algorithm of Exercise 5 uses the fact that 1293,
6789, or $abcd$ (meaning $1000a + 100b + 10c + d$), etc.
when multiplied by 10, is 12,930, 67,890, $ab,cd0$,
respectively.   Prove that this is so.

"Mental lightning" requires practice if you really want
to astound friends and acquaintances (not bad for those
students who have spare time).   The only writing allowed is the answer—no intermediate computations.
45×73:

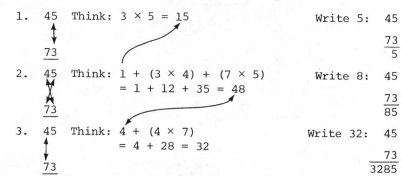

1.   45   Think: $3 \times 5 = 15$ Write 5:   45
     73   73
                                                    ————
                                                      5

2.   45   Think: $1 + (3 \times 4) + (7 \times 5)$ Write 8:   45
     73          $= 1 + 12 + 35 = 48$ 73
                                                             ————
                                                               85

3.   45   Think: $4 + (4 \times 7)$ Write 32:   45
     73          $= 4 + 28 = 32$ 73
                                                              ————
                                                              3285

Exercises   1.   Just write down the answers to the following multiplication exercises (no cheating, now!):

(a) 32   (b) 53   (c) 53   (d) 77   (e) 86
    14   24   87   5   9
    ——   ——   ——   ——   ——
      ,   ,   ,   ,   .

2.   Using the example $45 \times 73 = 3285$, explain why the
"mental lightning" method works.

3.   Try to devise a "mental lightning" method for multiplying a three-digit number by a two-digit number, say
312×45.

We digress, slightly, at this point to look at some methods of multiplication which are both fun and useful. With this in mind we establish the following objective.

● ●

Objective 23. To give the algebraic formulas underlying each of the following methods of multiplication: (a) Roman finger, (b) nines finger, (c) "little more than 100," (d) "little less than 100."

● ●

Nines finger multiplication may delight students but does have limited value. It only works for 9 times a one-digit number.

Number your fingers from 1 to 10, left to right, using both hands, of course.

Examples   1.   Then to multiply 6 × 9 count over to finger 6 and fold it down. The number of fingers preceding the folded finger, 5, is the number of tens, which makes 50, and the ones following, 4, are the units. So the answer is 54.

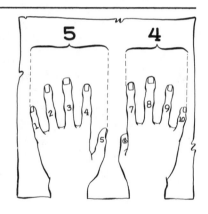

2.   Another example, 3 × 9. Fold down the 3 finger. There are two to the left of it and seven to the right, so the product is 27.

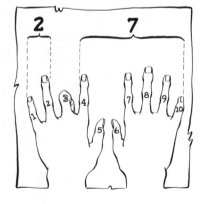

We can extend this multiplication to 9 times a two-digit number provided the tens digit is smaller than the ones digit.

Examples 1. 27 × 9. Leave a space be-tween the 2 and the 3 finger and fold down the 7 finger. Then the hundreds are the number of fingers to the left of the space, 2, and the tens are the number of fingers between the space and the folded finger, 4, with the fingers to the right as units, 3. So the answer is 243.

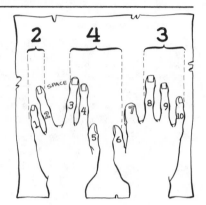

2. Consider 48 × 9 for another example. Peek at these hands!

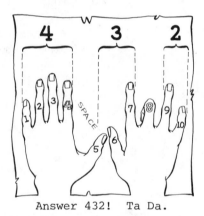

Answer 432! Ta Da.

Exercises 1. Verify nines finger multiplication by running through the products of 9 × 1, 9 × 2, . . . , 9 × 8, 9 × 9. Sketch pictures of each.

2. Multiply the following using the nines finger method: (a) 24 × 9, (b) 78 × 9, (c) 69 × 9, (d) 56 × 9.

3. Why does nines finger multiplication work? Find an algebraic formula for it. (Hint: In our first example, the problem is *does* 5(10) + (10 − 6) = 9 × 6?)

4. Try to find an algebraic formula for nines finger multiplication with two digits. (Harder!)

In *Roman finger multiplication* we number the fingers of each hand as follows:

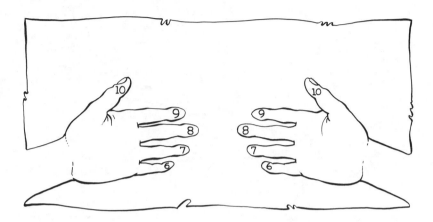

We can now use our hands as calculators, *providing* we know (a) how to multiply up to 5 × 5, (b) how to multiply by 10. (The old Romans presumably knew these facts, but 6 × 8, for example, was graduate work.) We'll illustrate with specific examples.

Examples   1.   6 × 8: Here a 6 finger and an 8 finger are held together stationary, along with the fingers under them, as illustrated below. The other fingers are wiggled. We take the number of stationary fingers times ten, plus the product of the numbers of wiggling fingers.

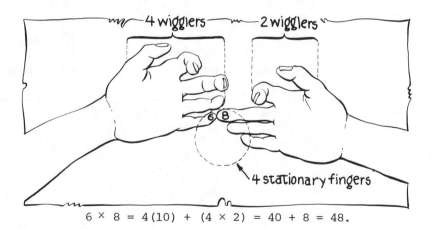

6 × 8 = 4(10) + (4 × 2) = 40 + 8 = 48.

2. 9×7:

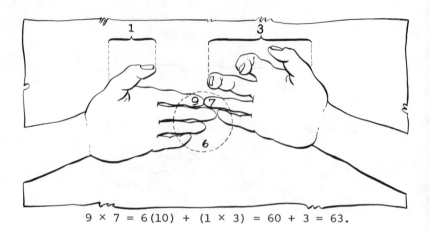

$$9 \times 7 = 6(10) + (1 \times 3) = 60 + 3 = 63.$$

3.   We look at *why* the trick in Example 2 works. To this
     end we reconsider the various numbers involved. We can
     think of 9 as $(5 + 4)$ and 7 as $(5 + 2)$, since each fin-
     ger is numbered 5 plus something. We think of 6 as 4 +
     2, and we consider 1 to be 5 − 4, 3 to be 5 − 2.   So
     the question is reduced to the following: Does
     $(5 + 4)(5 + 2) = (4 + 2)(10) + (5 − 4)(5 − 2)$?   The
     left-hand side equals:

   $$(5 + 4)(5 + 2) = 5^2 + 5(2) + 4(5) + 4(2).$$

And the right-hand side equals:

   $$(4 + 2)(10) + (5 − 4)(5 − 2)$$

   $$= 4(10) + 2(10) + 5^2 − 5(2) − 4(5) + 4(2)$$

   $$= 4(10 − 5) + 2(10 − 5) + 5^2 + 4(2)$$

   $$= 4(5) + 2(5) + 5^2 + 4(2)$$

   $$= \text{left-hand side.}$$

Since right-hand side equals left-hand side, QED.

Exercises   1.   Draw sketches (à la Examples 1 and 2) showing how to
                 Roman finger multiply (a) 6×7,   (b) 7×7,   (c)
                 8×9,   (d) 8×8,   (e) 9×10,   (f) 10×10,   (g)
                 6×6,   (h) 5×5.

            2.   Check the arithmetic structure (à la Example 3) of the
                 Roman finger multiplication of (a) 6×7,   (b) 8×9.

            3.   In general for Roman finger multiplication, $(5 + m) \times$
                 $(5 + n)$ represents our typical left-hand side. What
                 is our typical right-hand side?

            4.   Prove that the left-hand side and right-hand side in
                 Exercise 3 are always equal.

A more useful multiplication technique using complements follows. Suppose you are asked to multiply two numbers which are "a *Little Less than* 100."

Examples

1. Say 88 and 94. Then

    88   88 + 12 = 100; i.e., 12 is the complement of 88
    × 94   94 + 6 = 100; and 6 is the complement of 94.
    ────
    8272   The product of the complements is the tens and
            units position of our answer. Here 12 × 6 = 72.
            And the difference of one number and the complement of the other is the hundreds and thousands position. Here 88 - 6 = 82 or 94 - 12 = 82.

2. Try 96 × 87 for another example:

    96   96 + 4 = 100
    × 87   87 + 13 = 100   4 × 13 = 52 and 96 - 13 = 83.
    ────
    8352

    What happens if the product of the complements is larger than 99? Well, we just carry that 1, i.e., add it to the difference of the number and the other complement.

3. Consider 88 × 88:

    88   Now 88 + 12 = 100 and 12 × 12 = 144.
    × 88   Finally, 88 - 12 = 76, so
    ────
    144
    76
    ────
    7744

Exercises

1. Why does the "little less than 100" method work? Find an algebraic formula for it. (Hint: Let one number be 100 - m and the other be 100 - n.

2. Multiply the following using the "little less than 100" method. (a) 96 × 96, (b) 82 × 96, (c) 94 × 73, (d) 98 × 87, (e) 75 × 95.

3. Devise a multiplication method called "little less than 200."

4. Devise a multiplication method called "little less than 1000."

If we are asked to find the product of two numbers "*a little larger than* 100" we can use a similar method.

Examples	1.	$\begin{array}{r} 102 \\ \times\ 107 \\ \hline 10914 \end{array}$	$102 - 2 = 100$ where the complements' product
			$107 - 7 = 100$ is $7 \times 2 = 14$.

The difference of 102 and the complement of 107 is $102 - (-7) = 102 + 7 = 109$.   (Note: $107 - (-2) = 109$, also.)   So 14 is the tens and units position again, and the difference of the number and the complement of the other number is the hundreds, thousands, and higher positions.

2. $\begin{array}{r} 112 \\ \times\ 103 \\ \hline 11536 \end{array}$ $112 - 12 = 100$

   $103 - \ \ 3 = 100$ $12 \times 3 = 36$ and $112 - (-3)$
                                                              $= 115$.

3. $\begin{array}{r} 113 \\ \times\ 113 \\ \hline 169 \\ 126 \\ \hline 12769 \end{array}$ $113 - 13 = 100$; $13 \times 13 = 169$ and $113 - (-13)$
   $= 126$.   But what do we do with the hundreds position in 169?   Just carry it as before.

Exercises   1.   Why does the "little more than 100" method work?   Is this question any different from Exercise 1 of the preceding group of exercises?

2.   Multiply the following using the "little more than 100" method.   (a) 105×103,   (b) 111×102,   (c) 106×106, (d) 111×111,   (e) 102×108,   (f) 106×113.

3.   Devise a multiplication method called the "little more than 300" method.

4.   Devise a multiplication method called the "little more than 2000" method.

Although the multiplication algorithms *do* depend on a "polynomial" numeration system (i.e., with numbers expressed as sums of multiples of powers of some base: $8x^2 + 4x + 5$, where $x = 10$, is the familiar 845), they do *not* depend on the base being ten (except finger multiplication!), and thus they may be used to carry out computations with bases other than ten.

OTHER BASES

● ●

Objective   24.   To complete computation of given indicated products in bases other than ten (including the "eight-finger" system).

● ●

1. Base two;
   usual algorithm:

$$\begin{array}{r} 1101 \\ \underline{101} \\ 1101 \\ \underline{11010} \\ 1000001 \end{array}$$

2. Base eight;
   usual algorithm:

$$\begin{array}{r} \text{\textcircled{\#}} \ \# \\ \underline{\neq \ =} \\ - \ \text{\textcircled{\#}} \ \bullet \\ \underline{= \ \neq \ \#} \\ = \ \text{\textcircled{\#}} - \ \bullet \end{array}$$

3. Base three;
   grating algorithm:

	1	1	2	
1	0/2	0/2	1/1	2
0	0/1	0/1	0/2	1
	1	2	2	

$112 \times 21 = 10122$

4. Base twelve;
   grating algorithm:

	3	T	
3	2/9	9/2	E
7	1/3	4/2	5
	9	2	

$3T \times E5 = 3792$

5. Base five;
   duplication:

$$\begin{array}{rcl} 1 \times 34 &=& 34 \\ \overline{2} \times \overline{34} &\overline{=}& \overline{123} \\ 4 \times 34 &=& 301 \\ \overline{13} \times \overline{34} &\overline{=}& \overline{1102} \\ 31 \times 34 &=& 2204 \\ \underline{41 \times 34} &\underline{=}& \underline{3044} \quad \text{Answer} \end{array}$$

6. Base eight;
   duplication:

$$\begin{array}{rcl} - \ \times \ (\ \# \ \text{\textcircled{\#}} \ ) &=& \# \ \text{\textcircled{\#}} \\ = \ \times \ (\ \# \ \text{\textcircled{\#}} \ ) &=& - \ - \ = \\ \# \ \times \ (\ \# \ \text{\textcircled{\#}} \ ) &=& = \ = \ \# \\ - \ \bullet \ \times \ (\ \# \ \text{\textcircled{\#}} \ ) &=& \# \ \text{\textcircled{\#}} \ \bullet \\ = \ \bullet \ \times \ (\ \# \ \text{\textcircled{\#}} \ ) &=& - \ - \ = \ \bullet \end{array}$$

add all lines leaving out only these two lines

$$(\ = \ \neq \ ) \times (\ \# \ \text{\textcircled{\#}} \ ) = (- \ = \ \overline{\text{\textcircled{\#}}} \ \overline{\text{\textcircled{\#}}}) \quad \text{Answer}$$

Exercises

1. Carry out each of the following multiplications by (i) standard algorithm, (ii) grating, (iii) duplication:

   (a) Base two: $\begin{array}{r} 1011 \\ \underline{110} \end{array}$ (b) Base five: $\begin{array}{r} 231 \\ \underline{43} \end{array}$

(c) Base eight: ⊕ ⊕
  # =
  _____
  ,

(d) Base eight: ≠ ⊕̄
  ⊕ ≠
  _____
  ,

(e) Base eleven: 32
  4T
  ____
  ,

(f) Base twelve: 3TE
  45
  ____
  .

2. Fill in the next two entries:

(a) Base two: 11, 110, 1001, 1100, _____ , _____ ;

(b) Base five: 12, 24, 103, 211, _____ , _____ ;

(c) Base eight: #, =•, -••, #••, _____ , _____ ;

(d) Base twelve: 11, 55, 231, E35, _____ , _____ .

3. What possible base(s) (if any) yield the following multiplications?

(a) 33	(b) 111	(c) 312	(d) 3T2
4	11	21	2
242,	21,	6552,	E26.

_____

DIVISION

True Love in this differs from gold and clay, that to divide is not to take away.
  —Percy Bysshe Shelley,
  Epipsychidion

• •

Objective 25. To define the *quotient* (both with and without a *remainder*) of two cardinal numbers and illustrate these definitions with original examples.

• •

It turns out that mathematics is more like gold and clay than love; to divide is very like to take away. Recall that subtraction of cardinal numbers was defined in terms of addition. Let us use analogy (with a respectful nod to Professor Polya) in defining division in terms of multiplication and see if the analogy holds up (i.e., makes sense).
  Old statement, defining subtraction:

  For cardinal numbers a, b, c, $a - b = c$ means $a = b + c$.

  New analogous statement, defining division:

  For cardinal numbers a, b, c, $a \div b = c$ means $a = b \times c$.

(We substituted $\div$ for $-$, and $\times$ for $+$.)

Does this new statement make sense? Does $6 \div 3 = 2$ mean $6 = 3 \times 2$? Yes! So our analogy holds up. Of course, the expression $a \div b$ won't be defined in terms of cardinal numbers for just *any* old a and b, just as previously the expression $a - b$ wasn't for *all* cardinal numbers a and b.

Definition

For cardinal numbers a, b, c, the <u>quotient</u> $a \div b = c$ means $a = b \times c$. For cardinal numbers a, b, c, r, the <u>quotient</u> $a \div b = c$ with <u>remainder</u> r means $a = (b \times c) + r$.

The first part of that last definition has already been illustrated in a preceding paragraph, so let's look at examples of the second part:

Examples

1. $13 \div 4 = 3$, remainder 1 means $13 = (4 \times 3) + 1$.

2. $9 \div 2 = 4$ with remainder 1 means $9 = (2 \times 4) + 1$.

3. $8 \div 2 = 4$ means $8 = 2 \times 4$.

Exercises

1. Rewrite each of the following quotients in terms of multiplications and additions: (a) $10 \div 11 = 0$, r 10 (Answer: $10 = (11 \times 0) + 10$.); (b) $100 \div 11 = 9$, r 1; (c) $1000 \div 11 = 90$, r 10; (d) $10,000 \div 11 = 909$, r 1; (e) $100,000 \div 11 = 9090$, r 10; (f) $11 \div 3 = 3$, r 2; (g) $111 \div 3 = 37$; (h) $1111 \div 3 = 370$, r 1; (i) $11,111 \div 3 = 3703$, r 2; (j) $111,111 \div 3 = 37,037$; (k) $102 \div 3 = 34$; (l) $120 \div 3 = 67$; (m) $210 \div 3 = 70$.

2. Rewrite each of the following as a quotient: (a) $234 = 3 \times 78$ (Answer: $234 \div 3 = 78$); (b) $236 = 3 \times 78 + 2$; (c) $237 = 3 \times 79$; (d) $273 = 3 \times 91$; (e) $327 = 3 \times 109$; (f) $372 = 3 \times 124$; (g) $723 = 3 \times 241$; (h) $732 = 3 \times 244$.

Mathematics teachers are famous for saying "Division by zero is illegal!" They're *not* so famous, however, for explaining why.

Division by zero can lead to nasty surprises!

●●●

Objective 26.   To explain, with an example other than given in the
                 text, why division by zero is not allowed.

●●●

As background for an investigation of the cardinal sin of dividing by zero, let us note the following:

Let a be any cardinal number. Then $(a \times 3) \div 3 = a$, since by the definition of quotient $(a \times 3) \div 3 = a$ means $a \times 3 = 3 \times a$, which is true. Likewise, $(a \times 2) \div 2 = a$, and $(a \times 1) \div 1 = a$. Now if division by 0 were possible, we'd have $(a \times 0) \div 0 = a$; thus, for example, $(7 \times 0) \div 0 = 7$, and $(5 \times 0) \div 0 = 5$.

Notice that $7 \times 0 = 0 = 5 \times 0$. Therefore if division by 0 were legal, then $(7 \times 0) \div 0 = (5 \times 0) \div 0$, or $7 = 5$. Since supposition of the legality of division by zero leads to saying that $7 = 5$, we must do away with that supposition and declare that division by zero is *illegal*.

If this argument does not appeal to you, try another one:

Suppose this time that division by zero is legal, and $3 \div 0 = s$, some cardinal number. Then, using the definition of quotient, we'd have $3 = 0 \times s$. But $0 \times s = 0$. Therefore, $3 = 0$, nonsense once again!

Exercises

1. Contrive your own example (not $7 = 5$ or $3 = 0$) to show that division by zero is illegal.

2. "Prove" that $1 = 0$, and therefore every number equals zero, since every number is a multiple of 1.

3. For beginning algebra enthusiasts:

   Let $a = b$. Then

   $a^2 = ab$ (equals multiplied by equals)

   $a^2 - b^2 = ab - b^2$ (equals subtracted from equals)

   $(a - b)(a + b) = (a - b)b$ ("factoring"—CAD laws)

   $a + b = b$ (canceling $a - b$ on both sides of the equation).

   So if $a = b = 1$, then $2 = 1$. Explain what's wrong with this "paradox." (Between which two steps is an illegal maneuver made? What is the illegal maneuver?)

4. Concoct your own, original "paradox" of the type in Exercise 3.

5. What is $2 \div 2$? $1 \div 1$? $0 \div 0$?

ALGORITHMS

• •

Objective 27. To complete computation of a given indicated quotient according to (a) repeated subtraction, (b) the standard long division algorithm.

• •

Here we'll definitely ignore true love and go along with gold and clay, saying that to divide is indeed to take away. The fact is, most current textbooks consider division as repeated subtraction and use this point of view to plausibly develop the long division algorithm. Here are some examples of division by repeated subtraction:

Examples   1.   7)28:   28

$$\begin{array}{rl}
28 & \\
-\ 7 & \quad 1 \leftarrow \text{(For one 7 subtracted.)} \\
\hline
21 & \\
-\ 7 & \quad 1 \\
\hline
14 & \\
-\ 7 & \quad 1 \\
\hline
7 & \\
-\ 7 & \quad \underline{1} \quad \text{(Answer: 4, with no remainder.)} \\
\hline
0 & \quad 4
\end{array}$$

2.   7)18:   18

$$\begin{array}{rl}
18 & \\
-\ 7 & \quad 1 \\
\hline
11 & \\
-\ 7 & \quad \underline{1} \\
\hline
4 & \quad 2 \quad \text{(Answer: 2, with remainder 4.)}
\end{array}$$

3.   17)429:   429

$$\begin{array}{rl}
429 & \\
-\ 170 & \quad 10 \leftarrow \text{(We needn't restrict ourselves to} \\
\hline
259 & \quad \quad \quad \text{subtracting only single 17s; } any \\
-\ 170 & \quad 10 \quad \text{easily computed multiple will do.)} \\
\hline
89 & \\
-\ 34 & \quad 2 \\
\hline
55 & \\
-\ 34 & \quad 2 \\
\hline
21 & \\
-\ 17 & \quad \underline{1} \\
\hline
4 & \quad 25 \quad \text{(Answer: 25, with remainder 4.)}
\end{array}$$

4.   763)479,164:   479,164

$$\begin{array}{rl}
479,164 & \\
-\ 152,600 & \quad 200 \\
\hline
326,564 & \\
-\ 305,200 & \quad 400 \\
\hline
21,364 & \\
-\ 15,260 & \quad 20 \\
\hline
6,104 & \\
-\ 3,052 & \quad 4 \\
\hline
3,052 & \\
-\ 3,052 & \quad \underline{4} \\
\hline
0 & \quad 628, \quad \text{Answer.}
\end{array}$$

(Notice that we can use the knowledge of the result of multiplying by 200 to get easily the result of multiplying by 400, then 20, then 4.)

Alternative solution:

$$\begin{array}{rl}
479,164 & \\
-\ 228,900 & \quad 300 \\
\hline
250,264 & \\
-\ 228,900 & \quad 300 \\
\hline
21,364 & \\
-\ 15,260 & \quad 20 \\
\hline
6,104 & \\
-\ 4,578 & \quad 6 \\
\hline
1,526 & \\
-\ 1,526 & \quad \underline{2} \\
\hline
0 & \quad 628, \quad \text{Answer.}
\end{array}$$

Observe that using this strategy there is no single, uniquely correct way of dividing. While this may irritate the more pedantic element of the community, it is nevertheless psychologically sound: It allows for individuality and a touch of creativity; furthermore, it rewards unusual perception with a shorter process.

As you may have noticed, the most rewarding process (i.e., the shortest, most efficient process) possible is just the standard long division algorithm, which is easily illustrated with the hindsight gained from the last two "common sense" examples above:

```
                6
Step  1.  763)479164    which really means      479164
              4578                             - 457800   600
               213
```

```
               62
Step  2.  763)479164    which really means      479164
              4578                             - 457800   600
              2136                                21364
              1526                             -  15260    20
               610                                 6104
```

```
               628
Step  3.  763)479164    which really means      479164
              4578                             - 457800   600
              2136                                21364
              1526                             -  15260    20
              6104                                 6104
              6104                             -   6104     8
                 0                                    0   628.
```

Exercises 1. Compute each of the following by (i) repeated subtraction, (ii) another version of repeated subtraction, (iii) the standard long division algorithm. (a) 21)263, (b) 324)654728, (c) 729)8254967.

2. State advantages and disadvantages of the repeated subtraction approach in contrast to the long division algorithm.

3. Solve the following *alphametics* (or "cryptarithms"), that is; find correspondences of numerals with letters that result in correct division computations. These correspondences must be one-to-one; i.e., if you make s correspond to 3, then you cannot have another s correspond to 7, or any other letter correspond to 3.)

   (a) *six*)*a dozen*, with quotient *six* (b) (For women's libbers) *us*)*male*, with quotient *mud*

   (c) (For men's libbers) *tut*)*women!*, with quotient *tut* (Consider ! as a letter), (d) *quiz*)*zzzzzz*, with quotient *nap*.

FACTORS   At this point we know how to handle the operations of
addition, subtraction, multiplication, and division of
whole numbers. Hence we are in a position to explore
creatively some of the properties of specific numbers.
Creative exploration is one of the principal activities
of a mathematician; for this reason an elementary
teacher is not really teaching mathematics properly unless he or she is involving the students in "guessing
and proving" (a favorite phrase of Professor Polya).
There is lots of neat guessing and proving to be done
with the whole numbers. Many of the guesses and proofs
involve the concept of factors.

● ●

Objective   28.   To analyze the factors of a given cardinal number.

● ●

A *factor* of a cardinal number n is a number that divides into n and leaves no remainder (i.e., a remainder
of zero); thus, 3 is a factor of 6 because $6 \div 3 = 2$
with remainder 0 (i.e., $6 = 3 \times 2$), while 4 is not a
factor of 6 because $6 \div 4 = 1$ with remainder 2 (i.e.,
$6 = (4 \times 1) + 2$).

Examples   1.   Find all factors of (a) 1,   (b) 2,   (c) 4,   (d) 6,
(e) 0.
   (a) the only factor of 1 is 1 itself;   (b) the factors of 2 are 1 and 2;   (c) the factors of 4 are 1, 2,
and 4;   (d) the factors of 6 are 1, 2, 3, and 6;
(e) every whole number is a factor of 0, except 0 itself (since division by zero is undefined).

2.   How many factors has (a) $1 = 2^0$,   (b) $2 = 2^1$,   (c)
$4 = 2^2$,   (d) $8 = 2^3$,   (e) 2^n?
   (a) 1;   (b) 2;   (c) 3;   (d) 4—they are 1, 2, 4, 8;
(e) $n + 1$.

3.   How many elements of $\{1,2,3,4,5, \ldots , 56,57,58,59,
60\}$ have as a factor (a) 1,   (b) 2,   (c) 3,   (d) 4,
(e) 17?
   (a) 60;   (b) 30—they are $\{2,4,6, \ldots , 58,60\} =
\{2 \times 1, 2 \times 2, 2 \times 3, \ldots , 2 \times 29, 2 \times 30\}$;   (c) 20—
they are $\{3,6,9, \ldots , 57,60\} = \{3 \times 1, 3 \times 2, 3 \times 3,
\ldots , 3 \times 19, 3 \times 20\}$;   (d) 15;   (e) 3—they are
$\{17,34,51\} = \{17 \times 1, 17 \times 2, 17 \times 3\}$.

4.   What is the greatest factor *common to* (or shared by)
$2 = 1 \times 2$, $6 = 2 \times 3$, $12 = 3 \times 4$, $20 = 4 \times 5$, $n^2 + n
= n \times (n + 1)$? Here the answer is 2, since it divides
6, 12, 20, and $n \times (n + 1)$ and is the largest factor of
2 itself. (Why is 2 a factor of $n \times (n + 1)$?)

Exercises   1.   Find all factors of (a) 3,   (b) 5,   (c) 7,   (d) 9, (e) 11,   (f) 13,   (g) 15,   (h) 17,   (i) 19,   (j) 21, (k) 23,   (l) 25.

2.   Find all factors of (a) 10,   (b) 12,   (c) 14,   (d) 16, (e) 18,   (f) 20,   (g) 22,   (h) 24.

3.   How many factors has (a) 3,   (b) 9,   (c) 27,   (d) 81, (e) 3^n?

4.   How many factors has (a) 4,   (b) 16,   (c) 64,   (d) 256, (e) 4^n?

5.   How many elements of $\{117,118,119, \ldots, 6782,6783, 6784\}$ have as a factor (a) 2,   (b) 3,   (c) 5,   (d) 17, (e) 689?

6.   How many elements of $\{1,2,3, \ldots, 1198,1199,1200\}$ have as a factor (a) 1,   (b) 2,   (c) 3,   (d) 4,   (e) 5, (f) 6,   (g) 7,   (h) 8,   (i) 9,   (j) 10,   (k) 11, (l) 121,   (m) 234?

7.   What is the greatest factor common to

(a) $6 = 1 \times 2 \times 3, \quad 24 = 2 \times 3 \times 4, \quad 60 = 3 \times 4 \times 5,$
$n(n + 1)(n + 2)$;

(b) $18 = 3 \times 6, \quad 28 = 4 \times 7, \quad 40 = 5 \times 8, \quad 54 = 6 \times 9,$
$(n + 2)(n + 5)$;

(c) 24,   120,   360,   840,
$n(n + 1)(n + 2)(n + 3)$;

(d) all cardinal numbers of the form
$n(n + 1)(n + 2)(n + 3)(n + 4)$;

(e) all cardinal numbers of the form
$n(n + 2)(n + 3)(n + 4)$?

8.   The numbers 2, 3 and 5 are factors of how many of the numbers

(a) $1, 2, 3, \ldots, 8, 9, 10$;

(b) $1, 2, 3, \ldots, 98, 99, 100$;

(c) $1, 2, 3, \ldots, 998, 999, 1000$?

9.   The numbers 2, 3, *or* 5 are factors of how many of the numbers

(a) $1, 2, 3, \ldots, 8, 9, 10$;

(b) $1, 2, 3, \ldots, 98, 99, 100$;

(c) $1, 2, 3, \ldots, 998, 999, 1000$?

10.   How do Exercises 8 and 9 differ?

11.   Why did the Empress ask Emperor Maximilian to work some division problems using her lipstick instead of a pencil? (Answer: She wanted to see Max factor.)

| PRIME FACTORS | We cast about for another meaty aspect of cardinal numbers, and this time our choice is primes. A *prime number* is a whole number with precisely two factors (namely, itself and 1). |

● ●

| Objective   29. | To find prime factors of given (reasonably small) numbers. |

● ●

| Examples | 1. | Find all prime factors of (a) 1, (b) 2, (c) 4, (d) 6, (e) 0. |

(a) There are none, because 1 has only one factor and therefore is not a prime; (b) 2; (c) 2; (d) 2,3; (e) all primes.

2. To find the prime factors of (a) 40, (b) 41, (c) 42, (d) 43.

(a) $40 = 4 \times 10 = 2 \times 2 \times 2 \times 5$, so the prime factors are 2 and 5.

(b) 41 is a prime; hence its only prime factor is 41.

(c) $42 = 2 \times 21 = 2 \times 3 \times 7$; prime factors are 2, 3, 7.

(d) The only prime factor of 43 is 43. (Note: 41 and 43 are called *twin primes* because they are (i) prime and (ii) consecutive odd whole numbers.)

3. Find all prime numbers less than 50. Here we need only consider the numbers 2, 3, 4, . . . , 48, 49, 50 and discard those that are divisible by 2, 3, 5, or 7, excepting 2, 3, 5, and 7 themselves. (*Why* just 2, 3, 5, or 7?) We can do this systematically by circling each prime, then crossing out all of its subsequent multiples:

② ③ -4 ⑤ -6 ⑦ -8 -9 +0 ⑪
+2 ⑬ +4 +5 +6 ⑰ +8 ⑲ 20 2+
22 ㉓ 24 25 26 27 28 ㉙ 30 ㉛
32 33 34 35 36 ㊲ 38 39 40 ㊶
42 ㊸ 44 45 46 ㊼ 48 49 50

So the answer is 2, 3, 5, 7, 11, 13, 17, 19, 23, 29, 31, 37, 41, 43, 47. (Those that are underlined are twin primes.) This process for finding primes is called the "Sieve of Eratosthenes."

4. Find all primes of the form $n^2 - 1$. Besides $3 = 2^2 - 1$, there are none, because $n^2 - 1 = (n - 1)(n + 1)$.

1.   Find all prime factors of (a) 3,   (b) 5,   (c) 7,
         (d) 9,   (e) 11,   (f) 13,   (g) 15,   (h) 17,   (i) 19,
         (j) 21,   (k) 23,   (l) 25.

     2.   Find all prime factors of (a) 8,   (b) 10,   (c) 12,
         (d) 14,   (e) 16,   (f) 18,   (g) 20,   (h) 22,   (i) 24.

     3.   Find the prime factors of (a) 254,   (b) 255,   (c) 256.

     4.   Find 15 pairs of twin primes.

     5.   Find all prime numbers between (a) 50 and 100,   (b) 100
         and 150,   (c) 150 and 200,   (d) 200 and 250,   (e) 250
         and 300.

     6.   What is the largest prime we need to test in each part
         of Exercise 5? What is the general rule in this situ-
         ation?

     7.   3 is a prime, but 3 = (2 - 1)(2 + 1). Why is this not
         a contradiction?

     8.   Find all primes of the form $n^2 + 1$ that are less than
         1000.

     9.   Find all primes of the form $n^3 - 1$ that are less than
         1000.

    10.   Find all primes of the form $n^3 + 1$ that are less than
         1000.

    11.   Find all primes of the form $n^4 - 1$ that are less than
         1000.

    12.   Find all primes of the form $n^4 + 1$ that are less than
         1000.

    13.   Find all primes of the form $n^5 - 1$ that are less than
         1000.

    14.   Find all primes of the form $n^5 + 1$ that are less than
         1000.

    15.   Find all prime rib less than $2.00 per pound and tell
         us (Kelly and Logothetti) where to find it!

DIVISIBILITY   If, instead of a reasonably small whole number, we are
RULES   given an unreasonably large number, what do we do?
                 Well, we might try a divisibility rule.

● ●

Objective 30.   Given a divisibility rule, to explain why it works.

● ●

Examples   1.   Rule: If the sum of the digits of a number is divisible
                 by 3, then, and only then, so is the original number.

Consider 8154. 8 + 1 + 5 + 4 = 18, divisible by 3.
So 3 must be a (prime) factor of 8154; in fact,
8154 = 3 × 2718. Why does this work? We get insights
by writing 8154 in expanded notation:

$$8154 = 8(1000) + 1(100) + 5(10) + 4$$

$$= 8(999 + 1) + 1(99 + 1) + 5(9 + 1) + 4$$

$$= 8(999) + 1(99) + 5(9) + (8 + 1 + 5 + 4).$$

Since 8(999), 1(99) and 5(9) are all divisible by 3,
8154 is divisible by 3 if and only if (8 + 1 + 5 + 4)
is divisible by 3.

2. Rule: A number has 5 as a factor if and only if its
units digit is either 5 or 0.

Consider 8145 = 8(1000) + 1(100) + 4(10) + 5. Since 5
is a factor of 8(1000), 1(100), and 4(10), then it is a
factor of 8145 if and only if it is a factor of 5. A
similar explanation holds for 8140.

3. Rule: If both sums of alternate digits yield the same
total, then the original number is divisible by 11.

814506 has alternate sums of 8 + 4 + 0 and 1 + 5 + 6,
both of which equal 12. Hence, 814506 has 11 as a
factor; in fact, 814506 = 11 × 74,046.

Exercises 1. Explain why each of the following rules works:

(a) A number has 2 as a factor if and only if its units
digit is even;

(b) A number is divisible by 4 if and only if the number represented by its last two digits is divisible
by 4;

(c) An *even* number is divisible by 6 if and only if the
sum of its digits has 3 as a factor;

(d) A number is divisible by 8 if and only if the number represented by its last three digits is divisible by 8;

(e) A number has 9 as a factor if and only if the sum
of its digits has 9 as a factor;

(f) A number is divisible by 78,369 if and only if it
has 78,369 as a factor.

2. Use algebra to *prove* each of the rules in the examples
and in Exercise 1.

GREATEST
COMMON FACTOR
AND LEAST
COMMON
MULTIPLE

Armed with these rules you are now a champion at factoring into primes and are thus in a position to play
with two of the mathematicians' time-honored toys, the
greatest common factor (GCF) and the *least common multiple* (LCM).

*Objective 31.　　(a) To compute the GCF and LCM of a given set of num-
bers; (b) to explain why the product of the GCF and LCM
of two numbers equals the product of the two numbers.

Two cardinal numbers may have several common factors;
for example, 18 and 24 have 1, 2, 3, and 6 as common
factors. But only one of these factors is the *greatest*
common factor: here 6 is the GCF.

Examples　　1.　Find the GCF of the following sets of whole numbers:

(a) $\{1,3\}$. Here the GCF is 1.

(b) $\{2,3\}$. Here the GCF is also 1.

(c) $\{2,3,6\}$. Here the GCF is 1 once again.

(d) $\{2,6\}$. Here the GCF is 2.

(e) $\{3,6\}$. Here the GCF is 3. Compare (c), (d), and
(e).

(f) $\{12,15,24\}$. Here the GCF is 3 again.

(g) $\{12,18,30,42\}$. Here the GCF is 6.

2.　Find the GCF of 12,600 and 2,940. In a case like this
involving fairly large numbers it may be more efficient
to first find the prime factorization of each number:

$$12,600 = 2^3 \times 3^2 \times 5^2 \times 7^1$$
$$2,940 = 2^2 \times 3^1 \times 5^1 \times 7^2.$$

Now, to find the GCF we take the *smaller power of each
prime* that appears. Hence

$$\text{GCF}(12,600; 2,940) = 2^2 \times 3^1 \times 5^1 \times 7^1 = 420.$$

(GCF(12,600; 2,940) is read "the GCF of 12,600 and
2,940.")

3.　We use the technique of Example 2 to find
GCF(29,700; 90).

$$29,700 = 2^2 \times 3^3 \times 5^2 \times 11^1$$
$$90 = 2^1 \times 3^2 \times 5^1 = 2^1 \times 3^2 \times 5^1 \times 11^0.$$

Hence GCF(29,700, 90) = $2^1 \times 3^2 \times 5^1 \times 11^0 = 90$.

4.　Find GCF(24,45).

$$24 = 2^3 \times 3 = 2^3 \times 3^1 \times 5^0$$
$$45 = 3^2 \times 5 = 2^0 \times 3^2 \times 5^1.$$

Hence GCF(24,45) = $2^0 \times 3^1 \times 5^0 = 3$.

A *multiple* of a number is another number of which the
first number is a factor; e.g., a multiple of 5 is 35
because 5 is a factor of 35. A *common multiple* of two

numbers is a multiple of the first number and also a
multiple of the second number; e.g., 70 is a common
multiple of 5 and 7, since 70 = 5 × 14 and 70 = 7 × 10.
Two numbers have an infinity of common multiples, but
only one of these is the (positive) *least common multiple*; 35, 70, 140, 175, . . . , are all common multiples of 5 and 7, but only 35 is the *least* common multiple.

Examples   1.   Find the LCM of 2 and 3.
                     The positive multiples of 2 are 2, 4, ⑥, 8, 10,
                  . . . , and the positive multiples of 3 are 3, ⑥, 9,
                  12, . . . ,; so LCM(2,3) = 6.   (LCM(2,3) = 6 is read
                  "the LCM of 2 and 3 is (or 'equals') 6.")

             2.   Find the LCM of 4 and 6.

                     Multiples of 4:   4, 8, ⑫, 16, 20, 24, . . . ,
                     Multiples of 6:   6, ⑫, 18, 24, . . . ,

                  LCM(4,6) = 12.   Notice that sometimes LCM(a,b) = a × b,
                  and sometimes LCM(a,b) ≠ a × b.

             3.   We can use the prime factorization approach to find
                  LCMs.   LCM(12,600; 2,840):

                     $12{,}600 = 2^3 \times 3^2 \times 5^2 \times 7^1$
                     $2{,}940 = 2^2 \times 3^1 \times 5^1 \times 7^2$.

                  This time we take the *larger power of each prime* that
                  appears.   Hence LCM(12,600; 2,940) = $2^3 \times 3^2 \times 5^2 \times 7^2$
                  = 88,200.

             4.   Find LCM(29,700; 90).

                           $29{,}700 = 2^2 \times 3^3 \times 5^2 \times 11^1$
                               $90 = 2^1 \times 3^2 \times 5^1 \times 11^0$
                     LCM(29,700, 90) = $2^2 \times 3^3 \times 5^2 \times 11^1$ = 29,700.

             5.   Find LCM(18, 24, 40).

                     $18 \overset{.}{=} 2^1 \times 3^2 \times 5^0$
                     $24 = 2^3 \times 3^1 \times 5^0$
                     $40 = 2^3 \times 3^0 \times 5^1$.

                  So LCM(18, 24, 40) = $2^3 \times 3^2 \times 5^1$ = 360.

Exercises   1.   Find the GCF and LCM of each of the following sets of
                  numbers: (a) {2, 5, 11};   (b) {2, 10, 55};
                  (c) {44, 500};   (d) {90; 2,940; 12,600};
                  (e) {13; 90; 2,940; 12,600}.

             2.   (a) Find the LCM and GCF of 1,400 and 26,460;

                  (b) Find the product of LCM(1,400; 26,460) and
                      GCF(1,400; 26,460);

                  (c) Find the product of 1,400 and 26,460;

(d) Explain the relation between the answers in (b) and
(c) (*Why* do they turn out as they do?).

3. *Prove* algebraically that LCM(a,b) $\times$ GCF(a,b) = $a \times b$
for natural numbers a and b.

4. Why does or does not LCM(a,b,c) $\times$ GCF(a,b,c) =
$a \times b \times c$?

5. Which is easier to find PDQ, the LCM or the GCF?

6. Suppose $m = a \times b \times c$, where m, a, b, c are natural
numbers and a, b, c are primes; then can $m = d \times e \times f$,
where d, e, f are all primes and $\{a,b,c\} \neq \{d,e,f\}$?

7. *Prove*, algebraically, your answer to Exercise 6.

NUMBER LINE AND ORDER

So now we know what cardinal numbers are and how they
can be added, subtracted, multiplied, and divided. Another crucial aspect of these numbers is their order
and its connection with the concepts of "less than" and
"greater than." While these order relations could be
investigated axiomatically and numerically, it's more
concrete to look at them geometrically, on a number
line. Moreover, it is the notion of a one-to-one correspondence between numbers and points on a line that
has led to many of the advances in mathematics since
the early years of the Renaissance. Thus, it behooves
us to familiarize ourselves with properties of the number line.

● ●

Objective 32. To graph on the *number line* given sets of cardinal
numbers which may be defined in terms of multiples,
factors, and primes.

● ●

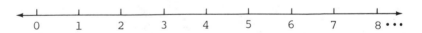

Here it doesn't matter how far apart 0 and 1 are, as
long as 1 is definitely to the right of 0; what's important is that the line segment from 0 to 1 is the
same length as that from 1 to 2, from 2 to 3, from 3
to 4, and so on.

Now let us look at some graphs of subsets of the
cardinal numbers.

Examples   1. $\{x: x \text{ is a multiple of } 3\}$:

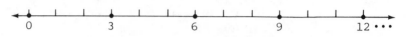

(Notice that $0 = 0 \times 3$ is a multiple of 3.)

2. $\{x: 3x - 9 = 0\}$:

3. $\{x: x \text{ is a multiple of } 2\} \cup \{x: x \text{ is a multiple of } 3\}$:

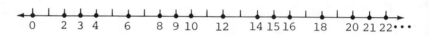

4. $\{x: x \text{ is a multiple of } 2\} \cap \{x: x \text{ is a multiple of } 3\}$:

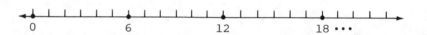

5. $\{x: x \text{ and } 12 \text{ share a common prime factor}\}$:

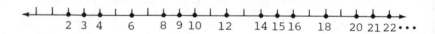

6. $\{x: x \text{ is a prime}\}$:

7. $\{x: x \text{ is a prime factor of } 12\}$:

Exercises   1.   Graph the following sets of cardinal numbers on the number line:

(a) $\{x: x \text{ is a multiple of } 6\}$,

(b) $\{x: 6 \text{ is a factor of } x\}$,

100   CHAPTER 2

(c) $\{x: x \text{ is a factor of } 6\}$,

(d) $\{x: x \text{ is a prime factor of } 6\}$,

(e) $\{x: x \text{ has a common factor with } 6\}$,

(f) $\{x: x \text{ is a mutliple of } 3\} \cup \{x: x \text{ is a multiple of } 4\}$,

(g) $\{x: x \text{ is a multiple of } 3\} \cap \{x: x \text{ is a multiple of } 4\}$,

(h) $\{1,2,3, \ldots , 18,19,20\} \sim \{x: x \text{ is prime}\}$,

(i) $\{x: x \text{ is prime}\} \cap \{x: x \text{ is even}\}$,

(j) $\{x: x \text{ is prime}\} \sim \{x: x \text{ is even}\}$,

(k) $\{x: x \text{ is prime}\} \cap \{x: x \text{ is a multiple of } 6\}$,

(l) $\{5 + x: x \text{ is a multiple of } 6\}$,

(m) $\{x: x \text{ is prime}\} \cap \{5 + x: x \text{ is a multiple of } 6\}$,

(n) $\{x: 2x - 4 = 6x - 28\}$,

(o) $\{x: 3x - 4 = 6x - 28\}$,

(p) $\{x: 4x - 4 = 6x - 28\}$,

(q) $\{x: 5x - 4 = 6x - 28\}$,

(r) $\{x: 6x - 4 = 6x - 28\}$ (careful!),

(s) $\{x: 7x - 4 = 6x - 28\}$ (careful!),

(t) $\{x: x - 4 = 6x - 28\}$ (careful!).

2. Consider the Six Bug; he hops exactly 6 units to the right on the number line. Thus, if he starts at 0, he hits 6, 12, 18, 24, ...

(a) If the six bug starts at 5, will he ever hit 14? 792? Why?

(b) If the six bug starts at 23, will he ever hit 279,954? Why?

(c) If a six bug met a sixteen bug at 96 and they fell in love, where (if any place) would they next meet?

(d) How many *times* will an n-bug meet an m-bug? Name at least three *places* at which they'll meet if they start at 0.

(e) If the six bug starts from an unknown point, what is the *maximum* number of times that he could land in the set $\{413,414,415,416,417,418,419\}$? What is the *minimum* number of times?

GRAPHING AND LATTICE POINTS   Geometric interpretation of the cardinal numbers need not be restricted to one dimension. We can move into a two-dimensional world if we take the Cartesian product $\{0,1,2,3, \ldots\} \otimes \{0,1,2,3, \ldots\}$, which results in

an infinite set of ordered pairs of cardinal numbers,
with these pairs corresponding to points, called *lattice
points*, arranged on a plane as in the following diagram:

y							
(0,5)	(1,5)	(2,5)	(3,5)	(4,5)	(5,5)	(6,5)	(7,5) ···
(0,4)	(1,4)	(2,4)	(3,4)	(4,4)	(5,4)	(6,4)	(7,4) ···
(0,3)	(1,3)	(2,3)	(3,3)	(4,3)	(5,3)	(6,3)	(7,3) ···
(0,2)	(1,2)	(2,2)	(3,2)	(4,2)	(5,2)	(6,2)	(7,2) ···
(0,1)	(1,1)	(2,1)	(3,1)	(4,1)	(5,1)	(6,1)	(7,1) ···
(0,0)	(1,0)	(2,0)	(3,0)	(4,0)	(5,0)	(6,0)	(7,0) ··· x

Exercise   The preceding diagram of lattice points looks like several copies of the number line (some horizontal, some
vertical) superimposed. Explain why this should be so,
according to the definition of $\{0,1,2,3, \ldots ,\} \otimes$
$\{0,1,2,3, \ldots ,\}$, viewing $\{0,1,2,3, \ldots ,\}$ as the
previously introduced number line.

● ●

*Objective 33.   To graph given sets of lattice points with cardinal
numbers as coordinates. Sets again may be defined in
terms of multiples, factors, and primes.

● ●

The elements of an ordered pair designating a point are
called the *coordinates* of that point. By custom, a
typical such point is given the coordinates (x,y); x
always stands for the first coordinate, y for the second coordinate.

Examples   1. $\{(x,y): y = 0\}$:

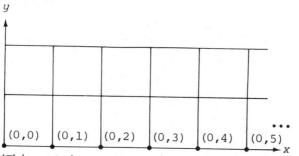

(This set is on what is customarily called the x-axis.)

2. $\{(x,y): x = 0\}$:

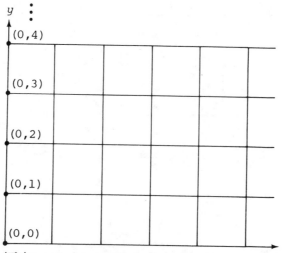

(This set is on what is usually called the y-axis.)

3. $\{(x,y): y = 0\} \cap \{(x,y): x = 0\}$:

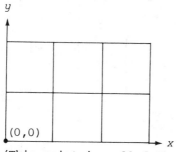

(This point is called the *origin*.)

4. $\{(x,y): x$ or y is a factor of $6\}$:

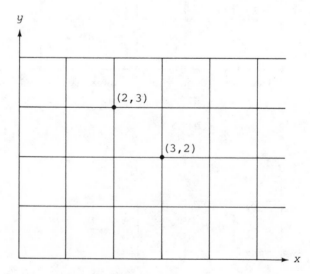

y

(0,6)	(1,6)	(2,6)	(3,6)	(4,6)	(5,6)	(6,6)
	(1,5)	(2,5)	(3,5)			(6,5)
	(1,4)	(2,4)	(3,4)			(6,4)
(0,3)	(1,3)	(2,3)	(3,3)	(4,3)	(5,3)	(6,3)
(0,2)	(1,2)	(2,2)	(3,2)	(4,2)	(5,2)	(6,2)
(0,1)	(1,1)	(2,1)	(3,1)	(4,1)	(5,1)	(6,1)
	(1,0)	(2,0)	(3,0)			(6,0)

x

5. $\{(x,y): x$ and y are prime and $xy = 6\}$:

y

(2,3)

(3,2)

x

6. {(x,y): x and y have common prime factors}:

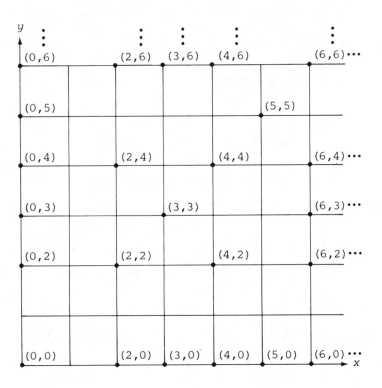

7. {(x,y): x + y = 0 or 1 or 2 or 3}:

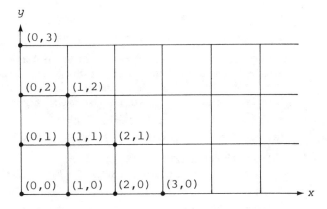

8. $\{(x,y): x^3 + y^3 = 8, x \neq 0 \neq y\}$: (Recall:

$x^3 = x \cdot x \cdot x$, so $4^3 = 4 \cdot 4 \cdot 4 = 64$.) (Answer: $\emptyset$.)

Exercises 1. Graph each of the following sets of lattice points:

(a) $\{(x,y): x = 3\}$,

(b) $\{(x,y): y = 4\}$,

(c) $\{(x,y): x + y = 0\}$,

(d) $\{(x,y): x + y + 2 = 0\}$ (careful!),

(e) $\{(x,y): x = 3\} \cap \{(x,y): x = 4\}$,

(f) $\{(x,y): xy = 12\}$,

(g) $\{(x,y): xy$ is a factor of $12\}$,

(h) $\{(x,y): xy$ is a multiple of $12\}$,

(i) $\{(x,y): x$ and y are prime factors of $12\}$,

(j) $\{(x,y): x$ and y have no common factors$\}$,

(k) $\{(x,y): x^4 + y^4 = 16\}$,

(l) $\{(x,y): x^4 + y^4 = 81\}$,

(m) $\{(x,y): x^4 + y^4 = 17\}$,

(n) $\{(x,y): x + y^2 = 2\}$,

(o) $\{(x,y): x^2 + y = 2\}$,

(p) $\{(x,y): x + y = 2\}$,

(q) $\{(x,y): x + y = 0$ or 1 or $2\}$,

(r) $\{(x,y): x + y - 5 = 0\}$,

(s) $\{(x,y): x + y - 5 = 0$ or 1 or $2\}$.

2. A two bug married a three beetle and the 2,3-couple now move as follows: They always jump 2 units to the right and then immediately, without pausing, 3 more units up. Thus, if they start at the origin, then they hit (2,3), (4,6), (6,9), (8,12), etc.

(a) Will they ever hit (122,182)? Why?

(b) If they start at (6,1), instead of the origin, will they ever hit (2006,3001)? Why? (3006,4001)? Why?

(c) If a 2,3-couple and 3,4-couple meet at the origin, like each other and agree to have a party when they next meet, where will they have their party?

(d) Where would the 2,3-couple and a 3,4-couple have to start on the x- and y-axes, respectively, in order that they meet at (306,408)?

(e) Where would they have had to start on the x- and y-axes, respectively, in order that they meet at (173,392)?

Let us now disregard the coordinates of these lattices and consider just the points themselves. A concrete manifestation of this array is the *geoboard*; an array of nails hammered into a board at the lattice points of a coordinate system:

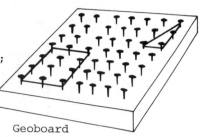

Geoboard

Rubber bands can then be stretched around nails to form "instant polygons," as illustrated in the figure.

Exercise   Construct a geoboard.

In leading up to the next objective, let's introduce the following notation: In any figure with its vertices ("corners") at lattice points, the number of points on the *boundary* is represented by b, while the number *within* the boundary is represented by w, as in the following examples.

Examples   1.

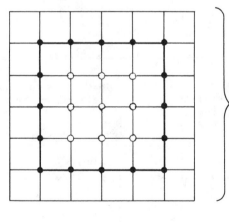

$b = 16$

$w = 9$

2.

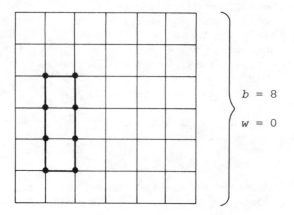

$b = 8$

$w = 0$

3.

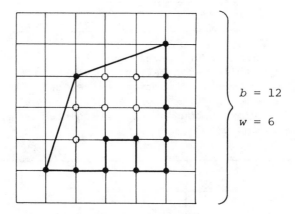

$b = 12$

$w = 6$

Furthermore, we will consider a "unit square" to be one of the smallest squares determined by the superimposed number lines:

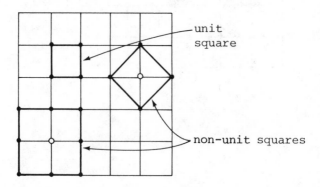

unit square

non-unit squares

Now let's do some "research," i.e., ask questions and form mathematical conjectures based on the answers.

How many unit squares are contained in the rectangles in Examples 1 and 2 above?

How many unit squares are in each of the following rectangles with vertices at lattice points?

Examples
(continued)

4.   5.

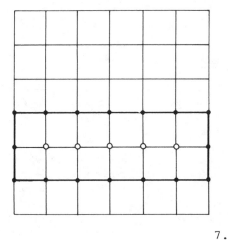

6.   7.

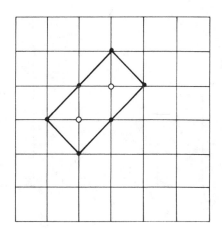 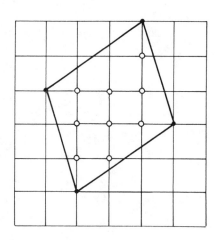

Next, let's calculate b and w for each of these examples and tabulate the resulting empirical evidence:

Rectangle Example	$A =$ No. Unit Squares	b	w
(1)	16	16	9
(2)	3	8	0
(4)	12	16	5
(5)	12	10	8
(6)	4	6	2
(7)	10	4	9

Exercise   Without looking at the following paragraphs, try to find a relationship between A, b, and w. Add at least five more rows to the table.

If you haven't already beat us to the punch, let's be a little more *systematic* in tracking down the relation (*if any*) between A, b, and w. Let's see what happens to A if b is increased by 2 but w remains constant:

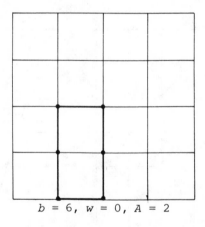   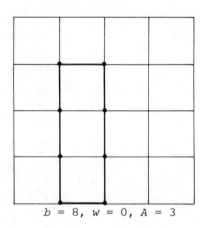

$b = 6$, $w = 0$, $A = 2$ $b = 8$, $w = 0$, $A = 3$

So here, at least, with w fixed an increase of 2 in b results in an increase of only 1 in A. This makes us suspect that $A = \frac{1}{2}b +$ (something-or-other). Now let's hold b fixed and let w increase by 3:

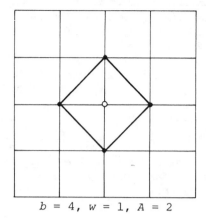 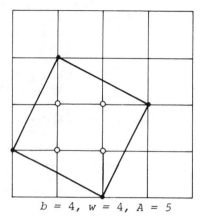

$b = 4$, $w = 1$, $A = 2$ $b = 4$, $w = 4$, $A = 5$

Here an increase of 3 in w results in an increase of 3 in A, too. Hence, we now suspect $A = \frac{1}{2}b + w \pm$ (who knows?).

Exercise   Figure out what that "$\pm$ (who knows?)" must be by checking all of the previous examples.

The formula determined in the last exercise is known as *Pick's theorem*, which brings us to the next objective.

● ●

*Objective 34.   To compute areas of given polygons with vertices at lattice points according to Pick's theorem.

● ●

Note: We've so far only got a *guess* for a formula for the areas of rectangles; no *proof* has been given, except for the specific examples examined. Guessing doesn't cost us anything and is a good and wholesome mathematical activity, so let's push our guess further.

Exercises   1.   Guess a formula for the area of *any* polygon with all of its vertices at lattice points.

        2.   Verify your formula from Exercise 1 with Example 3 back at the beginning of this discussion.

        3.   Draw at least five unusual polygons with vertices at lattice points and for each verify your formula of Exercise 1. (Good time to use your geoboard.)

        4.   Try to *prove* at least one fairly general case of Pick's theorem (for example, for all rectangles with vertices at lattice points). (Geoboard, anyone?)

ORDER RELATIONS	Cardinal numbers in one dimension on the number line can serve as a natural means of introducing the concepts of *order relations*. These are the relations that concern "less than" (symbol: < ; the smaller end points at the smaller number) and "greater than" (symbol: >). Technically, these relations are defined as follows:

Definition	*For cardinal numbers a, b, the* <u>order</u> <u>relation</u> *a < b (read "a is less than b") means b − a = c, for some nonzero cardinal number c. The* <u>order</u> <u>relation</u> *a > b (read "a is greater than b") means: b < a. Finally, a ≥ b means either a > b or a = b, and* <u>a ≤ b</u> *means either a < b or a = b.*

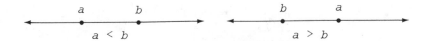

Examples	1.	99 < 201 since 201 − 99 = 102.
	2.	18 > 5 since 5 < 18, i.e., 18 − 5 = 13.

It turns out that while $a = b$ is illustrated by a one-to-one correspondence, $a < b$ is illustrated by a *many-to-one* correspondence.

We return to sets to help make these order relations more concrete. The statement 3 < 5 ("three is less than five") means, according to the definition, that 5 − 3 equals some cardinal number; in fact, 5 − 3 = 2, and this in turn is defined to mean that 5 = 3 + 2:

$$\{1,\ 2,\ 3,\ 4,\ 5\}$$
$$\updownarrow\ \updownarrow\ \updownarrow\ \ \searrow\ \searrow$$
$$\{a,\ b,\ c\}\ \cup\ \{d,\ e\}$$

Now our original relation involved just 5 and 3:

$$\{1,\ 2,\ 3,\ 4,\ 5\}$$
$$\updownarrow\ \updownarrow\ \updownarrow\ \updownarrow\ \updownarrow$$
$$\{a,\ b,\ c\}\ \ \underbrace{}_{?}$$

This last diagram is unsatisfying; it leaves some loose ends. If we tie those loose ends into the set $\{a,b,c\}$:

$$\{1,\ 2,\ 3,\ 4,\ 5\}$$
$$\updownarrow\ \updownarrow\ \updownarrow$$
$$\{a,\ b,\ c\}$$

the result is a many-to-one correspondence from $\{1,2,3,4,5\}$ to $\{a,b,c\}$.

Objective 35. Given some *order relations* between cardinal numbers, to illustrate them with correspondences between sets.

●●

Once more we'll forego verbiage in favor of examples in diagrams.

Examples   1. $4 > 2$: $\{a, b, c, d\}$ $\{a, b, c, d\}$
                                              or   or . . .
                          $\{*, \#\}$ $\{*, \#\}$

           2. $2 < 4$: Same as above.

           3. $2 + 3 = 5$: $\{a, h\} \cup \{e, a, t\}$

                                $\{l, u, n, c, h\}$

Exercise   Illustrate each of the following with correspondences between sets: (a) $3 < 4$, (b) $3 + 1 < 6$, (c) $3 + 4 \leqq 7$, (d) $4 > 1$, (e) $4 \geqq 1 + 3$, (f) $5 + 2 > 3 + 3$.

●●

Objective 36. To explain what given order relations mean on the number line.

●●

Again, we hope that a few examples in diagrams will suffice:

Examples   1. $4 > 2$:

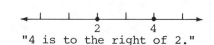

"4 is to the right of 2."

           2. $3 < 4$:

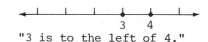

"3 is to the left of 4."

           3. $2 + 3 = 5$:

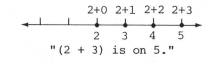

"(2 + 3) is on 5."

Exercises 1. Explain in words the following order relations on the number line: (a) $0 < 4$, (b) $3 + 1 < 6$,

(c) $3 + 4 \leq 7$,   (d) $4 > 1$,   (e) $4 \geq 1 + 3$,
(f) $5 + 2 > 3 + 3$.

THE LAW OF TRICHOTOMY

● ●

*Objective 37.   To state the *law of trichotomy* and illustrate it with examples on the number line, other than those in the text.

● ●

A quick sprint to the dictionary and we know that a trichotomy is a division into three cases. If we consider any two cardinal numbers a and b, the *law of trichotomy* says that exactly one of the following is the case:

Either   (i) $a < b$, i.e., a is to the left of b

or (ii) a is b,

or (iii) $a > b$, i.e., a is to the right of b.

Examples   1. $2 + 1 < 4$:

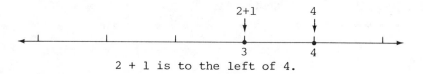

2 + 1 is to the left of 4.

2. $2 + 2 = 4$:

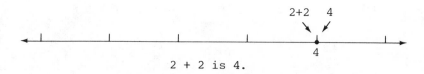

2 + 2 is 4.

3. $2 + 3 > 4$:

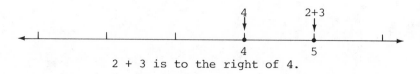

2 + 3 is to the right of 4.

4.   Let $a = 3 \times 17$, $b = 68 - 16$. Which of the cases of the trichotomy holds?

$a = 3 \times 17 = 51.$ $b = 68 - 16 = 52.$ Therefore $a < b$. On the number line,

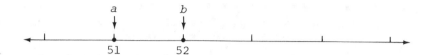

Exercises   1.   Find an eight-year-old and try to explain the law of trichotomy to him or her.

2.   Illustrate on the number line at least five essentially different cases in which $a < b$. (13 < 14 and 12 + 1 < 14 are essentially different. 2 × 6 < 14 and 3 × 3 < 14 are *not* essentially different because they both use multiplication of two cardinals on the left.)

3.   Illustrate on the number line at least five essentially different cases in which $a = b$.

4.   Illustrate on the number line at least five essentially different cases in which $a > b$.

5.   How can we generalize the law of trichotomy to any *three* cardinal numbers a, b, c? How many cases do we get? Is "trichotomy" still the apt word?

6.   How can we generalize the law of trichotomy to any four cardinal numbers a, b, c, d? How many cases do we get? Is "trichotomy" still the apt word?

7.   How many cases can we get with sets of n cardinal numbers?

8.   Make up a pun about "trichotomy."

LINEAR
DIOPHANTINE
EQUATIONS

DEFINITION   The fact that we're dealing with cardinal numbers (rather than rational or fractional or negative numbers, say) gives us more information than we'd have a right to expect with more general types of numbers. A glance at the number line immediately answers the question "What number is less than 1?" If our discussion is restricted to cardinal numbers, while on the other hand, 1/2, 1/3, 1/4, etc. are all equally eligible answers if we widen our consideration to all positive fractional numbers, for example. Equations in which the unknowns are guaranteed to be cardinal numbers were extensively studied by an ancient Greek named Diophantus and hence are referred to as Diophantine equations.

● ●

*Objective 38.   To solve given linear Diophantine equations for cardinal number solutions.

● ●

Examples   1.   In general, when you're faced with the task of solving, say, the equation $x + y = 3$, you reply, "I need *two* equations to solve for two unknowns, unless you want me to list an infinite set of solutions, such as $2\frac{2}{3} + \frac{1}{3}$, $2\frac{3}{4} + \frac{1}{4}$, $2\frac{4}{5} + \frac{1}{5}$, etc., not to mention $0 + 3$, $-1 + 4$, $-2 + 5$, $-3 + 6$, etc." But with cardinal solutions which are after all the most common in everyday life, you can always narrow down possible solutions, sometimes to a finite set of numbers. As noted in the section on graphing lattice points, $(0,3)$, $(1,2)$, $(2,1)$, and $(3,0)$ are the only pairs of cardinal numbers (x,y) that satisfy $x + y = 3$.

2.   Solve $x + y = 2$, given that $x < y$. For $x + y = 2$, the possible solutions in cardinal numbers are $(x,y) = (0,2)$, $(1,1)$, and $(2,0)$. Since only the first of these ordered pairs satisfies $x < y$, the unique answer is $x = 0$, $y = 2$.

3. $x = 4y + 2$, $y = 4z + 2$, $z = 4w + 2$. What's the smallest value of x such that these equations can be solved with cardinal numbers?
       If you don't know how to start on this problem, you might try discarding (temporarily) some of the conditions to be satisfied, and concentrate, say, on the first equation alone. What's the smallest value of x that satisfies this equation? Well, since $x = 4y + 2$, the smallest x would be yielded by the smallest possible value of y, i.e., $y = 0$: $x = 4(0) + 2 = 2$. Now, this is all well and good for the sole equation $x = 4y +2$, but it's unsatisfactory if we also take into account $y = 4z + 2$, which has no solution for z when $y = 0$. (Check this.) "Ha!" we hope you say, "All we have to do is skip to the last equation, let $w = 0$, so $z = 2$, whence $y = 10$ and $x = 42$." Another way of looking at this is to eliminate y and z via substitution and telescope the equations down to a single equation in x and w.

$x = 4y + 2 = 4(4z + 2) + 2 = 16z + 10 = 16(4w + 2) + 10$
$= 64w + 42 = 42$ when w takes its least value, 0.

Exercises   1.   Solve (*if possible*) the following Diophantine equations for cardinal solutions: (a) $x + 2y = 0$,

(b) $x + 2y + 1 = 0$,   (c) $x + 2y - 1 = 0$,
(d) $3x - 6y + 2 = 0$,   (e) $3x + 6y - 21 = 0$,
(f) $85x - 51y = 34$,   (g) $85x - 51y = 35$.

2. Solve (*if possible*) the following Diophantine equations for cardinal solutions, subject to the given order relations: (a) $2x + y - 4 = 0$; $xy > 0$,   (b) $x - y + 1 = 0$; $x \leq 2$,   (c) $x + y - 2 = 0$; $x < 3 - 6y$,   (d) $3x + 2y + 1 = 0$; $xy \leq 0$,   (e) $3x + 2y + z = 0$; $xy \leq 0$.

3. Find the smallest x such that the following Diophantine equations in cardinal numbers are satisfied:

(a) $x = 5y - 3$, $y = 5z - 3$, $z = 5w - 3$, $w = 5v - 3$;

(b) $x = 3y - 1$, $2y = 3z - 1$;

(c) $x = 3y + 2$, $2y = 3z + 2$, $2z = 3w + 2$;

(d) $x = 3 - 5y$, $y = 6z + 1$, $z = 2w$;

(e) $x = 3 - 5y$, $y = 6z$, $z = 2w$.

SOLUTION OF THE COCONUT PROBLEM	And now, as we approach the end of this long chapter we return to the example that began it, the Coconut Problem.

● ●

*Objective 39.   To solve the coconut problem for a given number of sailors and a given number of monkeys.

● ●

Examples   1. For a first helpful example, let's look at the relatively simple case of three sailors and two monkeys. What is the unknown? The minimum number of coconuts, call it x. What does x equal? Well

$$x = 3y + 2,$$

where y represents the number of coconuts in each sailor's true share, and 2 represents what's fed to the monkeys. So we have x in terms of y. What do we know about y? Ah, yes!

$$2y = 3z + 2; \text{ or } y = \frac{3z}{2} + 1,$$

where z is each sailor's share after the first sailor has tampered with the heap. Similarly,

$$z = \frac{3w}{2} + 1,$$

where w is the share after the second tampering. So we want to find the smallest cardinal numbers x, y, z, and w such that

$$x = 3y + 2$$

$$y = \frac{3z}{2} + 1$$

$$z = \frac{3w}{2} + 1.$$

Where have we seen this sort of problem before? In example 3 for Objective 38. Can we use that problem's method again? Let's try:

$$x = 3y + 2 = 3\left(\frac{3z}{2} + 1\right) + 2 = \frac{9z}{2} + 5$$

$$= \frac{9\left(\frac{3w}{2} + 1\right)}{2} + 5 = \frac{27w}{4} + \frac{19}{2} = \frac{27w + 38}{4}.$$

What is the smallest value of w that makes $x = (27w + 38)/4$ a cardinal number? Well,

$$x = \frac{(24w + 3w) + (36 + 2)}{4} = 6w + 9 + \frac{3w + 2}{4}$$

Since $6w$ and 9 are cardinal numbers, what we really need now is the smallest cardinal w such that $(3w + 2)/4$ is a cardinal number. $w = 2$ does the job, so

$$x = \frac{27w + 38}{4} = \frac{27(2) + 38}{4} = \frac{54 + 38}{4} = \frac{92}{4} = 23. \quad \text{Ta da!}$$

2. We'll look at the case of four sailors and one monkey. The unknown is x, of course, the minimum number of coconuts. What are the conditions upon x? Let's let y = the number of coconuts in each sailor's original share, z = the number after the first tampering, w = the number after the second tampering, v after the fourth. Originally, $x = 4y + 1$, and after the third sailor finished his skulduggery, $3y = 4z + 1$. The next two equations are

$$3z = 4w + 1$$

$$3w = 4v + 1.$$

Let's now solve for x in terms of u:

$$x = 4y + 1 = 4\frac{(4z + 1)}{3} + 1 = \frac{16z}{3} + \frac{7}{3}$$

$$= \frac{16}{3}\left(\frac{4w + 1}{3}\right) + \frac{7}{3} = \frac{64w}{9} + \frac{37}{9}$$

$$= \frac{64}{9}\left(\frac{4v + 1}{3}\right) + \frac{37}{9} = \frac{256v}{27} + \frac{175}{27}.$$

So what we want is the smallest cardinal number v such that 27 is a factor of $(256v + 175)/27$.

Now, $256 \div 27 = 9$ remainder 13 and $175 \div 27 = 6$, remainder 13. So what we're really after is the smallest cardinal number v such that 27 is a factor of $13v + 13$. Since $27 = 3^3$, 3 must be a factor of $13v + 13$.

But $13v + 13 = (12v + 12) + (v + 1)$, so 3 must be a factor of $v + 1$. Some values for v which work are $v = 2, 5, 8, 11, 14, 17, 20, 23, 26, 29, 32, 35$. We might try a few with sorry results, so let's look further for more clues to the value of v.

Now, 9 is also a factor of 27 so must divide $13v + 13$. Since $13v + 13 = (9v + 9) + (4v + 4)$, 9 must be a factor of $4(v + 1)$. Notice that 9 and 4 share no factors, thus 9 must be a factor of $v + 1$. This shortens our list of possible v considerably. Now v may be 8, 17, 26, 35, etc.

Trying these, we find $v = 26$ is the smallest value that works.

So $x = \dfrac{256 \times 26 + 175}{27} = \dfrac{6656 + 175}{27} = \dfrac{6831}{27} = 253$ at last!

Exercises

1. Why were we really after the smallest cardinal v such that 27 is a factor of $13v + 13$?

2. Why must 3 be a factor of $13v + 13$?

3. Why must 9 be a factor of $v + 1$ if we know that 9 is a factor of $4v + 4$?

4. Solve the Coconut Problem for three sailors and one monkey.

5. Solve the Coconut Problem for four sailors and two monkeys.

MODULAR ARITHMETIC

As noted in the preliminary chitchat before the treatment of Diophantine equations, the restriction of discussion to cardinal numbers makes some seemingly impossible problems a lot more accessible (although not always positively easy—recall the Coconut Problem). Life can be made even less complicated by restricting ourselves to only a finite subset of the cardinal numbers, by resorting to *modular* (or "*clock*") *arithmetic*. With a standard clock we throw away all numbers greater than 12 and restrict ourselves to $\{1,2,3,4,5,6,7,8,9,10,11,12\}$, a complete set of *residues* (*modulo 12*). If we use 0 instead of 12 to represent the beginning of a new day, then we get the mathematically more common set of residues $\{0,1,2,3,4,5,6,7,8,9,10,11\}$. This procedure can be generalized:

Definition	*For any cardinal numbers a, b, c(c ≠ 0), <u>a is congruent</u> <u>to b modulo c</u> (written "a ≡ b(mod c)") is defined to mean that a and b have the same remainder when divided by c (if the divisions are carried out so that the remainders are positive and less than c). Any set of cardinal numbers congruent to 0, 1, 2, . . . , c - 1 is a <u>complete</u> <u>set</u> <u>of</u> <u>residues</u> (<u>mod</u> <u>c</u>).*

Examples	1.	7 is congruent to 37 and 102 and 67 (mod 5), since if we divide 7, 37, 102, and 67 by 5, the remainder is always 2:

$$7 \div 5 = 1, \text{ r } 2$$
$$37 \div 5 = 7, \text{ r } 2$$
$$102 \div 5 = 20, \text{ r } 2$$
$$67 \div 5 = 13, \text{ r } 2.$$

So we write 7 ≡ 37 ≡ 102 ≡ 67 (mod 5). The usual complete set of residues (mod 5) is {0,1,2,3,4}, but we could use {3,4,5,6,7}, {0,11,22,33,44}, or {1,32,88, 94,130}.

2. 81 ≡ 0 ≡ 27 ≡ 18 (mod 9)
   10 ≡ 1 ≡ 19 ≡ 28 (mod 9)
   7 ≡ 16 ≡ 25 ≡ 70 (mod 9).

The usual complete set of residues (mod 9) is {0,1,2,3, 4,5,6,7,8}

3. Odd numbers are congruent to 1 (mod 2). Even numbers are congruent to 0 (mod 2).

   1 ≡ 3 ≡ 5 ≡ 37 ≡ 91 ≡ 129 (mod 2)
   0 ≡ 2 ≡ 4 ≡ 98 ≡ 112 ≡ 674 (mod 2).

The usual complete set of residues (mod 2) is {0,1}.

One advantage of modular arithmetic over cardinal number arithmetic is that *all* differences are defined, and *many more* quotients are defined. Thus, considering mod 9, for example:

$$2 - 7 = 2 - 7 + 0 \equiv 2 - 7 + 9 = 4$$

$$2 \div 7 = (2 + 0) \div 7 \equiv (2 + 9) \div 7 \equiv (2 + 18) \div 7$$

$$\equiv \bullet \bullet \bullet \equiv (2 + 54) \div 7 = 56 \div 7 = 8$$

but 7 ÷ 3 (mod 9) is not defined. (Suppose it were: $(7 + 9n)/3$ would be a cardinal number for some cardinal n, that is $(7 + 9n) \div 3$ would have no remainder, or, in modular language, $7 + 9n \equiv 0$ (mod 3). But $9n \equiv 0$ (mod 3), since 3 divides into $9n$ evenly. Therefore, we'd have 7 ≡ 0 (mod 3), which just isn't so. So 7 ÷ 3 (mod 9) is not defined.) Let's do something with this modular or clock arithmetic.

Objective   40.   To solve (if possible) given linear modular arithmetic
equations.

Examples   1. $3x + 4 \equiv 6x + 5$ (mod 7)

$$\begin{array}{rcl} -3x & & -3x \\ \hline 4 & \equiv & 3x + 5 \\ -5 & & -5 \\ \hline 4 - 5 & \equiv & 3x \end{array}$$

(just as in ordinary equation solving)

Now we can use the trick of adding cleverly disguised 0:

$$3x \equiv 4 - 5 = 4 - 5 + 0 \equiv 4 - 5 + 7 = 6.$$

Then $x = 3x \div 3 \equiv 6 \div 3 = 2$, Answer.

Check: $3(2) + 4 = 10 \equiv 3 \equiv 17 = 6(2) + 5.$

2. $7x + 5 \equiv 3x - 11$ (mod 13)

$$\begin{array}{rcl} -3x & & -3x \\ \hline 4x + 5 & \equiv & 0 - 11 \\ -5 & & -5 \\ \hline 4x & \equiv & 0 - 16 = 0 - 16 + 0 \equiv 0 - 16 + 26 = 10 \end{array}$$

So $x = 4x \div 4 \equiv 10 \div 4 = (10 + 0) \div 4$

$$\equiv (10 + 26) \div 4 = 36 \div 4 = 9, \text{ Answer.}$$

Check: $7(9) + 5 = 68 \equiv 3 \equiv 16 = 3(9) - 11.$

3. $5x + 2 \equiv 3x - 3$ (mod 6)

$$\begin{array}{rcl} -3x - 2 & \equiv & -3x - 2 \\ \hline 2x & \equiv & 0 - 5 \equiv 6 - 5 = 1. \end{array}$$

$x = 2x \div 2 \equiv (1 + 6) \div 2 \equiv (1 + 12) \div 2 \equiv (1 + 18) \div 2,$

etc.: impossible, since $1 + 6n$ is always odd and
therefore not a multiple of 2.

Exercises   1.   Solve for x, if possible:

(a) $2x + 3 \equiv 5 - 4x$ (mod 7),

(b) $2x + 3 \equiv 5 - 4x$ (mod 6),

(c) $15x + 3 \equiv 2x + 13$ (mod 16),

(d) $x + 2 \equiv 3x + 4$ (mod 5),

(e) $23x + 10 \equiv 4x - 12$ (mod 13),

(f) $7x + 3 \equiv 4 + 2x$ (mod 10).

2.   (a) What kinds of modulus permit *any* division (i.e.,
have all quotients defined)?

(b) What kinds of modulus give us trouble in division
(i.e., permit undefined quotients to arise)?

"But," you may object, "even though this clock arithmetic *is* easier to handle, so what? Is it useful in any real-life situations?" Yes, we answer smugly, it can be used to cut down the computation in the Coconut Problem, with one more look at which we'll finally draw this chapter on cardinal numbers to a close.

As an illustration, let's return to the previous solution of the four-sailor, one-monkey coconut problem. We pretty straightforwardly got $x = (256v + 175)/27$, and only then did things get really sticky. Let's now pick up this solution and apply modular arithmetic:

We want $(256v + 175)/27$ to be a cardinal number, that is, we want $256v + 175 \equiv 0 \pmod{27}$. Well, $256 \equiv 13$, and $175 \equiv 13$. Thus, we want $13v + 13 \equiv 0$ or $13v \equiv 0 - 13 \equiv 27 - 13 = 14$,

$$\text{so } v \equiv \frac{14}{13} = \frac{(14 - 0)}{13} \equiv \frac{14 - 27}{13} = \frac{-13}{13}$$

$$= -1 = 0 - 1 \equiv 27 - 1 = 26.$$

From here on the solution is as before.

Exercises   1. Solve the coconut problem using modular arithmetic:

(a) for three sailors and two monkeys,

(b) for five sailors and three monkeys,

(c) for six sailors and two monkeys,

(d) for four sailors and three monkeys,

(e) for five sailors and 1 monkey.

2. Find another "real-life" problem, solution of which is expedited by clock arithmetic.

3. Show that a general solution for the Coconut Problem with *s* sailors and *m* monkeys is

$$x = s^s - m(s - 1) \pmod{s^s}.$$

SUMMARY OF   6. To define the *cardinal number* of a set and illus-
OBJECTIVES   trate this definition for *zero* and for several
                     other cardinal numbers (page 33).

7. To explain what a *numeration system* is, as well as the relationship between a cardinal number and its *numeral* (page 38).

8. To explain the following types of numbers: *counting, natural, whole, ordinal* (page 38).

9. To define the *sum* of two cardinal numbers (page 39).

10. To use the foregoing definition to show, for example, that $3 + 4 = 7$ (page 39).

*11. To prove rigorously that $n + 0 = n$ for any cardinal number n (page 41).

12. (a) To illustrate with sets the *associative law* for addition of cardinal numbers; (b) to give examples other than those in the text illustrating the *usefulness* of this law (page 41).

13. (a) To illustrate with sets the *commutative law* for addition of cardinal numbers; (b) to give examples other than those in the text of the *usefulness* of this law (page 43).

*14. To explain *how* and *why* the "yes-no-maybe" trick works (page 50).

15. To complete the computations of given indicated sums in bases other than ten (including the "eight finger" or "Mickey Duck" system) (page 53).

16. To define the *difference* of two cardinal numbers and illustrate this definition with an example other than in the text (page 59).

17. To perform a given subtraction via (a) "regrouping," (b) "equal additions," (c) "complement" (page 60).

18. To define the *product* of two cardinal numbers and illustrate this definition with a result of the type $3 \times 5 = 15$. (page 64).

*19. To illustrate with sets the following multiplicative properties of cardinal numbers: (a) commutativity, (b) associativity, (c) $n \times 1 = n$ for any cardinal number n (page 65).

*20. (a) To illustrate with sets that multiplication is distributive over addition; (b) to state and prove whether or not addition is distributive over multiplication (page 67).

21. To cite examples other than those in the text illustrating the usefulness of the three multiplicative CAD properties (page 69).

22. To perform a given indicated multiplication (or "name the product") according to the following algorithms, explaining each step: (a) grating, (b) Napier's bones, (c) duplication, (d) "mental lightning" (page 73).

*23. To give the algebraic formulas underlying each of the following methods of multiplication: (a) Roman finger, (b) nines finger, (c) "little more than 100," (d) "little less than 100" (page 79).

24. To complete computation of given indicated products in bases other than ten (including the "eight-finger" system) (page 84).

25. To define the *quotient* (both with and without a *remainder*) of two cardinal numbers and illustrate these definitions with original examples (page 86).

26. To explain, with an example other than given in the text, why division by zero is not allowed (page 88).

27. To complete computation of a given indicated quotient according to (a) repeated subtraction, (b) the standard long division alogrithm (page 89).

28. To analyze the factors of a given cardinal number (page 92).

29. To find prime factors of given (reasonably small) numbers (page 94).

30. Given a divisibility rule, to explain why it works (page 95).

*31. (a) To compute the GCF and LCM of a given set of numbers; (b) to explain why the product of the GCF and LCM of two numbers equals the product of the two numbers (page 97).

32. To graph on the *number line* given sets of cardinal numbers which may be defined in terms of multiples, factors, and primes (page 99).

*33. To graph given sets of lattice points with cardinal numbers as coordinates. Sets again may be defined in terms of multiples, factors, and primes (page 102).

*34. To compute areas of given polygons with vertices at lattice points according to Pick's Theorem (page 111).

35. Given some *order relations* between cardinal numbers, to illustrate them with correspondences between sets (page 113).

36. To explain what given order relations mean on the number line (page 113).

*37. To state the *law of trichotomy* and illustrate it with examples on the number line, other than those in the text (page 114).

*38. To solve given linear Diophantine equations for cardinal number solutions (page 116).

*39. To solve the coconut problem for a given number of sailors and a given number of monkeys (page 117).

40. To solve (if possible) given linear modular arithmetic equations (page 121).

CHAPTER 3

NONNEGATIVE RATIONAL NUMBERS

$$\frac{old}{dad} = .donedonedone...$$

THE NEW YEAR PROBLEM	The problem here is to substitute numerals (base ten) for letters in the caption, that is, to solve the alphametic involving an infinite, repeating decimal expansion. It turns out that the property of having a repeating decimal expansion is characteristic of all rational numbers, in particular, the nonnegative rational or "fractional" numbers with which this chapter deals.

Challenge	Try to solve the preceding alphametic.

NONNEGATIVE
RATIONAL
(FRACTIONAL)
NUMBERS

● ●

Objective 41.	To define *nonnegative rational number* (or *fractional number*) and explain how a cardinal number may be considered to be nonnegative rational.

● ●

Definition	*A* <u>*nonnegative*</u> <u>*rational*</u> *(or* <u>*fractional*</u>*)* <u>*number*</u> *is a class of all ordered pairs a/b, b ≠ 0, of cardinal numbers a and b which are equivalent according to the following rule: a/b is equivalent to c/d(d ≠ 0) if and only if ad = bc. If a/b is equivalent to c/d, we write a/b = c/d. [Note: We have here another type of ordered pair, written a/b where a/b ≠ b/a if a ≠ b.]*

	How does this definition tie in with your previous experience with fractional numbers? Probably rather tightly, if you examine the definition closely. Look at some examples.

Examples 1.	Consider 2/3. This is certainly a pair of cardinal numbers, namely 2 and 3. Is it ordered? Yes, because 2/3 is quite a different number from 3/2. How about this "class of all ordered pairs" business? Well, don't you customarily think of 2/3, 4/6, 6/9, 8/12, 10/15, . . . as all representing the same number? Moreover, haven't you in the past considered the statement 2/3 = 8/12 equivalent to the statement 2 × 12 =

3 × 8? Finally, you've also got used to 2/3 representing 2 ÷ 3, so you can see that excluding 0 as the second (or "bottom") cardinal number in the representative of a rational number is merely a precaution against future division by 0.

2. The rational number 1/2 is the class of ordered pairs 1/2, 2/4, 3/6, 4/8, 5/10 . . . .

3. Consider the rational number 5/2. Is the ordered pair 10/4 in its class, i.e., is 10/4 = 5/2? Well, 2 • 10 = 20 = 4 • 5, so the answer is yes. What about the ordered pair 23/6? Is 23/6 = 5/2? Or is 2 • 23 = 46 ≠ 5 • 6? No!

Exercises

1. For each of the following, list at least five equivalent ordered pairs: (a) 3/4, (b) 4/3, (c) 28/21, (d) 15/9, (e) 2/1, (f) 5/1, (g) 14/7, (h) 0/1, (i) 0/12.

2. Prove that if neither b nor n is 0, then a/b is equivalent to na/nb.

3. If 2/3, for example, is an ordered pair, how come we don't write it (2,3)?

4. Consider the following rational numbers; which element does *not* belong in the class:

(a) 2/5, 4/10, 6/15, 14/35, 17/45, 30/75;

(b) 21/6, 28/8, 7/2, 64/18, 49/14;

(c) 3/2, 9/3, 27/9, 18/6;

(d) 10/22, 15/33, 3/11, 25/55, 50/110?

5. Using bars, demonstrate graphically that the following pairs are equivalent.
Example: 1/2 = 3/6

e.g., one bar divided into two equal pieces vs. one bar divided into six equal pieces

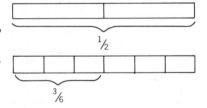

(a) 2/3 = 4/6, (b) 4/3 = 12/9, (c) 2/7 = 6/21, (d) 2/4 = 3/6, (e) 2/6 = 3/9.

6. Can you think of any graphic means (other than that in Exercise 5) to illustrate the idea of a rational number as a set of ordered pairs?

FRACTIONS

At this juncture you may groan, "Okay, I can see that a nonnegative rational number is a certain infinite class, just as a cardinal number is. Does this mean (sigh!) that we have to go through all the detailed rigmarole of establishing additive and multiplicative closure, commutativity, associativity, etc?" Our answer here is that while we could do this, and while it should be done in a high-powered, completely rigorous development of the fractional number system, we will nevertheless forgo this ordeal. This is partly because you've already had a strong taste of this kind of background in Chapter 2 and partly because of the following fact: It turns out that all of the CAD and related properties for nonnegative rational numbers reduce ultimately to these same properties for the cardinal numbers, about which we now assume you know everything. So relax; our treatment of the nonnegative rationals will be much briefer than that of the cardinals in order to avoid excessive repetition of the same ideas.

Another question that may be occurring to you is, "Why are they calling these numbers 'nonnegative rational' or 'fractional,' instead of plain old 'fractions'?" The answer is that in line with the distinction between a number and its numeral, we are reserving the term "fraction" for the numeral (or symbol) of a nonnegative rational.

Definition

A fraction, then, is composed of two numerals of cardinal numbers; the upper numeral is called the numerator, while the lower, nonzero numeral is called the denominator.

Examples

1. Thus 2/3, for example, is the numeral for the fractional number represented by two-thirds.

2. 7/2 is the numeral for the fractional number represented by seven halves.

3. 21/11 is the numeral for the fractional number represented by twenty-one elevenths.

In addition to possible number-numeral confusion, there is also a chance of perplexity in distinguishing between a nonnegative rational number and one of its representative ordered pairs. That is, the number commonly referred to as "two-thirds" is technically the whole class {2/3,4/6,6/9,8/12,10/15, . . .}, while the single ordered pair 2/3 is only one of the representatives of this class. Following current sloppy practice, we will in general not distinguish a nonnegative rational number from one of its representative ordered pairs. However, just in case we ever need notation to make this distinction, we will use {2/3} to represent the class which is the nonnegative rational number and 2/3 to represent one of the ordered pairs of cardinal numbers contained in it; thus $2/3 \; \varepsilon \; \{2/3\}$, $4/6 \; \varepsilon \; \{2/3\}$, $4/6 \; \varepsilon \; \{10/15\}$, and $\{2/3\} = \{4/6\} = \{10/15\}$, etc.

Let us return to the second half of Objective 36 and consider the cardinal number 3 and how it may be construed as a nonnegative rational. We've long been used to thinking of 3 as 3/1, or 6/2, or 9/3, etc., and that's the key here. Let us make the one-to-one correspondence

$$3 \leftrightarrow \{3/1\} = \{3/1, 6/2, 9/3, 12/4, 15/5, \; . \; . \; .\}$$

$$5 \leftrightarrow \{5/1\} = \{5/1, 10/2, 15/3, 20/4, 25/5, \; . \; . \; .\},$$

and in general

$$n \leftrightarrow \{n/1\} = \{n/1, 2n/2, 3n/3, \; . \; . \; .\}.$$

Exercises   1.   Exhibit one-to-one correspondences showing how the following cardinal numbers may be considered as nonnegative rationals. For each correspondence follow the examples just given, exhibiting at least five representatives of each class: (a) 1,   (b) 2,   (c) 0.

2.   Prove that the correspondence $n \leftrightarrow \{n/1\}$ really is one-to-one. That is, let a and b be two cardinals, with $a \leftrightarrow \{a/1\}$, $b \leftrightarrow \{b/1\}$; next show that if $\{a/1\} = \{b/1\}$, then $a = b$.

GEOMETRIC
INTERPRETATION

● ●

Objective 42.   To illustrate the definition of *nonnegative rational number* with a geometric interpretation.

● ●

To illustrate the definition of nonnegative rational number properly we need to keep two things in mind: (a) The number is a *class* and so should be represented by a collection of figures, not just one alone; (b) the class should contain *ordered pairs*.

Examples   1.   {2/3} = {2/3,4/6,6/9,8/12, . . .}:

          etc.

Here the numerator of each ordered pair represents the number of shaded "pieces of pie," while the denominator represents the total number of pieces. Another
way to represent the same
number: etc.

2.   1/2 = {1/2,2/4,3/6,4/8, . . .}:

 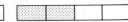   etc.

3.   {7/5} = {7/5,14/10,21/15,28/20, . . .}:

In this example, the left-
hand, shaded bars repre-
sent the numerators, while
the right-hand, unshaded
bars represent the denominators. This particular
representation is used
with the manipulative ma-
terials known as "Cuisen-
aire rods."

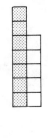 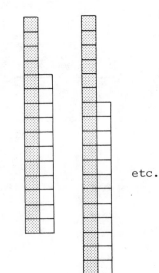   etc.

4. $\{3/4\} = \{3/4,6/8,9/12,12/16, \ldots\}$:

⊖⊖⊖○   ⊖⊖⊖⊖⊖⊘○○

⊖⊘⊖⊖○⊖⊖⊖⊖○○○   ○⊖⊖⊖⊖⊖⊖⊖⊖⊖⊖⊖○○○○   etc.

Here the totality of circles in each "chain" represents the denominator, while the shaded circles represent the numerator.

Definition   *The <u>reciprocal</u> of a fractional number is the new fractional number consisting of all of the original ordered pairs turned "upside down"—with all the numerators and denominators of the original number interchanged.*

Examples   1.   Thus the reciprocal of $\{2/3\} = \{2/3,4/6,6/9,8/12,10/15, \ldots\}$ is $\{3/2\} = \{3/2,6/4,12/8,15/10, \ldots\}$.

2.   The reciprocal of $\{2/7\} = \{2/7,4,14,6/21,8/28, \ldots\}$ is $\{7/2\} = \{7/2,14/4,21/6,28/8, \ldots\}$.

3.   And the reciprocal of $\{2\} = \{2/1,4/2,6/3,8/4, \ldots\}$ is $\{1/2\} = \{1/2,2/4,3/6,4/8, \ldots\}$.

Exercises   1.   Illustrate each of the following nonnegative rational numbers with a geometric interpretation: (a) 1/2, (b) 5/3,   (c) 4,   (d) 0.

2.   Explain how each of the preceding examples could just as well illustrate the reciprocal of the given nonnegative rational number.

3.   Estimate two nonequivalent fractional numbers represented by each of the following figures:

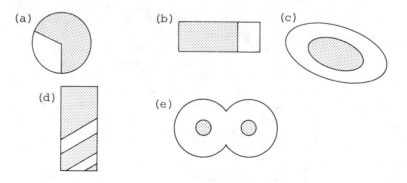

4. Estimate the shaded part of each of the drawings in Exercise 3: (a) to the nearest half, (b) to the nearest third, (c) to the nearest fifth, (d) to the nearest tenth.

5. Find the reciprocal of each of the following and list four representatives of its class: (a) 3/11, (b) 21/2, (c) 4/8, (d) 3, (e) 3/7, (f) 5/2.

MULTIPLICATION

• •

Objective 43. To define the *product* of two nonnegative rational numbers and illustrate this definition, showing how it includes previous results with cardinal numbers.

• •

Definition *Let a/b and c/d(b,d ≠ 0) represent two nonnegative rational numbers. Then the <u>product</u> of these two numbers is the rational number represented by (a × c)/(b × d).*

Examples 1. The product of 2/3 and 3/5 is

$$\frac{2}{3} \times \frac{3}{5} = \frac{2 \times 3}{3 \times 5} = \frac{6}{15}.$$

2. And the product of 7/11 and 2/5 is

$$\frac{7}{11} \times \frac{2}{5} = \frac{7 \times 2}{11 \times 5} = \frac{14}{55}.$$

3. The product of 5 and 2/3 is

$$5 \times \frac{2}{3} = \frac{5}{1} \times \frac{2}{3} = \frac{5 \times 2}{1 \times 3} = \frac{10}{3}.$$

"All well and good," you may say, "but why do we define the product of fractional numbers in this way?" One reason is that this definition preserves the multiplication of cardinal numbers. That is, suppose we think of the cardinals 3 and 5, for example, as nonnegative rationals 3/1 and 5/1; how might we define 3/1 × 5/1 so that we get as a result a fractional number representing 15/1, alias 15? The most natural answer to this question appears to be that we define 3/1 × 5/1 to be (3 × 5)/(1 × 1).

Let us look diagrammatically at another example that shows how this definition of the product of fractional numbers includes results with cardinal numbers:

Example

$$4 \times 6$$
$$\updownarrow \quad \updownarrow$$
$$\frac{8}{2} \times \frac{18}{3} = \frac{8 \times 18}{2 \times 3} = \frac{144}{6} \leftrightarrow 24$$

Exercises   1.   Illustrate the definition of product of nonegative
rational numbers and the results of the example above
with the following cardinal numbers: (a) 2 × 3 = 6,
(b) 1 × 4 = 4,   (c) 0 × 5 = 0,   (d) 2 × 3 × 5 = 30
(what multiplicative property is involved here?).

2.   Find the products: (a) 2/11 × 3/4,   (b) 3/8 × 16/2,
(c) 2/4 × 8/2,   (d) 7/11 × 5/4,   (e) 3/4 × 12/6.

The examples above provide an *arithmetic* reason for defining the product of nonnegative rational numbers as
we do.   But how about a geometric reason?

● ●

Objective   44.   To illustrate the definition of product of nonnegative
rational numbers geometrically.

● ●

Let us consider 3/5 × 2/4.   First of all, 3/5 may be
represented by

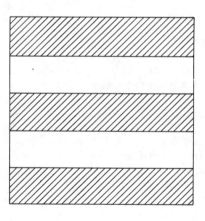

three shaded bars
of five total

while 2/4 may be pictured as

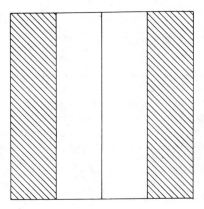

two shaded bars
of four total

If we follow the lead provided by the definition of
multiplication of cardinal
numbers via Cartesian
products of sets, we su-
perimpose one figure on
the other:

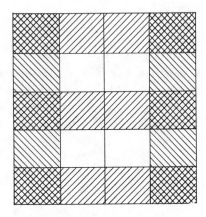

If we think of the number of double-hatched rectangles
compared to the total number of rectangles we get

$$\frac{6}{20} = \frac{3 \times 2}{5 \times 4},$$

in accordance with our definition.

   Another geometric interpretation of the product of
two fractional numbers is the following, which is
adaptable to illustration
with paper strips (for
example, cut from adding
machine tape). Consider
3/5 × 2/4 again. This
time represent 3/5 by

Then fold the 3/5 strip:

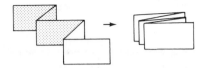

Take the resulting rectangle and either fold it or make marks with a marking pen that penetrate through all layers as follows:

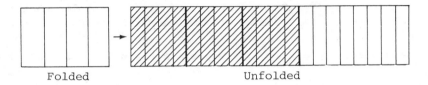

Folded   Unfolded

Then hatch the two left-hand subrectangles of each of the original five large rectangles:

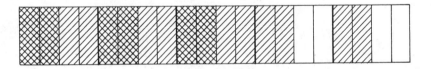

There are now six double-hatched small rectangles against a total of twenty:

$$\frac{3}{5} \times \frac{2}{4} = \frac{6}{20}.$$

How does this represent the definition of multiplication of fractional numbers? Well, through the second act of folding the initial folding we get 5 × 4 = 20 small rectangles altogether, while the hatching of the original three rectangles together with the hatching of the two left-hand subrectangles gives double-hatching on 3 × 2 = 6 small rectangles.

Exercises
1. Illustrate the following products geometrically by each of the methods just discussed: (a) 1/4 × 1/3, (b) 3/7 × 1/2, (c) 3/4 × 2/1 (careful!), (d) 0/1 × 2/5. In each case explain *how* your picture illustrates the given product.

2. Find another geometric way to illustrate products.

3. Using your method from Exercise 2, illustrate the products in Exercise 1.

GROUP
STRUCTURE OF
THE POSITIVE
RATIONALS

Let us turn from geometric considerations to algebraic structure.

● ●

*Objective 45.

To explain with original examples what is meant by "The positive rational numbers form a group under multiplication."

● ●

Definition

1. *The positive rational numbers are the nonnegative rational numbers except zero, i.e., {a/b: a and b are counting numbers, a ≠ 0 and b ≠ 0}.*

2. *A group is a set S ≠ ∅ and an operation ∗ such that (a) If a ε S and b ε S, then (a ∗ b) ε S ("closure"); (b) a ∗ (b ∗ c) = (a ∗ b) ∗ c ("associativity"); (c) There exists an element e ε S such that e ∗ a = a ∗ e = a for any a ε S ("identity"); (d) For each a ε S, there exists an element a' ε S such that a ∗ a' = a' ∗ a = e ("inverse").*

For Objective 45 we'll take $S = \{x: x$ is a positive rational$\}$ and $\ast = \times$ (multiplication of positive rationals). First of all, the positive rationals have closure under multiplication (the product of two positive rationals is a positive rational).

For instance, 2/5 and 3/7 are positive rationals, and so is $2/5 \times 3/7 = 6/35$. Second, the positive rationals have associativity under multiplication:

$$\left(\frac{2}{5} \times \frac{3}{7}\right) \times \frac{4}{11} = \frac{6}{35} \times \frac{4}{11} = \frac{24}{385} = \frac{2}{5} \times \frac{12}{77} = \frac{2}{5} \times \left(\frac{3}{7} \times \frac{4}{11}\right).$$

Third, the positive rationals have a multiplicative identity element, 1/1:

$$\frac{2}{5} \times \frac{1}{1} = \frac{2}{5} .$$

Finally, the positive rationals all have multiplicative inverses, namely, their reciprocals:

$$\frac{2}{5} \times \frac{5}{2} = \frac{10}{10} = \frac{1}{1} .$$

Exercises 1. Explain with examples other than those given in the text what is meant by "the positive rationals form a group under multiplication."

2. Why do we say "the positive rationals" rather than "the nonnegative rationals" form a group under multiplication?

3. Take each of the four properties of a group and explain why or why not the counting numbers (or "natural numbers") form a group under multiplication.

● ●

*Objective 46. To explain why group structure pops up so frequently in mathematics.

● ●

Notice that for Objective 46 an explanation such as "group structure appears so frequently because it is a fundamental concept" is inadequate. Such an explanation would be analogous to answering the question "Why does a cow have four legs?" with "Because it is a quadruped."

Exercise Ask at least three different mathematics professors why group structure pops up so frequently in mathematics and write down their answers.

This exercise may elicit several answers. If so, compare them with our official answer: *One of the reasons that mathematics was invented in the first place was to solve for unknowns, and a group provides just about the minimal structure for solving for unknowns.* In a sense, an unknown in a mathematical problem is all dressed up in a disguise, and it is up to the solver to strip off this dressing and reveal the naked unknown.

Thus, in solving an equation such as $(3/5)x = 4/7$, we need closure so that $(3/5) \cdot x$, for example, makes any sense. In general we need associativity for the same reason, although we won't need it here. We need an identity mainly so we can have inverses, and we need inverses to "undress" the unknown. Here the desired x is dressed up with the 3/5; to remove that 3/5, we merely multiply through by its inverse:

$$\frac{3}{5}x = \frac{4}{7} \Rightarrow \frac{5}{3} \cdot \frac{3}{5} \cdot x = \frac{5}{3} \cdot \frac{4}{7} \quad \text{(Here we use the inverse)}$$

$$\Rightarrow \frac{15}{15}x = \frac{20}{21} \quad \text{(Here we have a representative of identity on the left)}$$

$$\Rightarrow x = \frac{20}{21} \quad \text{(the "naked unknown")}.$$

Exercise   Solve each of the following equations, specifying each
                  group property as it is used:

(a) $\dfrac{2}{5}x = \dfrac{3}{5}$,   (b) $\dfrac{2}{3} \cdot \left(\dfrac{4}{5}x\right) = \dfrac{7}{8}$,   (c) $\dfrac{2}{3}x = \dfrac{3}{5}x$,

(d) $\dfrac{2}{3}x = \dfrac{1}{1}$,   (e) $\dfrac{2}{3} \cdot \left(\dfrac{4}{5}x\right) = \dfrac{4}{3} \cdot \left(\dfrac{2}{5}x\right)$,

(f) $\dfrac{2}{3} \cdot \left(\dfrac{4}{5}x\right) = \dfrac{4}{3} \cdot \left(\dfrac{1}{5}x\right)$,   (g) $\dfrac{2}{3} \cdot \left(\dfrac{4}{5}x\right) = \dfrac{1}{5} \cdot \dfrac{8}{3}$.

OTHER GROUPS

● ●

*Objective 47.   To cite an example of a group other than the positive
                  rationals under multiplication.

● ●

Of course, there are lots of groups other than the
positive rationals under multiplication. Many of these
consist of certain sets of numbers under such operations as addition and multiplication.

Other groups consist of sets of elements other than
numbers and operations other than arithmetic operations. For example, consider the following set of
symmetry transformations on an equilateral triangle:

 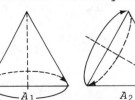 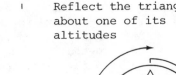

I A_1 A_2 A_3

Leave the   Reflect the triangle
triangle alone   about one of its
                              altitudes

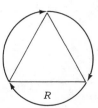   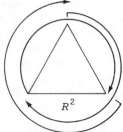

R R^2

Rotate the triangle   Rotate the triangle
around its center   around its center
through 120°   through 240°

The set we're dealing with here is $\{I, A_1, A_2, A_3, R, R^2\}$. It turns out that certain subsets of this set form groups under what is technically called "composition," which will be referred to here as $\textcircled{f}$, the "followed-by" operation. For example, $A_1 \textcircled{f} R$ means "A_1 followed by R"; let's see if we have closure, numbering vertices of the triangle to keep track of our transformations:

Start with: Apply A_1:   Apply R:

So $A_1 \textcircled{f} R$ takes into . We notice that vertex 3 stays fixed, and this leads us to the discovery that $A_1 \textcircled{f} R = A_3$. Here's a check:

Start with: Apply A_3:

Since $A_1 \textcircled{f} R$ and A_3 both effect the same transformation on the triangle, they are to be considered equal to each other.

Exercises

1. Invent a group using as your set the set of integers, that is, the set of all the positive and negative counting numbers together with zero. Be sure to state your operation!

2. Invent a group using modular (or "clock") arithmetic. State your operation.

3. (a) Why are R and R^2 written as they are, instead of R_1 and R_2?

   (b) What is A_1^2?   (e) What is $A_3 \textcircled{f} R^2$?

   (c) What is R^3?   (f) What is $(A_1 \textcircled{f} A_3) \textcircled{f} R^2$?

   (d) What is A_1^3?   (g) What is $A_1 \textcircled{f} (A_3 \textcircled{f} R^2)$?

4. Find a subset of $\{I, A_1, A_2, A_3, R, R^2\}$ which forms a group under $\textcircled{f}$. Explain in detail why it forms a group, giving examples for each of the four group properties.

5. Find at least three more different subsets of $\{I, A_1, A_2, A_3, R, R^2\}$ which form groups under $\text{\textcircled{f}}$.

6. Can two of the subsets in Exercise 5 be disjoint? Why?

7. Invent a group based on the symmetry transformations of a square. State your operation.

8. Invent a group based on the symmetry transformations of a regular tetrahedron—a four-faced solid with each face an equilateral triangle, as illustrated here. State your operation.

Regular tetrahedron

9. Let A be the set $\{a, b, c\}$ and define an operation $*$ by the following table:

$*$	a	b	c
a	a	b	c
b	b	c	a
c	c	a	b

Is this system, i.e., set A with operation $*$, a group?

10. Invent an operation based upon the symmetries of a line segment. Compare this group with the set $A = \{0,1\}$ and the operation of addition.

11. Invent a group not alluded to here. (You might try to *generalize* or *specialize* from some of the examples given here.)

12. What do you call ten simultaneous appendectomies? (Answer: group operation.)

OTHER
ARITHMETIC
OPERATIONS

ADDITION

● ●

Objective 48. To define the *sum* of two nonnegative rational numbers and illustrate with an original example how this definition includes previous results with cardinal numbers.

● ●

One of the most difficult tasks that an elementary school teacher faces is teaching addition of fractional numbers. This is probably because adding with fractions, as opposed to multiplying with them, is so counterintuitive and relatively complicated. While students may easily learn, for example, that $1/5 + 3/5 = 4/5$, they have a much harder time learning how to compute $2/5 + 3/7$, say. This may be because they neglect to think of $2/5$ as $\{2/5\}$, a whole class of representatives. For if they did, they could ask, "Which representatives of $\{2/5, 4/10, 6/15, 8/20, 10/25, 12/30, 14/35, \ldots\}$ and $\{3/7, 6/14, 9/21, 12/28, 15/35, \ldots\}$ should be selected?" The answer here is $14/35$ and $15/35$, resulting in the sum

$$\frac{2}{5} + \frac{3}{7} = \frac{14}{35} + \frac{15}{35} = \frac{14 + 15}{35} = \frac{29}{35}.$$

Or suppose we wish to add $2/3$ and $5/11$. Well, $\{2/3\} = \{2/3, 4/6, 6/9, \ldots, 22/33, \ldots\}$ and $\{5/11\} = \{5/11, 10/22, 15/33, 20/44, \ldots\}$. So $2/3 + 5/11 = 22/33 + 15/33 = 37/33$. A rather large set of representatives of the class of $2/3$ is needed here. But patience pays its reward.

If, however, we wish to add $3/4$ and $5/3$, we need only see that $\{3/4\} = \{3/4, 6/8, 9/12, \ldots\}$ and $\{5/3\} = \{5/3, 10/6, 15/9, 20/12, \ldots\}$, to get $3/4 + 5/3 = 9/12 + 20/12 = 29/12$.

Exercise	Add the following by first writing out several representatives of each nonnegative number involved: (a) $5/2 + 3/7$, (b) $3/4 + 4/5$, (c) $3/1 + 1/3$, (d) $3/6 + 1/2$, (e) $5/8 + 6/7$, (f) $7/12 + 3/8$.

The procedure used in this exercise can, as you may suspect, become tedious. How might we shorten it? In particular, how might we figure out which representatives to choose without actually writing out so many? For an answer, let us look more closely at the foregoing examples:

$$\frac{2}{5} + \frac{3}{7} = \frac{14}{35} + \frac{15}{35} = \frac{29}{35}.$$

First of all, how is that 35 related to $2/5$ and $3/7$? Yes! It's 5×7. How about the 14; where did it come

from? Quite right: 2×7. And the 15 came from 3×7
In the example

$$\frac{2}{3} + \frac{5}{11} = \frac{22}{33} + \frac{15}{33} = \frac{37}{33} ,$$

$33 = 3 \times 11$ and 22 is 2×11, while 15 is 3×5.
In the example

$$\frac{3}{4} + \frac{5}{3} = \frac{9}{12} + \frac{20}{12} = \frac{29}{12} ,$$

again 12 is 4×3, while 9 is 3×3 and 20 is 4×5.
Does the method or pattern begin to rear its head?

Let us now pass from the particular to the general
and attack Objective 48.

Definition

*Let a/b and $c/d (b,d, \neq 0)$ represent two nonnegative
rational numbers. Then the <u>sum</u> of these two numbers
is the rational number represented by*

$$\frac{(a \times d) + (b \times c)}{b \times d} .$$

So we can shorten our work in this summing process.
Some more examples follow:

Examples

1. $\dfrac{2}{3} + \dfrac{4}{5} = \dfrac{2 \times 5 + 3 \times 4}{3 \times 5} = \dfrac{10 + 12}{15} = \dfrac{22}{15} .$

2. $\dfrac{2}{11} + \dfrac{3}{7} = \dfrac{2 \times 7 + 11 \times 3}{11 \times 7} = \dfrac{14 + 33}{77} = \dfrac{47}{77} .$

3. $\dfrac{21}{101} + \dfrac{8}{111} = \dfrac{21 \times 111 + 101 \times 8}{101 \times 111} = \dfrac{2331 + 808}{11,211} = \dfrac{3,139}{11,211} .$

Exercises

1. If a/b and c/d do not have zero denominators, can their
sum? Why?

2. Prove that it would make no difference if we took an
equivalent representative instead of a/b and also another equivalent representative for c/d; we would still
get the same sum as we get with a/b and c/d.

3. Find the following sums: (a) $1/2 + 2/5$, (b) $3 + 1/8$,
(c) $2/4 + 6/9$, (d) $11/5 + 5/11$, (e) $27/4 + 3/2$.

4. Using a different representative for the numbers in
Exercise 3, find their sums and show that you have obtained the same answer.

Now does this definition include previous results with
cardinal numbers?

Examples	1.	$2 + 3 = 5$:	$\begin{matrix} 2 & 3 \\ \updownarrow & \updownarrow \end{matrix}$

$$\frac{2}{1} + \frac{3}{1} = \frac{2 \cdot 1 + 1 \cdot 3}{1 \cdot 1} = \frac{2 + 3}{1} = \frac{5}{1} \leftrightarrow 5$$

2. $3 + 4 = 7$: $\begin{matrix} 3 & 4 \\ \updownarrow & \updownarrow \end{matrix}$

$$\frac{15}{5} + \frac{8}{2} = \frac{15 \cdot 2 + 5 \cdot 8}{5 \cdot 2} = \frac{30 + 40}{10} = \frac{70}{10} \leftrightarrow 7$$

Exercise	Illustrate the definition of addition of fractional numbers using the results of Examples 1 and 2 above with cardinal numbers: (a) $3 + 5 = 8$, (b) $1 + 4 = 5$, (c) $0 + 5 = 5$, (d) $2 + 3 + 5 = 10$ (what additive property is involved here?).

LCD AND PRIME FACTORS

At this point your reaction may be, "Okay, okay; I get this. But what about all of that 'least common denominator' stuff that I was tortured with when I was in elementary school?"

Our answer is first that the LCD is not as holy as some teachers trump it up to be, and second that it is connected to our definition as follows. Consider adding two nonnegative rational numbers with representatives that have the same denominator, for instance $3/7 + 2/7$:

Step 1. $\dfrac{3}{7} + \dfrac{2}{7} = \dfrac{3 \cdot 7 + 7 \cdot 2}{7 \cdot 7}$

Step 2. $= \dfrac{7(3 + 2)}{7 \cdot 7}$

Step 3. $= \dfrac{7}{7} \cdot \dfrac{(3 + 2)}{7}$

Step 4. $= \dfrac{3 + 2}{7}$

So it turns out that representatives of fractional numbers with the same denominator may be added in the "natural way," by adding the numerators and leaving the denominators alone:

$$\frac{3}{7} + \frac{2}{7} = \frac{3 + 2}{7} = \frac{5}{7} \; ; \quad \frac{1}{2} + \frac{5}{2} = \frac{6}{2} \; ; \quad \frac{2}{9} + \frac{4}{9} = \frac{6}{9} \; , \text{ etc.}$$

Exercises	1.	What is the justification for Step 1 above?
	2.	What two laws of cardinal numbers are used in Step 2?
	3.	What is the justification for Step 3?
	4.	What is the justification for Step 4?

Let's return to our transition between adding by definition and adding through use of lowest common denominators.

Examples   1.   This time consider 3/5 + 2/7, where {3/5} = {3/5,6/10, 9/15,12/20,15/25,18/30,21/35, . . .} and {2/7} = {2/7, 4/14,6/21,8/28,10/35, . . .}. Now since it doesn't make any difference which representatives of {3/5} and {2/7} we select, we may choose 21/35 and 10/35, respectively:

$$\frac{3}{5} + \frac{2}{7} = \frac{21}{35} + \frac{10}{35} = \frac{21 + 10}{35} = \frac{31}{35} \cdot$$

"Okay," you may say, "but how can I select appropriate representatives without writing out long lists of representatives?" The key is to look at the *prime factors* of the final denominator: 35 = 5 • 7. Going back to 3/5 and 2/7, we may reason that we need a 7 in the denominator of 3/5, so we'll take (3/5) • (7/7) instead of 3/5, using 7/7 as a representative of the multiplicative identity; and we need a 5 in the denominator of 2/7, so we'll take (2/7) • (5/5) instead of 2/7, this time letting 5/5 represent the multiplicative identity.

2.   Let's consider another example, 5/6 + 7/10:

Step 1. $\dfrac{5}{2 \cdot 3} + \dfrac{7}{2 \cdot 5}$

Step 2. $\dfrac{5}{2 \cdot 3} \cdot \dfrac{5}{5} + \dfrac{7}{2 \cdot 5} \cdot \dfrac{3}{3}$

Step 3. $\dfrac{5 \cdot 5 + 7 \cdot 3}{2 \cdot 3 \cdot 5}$

Step 4. $\dfrac{25 + 21}{30} = \dfrac{46}{30} \cdot$

This addition with least common denominators may be summarized as follows: *Factor the denominator of each term into its prime factors; then multiply each term by appropriate representatives of multiplicative identity so that all denominators have the same factors, but they don't have any more in common than is necessary.*

3.   Let's look at another example, 2/15 + 7/10 + 13/20.

Step 1. *Factor the denominator of each term into its prime factors:*

$$\frac{2}{15} + \frac{7}{10} + \frac{13}{20} = \frac{2}{3 \cdot 5} + \frac{7}{2 \cdot 5} + \frac{13}{2^2 \cdot 5}$$

Step 2. *Multiply each term by appropriate representatives of multiplication identity so that all denominators have the same factors:*

$$\frac{2}{3 \cdot 5} + \frac{7}{2 \cdot 5} + \frac{13}{2^2 \cdot 5} = \frac{2}{3 \cdot 5} \cdot \frac{2^2}{2^2} + \frac{7}{2 \cdot 5} \cdot \frac{3 \cdot 2}{3 \cdot 2}$$

$$+ \frac{13}{2^2 \cdot 5} \cdot \frac{3}{3} \, ,$$

Step 3. *but they don't have any more in common than is necessary:*

$$not \quad \frac{2}{3 \cdot 5} + \frac{7}{2 \cdot 5} + \frac{13}{2^2 \cdot 5}$$

$$= \frac{2}{3 \cdot 5} \cdot \frac{2 \cdot 5 \cdot 2^2 \cdot 5}{2 \cdot 5 \cdot 2^2 \cdot 5} + \frac{7}{2 \cdot 5} \cdot \frac{3 \cdot 5 \cdot 2^2 \cdot 5}{3 \cdot 5 \cdot 2^2 \cdot 5}$$

$$+ \frac{13}{2^2 \cdot 5} \cdot \frac{2 \cdot 5 \cdot 3 \cdot 5}{2 \cdot 5 \cdot 3 \cdot 5} \, ,$$

for example.

4. Nor $\dfrac{5}{42} + \dfrac{7}{60} = \dfrac{5}{2 \cdot 3 \cdot 7} + \dfrac{7}{2 \cdot 2 \cdot 3 \cdot 5}$

$$= \frac{5}{2 \cdot 3 \cdot 7} \cdot \frac{2 \cdot 5}{2 \cdot 5} + \frac{7}{2 \cdot 2 \cdot 3 \cdot 5} \cdot \frac{7}{7}$$

$$= \frac{5 \cdot 2 \cdot 7 + 7 \cdot 7}{2 \cdot 2 \cdot 3 \cdot 5 \cdot 7} = \frac{50 + 49}{420} = \frac{99}{420} \, .$$

ALGORITHMS   Of course, an objective lurks behind all of this.

● ●

Objective 49.   To perform a given indicated addition of nonnegative rationals according to the following methods: (a) definition, (b) least common denominator, (c) grating.

● ●

You already know methods (a) and (b), and they might possibly suffice throughout your career as a teacher. They also might not. Many elementary teachers consider adding with fractions the most difficult phase of mathematics to teach, one which must be returned to again and again. Perhaps on your third or fourth visit you and your students may want to try the grating method, for novelty if nothing else.

Examples   1.   Let's look at an example, 3/5 + 2/7 again, which we'll write here as

$\dfrac{3}{5}$ and 2/7:

Step 1.
```
        2  / 7
    3 |  +  |     |
    5 |     |     |
```

Step 2.
```
        2  / 7
    3 |  +  | 21 |
    5 | 10  | 35 |
```

Step 3.
```
        2  / 7
    3 |  +  | 21 | 31 |
    5 | 10  | 35 | 35 |   ,
```

where 31/35 is the answer. We multiply 3 × 7 and place the answer in the box below 7 opposite 3. Next multiply 2 × 5 and place the answer in the box below 2 opposite 5. Continuing, multiply 5 × 7 and place the answer in the box below 7 opposite 5. Finally, add the boxes along the main diagonal, 10 + 21 = 31, for the numerator of our answer, with the lower right-hand box as the denominator.

2. Let's try this again, this time with 2/15 + 7/10.

Step 1.
```
        7  /10
    2  |  +  | 20 |
    15 |     |    |   ,
```

Step 2.
```
        7  /10
    2  |  +  | 20  |
    15 | 105 | 150 |
```

Step 3.
```
        7  /10
    2  |  +  | 20  | 125 |
    15 | 105 | 150 | 150 |
```

3. Another example, with three fractions: 2/3 + 9/5 + 4/7:

Step 1.
```
        9  / 5          4  / 7
    2 |  +  |     |     |  +  |     |
    3 |     |     |     |     |     |
```

Step 2.
```
        9  / 5          4  / 7
    2 |  +  | 10  |     |  +  |     |
    3 | 27  | 15  |     |     |     |
```

Step 3.
```
        9  / 5            4  / 7
    2 |  +  | 10 | 37 |  +  | 259 | 319 |
    3 | 27  | 15 | 15 | 60  | 105 | 105 |   ,
```

where 319/105 is the answer.

4. Again, with 2/5 + 4/3 + 5/6:

Step 1.
```
        4  / 3          5  / 6
    2 |  +  |     |     |  +  |     |
    5 |     |     |     |     |     |
```

Step 2.
```
        4  / 3            5  / 6
    2 |  +  | 6  | 26 |  +  |     |
    5 | 20  | 15 | 15 |     |     |
```

Step 3.
```
        4  / 3            5  / 6
    2 |  +  | 6  | 26 |  +  | 156 | 231 |
    5 | 20  | 15 | 15 | 75  | 90  | 90  |
```

1. Add each of the following by all three methods:
(a) 5/6 + 1/2, (b) 5/6 + 1/2 + 3/4, (c) 1/2 + 1/3 + 1/4 + 1/5, (d) 2/7 + 5/6, (e) 3/4 + 2/5 + 6/13, (f) 1/4 + 4/6 + 1/8 + 4/11.

2. *Prove* that the grating method follows from the definition of sum. (Hint: Look at the following diagram.)

3. State advantages and disadvantages of each of the three methods of adding fractional numbers.

4. Find the LCDs of each of the following sets of fractional numbers: (a) 1/2,1/3,1/12,1/30, (b) 1/24,1/50, 1/144,1/300, (c) 1/12,1/36,1/49,1/126, (d) 1/38/1/28, 1/18,1/8.

SUBTRACTION

• •

Objective 50. To define the *difference* of two nonnegative rational numbers.

• •

Here we lazily copy what we did with cardinal numbers:

Definition

For fractional numbers a/k,b/m,c/n, the <u>difference</u> *a/k - b/m is defined as follows: a/k - b/m = c/n means a/k = b/m + c/n.*

Notice again that this definition does not guarantee the existence of every difference $a/k - b/m$. It merely states that if $a/k - b/m = c/n$ makes any sense, then it's just another way of writing $a/k = b/m + c/n$. Thus $1/2 - 1/3 = 1/6$ means $1/2 = 1/3 + 1/6$, but $1/5 - 1/4$ so far has no meaning, inasmuch as we have not introduced the negative rational numbers yet.

Exercises 1. One of the following is incorrect; find it, correct it, and rewrite the sums as differences:

(a) $\frac{1}{5} + \frac{1}{20} = \frac{1}{4}$, (b) $\frac{3}{10} + \frac{5}{12} = \frac{43}{60}$, (c) $\frac{2}{3} + \frac{3}{5} = \frac{13}{15}$,

(d) $\frac{3}{4} + \frac{5}{16} = \frac{17}{16}$.

2. Rewrite the following differences as sums:

(a) $\dfrac{1}{2} - \dfrac{1}{3} = \dfrac{1}{6}$, (b) $\dfrac{1}{3} - \dfrac{1}{4} = \dfrac{1}{12}$, (c) $\dfrac{1}{4} - \dfrac{1}{5} = \dfrac{1}{20}$,

(d) $\dfrac{1}{5} - \dfrac{1}{6} = \dfrac{1}{30}$.

3. What general rule emerges from the examples in Exercise 2? *Prove* this general rule.

The definition just given isn't really a "working definition," i.e., a definition used often in the course of work with fractional numbers. The next objective involves such a working form.

● ●

*Objective 51.

To prove $\dfrac{a}{m} - \dfrac{b}{n} = \dfrac{a \cdot n - m \cdot b}{m \cdot n}$

● ●

Exercises 1-3 will satisfy this objective, but first let us look at some examples to convince ourselves of its validity and usefulness.

Examples

1. $\dfrac{2}{5} - \dfrac{1}{4} = \dfrac{2 \cdot 4 - 5 \cdot 1}{5 \cdot 4} = \dfrac{8 - 5}{20} = \dfrac{3}{20}$.

Check: $\dfrac{1}{4} + \dfrac{3}{20} = \dfrac{1 \cdot 5 + 3}{20} = \dfrac{8}{20} = \dfrac{2}{5}$. Yes!

2. $\dfrac{9}{11} - \dfrac{3}{4} = \dfrac{9 \cdot 4 - 11 \cdot 3}{11 \cdot 4} = \dfrac{36 - 33}{44} = \dfrac{3}{44}$.

Check: $\dfrac{3}{4} + \dfrac{3}{44} = \dfrac{3 \cdot 11 + 3}{4 \cdot 11} = \dfrac{33 + 3}{44} = \dfrac{36}{44} = \dfrac{9}{11}$. Yes!

3. $\dfrac{7}{8} - \dfrac{5}{6} = \dfrac{7 \cdot 6 - 8 \cdot 5}{8 \cdot 6} = \dfrac{42 - 40}{48} = \dfrac{2}{48}$.

Check: $\dfrac{5}{6} + \dfrac{2}{48} = \dfrac{5 \cdot 8 + 2}{48} = \dfrac{42}{48} = \dfrac{7}{8}$. Yes!

Exercises

1. Rewrite $\dfrac{a}{m} - \dfrac{b}{n} = \dfrac{an - mb}{mn}$ as a sum.

2. Express the right-hand side of the answer to Exercise 1 with a lowest common denominator.

3. (a) $bm + (an - mb) = (bm + an) - mb$. Why?

   (b) $(bm + an) - mb = (an + bm) - mb$. Why?

   (c) $(an + bm) - mb = (an + bm) - bm$. Why?

   (d) $(an + bm) - bm = an + (bm - bm)$. Why?

4. Write a detailed proof, *including reasons*, that

$$\frac{a}{m} - \frac{b}{n} = \frac{an - mb}{mn} .$$

5. Prove the following law for cardinal numbers: $(a + b) - c = a + (b - c)$, assuming $b - c$ makes sense. (First show that for any cardinal number n, $(n - c) + c = n$. Then use this fact to show that the proposed law is equivalent to $a + b = a + b$, which is certainly true.)

6. Subtract (if possible): (a) 3/4 - 1/3, (b) 2/11 - 3/13, (c) 5/7 - 6/11, (d) 5/8 - 3/4, (e) 7/40 - 11/65, (f) 20/21 - 8/11.

DIVISION

● ●

Objective 52. To define the *quotient* of two fractional numbers.

● ●

Definition

For nonnegative rational numbers a/k, b/m, c/n with b ≠ 0 (as well as k,m,n ≠ 0), the quotient *a/k ÷ b/m is defined as follows: a/k ÷ b/m = c/n means a/k = b/m × c/n.*

Examples

1. $\frac{1}{2} \div \frac{1}{3} = \frac{3}{2}$ since $\frac{1}{2} = \frac{1}{3} \times \frac{3}{2}$.

2. Or $\frac{3}{8} \div \frac{2}{3} = \frac{9}{16}$ since $\frac{3}{8} = \frac{18}{48} = \frac{2}{3} \times \frac{9}{16}$.

3. And $\frac{2}{7} \div \frac{7}{12} = \frac{24}{49}$ since $\frac{2}{7} = \frac{7}{12} \times \frac{24}{49}$.

Exercises

1. How is the definition of quotient similar to the definition of difference? How are the two definitions dissimilar?

2. Show with examples how the definitions of difference and quotient for fractional numbers include previous results with whole numbers.

3. Divide the following: (a) 1/2 ÷ 1/6, (b) 3/4 ÷ 4/3, (c) 1/8 ÷ 8/7.

What about "invert and multiply"? What, indeed, about that old grammar school wheeze? The next objective establishes that rule.

*Objective 53. To prove $\dfrac{a}{m} \div \dfrac{b}{n} = \dfrac{an}{bm}$, where $b \neq 0$ (as well as $m, n \neq 0$).

Examples

1. $\dfrac{2}{3} \div \dfrac{4}{5} = \dfrac{2 \cdot 5}{4 \cdot 3} = \dfrac{10}{12} = \dfrac{5}{6}$.

2. $\dfrac{3}{7} \div \dfrac{4}{11} = \dfrac{3 \cdot 11}{4 \cdot 7} = \dfrac{33}{28}$.

3. $\dfrac{3}{8} \div \dfrac{1}{2} = \dfrac{3 \cdot 2}{1 \cdot 8} = \dfrac{6}{8}$.

Exercises

1. Rewrite $a/m \div b/n = an/bm$ as a product.

2. Explain why $(b \cdot an)/(n \cdot bm) = a/m$.

3. Prove that the statement $a/m \div b/n = an/bm$ is equivalent to the statement $a/m = a/m$.

4. $\dfrac{\frac{a}{m}}{\frac{b}{n}}$ means $\dfrac{a}{m} \div \dfrac{b}{n}$. Explain why the "outside-over-inside" rule illustrated below is valid.

$$\left.\dfrac{\frac{a}{m}}{\frac{b}{n}}\right\} \;\begin{array}{l} \longrightarrow an \\ \longrightarrow bm \end{array} = \dfrac{an}{bm} \; ; \qquad \left.\dfrac{\frac{3}{4}}{\frac{5}{7}}\right\} \;\begin{array}{l} \longrightarrow 3 \cdot 7 \\ \longrightarrow 4 \cdot 5 \end{array} = \dfrac{3 \cdot 7}{4 \cdot 5} = \dfrac{21}{20} \; .$$

5. Explain how the "outside-over-inside" rule may be applied to each of the following:

   (a) $\dfrac{3}{\frac{4}{5}}$, (b) $\dfrac{\frac{3}{4}}{5}$.

6. Compute: (a) $2/3 \div 1/2$, (b) $3/8 \div 1/3$,
   (c) $6/11 \div 2/11$, (d) $4/7 \div 7/3$, (e) $9/8 \div 1/9$.

7. Simplify: (a) $\dfrac{\frac{2}{3}}{\frac{1}{8}}$, (b) $\dfrac{\frac{3}{7}}{\frac{7}{3}}$, (c) $\dfrac{\frac{6}{8}}{\frac{2}{3}}$, (d) $\dfrac{\frac{7}{8}}{\frac{1}{7}}$,

   (e) $\dfrac{\frac{1}{2}}{\frac{4}{5}}$, (f) $\dfrac{\frac{3}{4}}{\frac{1}{2}}$.

ORDER RELATIONS	The order relations between the fractional numbers are essentially the same as those between the cardinals.

Definition	*For nonnegative rational numbers a/m, b/n, a/m < b/n means b/n − a/m = c/k for some positive rational c/k; a/m > b/n means b/n < a/m; a/m ≤ b/n means a/m < b/n or a/m = b/n; and a/m ≥ b/n means a/m > b/n or a/m = b/n.*

Do these definitions preserve previous relations among the integers? Yes. For instance, 3 < 5 means 5 − 3 = 2, which is a nonnegative cardinal number, and 3/1 < 10/2 means 10/2 − 3/1 = (10 • 1 − 2 • 3)/2 • 1 = (10 − 6)/2 = 4/2, which is a positive rational number. So 3 < 5 is preserved as 3/1 < 10/2.

Examples	1.	2/3 < 3/4 since 3/4 − 2/3 = (3 • 3 − 2 • 4)/12 = (9 − 8)/12 = 1/12.
	2.	Or 1/2 < 5/8 since 5/8 − 1/2 = 1/8.
	3.	Or if $1/x < 1/2$, $x > 0$, then $1/2 - 1/x = (x - 2)/2x > 0$ implies that x must be larger than 2.
	4.	Similarly, if $1/x \leq 1/3$, $x > 0$, then $1/3 - 1/x = (x - 3)/3x \geq 0$ implies that x must be larger than or equal to 3: $x \geq 3$.

• •

Objective 54.   Given a pair of nonnegative rational numbers, to state with proof whether or not they are equal, and if not, which is the larger.

• •

Let us check, as an early example, the relation between 3/13 and 4/17. Are these two numbers equal? If not, which is larger? As of now, the only way to check is to check first for equality, then if necessary for inequality:

Equality:

(a) $\frac{3}{13} = \frac{4}{17}$?   (b) 3 • 17 = 13 • 4?   (c) 51 = 52?   No.

Inequality:

$$\frac{4}{17} - \frac{3}{13} = \frac{4 \cdot 13 - 17 \cdot 3}{17 \cdot 13} = \frac{52 - 51}{221} = \frac{1}{221}$$, which is

positive; so $\frac{3}{13} < \frac{4}{17}$.

It may have occurred to you that both of these checks could be combined into one test, as is formally stated in the following theorem.

| Theorem | *Whatever order relation holds between two fractional numbers a/m and b/n, this is exactly the same relation as holds between a • n and m • b, respectively.* |

Thus, using this theorem on the preceding example, we may write

(a) $\dfrac{3}{13}$? $\dfrac{4}{17}$,   (b) 3 • 17 ? 13 • 4,   (c) 51 ? 52.

Ah! The unknown relation is "less than": $\dfrac{3}{13} < \dfrac{4}{17}$.

Exercises   1. For each of the following pairs of fractional numbers, state with proof whether or not they are equal, and if not, which is the larger: (a) 12/23 ? 20/155, (b) 3/10 ? 11/37,   (c) 29/2 ? 46/6,   (d) 30/78 ? 45/117,   (e) 6/23 ? 5/19.

2. (a) 2/3 ? 2/4,   (b) 2/4 ? 2/5,   (c) 2/5 ? 2/6,

(d) What is the most general law that can be inferred from these examples?

(e) Prove this law.

3. Find all possible values of x if (a) $1/x < 3/4$, (b) $3/x > 1/2$,   (c) $x/2 \leq 3/4$,   (d) $1/x \geq 1/2$, (e) $2/x < 3/4$; x a whole number.

DECIMAL
REPRESENTATION

Let us consider a fractional number, say 3/8, not quite chosen by chance.

$$\frac{3}{8} = \frac{3}{8} \cdot \frac{125}{125} = \frac{375}{1000} = \frac{300 + 70 + 5}{1000}$$

$$= \frac{300}{1000} + \frac{70}{1000} + \frac{5}{1000} = \frac{3}{10} + \frac{7}{100} + \frac{5}{1000} ,$$

which is abbreviated to the following *decimal representation*:

$$\frac{3}{10} + \frac{7}{100} + \frac{5}{1000} = .375 .$$

Why was the unit representative 125/125 used in this computation? Yes, 8 • 125 = 1000. Is 125 the smallest number x such that $8x = 10^n$, i.e., 8 times this number yields a power of 10? Would it change the decimal representation if 125 were not the smallest such number?

Let's look at another problem. What is the decimal representation of 3/4?

$$\frac{3}{4} \times \frac{25}{25} = \frac{75}{100} = .75.$$

Again, why use 25/25? Yes, $4 \times 25 = 10^2$. And what is the decimal representation of 5/16?

$$\frac{5}{16} \times \frac{625}{625} = \frac{3125}{10,000} = .3125.$$

Any fraction written with only a power of 10 in the denominator is called a *decimal fraction*, while other, nondecimal fractions are called *common fractions*. A *decimal* is a decimal fraction.

Exercises   1.   Find decimal equivalents (or representatives) of the following common fractions: (a) 1/2, (b) 5/2, (c) 1/4, (d) 3/4, (e) 7/4, (f) 1/5, (g) 2/5, (h) 23/5, (i) 1/8, (j) 3/8, (k) 5/8, (l) 27/8.

2.   Find at least two common fraction equivalents for each of the following decimals: (a) .125, (b) .123, (c) 2.75, (d) 47.34, (e) .004, (f) 1.0007, (g) 942.13, (h) .123456.

These examples and problems do allow us to find some decimals, but each is a special, nice number. And finding the unit representative which gives a power of 10 in the denominator is not easy. So we need a more usable means. Let's work toward that goal.

● ●

Objective 55.   To convert, if possible, given fractions to repeating decimals and to percents, and vice versa.

● ●

Definition   *Percent means "hundredths," and a percent means either "one hundredth" or a fraction with only 100 in the denominator. In symbols, "x percent" is written "x%" and means x/100.*

Here are some illustrations:

Common Fraction	Decimal Fraction	Percent
$\frac{3}{8}$	.375	37.5%
$\frac{3}{25}$	.12	12%
$\frac{412}{10}$	41.2	4120%

None of the examples we have seen is completely general (in fact, they're not even completely private!). The singularity of each of them lies in the fact that each denominator of the given fraction is a factor of a power of 10—8 is a factor of 1000, 25 a factor of 100, 10 a factor of 10—and this makes it relatively easy to derive neat decimal and percent equivalents. But how do we handle less convenient denominators?

Let us sneak up on an answer to that question, considering some special cases first.

$$\frac{20}{5} = \frac{4}{1} \leftrightarrow 4, \text{ and } 4 = 20 \div 5$$

$$\frac{12}{4} = \frac{3}{1} \leftrightarrow 3, \text{ and } 3 = 12 \div 4$$

$$\frac{6}{3} = \frac{2}{1} \leftrightarrow 2, \text{ and } 2 = 6 \div 3.$$

Thus it appears (but certainly *hasn't been proved*) that for a nonnegative rational a/b with $b \neq 0$, a/b and $a \div b$ represent the same number. To check this, let's first make the usual correspondence $a \leftrightarrow a/1$, $b \leftrightarrow b/1$. Then

$$a \div b \leftrightarrow \frac{a}{1} \div \frac{b}{1} = \frac{a \cdot 1}{1 \cdot b} = \frac{a}{b}.$$

Exercise	On the basis of this last paragraph, we write $a \div b = a/b$. But there is a previous definition of $a \div b$, namely "$a \div b = c$ with remainder r" means "$a = (b \times c) + r$." Connect these two conceptions of $a \div b$ by expressing a/b as a sum of fractional numbers involving b, c, and r.

Okay, so $a/b = a \div b$. But how are we going to get power-of-10 denominators into the act? Well, we'll use a common mathematical ploy: inserting what we want and inserting something else to make up for it. The fact we want is that

$$a \div b = (10a \div b) \times \frac{1}{10}.$$

Exercises	1.	Illustrate the above fact with at least three different examples.
	2.	Prove that fact.

Examples	1.	Let's now use this famous fact on a fairly general example:

$$\frac{3}{7} = 3 \div 7 = (30 \div 7) \cdot \frac{1}{10} = \left(4 + \frac{2}{7}\right) \cdot \frac{1}{10}$$

$$= 4\left(\frac{1}{10}\right) + \frac{2}{7} \cdot \frac{1}{10} = 4\left(\frac{1}{10}\right) + (2 \div 7) \cdot \frac{1}{10}$$

$$= 4\left(\frac{1}{10}\right) + \left((20 \div 7) \cdot \frac{1}{10}\right) \cdot \frac{1}{10}$$

$$= 4\left(\frac{1}{10}\right) + \left(2 + \frac{6}{7}\right) \cdot \frac{1}{100}$$

$$= 4\left(\frac{1}{10}\right) + 2\left(\frac{1}{100}\right) + \frac{6}{7} \cdot \frac{1}{100}$$

$$= 4\left(\frac{1}{10}\right) + 2\left(\frac{1}{100}\right) + (6 \div 7) \cdot \frac{1}{100}$$

$$= 4\left(\frac{1}{10}\right) + 2\left(\frac{1}{100}\right) + (60 \div 7) \cdot \frac{1}{1000}$$

$$= 4\left(\frac{1}{10}\right) + 2\left(\frac{1}{100}\right) + \left(8 + \frac{4}{7}\right) \cdot \frac{1}{1000}$$

$$= 4\left(\frac{1}{10}\right) + 2\left(\frac{1}{100}\right) + 8\left(\frac{1}{1000}\right) + \frac{4}{7} \cdot \frac{1}{1000}$$

$$= 4\left(\frac{1}{10}\right) + 2\left(\frac{1}{100}\right) + 8\left(\frac{1}{1000}\right) + (4 \div 7) \cdot \frac{1}{1000}$$

$$= 4\left(\frac{1}{10}\right) + 2\left(\frac{1}{100}\right) + 8\left(\frac{1}{1000}\right) + (40 \div 7) \cdot \frac{1}{10,000}$$

$$= 4\left(\frac{1}{10}\right) + 2\left(\frac{1}{100}\right) + 8\left(\frac{1}{1000}\right) + \left(5 + \frac{5}{7}\right) \cdot \frac{1}{10,000}$$

$$= 4\left(\frac{1}{10}\right) + 2\left(\frac{1}{100}\right) + 8\left(\frac{1}{1000}\right) + 5\left(\frac{1}{10,000}\right) + \frac{5}{7} \cdot \frac{1}{10,000}$$

$$= 4\left(\frac{1}{10}\right) + 2\left(\frac{1}{100}\right) + 8\left(\frac{1}{1000}\right) + 5\left(\frac{1}{10,000}\right) + (50 \div 7)$$
$$\cdot \frac{1}{100,000}$$

$$= 4\left(\frac{1}{10}\right) + 2\left(\frac{1}{100}\right) + 8\left(\frac{1}{1000}\right) + 5\left(\frac{1}{10,000}\right) + 7\left(\frac{1}{100,000}\right)$$
$$+ \frac{1}{7} \cdot \frac{1}{100,000}$$

$$= 4\left(\frac{1}{10}\right) + 2\left(\frac{1}{100}\right) + 8\left(\frac{1}{1000}\right) + 5\left(\frac{1}{10,000}\right) + 7\left(\frac{1}{100,000}\right)$$
$$+ 1\left(\frac{1}{1,000,000}\right) + \frac{3}{7} \cdot \frac{1}{1,000,000} \; .$$

At this point we've returned to 3/7 again, as the coefficient of 1/1,000,000. This means we'll just get a repetition of the coefficients computed so far. All of the above computation may be concisely written as follows:

$$
\begin{array}{r}
.428571428571\ldots \\
7)\overline{3.00000000000} \\
\underline{2\ 8} \\
20 \\
\underline{14} \\
60 \\
\underline{56} \\
40 \\
\underline{35} \\
50 \\
\underline{49} \\
10 \\
\underline{7} \\
3\ \ldots
\end{array}
$$

For additional shorthand we write $.\overline{428571}$ for $.428571428571\ldots\ldots$

2. Let's look at one more example, comparing development in the horizontal notation and in the long division:

$\dfrac{3}{8} = 3 \div 8$

$\quad = (30 \div 8)\left(\dfrac{1}{10}\right)$

$\quad = 3\left(\dfrac{1}{10}\right) + \dfrac{6}{8} \cdot \dfrac{1}{10}$

$\quad = 3\left(\dfrac{1}{10}\right) + \dfrac{60}{8} \cdot \dfrac{1}{100}$

$\quad = 3\left(\dfrac{1}{10}\right) + 7\left(\dfrac{1}{100}\right)$

$\qquad\qquad + \dfrac{4}{8} \cdot \dfrac{1}{100}$

$\quad = 3\left(\dfrac{1}{10}\right) + 7\left(\dfrac{1}{100}\right)$

$\qquad\qquad + \dfrac{40}{8} \cdot \dfrac{1}{1000}$

$\quad = 3\left(\dfrac{1}{10}\right) + 7\left(\dfrac{1}{100}\right)$

$\qquad\qquad + 5\left(\dfrac{1}{1000}\right)$

$\dfrac{3}{8} = 8)\overline{3.000}$

$= 8)\overline{3.000}\quad\begin{array}{r}.3\\ \underline{2\ 4}\\ 6\end{array}$

$= 8)\overline{3.000}\quad\begin{array}{r}.3\\ \underline{2\ 4}\\ 60\end{array}$

$= 8)\overline{3.0000}\quad\begin{array}{r}.37\\ \underline{2\ 4}\\ 60\\ \underline{56}\\ 4\end{array}$

$= 8)\overline{3.0000}\quad\begin{array}{r}.37\\ \underline{2\ 4}\\ 60\\ \underline{56}\\ 40\end{array}$

$= 8)\overline{3.0000}\quad\begin{array}{r}.375\\ \underline{2\ 4}\\ 60\\ \underline{56}\\ 40\\ \underline{40}\\ 0\end{array}$

$$= 3\left(\frac{1}{10}\right) + 7\left(\frac{1}{100}\right)$$

$$+ 5\left(\frac{1}{1000}\right)$$

$$= 8\overline{)3.0000}^{.375\overline{0}}$$

```
        .3750
8 ) 3.0000
    2 4
      60
      56
      40
      40
       0
```

Exercises

1. Rewrite each of the following fractions in infinitely repeating decimal form, *if possible*: (a) 1/3, (b) 1/6, (c) 1/7, (d) 1/9, (e) 1/11, (f) 1/12, (g) 22/7, (h) 1/1, (i) 2/1, (j) 1/2, (k) 3/4.

2. Rewrite 1/7, 2/7, 3/7, 4/7, 5/7, 6/7 in repeating decimal expansion. What is there to notice here?

3. What kinds of fractions have infinitely repeating contiguous zeros in their expansions?

4. Rewrite each of the fractions of Exercise 1 in percents, rounded off (if necessary) to the nearest tenth of a percent.

We turn now to the converse of the preceding exercises: finding common fraction equivalents of given decimals. We'll plunge right into some examples:

Examples

1. $4.035 = \dfrac{4035}{1000} = \dfrac{807}{200}$

2. $2.122 = \dfrac{2122}{1000} = \dfrac{1061}{500}$

Notice that in these examples the denominator of the unreduced fraction has as many zeros as the numerator has digits to the right of the decimal point.

3. $4.\overline{035} = 4.035035035. \ldots$

There's a neat trick to handle this sort of decimal. The idea is to get another number with the same "infinite decimal tail" and cancel the two tails via subtraction, as in Example 4.

4. $.33\overline{3} = .33333 \ldots \ldots :$

Let $x = .333 \ldots$
$\underline{10x = 3.333 \ldots}$
$9x = 3$
$x = \dfrac{3}{9} = \dfrac{1}{3}$

5. Let's try $6.\overline{12}$:

$$x = 6.12121212 \ldots$$
$$\underline{100x = 612.12121212 \ldots}$$
$$99x = 606$$
$$x = \frac{606}{99} = \frac{202}{33}.$$

Exercises
1. Why did we multiply by 1000 in Example 3 and by only 10 in Example 4?

2. What is another power of 10 that would have worked in Example 3? In Example 4?

3. In this process, which is subtracted from what?

Let's consider another method:

$4,0\overline{35} = 4.0353535 \ldots$:

$$x = 4.0\overline{35} = 4.0353535 \ldots$$
$$10x = 40.\overline{35} = 40.3535353 \ldots$$
$$\underline{1000x = 4035.\overline{35} = 4035.3535353 \ldots}$$
$$990x = 3995.$$
$$x = \frac{3995}{990}$$

Exercises
1. Why does this example have an extra step?

2. In this process, which is subtracted from what?

Still another example:

$4.03\overline{5} = 4.0355555555 \ldots$:

$$\text{Let} \quad x = 4.03\overline{5}$$
$$100x = 403.\overline{5}$$
$$\underline{1000x = 4035.\overline{5}}$$
$$900x = 3632.$$
$$x = \frac{3632}{900}$$

THE NEW YEAR
PROBLEM SOLVED
AND
ALPHAMETICS

Let's look at the alphametic with which this chapter begins:

$$\frac{old}{dad} = .donedonedone \ldots .$$

If we let x be the Mystery Number, then

$$x = .donedonedone \ldots .$$

and

$$10000x = done.donedonedone \ldots \ ,$$

and therefore

$$9999x = done, \text{ or } x = \frac{done}{9999} = \frac{done}{3^2 \cdot 11 \cdot 101} \ .$$

Noting that

$$\frac{old}{dad} = x = \frac{done}{3^2 \cdot 11 \cdot 101}$$

we *suspect* (but certainly not beyond the shadow of a doubt) that $a = 0$, and *dad* is some multiple of 101: 202 or 303 or 404 or 505 or . . . . This would mean that 11 is a factor of DONE, so $d + n = o + e$ or $d + n = o + e \pm 11$. Now solving an alphametic is largely trial and error, with some opportunity for deduction only if you're lucky. Most of the time you make a guess and try it out; about the only inside tips for this are (a) to be *systematic*, and (b) to try the *simple cases first*. (You might be lucky and hit an easy winner.) So let's try $d + n = o + e$ first. Meanwhile, what about that 3^2? It either divides evenly into *done*, or it doesn't, in which case we'd think about *dad* being 303 or 606 or 909. First, however, let's see what would happen if 9 were a factor of *done*: Then $d + o + n + e =$ either 9 or 18 or 27. (Why not 36?) But if we're temporarily assuming that $d + n = o + e$, then we have that $d + o + n + e = 2(o + e) = 18$, the only possibility, since 18 is even, while 9 and 27 are odd. Hence we try $o + e = 9 = d + n$. Since $a = 0$ (we think), we should try the most frequent $d = 1,2,3,4,5,$ 6,7 or 8. (Why not 9?) Then d would be 8,7,6,5,4,3, 2 or 1, respectively, and o,e would be a different pair that also add up to 9. To save space, we won't show you here our trials of $d = 1,2,3,4$, but will jump into our successful $d = 5$ (so that $n = 4$):

$$\frac{o15}{5o5} \stackrel{?}{=} .\overline{5o4e} \ .$$

(Those are *letter os*, not *numeral* 0s.) Since $o/5$ is approximately $.5 = 1/2$, let's try $o = 2$ (and therefore $e = 7$):

$$\frac{215}{5o5} \stackrel{?}{=} .\overline{5247}$$

Now,

$$.\overline{5247} = \frac{5247}{9999} = \frac{9 \cdot 11 \cdot 53}{9 \cdot 11 \cdot 101} = \frac{265}{505} \ ,$$

so $l = 6$ would give us one solution. There may be others, and we leave to you the fun of deciding whether or not there are any.

Exercises   1.   Convert the following decimals to common fractions:
(a) .684<u>2</u>,   (b) .684<u>2</u>,   (c) .68<u>42</u>,   (d) .68$\overline{42}$,
(e) .684$\overline{2}$,   (f) 35.53,   (g) 35.$\overline{53}$,   (h) 35.5$\overline{3}$.

2.   Convert to common fractions: (a) .1$\overline{0}$,   (b) .0$\overline{9}$,
(c) .0$\overline{8}$,   (d) .$\overline{9}$.

3.   What kinds of numbers have two different decimal expansions?

4.   Convert to common fractions: (a) 12%,   (b) 12.34%,
(c) 12.3$\overline{4}$%,   (d) 12.$\overline{34}$%.

5.   Find at least one solution of each of the following alphametics:

(a) $\dfrac{so}{he}$ = .ranranran . . . ,

(b) $\dfrac{mom}{dad}$ = .walkwalkwalk . . . ,

(c) $\dfrac{old}{dad}$ = .donedonedone . . . ,

6.   Prove that it is impossible to solve $\dfrac{he}{she}$ = .wheeee
. . . .

7.   Invent your own alphametic involving an infinite repeating decimal expansion.

GRAPHING

● ●

Objective 56.   To graph given fractional numbers, expressed as common fractions or decimals or percents, on the number line.

● ●

Once again, it's "damned be him that first cries 'hold, enough!'" as we launch immediately into some examples.

Examples   1.

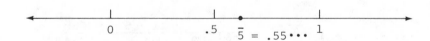

$$0 \qquad .5 \quad \overline{5} = .55\cdots \quad 1$$

2.

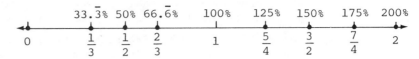

3. $S = \{1/b: b = 2^n$ for some cardinal $n\}$.

4. $S = \{x: x = n .\overline{9}, n =$ cardinal number$\}$

5.

6. $S = \{n/(n + 1): n$ a cardinal$\}$

Exercises
1. Graph on the same number line: (a) $.519$, $.51\overline{9}$, $.5\overline{19}$, $.\overline{519}$; (b) $.591$, $.59\overline{1}$, $.5\overline{91}$, $.\overline{591}$.

2. Graph on the same number line: 10%, $1/6$, $.160$, $.20$, $2/5$, 50%, 70%, $4/5$, $5/6$, $.90$.

3. In Example 3 above, is $0 \,\varepsilon\, S$? Why? In Example 6, is $1 \,\varepsilon\, S$? Why?

4. Graph $S = \left\{ \dfrac{2n + 1}{n} : n \text{ cardinal} \right\}$.

5. Graph $S = \left\{ x: x = 1 - \dfrac{1}{3^n}, \ n \text{ cardinal} \right\}$.

6. Graph $S = \left\{ \dfrac{a}{b} : \dfrac{0}{1} \le \dfrac{a}{b} \le \dfrac{1}{1}, \ b = 2^n \text{ for cardinal } n \right\}$.

7. $F_0 = \left\{ \dfrac{0}{1} \right\}$, $F_1 = \left\{ \dfrac{0}{1}, \dfrac{1}{1} \right\}$, $F_2 = \left\{ \dfrac{0}{1}, \dfrac{1}{2}, \dfrac{1}{1} \right\}$,

$F_3 = \left\{ \dfrac{0}{1}, \dfrac{1}{3}, \dfrac{1}{2}, \dfrac{2}{3}, \dfrac{1}{1} \right\}$, $F_4 = \left\{ \dfrac{0}{1}, \dfrac{1}{4}, \dfrac{1}{3}, \dfrac{1}{2}, \dfrac{2}{3}, \dfrac{3}{4}, \dfrac{1}{1} \right\}$.

(a) What is F_5? F_6? (b) Graph F_9.

8. What nonnegative rational is immediately to the right of 1.234 on the number line? (Careful!)

9. For each of the following sequences find three more fractional numbers consistent with those that are given. Then graph all seven numbers on the number line.

   (a) 45/4, 15/4, 5/4, 5/12, _____ , _____ , _____ .

   (b) 13%, 15%, 19%, 24%, _____ , _____ , _____ .

   (c) .25$\overline{0}$, .2$\overline{0}$, .1$\overline{6}$, .$\overline{142857}$, _____ , _____ , _____ .

   (d) 12.8, 160/25, 320%, 1.6, _____ , _____ , _____ .

10. Explain advantages and disadvantages of (a) common fractions, (b) decimals, (c) percents, as compared with each other.

50. To define the *difference* of two nonnegative rational numbers (page 149).

*51. To prove $\dfrac{a}{m} - \dfrac{b}{n} = \dfrac{a \cdot n - m \cdot b}{m \cdot n}$ (page 150).

52. To define the *quotient* of two fractional numbers (page 151).

*53. To prove $\dfrac{a}{m} \div \dfrac{b}{n} = \dfrac{an}{bm}$, where $b \neq 0$ (as well as

$m,n \neq 0$) (page 152).

54. Given a pair of nonnegative rational numbers, to state with proof whether or not they are equal, and if not, which is the larger (page 153).

55. To convert, if possible, given fractions to repeating decimals and to percents, and vice versa (page 155).

56. To graph given fractional numbers, expressed as common fractions or decimals or percents, on the number line (page 162).

WORDS TO KNOW

nonnegative rational
  number   (page 128)
fractional number
  (page 128)
numerator   (page 130)
denominator   (page 130)
class   (page 131)
reciprocal   (page 133)
positive   (page 138)
group   (page 139)
least common denominator
  (page 145)
prime factors   (page 146)
grating   (page 147)
percent   (page 155)

hundredths   (page 155)
graph   (page 162)
fraction   (page 130)
product   (page 134)
sum   (page 144)
difference   (page 149)
quotient (page 151)
order relation   (page 153)
decimal representation
  (page 154)
decimal fraction   (page
  155)
common fraction   (page
  155)
decimal   (page 155

CHAPTER 4

INTEGERS

Suppose we count the number of hairs on the head of the guy at the left on page 167, then multiply that by the number of hairs on the head of the guy in the middle, then multiply that result by the number of hairs on the head of the girl, etc., until we've done this for every person that has ever lived. What is the answer, to the nearest billion, say?

Challenge

Try to solve the Hair Problem.

The answer to the Hair Problem involves a characteristic property of a mathematical structure called an "integral domain," so called because it is essentially the structure of the integers, which are, only roughly speaking, what we might call "the positive, negative, and zero whole numbers": . . . , -3, -2, -1, 0, 1, 2, 3, ...

DEFINITION AND INTERPRETATION

Before plunging into the definition of the integers, let us ask ourselves, "Why do we want integers, anyway?" Since the integers essentially consist of the cardinal numbers and their negatives, this question amounts to "Why do we want the negative integers?"

We can begin to formulate an answer by thinking of the answer to a previous question, "Why do we need the positive rationals?" In that case the answer was to complete a group structure under multiplication, thereby introducing multiplicative inverses with which we might solve any equation of the form $ax = b$, where a and b are positive and rational. For instance: Suppose

$$\frac{2}{3} x = \frac{5}{7} .$$

To get rid of that 2/3 we multiply by

$$\frac{1}{\frac{2}{3}} = \frac{3}{2} : \quad \frac{3}{2}\left(\frac{2}{3}x\right) = \frac{3}{2} \cdot \frac{5}{7}$$

$$\left(\frac{3}{2} \cdot \frac{2}{3}\right)x = \frac{15}{14}$$

$$\frac{6}{6}x = \frac{15}{14}$$

$$x = \frac{15}{14} , \text{ answer.}$$

1. Solve for x, if possible:

(a) $\frac{3}{4}x = \frac{6}{7}$, (b) $\frac{3}{4}x = \frac{6}{8}$, (c) $3x = \frac{1}{4}$, (d) $2x = 3$,

(e) $0 \cdot x = 3$, (f) $3 \cdot x = 0$, (g) $\frac{3}{4}x = 0$,

(h) $\frac{3}{4}x = 1$.

2. Copy down the example above, and opposite each step state which group property, if any, is being used.

3. (a) What is the multiplicative inverse of a?

(b) How do we use it to solve $ax = b$?

(c) What other group properties are used in the solution of this equation?

Analogy is a standard developmental principle in mathematics; let us use it here and attempt to complete another group structure, this time under addition. As before, we'll start with the cardinal (or whole) numbers, and we'll use our earlier development of fractional numbers as a guide. Let's do this first in attacking the next objective.

● ●

Objective 57. To define *integer* and explain how a cardinal number may be considered to be an integer.

● ●

In this definition, we'll blindly follow what we did earlier with nonnegative rationals, merely substituting addition for multiplication, and see if what results makes any sense.

Earlier definition:
A *nonnegative* (or *fractional*) *number* is a class of all ordered pairs a/b, $b \neq 0$, of cardinal numbers a and b which are equivalent according to the following rule: $a/b = c/d$ if and only if $a \times d = b \times c$.

Blind analogy:
An *integer* is a class of all ordered pairs $a - b$, $b \neq 0$, of cardinal numbers a and b which are equivalent according to the following rule: $a - b = c - d$ if and only if $a + d = b + c$.

Does this blind analogy make sense? At first glance it may seem not to make sense; we are used to ordered pairs representing fractional numbers, but we are not used to thinking of integers as ordered pairs. If we do consent to consider integers as ordered pairs, we'll of course have to use different symbols, so as to avoid confusion between nonnegative rationals and integers.

Hence, we introduce $a - b$ instead of a/b as our ordered pairs.

What about $b \neq 0$? Earlier we stipulated this because we anticipated ultimately interpreting a/b as $a \div b$, and we knew that we did not want to allow division by zero. With the integers we may anticipate that $a - b$ will ultimately be interpreted as "a subtract b," and then ask if we want to rule out subtraction of zero. Well, no, we don't. Is there another analogous cardinal whose subtraction we'll want to rule out? No, so "$b \neq 0$" is not necessary here.

How about the definition of equivalence? Does that make any sense? Let's check some special cases:

Does $5 - 3 = 4 - 2$ mean $5 + 2 = 4 + 3$?
Does $6 - 0 = 9 - 3$ mean $6 + 3 = 0 + 9$?
Does $0 - 8 = 1 - 9$ mean $0 + 9 = 8 + 1$?

Since we know from experience that the answer to all of these questions is yes, let's accept this definition of equivalence.

Definition	An *integer* is a class of all ordered pairs $a - b$ of cardinal numbers equivalent according to the following rule: $a - b = c - d$ means $a + d = b + c$.

Thus $p = \{2 - 0, 3 - 1, 4 - 2, 5 - 3, 6 - 4, \ldots\}$
$q = \{0 - 0, 1 - 1, 2 - 2, 3 - 3, 4 - 4, \ldots\}$
$r = \{0 - 8, 1 - 9, 2 - 10, 3 - 11, 4 - 12,$
$\ldots\},$

are three examples of integers according to this definition.

The foregoing analogy is not the only possible approach to the definition of integers. Another equally valid approach is to define:

0 as the solution of $x - 0 = 0$
$^+1$ as the solution of $x - 1 = 0$
$^+2$ as the solution of $x - 2 = 0,$

in general,

^+n as the solution of $x - n = 0$;

and also

$^-1$ as the solution of $x + 1 = 0$
$^-2$ as the solution of $x + 2 = 0$
$^-3$ as the solution of $x + 3 = 0,$

and in general

^-n as the solution of $x + n = 0.$

That is, for any positive cardinal number n, ^-n is defined into existence as the additive inverse of n. We then form the union $\{0,1,2,3, \ldots\} \cup \{^-1,^-2,^-3, \ldots\} = \{\ldots, {}^-3,{}^-2,{}^-1,0,1,2,3 \ldots\}$, called *the integers*. Note: We'll write "$^-2$" for "negative 2," to distinguish it from "-2," meaning "subtract 2."

Examples

1. We might define $^-1$ as *either* $\{0 - 1, 1 - 2, 2 - 3, 3 - 4, \ldots\}$ *or* as the (unique) solution of $x + 1 = 0$.

2. We might define $^-2$ as *either* $\{0 - 2, 1 - 3, 2 - 4, 3 - 5, \ldots\}$ *or* as the solution of $x + 2 = 0$.

3. We might define $^+1$ as *either* $\{1 - 0, 2 - 1, 3 - 2, 4 - 3, \ldots\}$ *or* as the solution of $x - 1 = 0$.

Exercises

1. What are the numerals for the integers p, q, r defined above?

2. The second half of Objective 57 is to explain how a cardinal number may be considered to be an integer. Using our first definition of "integer," copy down the previous explanation of how a cardinal number may be considered to be a fractional number, then construct its "blind analogy." Finally, alter that analogy, if necessary, so that it makes sense.

3. Show how a cardinal number may be considered to be an integer under the second definition of "integer."

4. We saw that $^-1$, for example, is the solution of $x + 1 = 0$, and also of $x + 2 = 1$, $x + 3 = 2$, $x + 4 = 3$, etc. How does this observation connect our two different definitions of cardinal numbers?

INTEGERS ON
THE NUMBER
LINE

Let's now turn to geometric consideration of the definition of integers.

● ●

*Objective 58. To illustrate a given integer as a class of jumps on the cardinal number line.

● ●

We attack this objective immediately by considering interpretations of the symbols in our first definition.

Examples   1.

                                               2.

3 − 0: A jump three units
to the right, from 0 to 3.

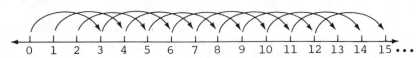

2 − 2: A jump from 2 back
onto 2.

3.

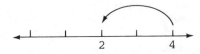

2 − 4: A jump two units to
the left starting at 4 and
ending at 2.

4.

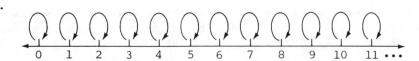

$^{+}3 = \{3 - 0, 4 - 1, 5 - 2, 6 - 3, 7 - 4, 8 - 5, 9 - 6,$
$\quad\quad 10 - 7, \ldots\}$

Thus the integer $^{+}3$ may be thought of as the class of
all jumps of three units to the right, starting from
some whole number.

5.

$^{0}0 = \{0 - 0, 1 - 1, 2 - 2, 3 - 3, 4 - 4, 5 - 5, 6 - 6,$
$\quad\quad \ldots\}$

Let's write the integer zero, temporarily at least, as
$^{0}0$ to distinguish it from the cardinal zero, 0. The
integer $^{0}0$ may be thought of as the class of all jumps
from a cardinal on the number line back onto itself.

6.

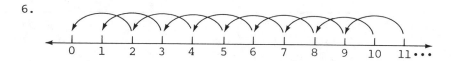

$$^-2 = \{0 - 2, \ 1 - 3, \ 2 - 4, \ 3 - 5, \ 4 - 6, \ 5 - 7, \ 6 - 8,$$
$$\ldots\};$$

the integer ‾2 may be thought of as the class of all jumps of two units to the left, ending at some whole number.

Exercises 1. Illustrate each of the following ordered pairs with a jump on the cardinal number line: (a) 5 - 6, (b) 1 - 0, (c) 9 - 5, (d) 100 - 100, (e) 4 - 5, (f) 0 - 1, (g) 3 - 10.

2. For each of the following integers, (i) indicate it as a class of ordered pairs of cardinals, (ii) illustrate it with a class of jumps on the number line: (a) ‾3, (b) ‾1, (c) ⁺1, (d) ⁺2.

Now that we're adept at jumping about on the cardinal number line, let's in effect extend our jumping to the integer number line, redrawing our jumps so that they all start at zero (that is, so that zero is the *origin* of each jump):

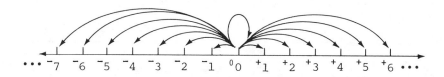

Here we may think of all jumps of one unit to the left as being superimposed on the jump from ⁰0 to ‾1, all jumps from a number onto itself as being superimposed on the jump from ⁰0 to ⁰0, all jumps of two units to the right as being superimposed on the jump from ⁰0 to ⁺2, etc. Finally, omitting the jumps, we end up with the customary depiction of the integer number line:

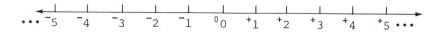

1.   What does the picture of the set of jumps from the origin look like? How might you use this in your teaching of the integer number line?

2.   Consider the second definition of ⁻1: the solution of $x + 1 = 0$. A geometric interpretation of this might be "that jump which goes from 1 to 0." Give geometric interpretations of the solutions of (a) $x + 2 = 0$, (b) $x + 3 = 0$,   (c) $x + n = 0$ (n a cardinal number), (d) $x + 0 = 0$,   (e) $x - 1 = 0$,   (f) $x - 2 = 0$, (g) $x - 3 = 0$,   (h) $x - n = 0$ (n a cardinal number).

3.   Which integers are represented by the following jumps on the number line?

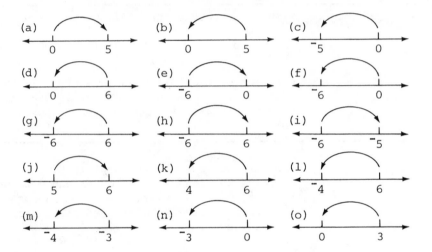

We are now in a position to consider the next objective.

● ●

Objective   59.   To graph given sets of integers on the integer number line.

● ●

Once again we dive into examples. Here x is the generic symbol for an integer.

Examples   1.

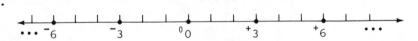

$\{x: x \text{ is a multiple of } 3\}$

2.

$$\{x: x \equiv 1 \pmod 3\}$$

3.

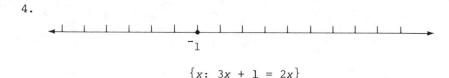

$$\{x: 3x + 1 \equiv 2x \pmod 5\}$$

4.

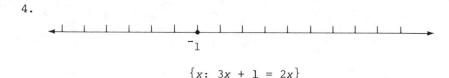

$$\{x: 3x + 1 = 2x\}$$

5.

$$\{x: 3x + 1 = 0\} = \emptyset$$

Exercises   Graph each of the following sets of integers:

1. $\{x: x = 3n + 1,\ n = 0,1,2,3,\ .\ .\ .\}$.

2. $\{x: x \text{ is odd}\}$.

3. $\{x: x \text{ is even}\}$.

4. $\{x: x \equiv 3 \pmod 5\}$.

5. $\{x: 3x + 2 = 0\}$.

6. $\{x: 3x + 2 \equiv 0 \pmod 5\}$.

7. $\{x: 3x + 2 \equiv 0 \pmod 4\}$.

8. $\{x: 2x \equiv 0 \pmod 5\}$.

9. $\{x: 2x \equiv 0 \pmod 4\}$.

10. $\{x: x = {}^-2 + n,\ n = 0,1,2,\ .\ .\ .\}$.

11. $\{x: x = n({}^-2 + n),\ n = 0,1,2,3,\ .\ .\ .\}$.

12. $\{x: x = \dfrac{3 - n}{n},\ n = 1,2,3,\ .\ .\ .\}$.

13. $\{x: x = 3 - ({}^-n),\ n = 0,1,2,3,\ .\ .\ .\}$ (careful!).

14. $\{x: x = n^2\} \cup \{x: x = {}^-(n^2)\}$.

15. $\{x: x = n^2\} \cap \{x: x = {}^-(n^2)\}$.

<table>
<tr><td>ARITHMETIC
OPERATIONS</td><td>We could carefully develop the integers with logical rigor, but we won't, lest the rigor result in mortis. Instead we'll content ourselves with some definitions and just a few properties of the integers under these operations, in order to give the flavor of foundational considerations.</td></tr>
</table>

● ●

Objective 60. To define addition, subtraction, multiplication, and division of integers.

● ●

Here again we have the problem of two different possible definitions, depending on which definition of "integer" we take.

Definitions *Let x and y be integers with x represented by a − b, y represented by c − d. Then (a) the <u>sum</u> x + y of x and y is the integer represented by (a + c) − (b + d); (b) for integer z, "x − y = z" means x = y + z; (c) the <u>product</u> x • y of x and y is the integer represented by (ac + bd) − (ad + bc); (d) "x ÷ y = z" means x = y • z.*

These definitions, based on our first definition of "integer," are not very palatable because they are not very natural. Why, then, you may ask, are they made as they are? The answer is that, as is often the case in mathematics, a seemingly complex definition results in easier proofs later on. Before looking at some such proofs, however, let's try to get more comfortable with these admittedly complex-appearing definitions.

Examples? Let's consider the definition of "sum" and relate it to the cardinal number line, looking at the specific example (5 − 2) + (7 − 3). As a jump, (5 − 2) is interpreted as starting at 2 and ending at 5:

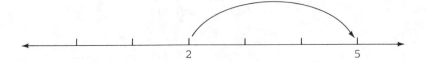

We can think of this as being performed by a little cricket, Hy Quimby Cricket (more commonly known as Hy Q.), working out of the origin.

Hy's assignment consists of two parts: (a) "Go to 2" and (b) "jump to 5." Similarly, the assignment for (7 − 3) is (a) "Go to 3" and (b) "jump to 7." Obediently, Hy Q. goes to 2 and jumps to 5. Now, Hy Q. is not only well behaved but smart. He knows that (7 - 3) is the same as (9 - 5), so being already at 5 he completes his assignment by jumping to 9. Thus (5 - 2) + (7 - 3) is the same as (9 - 2). And since (9 - 2) = (12 - 5), we satisfy our complex definition.

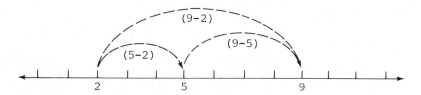

Being versatile, as well as smart, Hy reworks the example. He scurries to the origin and runs out to 2, then asks, "Why not continue on out 3 more, doing all of my 'going' first?" Then, since all of his "going" is done, he decides to do all of his "jumping" next. So he jumps to 12, the sum of 7 and 5, showing directly that (5 - 2) + (7 - 3) = (12 - 5) as per the definition.

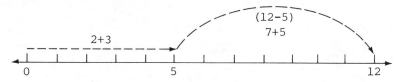

Hy Q. is not one to be satisfied with one example, so he suggests we try adding (3 - 6) + (4 - 2). He walks out to 6 and jumps back to 3. Again he knows (4 - 2) is the same as (5 - 3). So being at 3 he finishes his job by hopping to 5. His conclusion is that (3 - 6) + (4 - 2) = (5 - 6) = (7 - 8).

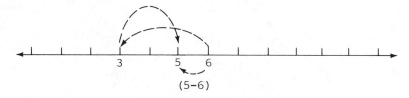

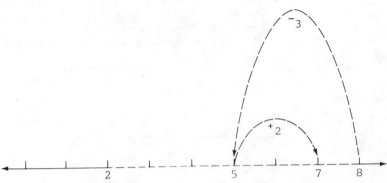

Hy 2. going from 2 to 8 then jumping -3 and +2
using the definition

In this last example Hy is trying to tell us something. Can you see his message? When executing a
jump $(a - b)$, if b is larger than a, i.e., to the right
of a on the integer line, Hy jumps to the left. But
when b is to the left of a, he jumps to the right.

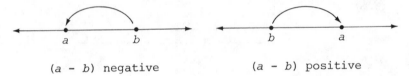

$(a - b)$ negative $(a - b)$ positive

Thus according to Hy, a jump to the left, goes down the
line so is *negative*, while a jump to the right goes up
the line and is *positive*.

Let's give Hy a bit more exercise and try the example
$(8 - 12) + (2 - 5)$. Hy goes to 12 and jumps to 8.
Since $(2 - 5)$ is the same as $(5 - 8)$, he jumps on to 5,
thus completing his job and getting the answer
$(5 - 12)$, which is the same as $(10 - 17)$ as in our definition.

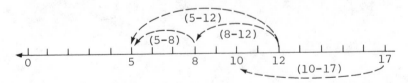

Here is one of the easier proofs we wrote of earlier:
Prove that $(a - b) = \big((a + c) - (b + c)\big)$, where a, b, c
are cardinal numbers and $(a - b)$ and $\big((a + c) - (b + c)\big)$
represent integers. As we often do in mathematics, we

start with the more complicated side, apply a definition and simplify, and hope that it all turns out to
be the simpler side. $\big((a + c) - (b + c)\big) = (a - b) +$
$(c - c)$, by the definition of $(a - b) + (c - c)$. And
$(c - c)$ represents $^0 0$. Therefore $\big((a + c) - (b + c)\big)$
$= (a - b) + (c - c) = (a - b) + {}^0 0 = a - b$.

Exercises 1. Give a Hy Q. Cricket explanation of why $(3 - 6) +$
$(4 - 8) = (7 - 14)$.

2. Prove that $(a - b) = \big((c + a) - (c + b)\big)$, where a, b, c
represent cardinal numbers and $(a - b)$ and $\big((c + a) -$
$(c + b)\big)$ represent integers.

3. Prove from definitions that $(a - b) + (b - c) = (a - c)$
for integers represented by $(a - b)$, $(b - c)$, $(a - c)$.

4. Demonstrate commutativity of integers under addition by
looking at (a) $^-5 + {}^+1$, (b) $^+5 + {}^-7$, (c) $^-5 + {}^-7$,
using jumps on the number line.

5. Demonstrate associativity of integers under addition by
looking at: (a) $^-5 + ({}^+7 + {}^+3)$, (b) $^-5 + ({}^-7 + {}^+3)$,
(c) $^-5 + ({}^-7 + {}^-3)$, (d) $^+5 + ({}^-7 + {}^-3)$,
(e) $^+5 + ({}^-7 + {}^+3)$.

6. (a) Prove that every ordered pair representing the
integer represented by $(3 - 5)$ is either of the
form $\big((3 - c) - (5 - c)\big)$ or of the form $\big((3 + c) -$
$(5 + c)\big)$, for some cardinal number c.

(b) Prove part (a) in general, substituting $(a - b)$ for
$(3 - 5)$.

7. Prove that addition of integers is well defined, that
is, that it does not matter *which* representative of two
integers we choose when we apply the definition of the
sum of the integers.

8. How does the definition of subtraction for integers
compare with the definition of subtraction for cardinals?

9. Illustrate the following subtractions with jumps on the
number line: (a) $^+6 - {}^+3$, (b) $^+6 - {}^-3$, (c) $^-6 - {}^-3$,
(d) $^-6 - {}^+ 3$. (Hint: Start by letting $^+6 - {}^+3 = a$, then
rewriting $^+6 = {}^+3 + a$ and figuring out what a is.)

10. Go jump in the lake if you don't like integers.

Turning to an explanation of the definition of multiplication of integers, we'll rely on arithmetic-
algebraic, rather than geometric, intuition. We'll
start by reviewing some distributive laws of cardinal
numbers:

$\quad$ (a) $a \times (b + c) = (a \times b) + (a \times c)$

(b) $a \times (b - c) = (a \times b) - (a \times c)$ (*if $b - c$ is defined*)

(c) $(a - b) \times c = (a \times c) - (b \times c)$ (*if $a - b$ is defined*).

Examples   1. $3 \times (5 + 7) = 3 \times 12 = 36$

$(3 \times 5) + (3 \times 7) = 15 + 21 = 36$

Thus $3 \times (5 + 7) = (3 \times 5) + (3 \times 7)$.

2. $3 \times (7 - 5) = 3 \times 2 = 6$

$(3 \times 7) - (3 \times 5) = 21 - 15 = 6$

Thus $3 \times (7 - 5) = (3 \times 7) - (3 \times 5)$.

Here's a proof that $a \times (b + c) = (a \times b) + (a \times c)$ for cardinal numbers a, b, c. Let sets A, B, C represent a, b, c, respectively, with B and C disjoint. From set theory we know that $A \otimes (B \cup C) = (A \otimes B) \cup (A \otimes C)$ (see page 25). Moreover, since $B \cap C = \emptyset$, $(A \otimes B) \cap (A \otimes C) = \emptyset$. (Remember in our definition of addition, the sets must be disjoint.) Therefore the cardinal number representing $A \otimes (B \cup C)$ is also the cardinal number representing $(A \otimes B) \cup (A \otimes C)$. That is, $a \times (b + c) = (a \times b) + (a \times c)$, QED.

Exercises   1.   Illustrate the three distributive laws with examples other than those in the text.

2.   Prove the laws in Examples 1 and 2.

Armed with these facts, we can attack $(a - b) \times (c - d)$, again assuming both the parenthetical expressions are fulfilled for cardinal numbers. First, to ensure that we think of $(a - b)$ as a single entity, let's shade it in:

$$(a - b) = \text{⬭}$$

$$\text{Then } (a - b) \times (c - d) = \text{⬭} \times (c - d)$$

$$= (\text{⬭} \times c) - (\text{⬭} \times d).$$

Now let's "erase" the shading:

$$(a - b) \times (c - d) = \big((a - b) \times c\big) - \big((a - b) \times d\big)$$

$$= (ac - bc) - (ad - bd)$$

$$= (ac + bd) - (ad + bc).$$

Justify each of the steps in the computation. (Going
                            from the next-to-the-last step to the last one will
                            probably require several steps in itself.)

                            The message in the foregoing computation is that for
                            cardinal numbers a, b, c, d, with both $a - b$ and $c - d$
                            defined, the following holds:

                            $(a - b) \times (c - d) = (ac + bd) - (ad + bc)$.

                            To retain this earlier result, it is thus natural to
                            define the integer represented by $\big((ac + bd) -$
                            $(ad + bc)\big)$ to be the product of the integers repre-
                            sented by $(a - b)$ and $(c - d)$.

MULTIPLICATION
AND SIGNS

● ●

Objective 61.   (a) To formally prove, (b) to informally explain, that
                            the product of a negative integer and a negative inte-
                            ger is positive.

● ●

                            Attending first to the proof, instead of giving you the
                            proof of the general case we will give a fairly general
                            specific case. (This is a standard procedure in the
                            development of mathematics.)

Examples   1.   Proof that $(^-2) \times (^-3) = {}^+6$: Let $^-2$ be represented by
                            $(0 - 2)$ and $^-3$ by $(4 - 7)$. Then $(^-2) \times (^-3)$ is repre-
                            sented by

                            $(0 \times 4 + 2 \times 7) - (2 \times 4 + 0 \times 7)$

                                                $= (0 + 14) - (8 + 0)$
                                                $= (14 - 8)$,
                            which represents $^+6$.

             2.   Proof that $^-2 \times {}^-n$ is positive, where n represents a
                            positive whole number (so that ^-n represents a negative
                            integer): $^-2 \times {}^-n$ is represented by

                            $(0 - 2) \times (0 - n) = (0 \times 0 + 2 \times n) - (2 \times 0 + 0 \times n)$

                                                $= (0 + 2n) - (0 + 0) = 2n$,
                            which is positive.

Exercises	1.	Define "positive integer." (Hint: One way to represent such an integer is $(c - 0)$.)
	2.	Define "the integer zero."
	3.	Define "negative integer."
	4.	Prove, in the general case, that the product of two negative integers is positive. (*Hint*: Let $(0 - a)$ and $(0 - b)$ represent the two negative integers, where a and b are *positive* whole numbers.)
	5.	Prove, in the general case, that the product of a negative integer and a positive integer is negative.
	6.	How are fights between two pairs of elderly mares related to a fight among a bunch of deputy sheriffs? (Answer: A naggy tiff times a naggy tiff equals a posse tiff.)

The preceding explanations and exercises apply to part (a) of Objective 61. They, and indeed much of what has so far come up in this chapter, constitute material that you as an elementary teacher will in general *not* pass on to most of your students. Instead, knowing what lies behind the integers, you'll probably satisfy yourself (and us two authors) with the *results* of most of the foregoing, together with a discussion of the *plausibility* of these results (perhaps demonstrated on the number line). Thus, of what has come before in this chapter, about all that you'll relay is that:

1. the integers broaden our powers of equation solving,

2. the integers, like the fractional numbers, extend from the cardinal numbers,

3. the integers may be interpreted as either jumps or points on the number line (which for integers is extended from that for whole numbers),

4. the integers may be added, subtracted, multiplied (all of the time), and divided (sometimes).

The remainder of this chapter consists of material you'll be more likely to relay, beginning with part (b) of Objective 61. One of the most difficult tasks of an elementary teacher is to give a plausible explanation of why a negative times a negative is positive. (The kids usually readily accept that a positive times a negative, for example, is negative.) Here are a couple of strategies that *might* (we promise nothing!) help.

$$
\begin{array}{rcl}
\text{(a) Via patterns:} \quad 3 \times {}^{-}1 &=& {}^{-}3, \\
2 \times {}^{-}1 &=& {}^{-}2, \\
1 \times {}^{-}1 &=& {}^{-}1, \\
\underline{0 \times {}^{-}1} &=& \underline{\ 0} \\
\end{array}
$$

(pause)

What comes next on the left? (Answer: $^-1 \times {}^-1$.)
What comes next on the right? (Answer: $^+1$). Voila!

(b) Via "opposites": $^-1 \times {}^+3 = {}^-3$, the opposite of $^+3$
$^-1 \times {}^+5 = {}^-5$, the opposite of $^+5$.

Therefore $\quad {}^-1 \times {}^-4 =$ the opposite of $^-4 = {}^+4$,
and then $\quad {}^-2 \times {}^-4 = ({}^+2 \times {}^-1) \times {}^{--}4$
$\qquad\qquad\qquad = {}^+2 \times ({}^-1 \times {}^-4)$
$\qquad\qquad\qquad = {}^+2 \times {}^+4 = {}^+8$.

(c) Via jumps on the number line:

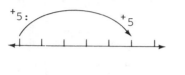

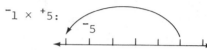

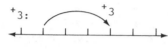

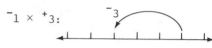

(Multiplying by $^-1$ changes the direction of the jump.)

(d) Via the distributive law:

$0 = {}^-3 \times 0 = {}^-3 \times ({}^+2 + {}^-2) = ({}^-3 \times {}^+2) + ({}^-3 \times {}^-2)$
$\qquad = {}^-6 + \underline{\quad ? \quad}$ (The answer here must be $^+6$.)

Exercise   Find or invent an explanation that a negative times a
negative is positive using: (a) the idea of money in
hand and money owed; (b) the idea that leaving a town
is negative, while staying is positive if the person in
question is good (positive), then considering what happens when a bad (i.e., negative) guy leaves town; (c)
an idea of your own; (d) *another* idea of your own.

SUBTRACTION   The following objective is closely related to what
we've just been thinking about:

● ●

Objective 62.   (a) To informally explain, (b) to formally prove that
subtracting a negative integer is equivalent to adding
a positive integer.

● ●

That is, we're interested in why, for example, $^+5 - {}^-3$
$= {}^+5 + {}^+3$. The informal explanations will be left for

you to devise. The formal proof will also be left for you to devise, but we *will* give the following proof: For integers, subtracting a positive number is equivalent to adding some negative number.

Proof: Let $(p - 0)$ represent the positive integer and $(a - b)$ represent an arbitrary integer. Then we want $(a - b) - (p - 0) = (a - b) + (0 - p)$, or, by the definition of subtraction,

$$(a - b) = (p - 0) + \big((a - b) + (0 - p)\big)$$

Step 1. $\quad\quad\quad = (p - 0) + \big((0 - p) + (a - b)\big)$

Step 2. $\quad\quad\quad = \big((p - 0) + (0 - p)\big) + (a - b)$

Step 3. $\quad\quad\quad = (p - p) + (a - b)$

Step 4. $\quad\quad\quad = (a - b).$

Since $(a - b)$ does equal $(a - b)$, we may start by writing $(a - b) = (a - b)$, then write the steps in the order 4, 3, 2, 1, and finally end up with what we wanted:

$(a - b) - (p - 0) = (a - b) + (0 - p)$. QED.

This method of working backward is a standard approach in *devising* mathematical proofs. But in *writing* the proofs, it is better to work forward, in this case starting with $(a - b) = (a - b)$ and then showing it follows that $(a - b) - (p - 0) = (a - b) + (0 - p)$. Otherwise, it may appear that you are *assuming* $(a - b) - (p - 0) = (a - b) + (0 - p)$ and from that *proving* that $(a - b) = (a - b)$, which, though true, is not too profound.

Exercises

1. Give the justifications for Steps 1, 2, 3, and 4 above.

2. Prove that subtracting a negative integer is equivalent to adding a positive integer.

3. Rewrite the following subtraction exercises as addition exercises: (a) $^-3 - {}^+2$, (b) $^+5 - {}^+3$, (c) $^-7 - {}^+4$, (d) $^-9 - {}^-3$, (e) $^+11 - {}^+6$.

4. Carry out the subtractions of Exercise 3.

5. Explain what is wrong with this "proof" that $^+1 = {}^-1$: $^+1 = {}^-1$; therefore $(^+1)^2 = (^-1)^2$, or $^+1 = {}^+1$.

6. How are $(^-1) \times (^-1) = {}^+1$ and $-(^-1) = {}^+1$ related?

7. How can two wrongs make a right? (Answer: Sam Wrong and Joe Wrong can turn their car the opposite of left.)

ABSOLUTE VALUE   Let's turn now to a very interesting and useful concept of measure, the "absolute value" of an integer.

● ●

Objective 63.   To define the *absolute value* of an integer and compute
absolute values of given integers.

● ●

In a sense, +7 and -7 are both the "same size," as are
-252 and 252, -62 and 62, etc. The following definition makes this "same-sizedness" more precise.

Definition   *Let n be any nonnegative integer. Then the <u>absolute
value</u> <u>of</u> <u>n</u>, denoted $|n|$, is defined as follows:*

(a) $|n| = n$,

(b) $|-n| = n$.

Examples   1. $|+7| = 7$.

2. $|-7| = 7$.

3. $|23| = 23$.

4. $|-23| = 23$.

5. $|0| = 0$.

6. $|-3| = 3$.

Exercises   1.   Compute the absolute values of: (a) -3,   (b) (7),
(c) (-7),   (d) (-3)(-4),   (e) (-3)(4),   (f) -3 + 4,
(g) -3 + (-4),   (h) 3 + (-4),   (i) 3 + 4,
(j) 3 + (-3).

2.   Prove that (i) $|x| = x$ if $x \geq 0$,   (ii) $|x| = -x$ if
$x < 0$, where x is an integer.

3.   How is $|a \times b|$ related to $|a|$ and $|b|$?   (See Exercises
1(d) and 1(e).)

4.   How is $|a + b|$ related to $|a|$ and $|b|$?   (See Exercises
1(f), 1(g), 1(h), and 1(i).)

5.   What solutions are there to $|x| = 0$ besides $x = 0$?

● ●

Objective 64.   To give a geometric interpretation of absolute value of
integers.

● ●

Examples

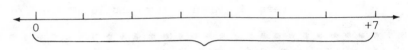

$$|+7| = 7 = \text{distance } +7 \text{ is from 0, the "origin"}$$

2.

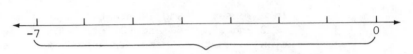

$$|-7| = 7 = \text{distance } -7 \text{ is from the origin}$$

3.

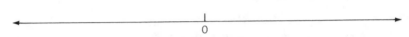

$$|0| = 0 = \text{distance } 0 \text{ is from the origin}$$

4.

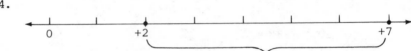

$$|^+7 - {}^+2| = 5 = \text{distance } {}^+7 \text{ is from } {}^+2$$

5.

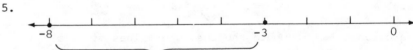

$$|^-8 - {}^-3| = 5 = \text{distance } {}^-8 \text{ is from } {}^-3$$

6.

$$|^-5 - {}^+3| = 8 = \text{distance } {}^-5 \text{ is from } {}^+3$$

7.

$$|^-5 - 0| = |^-5| = \text{distance } {}^-5 \text{ is from the origin}$$

Exercises   1.   Geometrically, $|x|$ stands for the distance from   ?   to   ? .

2.   Geometrically, $|x - a|$ stands for the distance from   ?   to   ? .

3.   Solve for x, if possible: (a) $|x| = 3$, (b) $|x| = -3$, (c) $|x| = 0$, (d) $|-x| = 5$, (e) $|0 - x| = 5$, (f) $|x - 0| = 5$, (g) $|x - 3| = 2$, (h) $|3x - 2| = 5$, (i) $|2 - 3x| = 5$, (j) $|3 - x| = 2$, (k) $|5x - 2/3| = 1$, (l) $|x + 4| = 2$ (hint: $|x + 4| = |x - (^-4)|$), (m) $|2x + 3| = 1$, (n) $|x^2 - 2| = 7$, (o) $|x^2 + 2| = 6$, (p) $|x^2 - 1| = 2$, (q) $|x^2 - 1| = -2$, (r) $|x^3 - 1| = 1$.

DIOPHANTINE EQUATIONS

We stated earlier that integers were invented to extend the solvability of certain equations. The following objective is written with this goal in mind.

● ●

*Objective 65.   To solve, if possible, given Diophantine equations linear in either x or some other power of x.

● ●

Recall that a Diophantine equation is one of which the unknowns are integers. Such equations are linear in some power x^p of x, if they are equivalent to $ax^p = b$. Finally, a power of x is a multiple of x by itself: $x^2 = x \cdot x$, $x^3 = x \cdot x \cdot x$, $x^p = \underbrace{x \cdot x \cdot x \cdot \ldots \cdot x}_{p \text{'}xs}$

Examples   We will solve, if possible, the following equations for all possible values of x, x an integer:

1. $3(x + 2) = 4x + 5$

By the distributive law, $3x + 6 = 4x + 5$. Adding ^-3x and $^-5$ to both sides of the equation, we get

$$
\begin{array}{rcrc}
3x + & 6 = & 4x + & 5 \\
^-3x & ^-5 & ^-3x & ^-5 \\
\hline
& 1 = & x &
\end{array}
$$

Check: $3(1 + 2) = 9 = 4 \cdot 1 + 5$.

2. $3(x + 2) = 3x + 5$.

$$\begin{array}{rcrr}
3x + & 6 = & 3x + & 5 \\
^-3x & ^-6 & ^-3x & ^-6 \\
\hline
& 0 = & & ^-1
\end{array}$$

Impossible; there are *no* values of x such that $0 = {}^-1$.

3. $3(x + 2) = (3x + 6)$. If we use the distributive law on the left side, we get $3x + 6 = 3x + 6$; which holds for any value of x. So let $x = a$ (for "anything"—as long as it's an integer).

4. $3(4x - 2(x + 3)) = 5$

In situations like this it's best to work, like Houdini, from the inside out:

$$\begin{array}{rclcr}
3(4x - & 2x - 6) & = & & 5 \\
3(2x - & 6) & & = & 5 \\
6x - & 18 & & = & 5 \\
& {}^+18 & & & {}^+18 \\
\hline
6x & & & = & 23
\end{array}$$

Alas! This equation has no integers as solutions: Impossible.

5.
$$\begin{array}{rcr}
x + & 3 = & 5 \\
& ^-3 & ^-3 \\
\hline
x & = & 2
\end{array}$$

6.
$$\begin{array}{rcr}
x^2 + & 3 = & 5 \\
& ^-3 & ^-3 \\
\hline
x^2 & = & 2
\end{array}$$

No integers as solutions: Impossible.

7.
$$\begin{array}{rcr}
x^2 + & 3 = & 12 \\
& ^-3 & ^-3 \\
\hline
x^2 & = & 9; \quad x = \pm\, 3.
\end{array}$$

Check: $(^+3)^2 = 3 \times 3 = 9$; $(^-3)^2 = (^-3) \times (^-3) = {}^+9 = 9$.

8.
$$\begin{array}{rcr}
x^3 - & 2 = & 6 \\
& ^+2 & ^+2 \\
\hline
x^3 & = & 8; \quad x = 2.
\end{array}$$

Check: $2^3 = 2 \times 2 \times 2 = 8$.

9. $3(1 - 2(^-3x^4 + 2)) = 2(x^4 + 123) + 1$

Inside out on the left-hand side:

$$\begin{aligned}
3(1 - 2(^-3x^4 + 2)) &= 3(1 + 6x^4 - 4) \\
&= 3(6x^4 - 3) \\
&= 18x^4 - 9.
\end{aligned}$$

So $18x^4 - 9 = 2(x^4 + 123) + 1 = 2x^4 + 246 + 1$
$$= 2x^4 + 247.$$

$$\begin{array}{rcr}
18x^4 - & 9 = & 2x^4 + 247 \\
^-2x^4 & ^+9 & ^-2x^4 \quad {}^+9 \\
\hline
16x^4 & = & 256 = 16(16); \quad x^4 = 16; \quad x = \pm 2.
\end{array}$$

Exercises   Solve for all possible values of x, x an *integer*.

1. $5(2 - 3(x - 2)) = {}^{-}15x - 10$.

2. $3(x - 4) = {}^{-}4(2 + x) - 25$.

3. $3(2 - (3 + 4x)) = 4 - 12x$.

4. $2(1 + 3(x^2 - 1)) = 3x^2 + 17$.

5. $2(x^2 - 4) = x^2 - 7$.

6. $2(x^3 - 4) = x^3 - 7$.

7. $5x^4 + 3 = {}^{-}5(2 - x^4) + 13$.

8. $3x^2(x^3 - 2) = 3x^5 - 6(x^2 + 1)$.

9. $4x(x^3 - 27) = 3x^4 - 108x + 81$.

10. $4x(x^3 - 27) = 2x^4 - 108x + 81$.

ABSTRACT
STRUCTURE OF
THE INTEGERS

● ●

*Objective 66.   To explain with examples what is meant by "The integers form a *commutative group* under addition."

● ●

Definition   *First we define a <u>commutative</u> <u>group</u> (or <u>Abelian</u>** <u>group</u>) to be a group whose operation satisfies the commutative law. Thus the positive rationals form a commutative group under multiplication because for any two fractional numbers a/b and c/d, a/b × c/d = ac/bd = ca/db = c/d × a/b.*

Exercise   Explain with examples what is meant by "The integers form a commutative group under addition."

There are other abstract mathematical structures besides groups, many of them involving more than one operation. One such structure is the one inspired by the properties of the integers, the integral domain.

**After Niels Henrik Abel (1802-1829), who was very able in algebra.

Definition

An *integral domain* is a set *S* of elements and two operations # and ∗, such that: (a) *S* forms a commutative
group under #, with the identity element 0;   (b) *S* is
closed, associative, and commutative under ∗ and has an
identity element *e* (relative to ∗);   (c) *The following
distributive law holds for elements a, b, c ε S: a ∗
(b # c) = (a ∗ b) # (a ∗ c)*;   (d) *If 0 ≠ a ε S and 0 ≠
b ε S, then a ∗ b ≠ 0.*

This definition will be easier to follow if you take *S*
to be the integers, # to be +, and ∗ to be ×, with *e*
= 1. To illustrate part (b) of the definition, we may
write:

S is closed under ×:   2 ε *S*, ⁻3 ε *S*, and 2 × ⁻3 =
⁻6 ε *S*.

S is associative under ×:   2, ⁻3, ⁻5 ε *S*, and
2 × (⁻3 × ⁻5) = 2 × 15 = 30 = ⁻6 × ⁻5 = (2 × ⁻3) × ⁻5.

S is commutative under ×:   2 × ⁻3 = ⁻6 = ⁻3 × 2.

S has an identity element under ×:   ⁻3 × 1 = ⁻3 =
1 × ⁻3.

Exercises 1. Instead of what was written in part (b) of the definition of an integral domain, why don't we just write "*S*
forms a commutative group under ∗, with the identity
element *e*"?

2. Explain, with examples other than those in the text,
what an integral domain is.

3. Give an example of an integral domain other than the
integers under + and ×.   (Hint: Clock arithmetic.
Alternate hint: Polynomials.)

4. Prove that for any element *a* in an integral domain *S*,
a ∗ 0 = 0.   (Hint: Show that (*a* ∗ *a*) # (*a* ∗ 0) = *a* ∗ *a*,
so that *a* ∗ 0 must be the identity under #.)

5. Solve the hair problem that introduced this chapter.
(Hint: See Exercise 4.)

6. Prove that for *a, b* ε *S*, an integral domain, if
a ∗ *b* = 0, then either *a* = 0 or *b* = 0.   (Hint: Suppose,
contrary to all hopes, that neither *a* nor *b* is 0, and
try to derive something contrary to what is given.)

7. How is the result of Exercise 6 used to solve an equation such as (*x* − 1)(*x* + 2) = 0?

8. Solve, if possible, each of the following equations, if x is to be an integer: (a) $(x - 1)(x - 2)(x - 3) = 0$, (b) $(x + 1)(x - 1)(x + 3) = 0$, (c) $(x^2 - 1)(x - 1)$ $(x + 3) = 0$, (d) $(x^2 - 4)(x - 2) = 0$, (e) $(x^2 + 4)$ $(x^2 - 1) = 0$, (f) $(x^2 + 4)(x^2 + 1) = 0$ (Careful!).

SOLUTION TO
THE HAIR
PROBLEM

The solution to the Hair Problem might be called the Yul Bryner principle. Need we say more? This property of the additive identity, 0, of annihilating all other elements under multiplication crops up again in Chapter 5 when we discuss fields.

MATRICES

The question "why bother with all of these obvious facts that are true for all mathematical systems—isn't it like teaching people to breathe?" so typically asked by students, is partly answered by consideration of *matrices*, which for our purposes will be considered to be rectangular arrays of numbers, such as

$$\left.\begin{pmatrix} 1 & 2 & 0 & -1 \\ 3 & 0 & 1 & -2 \\ -2 & 1 & 2 & -3 \end{pmatrix}\right\} \text{ 3 rows : a "3-by-4 matrix"}$$

$$\underbrace{}_{\text{4 columns}}$$

These matrices are added as follows:

$$\begin{pmatrix} 1 & 2 & 0 & -1 \\ 3 & 0 & 1 & -2 \\ -2 & 1 & 2 & -3 \end{pmatrix} + \begin{pmatrix} 4 & 5 & -6 & 4 \\ 5 & -4 & 4 & 6 \\ -6 & 4 & 5 & 5 \end{pmatrix}$$

$$= \begin{pmatrix} 1 + 4 & 2 + 5 & 0 + {}^-6 & -1 + 4 \\ 3 + 5 & 0 + {}^-4 & 1 + 4 & -2 + 6 \\ -2 + {}^-6 & 1 + 4 & 2 + 5 & -3 + 5 \end{pmatrix}$$

$$= \begin{pmatrix} 5 & 7 & -6 & 3 \\ 8 & -4 & 5 & 4 \\ -8 & 5 & 7 & 2 \end{pmatrix}$$

Matrices are also multiplied, providing the number of *rows* in the second matrix is the same as the number of *columns* in the first matrix. In such cases we multiply "row-by-column" as follows:

$$\begin{pmatrix} 1 & 2 & 0 & -1 \\ 3 & 0 & 1 & -2 \\ -2 & 1 & 2 & -3 \end{pmatrix} \times \begin{pmatrix} 4 & 5 \\ 5 & -4 \\ -6 & 4 \\ 4 & 6 \end{pmatrix} =$$

$$= \begin{pmatrix} 1(4)+2(5)+0(^-6)+(^-1)4 & 1(5)+2(^-4)+0(4)+(^-1)6 \\ 3(4)+0(5)+1(^-6)+(^-2)4 & 3(5)+0(^-4)+1(4)+(^-2)6 \\ (^-2)4+1(5)+2(^-6)+(^-3)4 & (^-2)5+1(^-4)+2(4)+(^-3)6 \end{pmatrix}$$

$$= \begin{pmatrix} 10 & -9 \\ -2 & 7 \\ -27 & -24 \end{pmatrix}$$

A matrix such as

$$\begin{pmatrix} 1 & 0 & 0 \\ 0 & 1 & 0 \\ 0 & 0 & 1 \end{pmatrix}$$

is a multiplicative identity; you can probably guess
what kind of matrix is an additive identity.

Exercises 1. Add:

(a) $\begin{pmatrix} 3 & 0 & 2 \\ 1 & 1 & 0 \end{pmatrix} + \begin{pmatrix} -1 & 2 & 1 \\ 0 & -2 & 0 \end{pmatrix}$

(b) $\begin{pmatrix} 3 \\ 1 \\ 0 \end{pmatrix} + \begin{pmatrix} 2 \\ -2 \\ 4 \end{pmatrix}$

(c) $\begin{pmatrix} 4 & 5 \\ 0 & 1 \end{pmatrix} + \begin{pmatrix} -4 & -5 \\ 0 & -1 \end{pmatrix}$

2. Multiply:

(a) $\begin{pmatrix} 3 & 0 & 2 \\ 1 & 1 & 0 \end{pmatrix} \times \begin{pmatrix} 1 & 1 & 0 \\ -1 & 1 & 1 \\ 0 & -1 & 1 \end{pmatrix}$

(b) $(5 \quad 0 \quad 3 \quad -2) \times \begin{pmatrix} 1 & -1 & -2 & 1 \\ 0 & 1 & 3 & 0 \\ 1 & 1 & 1 & 0 \\ 0 & 0 & 0 & 2 \end{pmatrix}$

3. Write down matrices which are additive identities of
the following dimensions ("row-by-column"): (a) 2 by
3, (b) 3 by 2, (c) 2 by 2.

4. Explain why or why not the set of 2-by-2 matrices with
integer entries forms a commutative group under addition.

5. Explain why or why not the set of 2-by-2 matrices with
integer entries forms a commutative group under multiplication.

6. Explain why or why not the set of 2-by-2 matrices with
integer entries forms an integral domain.

● ●

*Objective 68. To cite an example of a mathematical structure in which
the product of two elements equaling zero does *not* imply one or the other of the elements is itself zero.

● ●

Exercises   1.   Cite such an example.   (Hint: 2-by-2 matrices.)

2.   Cite another example.

SUMMARY OF   57.   To define *integer* and explain how a cardinal num-
OBJECTIVES   ber may be considered to be an integer (page 169).

*58.   To illustrate a given integer as a class of jumps
       on the cardinal number line (page 171).

59.   To graph given sets of integers on the integer
      number line (page 174).

60.   To define addition, subtraction, multiplication,
      and division of integers (page 176).

61.   (a) To informally explain, (b) to formally prove
      that the product of a negative integer and a
      negative integer is positive (page 181).

62.   (a) To informally explain, (b) to formally prove
      that subtracting a negative integer is equivalent
      to adding a positive integer (page 183).

63.   To define the *absolute value* of an integer and
      compute absolute values of given integers (page
      185).

64.   To give a geometric interpretation of absolute
      value of integers (185).

*65.   To solve, if possible, given Diophantine equations
       linear in either x or some other power of x (page
       187).

*66.   To explain with examples what is meant by "The
       integers form a *commutative group* under addition"
       (page 189).

*67.   To explain with examples what an *integral domain*
       is (page 190).

*68.   To cite an example of a mathematical structure in
       which the product of two elements equaling zero
       does *not* imply one or the other of the elements is
       itself zero (page 192).

WORDS TO KNOW   integer (page 168)   product of integers   (page
                  positive integer   (page   176)
                    168)   quotient of integers
                  integer number line   (page   (page 176)
                    173)

CHAPTER 5

RATIONAL NUMBERS

THE FAKE PIG PROBLEM	Members of the Pig Civil Defense league were taking time off from lobbying against pork consumption to mix up several vats of wolfsbane. Andrew and Bruce took six hours to mix one vat of bane; Bruce and Cyril took three hours to mix one vat; and Andrew, Bruce, and Cyril working together took three hours to make two vats. (We assume that each pig works at a constant rate.) One of these three pigs, it turns out, was a fake, really another agent of the big bad wolf. Which one was it?
Challenge	Try to solve the Fake Pig Problem, (i.e., find out who mixed a negative amount of wolfsbane per hour.)

The Fake Pig Problem represents a whole collection of problems in which information is given in integers and an answer is to be found via addition, subtraction, multiplication, and division (but *not* via square roots, for example). Solution of such problems typically involves most of the properties of a mathematical structure called a "field," of which a familiar example is the rational numbers (or, in loose language, the positive, zero, and negative fractional numbers). The purpose of this chapter is to examine properties of fields in general and the rational number system in particular.

RATIONAL
NUMBERS AND
FIELD
PROPERTIES

● ●

Objective 69. To define *rational number* in terms of integers.

● ●

You can probably figure out much of this for yourself, copying the development of the fractional numbers in Chapter 3, but this time assuming that you know all about the integers rather than just the cardinal numbers.

Exercise	Complete the following definition: A rational number is a class of all ordered pairs. . . . (This should look pretty familiar to you by now.)

●●

*Objective 70. To explain with examples what is meant by "The rational numbers form a field under addition and multiplication."

●●

Again, we'll let you, with the mathematical maturity you've accumulated so far from this book, do most of the work, after we give the definition of a field, a mathematical structure that's sort of an "ultra integral domain."

Definition   A *field* is a set S (S ≠ ∅) and two operations # and *, such that: (a) S forms a commutative group under #, with an identity element 0; (b) the elements of S other than 0 form a commutative group under *, with an identity element e, and (c) the following distributive law holds for any elements a, b, c ε S: a * (b # c) = (a * b) # (a * c).

Examples   The rational numbers (0,±1,±2,±3, . . . , ±1/2, ±2/3, ±1/4,±3/4, . . .) form a field, if we take # to be addition and * to be multiplication. You can check this out as an exercise, but we'll illustrate some of the properties.

1. Multiplicative inverses (one of the five properties of the commutative group under multiplication): The multiplicative inverse of -3/4 is -4/3, since

$$\frac{-3}{4} \times \frac{-4}{3} = \frac{(-3) \times (-4)}{4 \times 3} = \frac{12}{12} = 1,$$

and 1 is the multiplicative identity.

2. Distributive law:

$$-\frac{2}{3} \times \left(\frac{3}{4} + \frac{-5}{6}\right) = \frac{-2}{3} \times \left(\frac{18 + -20}{24}\right) = -\frac{2}{3} \times \frac{-2}{24}$$

$$= -\frac{2}{3} \times \frac{-1}{12} = \frac{-2 \times -1}{3 \times 12} = \frac{2}{36} = \frac{1}{18} = \frac{-9 + 10}{18} = \frac{-1}{2} + \frac{5}{9}$$

$$= \frac{-6}{12} + \frac{10}{18} = \left(\frac{-2 \times 3}{3 \times 4}\right) + \left(\frac{-2 \times -5}{3 \times 6}\right)$$

$$= \left(\frac{-2}{3} \times \frac{3}{4}\right) + \left(\frac{-2}{3} \times \frac{-5}{6}\right).$$

These illustrate two of the eleven axioms of a field.

Exercises   1. Explain the difference between a field and a mere integral domain.

2. Explain with examples other than those given above how the rational numbers form a field under addition and

multiplication (i.e., illustrate each of the eleven axioms of a field as was done in our example).

3. Give an example of a field other than the rational numbers. (Hint: Consider clock arithmetic.)

4. Is it true that in a field if the product (under *) of two elements is 0, then one or the other or both of the elements is 0? Prove your answer.

5. Why is the multiplicative inverse of 0 not defined in a field?

6. Why is 0 not poetic, multiplicatively speaking? (Answer: It's not in verse.)

Instead of developing the field of rational numbers as we did, we might just as well have built them as is indicated in the following Venn diagram:

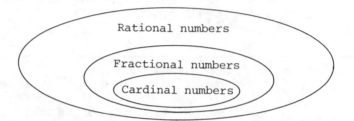

According to this scheme we would have first completed the multiplicative group structure of nonzero elements to form, with zero, the fractional (or "nonnegative rational") numbers, then completed the additive group structure of all elements to form the field of rational numbers.

The preceding diagram is part of the next objective.

● ●

Objective 71. To illustrate with Venn diagrams two different developments of the rational numbers from the cardinal numbers.

● ●

Exercises 1. Draw a Venn diagram of the development of the rational numbers different from the one in the text. (Hint: What's an alternative order of completing the various group structures?)

2. Copy the diagrams in Exercise 1 and the text and on each divide the universe (or rational numbers) into negative and nonnegative numbers.

The system of rational numbers is not by any means the
only example of a field structure. This observation
leads us to the next objective.

● ●

*Objective 72.   To cite a modular arithmetic not given in the text and
explain with examples how it forms a field.

● ●

In order to attack this objective it's probably a good
idea to familiarize ourselves with some finite fields
and nonfields. (The rationals form an *infinite* field,
because they constitute an infinite set of elements.)
And what better way to familiarize ourselves than by
leaping into examples?

Examples   1.   Integers, mod 2: Let's build addition and multiplication tables to use for reference in checking whether
this modular arithmetic is a field:

+	0	1		×	0	1
---	---	---		---	---	---
0	0	1		0	0	0
1	1	0		1	0	1

Do all elements form a commutative group under addition? Let's see: There's certainly closure, because
the elements in the body of the addition table are exactly those in the margin. There's associativity:

$0 + (0 + 0) = 0 = (0 + 0) + 0$
$0 + (0 + 1) = 1 = (0 + 0) + 1$
$0 + (1 + 1) = 0 = (0 + 1) + 1$
$0 + (1 + 0) = 1 = (0 + 1) + 0$
$1 + (0 + 0) = 1 = (1 + 0) + 0$
$1 + (0 + 1) = 0 = (1 + 0) + 1$
$1 + (1 + 0) = 0 = (1 + 1) + 0$
$1 + (1 + 1) = 1 = (1 + 1) + 1.$

There is an identity, 0: $0 + 0 = 0$, $1 + 0 = 1$. There
are inverses: $0 + 0 = 0$, $1 + 1 = 0$. These are reflected in the table by the presence of each element in
each row and column. There is commutativity: $1 + 0 =$
$0 + 1$; the table shows this by its symmetry about the
diagonal moving downhill as you go from left to right
(the "main diagonal"). Yes, we do have an additive
commutative group.
    Do the nonzero elements form a commutative group un-
der multiplication? There's closure: $1 × 1 = 1$.
There's associativity: $1 × (1 × 1) = 1 = (1 × 1) × 1$.
There's identity: $1 × 1 = 1$. There are inverses:
$1 × 1 = 1$. And there's sort of de facto commutativity.
So we also have a multiplicative commutative group.

How about distributivity?

$$0 \times (0 + 0) = 0 = (0 \times 0) + (0 \times 0)$$
$$0 \times (1 + 0) = 0 = (0 \times 1) + (0 \times 0)$$
$$0 \times (1 + 1) = 0 = (0 \times 1) + (0 \times 1)$$
$$1 \times (0 + 0) = 0 = (1 \times 0) + (1 \times 0)$$
$$1 \times (1 + 0) = 1 = (1 \times 1) + (1 \times 0)$$
$$1 \times (1 + 1) = 0 = (1 \times 1) + (1 \times 1).$$

So the integers, mod 2, *do* form a field.

2. Integers, mod 4:

+	0	1	2	3
0	0	1	2	3
1	1	2	3	0
2	2	3	0	1
3	3	0	1	2

×	0	1	2	3
0	0	0	0	0
1	0	1	2	3
2	0	2	0	2
3	0	3	2	1

Here the additive group is okay, but the multiplicative group is not: For instance, 2 has no inverse. So the integers, mod 4, do *not* form a field.

3. Field with four elements: The integers, mod 4, do not form a field, but there *is* a field of order 4 (i.e., with four elements). It is defined by the following tables. (Don't ask what *a* and *b* are; they are just elements of this field and are not equivalent to any numbers.)

+	0	1	*a*	*b*
0	0	1	*a*	*b*
1	1	0	*b*	*a*
a	*a*	*b*	0	1
b	*b*	*a*	1	0

×	0	1	*a*	*b*
0	0	0	0	0
1	0	1	*a*	*b*
a	0	*a*	*b*	1
b	0	*b*	1	*a*

Exercises 1. (a) Without writing them all out, how should we know that there are eight cases to check in the additive associativity of the integers, mod 2?

(b) How many cases are there in the distributivity of the integers, mod 2?

(c) Why is it necessary to check only six cases for distributivity, mod 2?

2. Give at least three other reasons that the integers, mod 4, do not form a field.

3. Prove or disprove that each of the following forms a field: (a) integers, mod 3; (b) integers, mod 5; (c) integers, mod 6; (d) integers, mod 7; (e) integers, mod 8.

4. Which modular arithmetics form a field?

5. Construct a field of order 8 (i.e., with eight elements).

6. What are the possible orders of finite fields?

SOLUTION OF
LINEAR
EQUATIONS AND
THE FAKE PIG
PROBLEM

What are fields good for? Among other things, they provide the machinery to solve linear equations, that is, equations of the form $ax + b = cx + d$, where a, b, c, d are elements of the given field.

● ●

Objective 73. To solve, if possible, given linear equations with rational coefficients or linear congruences in a given modular arithmetic.

● ●

Once again we can probably help most by charging right into some examples. In these we will draw attention to the field properties as they are used. First, some examples of linear equations.

Examples

1. $\dfrac{3}{4}x - \dfrac{5}{3} = \dfrac{2}{5}\left(x + \dfrac{1}{2}\right)$

What offends our aesthetic eyes most in this example is the presence of all those fractions. How do we rid ourselves of these loathsome fractions? Of course! By multiplying both sides of the equation by the same, suitable number. What is suitable? The answer here is a number which is a multiple of the denominators of all of the obnoxious fractional numbers: in this case 60, the LCM or least common (positive) multiple of 4, 3, 5, 2. "Clearing fractions" is the principal function of the LCM in elementary mathematics. We don't really need the *least* common multiple; *any* old CM would do, but we usually prefer the LCM because it leads to simpler computation.

$$\frac{3}{4}x - \frac{5}{3} = \frac{2}{5}\left(x + \frac{1}{2}\right) \qquad \text{(Original equation)}$$

$$\Updownarrow$$

$$60\left(\frac{3}{4}x - \frac{5}{3}\right) = 60\left(\frac{2}{5}\left(x + \frac{1}{2}\right)\right)$$

$$\Updownarrow$$

$$45x - 100 = 24\left(x + \frac{1}{2}\right) \qquad \text{(Multiplying by 60)}$$

$$\Updownarrow$$

$$45x - 100 = 24x + 12 \qquad \text{(Distributive law)}$$

$$\Updownarrow$$

$$45x - 100 = 24x + 12$$
$$\underline{+ 100 = \qquad + 100}$$
$$45x \qquad = 24x + 112$$

(Adding additive inverse of ⁻100)

$$\Updownarrow$$

$$45x = 24x + 112$$
$$\underline{-24x \quad -24x}$$
$$21x = \qquad\qquad 112$$

(Adding additive inverse of 24x)

$$\Updownarrow$$

$$\frac{1}{21}(21x) = \frac{1}{21}(112)$$

(Multiplying by multiplicative inverse of 21)

$$\Updownarrow$$

$$x = \frac{112}{21} = \frac{16}{3}$$

("Reducing"—substituting for a rational number its equivalent)

Answer: $x = \dfrac{16}{3}$.

Check: $\dfrac{3}{4}\left(\dfrac{16}{3}\right) - \dfrac{5}{3} = 4 - \dfrac{5}{3} = \dfrac{7}{3}$, on the left-hand side.

$\dfrac{2}{5}\left(\dfrac{16}{3} + \dfrac{1}{2}\right) = \dfrac{32}{15} + \dfrac{1}{5} = \dfrac{35}{15} = \dfrac{7}{3}$, on the right. It must be

right!

2. $3(2x - 6) = 6x + 2$

$$\Updownarrow$$

$$6x - 18 = 6x + 2$$
$$\underline{+ 18 \qquad + 18}$$

(Distributive law)

$$6x \qquad = 6x + 20$$
$$\underline{-6x \qquad -6x}$$

(Additive inverse)

$$0 \qquad = \qquad 20$$

(Additive inverse)

Since $0 \neq 20$, a solution to this equation is *impossible*.

Examples of linear congruences, or congruences in which all variable terms are of the first degree, follow.

Examples   1. $3(2x - 6) \equiv 4x + 5 \pmod 7$

$$\Updownarrow$$

$6x - 18 \equiv 4x + 5 \pmod 7$ (Distributive law)

$$\Updownarrow$$

$6x - 4 \equiv 4x + 5 \pmod 7$ ($18 \equiv 4$, mod 7)

$$\Updownarrow$$

$$6x - 4 \equiv 4x + 5$$
$$\underline{-4x + 4 \quad -4x + 4}$$
$$2x \qquad \equiv \qquad 9 \pmod 7$$

(Additive inverses)

$$\Updownarrow$$

$$\frac{2x}{2} \equiv \frac{9}{2} \ (\text{mod}\ 7) \qquad\qquad (\text{Multiplicative inverses})$$

$$\Updownarrow$$

$$x \equiv \frac{9}{2} \equiv \frac{9 + 7}{2} = \frac{16}{2} = 8 \equiv 1 \ (\text{mod}\ 7)$$

Answer: $x \equiv 1 \ (\text{mod}\ 7)$.

Check: $3(2 - 6) = 3(-4) = -12 \equiv 2 \ (\text{mod}\ 7)$
$\qquad\qquad 4 + 5 = 9 = 2 \ (\text{mod}\ 7)$.

2. $4x - 2 \equiv 2x + 3 \ (\text{mod}\ 6)$

$$\Updownarrow$$

$$
\begin{array}{ll}
4x - 2 \equiv 2x + 3 & (\text{Additive inverses}) \\
\underline{-2x + 2 \quad\ -2x + 2} & \\
\ 2x \quad\ \equiv \quad\quad\ 5 \ (\text{mod}\ 6) &
\end{array}
$$

This is *impossible*, since 2 has no multiplicative inverse, mod 6:

$$x \equiv \frac{5}{2} \equiv \frac{5 + 6}{2} \equiv \frac{5 + 12}{2} \equiv \cdot\ \cdot\ \cdot \equiv \frac{5 + 6n}{2}, \ \text{which is}$$

never an integer.

We now turn to some examples of systems of linear equations.

Examples 1. Suppose the following equations hold simultaneously:

$$\frac{-2}{3} x + 3y = \frac{1}{2}$$

$$2x + \frac{5}{3} y = -\frac{3}{4}$$

Here we want an x and a y that satisfy both of these equations. If this baffles you, you might ask the routine mathematical question, "How can I make this look like a problem I can already solve?" One answer to this question is to combine the two original equations in such a way as to eliminate one of the unknowns so that we are left with a single equation in one unknown. *Regardez*:

$$\dfrac{^-2}{3}x + 3y = \dfrac{1}{2} \left.\right\} \qquad\longleftrightarrow\qquad 3\left(\dfrac{^-2}{3}x\right) + 3(3y) = 3\left(\dfrac{1}{2}\right)$$

$$2x + \dfrac{5}{3}y = \dfrac{^-3}{4} \qquad\qquad\qquad 2x + \dfrac{5}{3}y = \dfrac{^-3}{4}$$

$$-2x + 9y = \dfrac{3}{2} \qquad\qquad -2x + \dfrac{27}{3}y = \dfrac{6}{4}$$

$$2x + \dfrac{5}{3}y = \dfrac{^-3}{4} \qquad\longleftrightarrow\qquad 2x + \dfrac{5}{3}y = \dfrac{^-3}{4}$$

$$0 + \dfrac{32}{3}y = \dfrac{3}{4} \quad\longleftrightarrow\quad \dfrac{3}{32}\left(\dfrac{32}{3}y\right) = \dfrac{3}{32}\left(\dfrac{3}{4}\right) \quad\longleftrightarrow\quad y = \dfrac{9}{128}$$

Now that we know what y is we can go back to the original equations to track down x:

$$-\dfrac{2}{3}x + 3y = \dfrac{1}{2} \qquad\qquad\qquad 2x + \dfrac{5}{3}y = -\dfrac{3}{4}$$
$$\Updownarrow \qquad\qquad\qquad\qquad\qquad \Updownarrow$$
$$\dfrac{-2}{3}x + 3\left(\dfrac{9}{128}\right) = \dfrac{1}{2} \quad \text{and} \quad 2x + \dfrac{5}{3}\left(\dfrac{9}{128}\right) = \dfrac{-3}{4}$$
$$\Updownarrow \qquad\qquad\qquad\qquad\qquad \Updownarrow$$
$$\dfrac{-2}{3}x + \dfrac{27}{128} = \dfrac{1}{2} \quad \text{and} \quad 2x + \dfrac{15}{128} = \dfrac{-3}{4}$$
$$\Updownarrow \qquad\qquad\qquad\qquad\qquad \Updownarrow$$
$$\dfrac{-2}{3}x = \dfrac{64}{128} - \dfrac{27}{128} \quad \text{and} \quad 2x = \dfrac{-96}{128} - \dfrac{15}{128}$$
$$\Updownarrow \qquad\qquad\qquad\qquad\qquad \Updownarrow$$
$$\dfrac{-3}{2}\left(\dfrac{-2}{3}x\right) = \dfrac{-3}{2}\left(\dfrac{37}{128}\right) \quad \text{and} \quad \dfrac{1}{2}(2x) = \dfrac{1}{2}\left(\dfrac{-111}{128}\right)$$
$$\Updownarrow \qquad\qquad\qquad\qquad\qquad \Updownarrow$$
$$x = \dfrac{-111}{256} \qquad \text{and} \qquad x = \dfrac{-111}{256}$$

Ho! We get the same value for x, *and this will always be so*. Thus, the final answer is $(x,y) = (-111/256, 9/128)$. (Notice: The answers here are rather ugly—not whole numbers—and this is the way it usually is in real life problems.)

2. $\left.\begin{array}{l} \dfrac{1}{x} + \dfrac{1}{y} - 2\left(\dfrac{1}{z}\right) = \dfrac{2}{3} \\[2em] 3\left(\dfrac{1}{x}\right) \qquad + \dfrac{1}{z} = \dfrac{-1}{2} \\[2em] 2\left(\dfrac{1}{y}\right) - \left(\dfrac{1}{z}\right) = \dfrac{1}{6} \end{array}\right\} \to \left\{\begin{array}{l} \dfrac{1}{x} + \dfrac{1}{y} - 2\left(\dfrac{1}{z}\right) = \dfrac{2}{3} \\[2em] 6\left(\dfrac{1}{x}\right) + 2\left(\dfrac{1}{z}\right) = \dfrac{-2}{2} \\[2em] 3\left(\dfrac{1}{x}\right) + 2\left(\dfrac{1}{y}\right) = \dfrac{-1}{3} \leftrightarrow 3\left(\dfrac{1}{x}\right) + 2\left(\dfrac{1}{y}\right) = \dfrac{-1}{3} \end{array}\right.$

$\to 7\left(\dfrac{1}{x}\right) + \dfrac{1}{y} = \dfrac{-2}{6}$

$\left\{\begin{array}{l} -14\left(\dfrac{1}{x}\right) - 2\left(\dfrac{1}{y}\right) = \dfrac{2}{3} \\[2em] 3\left(\dfrac{1}{x}\right) + 2\left(\dfrac{1}{y}\right) = \dfrac{-1}{3} \end{array}\right.$

$-11\left(\dfrac{1}{x}\right) = \dfrac{1}{3}$

$\dfrac{1}{x} = \dfrac{-1}{33}$

$x = -33$

Returning to the second equation, say,

$3\left(\dfrac{1}{x}\right) + \dfrac{1}{z} = \dfrac{-1}{2} \;\Rightarrow\; 3\left(\dfrac{-1}{33}\right) + \dfrac{1}{z} = \dfrac{-1}{2}$

$z = \dfrac{-22}{9} \iff \dfrac{1}{z} = \dfrac{-1}{2} + \dfrac{1}{11} = \dfrac{-9}{22}$

Finally, we return to the third equation, say:

$2\left(\dfrac{1}{y}\right) - \left(\dfrac{1}{z}\right) = \dfrac{1}{6} \iff 2\left(\dfrac{1}{y}\right) - \left(\dfrac{-9}{22}\right) = \dfrac{1}{6}$

$y = \dfrac{-33}{8} \iff \dfrac{1}{y} = \dfrac{-8}{33} \iff 2\left(\dfrac{1}{y}\right) = \dfrac{1}{6} - \dfrac{9}{22} = \dfrac{-16}{66} = \dfrac{-8}{33}\ .$

Thus, we get $(x,y,z) = (-33,-33/8,-22/9)$.

3. $\left.\begin{array}{l} 2x + \dfrac{1}{2}y = \dfrac{-3}{4} \\[2em] -4x - y = \dfrac{3}{2} \end{array}\right\} \iff \left\{\begin{array}{l} 4x + y = \dfrac{-3}{2} \\[2em] -4x - y = \dfrac{3}{2} \end{array}\right\} \to 0 = 0.$

In this case we can think of the $0 = 0$ as $0 \cdot y = 0$, in which case y can be *any* number. Thus there are an *infinite number of solutions*.

4. $2x + \dfrac{1}{2}y = \dfrac{-3}{5}$ $\left.\begin{array}{c}\\\\\\\\-4x - y = \dfrac{3}{2}\end{array}\right\}$ $\Longleftrightarrow$ $\left\{\begin{array}{c}4x + y = \dfrac{-6}{5}\\\\\\-4x - y = \dfrac{3}{2}\end{array}\right\}$ $\to 0 = \dfrac{-12}{10} + \dfrac{15}{10} = \dfrac{3}{10}.$

In *this* case, we get $0 = 3/10$, which is impossible. No solution.

Meanwhile, back to the wolfsbane mixers, who is the fake? If we let a, b, and c represent the work done in one hour by our heroes we have the equations

$6a + 6b = 1$
$3b + 3c = 1$
$3a + 3b + 3c = 2.$

So $\left.\begin{array}{c}3a + 3b + 3c = 2\\3b + 3c = 1\end{array}\right\}$ $3a = 1$ or $a = \dfrac{1}{3},$

and $\left.\begin{array}{c}2(3a + 3b + 3c) = 2 \times 2\\6a + 6b = 1\end{array}\right\}$ $6c = 4 - 1$ or $c = \dfrac{3}{6} = \dfrac{1}{2};$

but $6a + 6b = 6\left(\dfrac{1}{3}\right) + 6b = 1$ or $b = \dfrac{1 - 2}{6} = \dfrac{-1}{6}$

Bruce is our fake as he did a negative amount of work.

Exercises

Solve for x, if possible. Many of these equations are almost the same as their predecessors. Think about the differences and similarities and what effect they'll have as the solutions unfold.

1. $5x - 2 = 2x + 4.$

2. $5x - 2 = -2x - 4.$

3. $5(x - 2) = -2x - 4.$

4. $5(x - 2) = 5x - 4.$

5. $5(x - 2) = -2(4x - 1).$

6. $\dfrac{5}{3}x - 2 = \dfrac{2}{5}x + \dfrac{1}{4}.$

7. $\dfrac{5}{3}x - \dfrac{2}{5} = \dfrac{2}{5}x + \dfrac{1}{4}.$

8. $\dfrac{5}{3}\left(x - \dfrac{2}{5}\right) = \dfrac{2}{5}x + \dfrac{1}{4}.$

9. $\dfrac{5}{3}\left(x - \dfrac{2}{5}\right) = \dfrac{-2}{5}\left(5x - \dfrac{1}{4}\right).$

10. $\dfrac{5}{3}\left(x - \dfrac{2}{5}\right) = 5\left(\dfrac{x}{3} + 1\right).$

11. $\frac{5}{3}\left(x - \frac{2}{5}\right) = 5\left(\frac{x}{3} - \frac{2}{25}\right)$.

12. $\frac{5}{3}\left(x - \frac{2}{5}\right) = 2\left(x - \frac{1}{5}\right)$.

13. $5x - 2 \equiv 2x - 4 \pmod 7$.

14. $5x - 2 \equiv 2x - 4 \pmod 6$.

15. $5x - 2 \equiv 4x - 3 \pmod 6$.

16. $5(x - 2) \equiv -2x - 4 \pmod{11}$.

17. $5(x - 2) \equiv -2x - 4 \pmod{12}$.

18. $5(x - 2) \equiv -2x - 4 \pmod{13}$.

19. $3(2x - 3) \equiv -3(4x + 5) \pmod 9$.

20. $3(2x - 3) \equiv -3(4x + 5) \pmod 8$.

21. $3(2x - 3) \equiv -3(4x + 5) \pmod 7$.

22. $3(2x - 3) \equiv -3(4x + 5) \pmod 6$.

23. In the first linear system example, explain what was done at each double arrow and why one arrow is single rather than double.

24. Why, after solving for y in an exercise like the first linear system example, is it true that it doesn't matter which of the original equations we use to find x?

25. Why, in the third linear system example, can y be *any* number?

26. Solve the following linear systems, if possible:

(a) $3x - y = 6$
$-2x + y = -4$

(b) $3x - y = 6$
$x - \frac{1}{3}y = 1$

(c) $3x - y = 6$
$x - \frac{1}{3}y = 2$

(d) $\frac{2}{3}x - \frac{3}{4}y = \frac{1}{2}$
$4x + \frac{1}{2}y = \frac{-2}{3}$

(e) $\frac{2}{3}x - \frac{3}{4}y = \frac{1}{2}$
$\frac{-8}{3}x + 3y = 2$

(f) $x + y = \frac{2}{3}$
$y + z = \frac{2}{3}$
$x + y + z = \frac{1}{3}$

(g) $x - 2y + 3z = 8$
$-2x + 3y + z = 8$
$3x + y - 2z = 8$

(h) $x - 2y + 3z = 8$
$3x + 2y + z = 8$
$3x - 2y + 2z = 8$

(i) $\dfrac{1}{x} + \dfrac{1}{y} + \dfrac{1}{z} = \dfrac{-1}{6}$ (j) $\dfrac{1}{x} + \dfrac{1}{y} + \dfrac{1}{z} = \dfrac{-1}{6}$

$\dfrac{1}{x} - \dfrac{1}{y} + \dfrac{1}{z} = \dfrac{1}{3}$ $\dfrac{1}{x} - \dfrac{1}{y} + \dfrac{1}{z} = \dfrac{1}{3}$

$\dfrac{-1}{x} + \dfrac{1}{y} + \dfrac{1}{z} = \dfrac{1}{2}$ $2\left(\dfrac{1}{x}\right) + 2\left(\dfrac{1}{z}\right) = \dfrac{1}{2}$

27. Resolve (g) and (h) of Exercise 26 *in a clever way*. (Look at the equations closely; what is peculiar about them? What does this peculiarity imply about solutions?)

28. If you mastered Exercises 24(i) and (j), you are in a position to solve the Fake Pig Problem. Do this. (Hint: To set up equations, figure out two different expressions for the number of vats of wolfsbane manufactured in *one* hour.)

GRAPHING SETS
OF RATIONAL
NUMBERS ON THE
NUMBER LINE

• •

Objective 74. To graph given sets (possibly elements of sequences) of rational numbers, indicating accumulation points, if any.

• •

Before you can properly attack Objective 74, you have to know what a sequence is and what an accumulation point is.

Definition   A *sequence is a rule associating to each counting num-ber n an element a_n*:
$$1 \longrightarrow a_1$$
$$2 \longrightarrow a_2$$
$$3 \longrightarrow a_3$$
$$\cdots$$
$$n \longrightarrow a_n$$
$$\cdots.$$

Another way of saying this is to say that a sequence is an ordered set $\{a_1, a_2, a_3, \ldots\}$ with a first element a_1, a second element a_2, a third element a_3, etc.

Definition   *For a more precise definition, we may say that: accumu-lation point (or cluster point) a of a sequence S =*

$\{a_1, a_2, a_3, \ldots\}$ *is a point, not necessarily an element of S, such that an infinite number of elements of S are arbitrarily close to a.*

Example

$$a_1 = \frac{-5}{2} = -2\frac{1}{2} \quad \left(\text{or, to write it differently, } 1 \to \frac{-5}{2}\right)$$

$$a_2 = \frac{9}{4} = 2\frac{1}{4} \quad \left(\text{or } 2 \to \frac{9}{4}\right)$$

$$a_3 = \frac{-17}{8} = -2\frac{1}{8} \quad \left(\text{or } 3 \to \frac{-17}{8}\right)$$

$$a_4 = \frac{33}{16} = 2\frac{1}{16} \quad \left(\text{or } 4 \to \frac{33}{16}\right)$$

$$a_5 = \frac{-65}{32} = -2\frac{1}{32} \quad \left(\text{or } 5 \to \frac{-65}{32}\right)$$

$$a_6 = \frac{129}{64} = 2\frac{1}{64} \quad \left(\text{or } \to \frac{129}{64}\right), \text{ etc.}$$

The graph of this sequence is as follows:

In this particular case there are two "accumulation points," -2 and 2. That is, an infinite number of elements of the sequence sooner or later accumulate as close to -2 and 2 as anyone might wish. While such sequences and accumulation points belong principally to the realm of college calculus, they also have some place in elementary school mathematics, in that they can be used to help the kids develop pattern recognition.

Examples   1. $S = \{a_n\} = \{(-1)^n\}$.

Let's write out the first few elements of S:

$$a_1 = (-1)^1 = -1$$

$$a_2 = (-1)^2 = (-1) \times (-1) = +1$$

$$a_3 = (-1)^3 = (-1) \times (-1) \times (-1) = -1$$

$$a_4 = (-1)^4 = (-1) \times (-1) \times (-1) \times (-1) = +1, \text{ etc.}$$

In this case the graph is merely

and both 1 and -1 are accumulation points.

2. Consider the sequence defined by $a_n = (-1)^n(2 + 1/2^n)$. If we write out the first few terms we'll see that this is just the sequence of Example 1 expressed differently.

3. Consider the sequence defined by $a_n = 1/n$. The first few terms of this sequence are 1/1, 1/2, 1/3, 1/4, 1/5, 1/6, and the graph looks like

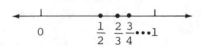

The accumulation point of this sequence is 0.

4. Try this sequence on for size:

$a_1 = 0$, $a_2 = 1/2$, $a_3 = 2/3$, $a_4 = 3/4$, ... ,
$a_n = (n - 1)/n$.

The graph is

and the accumulation point is 1.

Exercises

1. In the Example 2, are -2 and 2 accumulation points? Why?

2. What effect does a factor of $(-1)^n$ in a_n have on the sequence $\{a_n\} = \{a_1, a_2, a_3, \ldots\}$?

3. Graph each of the following sets of rational numbers, indicating any accumulation points:

   (a) $\{a/b$: a, b are integers, a is a factor of 1$\}$,

   (b) $\{a/b$: a, b are integers, a is a factor of 3$\}$,

   (c) $\{a/b$: a, b are integers, b is a power of 2$\}$,

   (d) $\{a/b$: a, b are integers, b is a power of 3$\}$,

   (e) $\{a/b$: a, b are integers, b is a power of -3$\}$,

   (f) $\{x$: $24x$ is an integer and $-24 \leq 24x \leq 48\}$,

   (g) $\{x$: $-36x$ is a positive integer and $x < 1\}$,

   (h) $\{x$: $6x$ is an integer$\}$,

   (i) $\{x$: $x = (-1/2)^n$, $n = 1,2,3, \ldots\}$,

   (j) $\{x$: $x = \dfrac{2n}{n + 1}$, $n = 1,2,3, \ldots\}$,

   (k) $\{x$: $x = (-1)^n\left(3 + \dfrac{5}{n}\right)$, $n = 1,2,3, \ldots\}$,

(1) $\{x: \quad x = (-1)^n(\frac{5}{n}), \quad n = 1,2,3, \ldots\}$,

(m) $\{x: \quad x = (-1)^n(\frac{2n + 1}{3n + 4}), \quad n = 1,2,3, \ldots\}$,

(n) $\{x: \quad x = \frac{5n - 3}{2 + 4n}, \quad n = 1,2,3, \ldots\}$,

(o) $\{x: \quad x \equiv n \pmod 3 + \frac{1}{2^n}, \quad n = 1,2,3, \ldots\}$,

(p) $\{x: \quad x \equiv n \pmod 4 + (-1)^n \frac{1}{n}, \quad n = 1,2,3, \ldots\}$,

(q) $\{a/b: \quad a, b$ are integers, b is a factor of $6\}$,

(r) $\{a/b: \quad a, b$ are integers, b is a multiple of $6\}$,

(s) $\{a/b: \quad a, b$ are integers$\}$.

We now focus on pattern recognition.

● ●

Objective   75.   Given the first five terms a_1, a_2, a_3, a_4, a_5 of a sequence, to find a formula for a_n that is consistent with these terms.

● ●

Examples   1. $a_1 = 2$, $a_2 = 3$, $a_3 = 4$, $a_4 = 5$, $a_5 = 6$. $a_n = ?$

The clue here is the relation between the subscript of a term and the value of the term. Here the value is always one more than the subscript. Hence a_n could be $n + 1$.

2. $a_1 = 1$, $a_2 = 4$, $a_3 = 9$, $a_4 = 16$, $a_5 = 25$. $a_n = ?$

What do 1, 4, 9, 16, 25 all have in common? Right! They're all squares of integers: $a_1 = 1^2$, $a_2 = 2^2$, $a_3 = 3^2$, $a_4 = 4^2$, $a_5 = 5^2$. Thus $a_n = n^2$ is consistent with a_1, a_2, a_3, a_4, a_5.

3. $a_n = n^2 + (n - 1)(n - 2)(n - 3)(n - 4)(n - 5)$ is also consistent with a_1, a_2, a_3, a_4, a_5 of Example 2. See the exercises for further discussion.

4. $a_1 = 1$, $a_2 = 6$, $a_3 = 13$, $a_4 = 22$, $a_5 = 33$. $a_n = ?$

The 1 and the 6 don't tell us much. But 13, 22, 33 are fairly close to the famous numbers 16, 25, 36. Ah, yes! $13 = 4^2 - 3$, $22 = 5^2 - 3$, $33 = 6^2 - 3$; and $1 = 2^2 - 3$ and $6 = 3^2 - 3$. Thus we have $a_1 = 2^2 - 3$, $a_2 = 3^2 - 3$, $a_3 = 4^2 - 3$, $a_4 = 5^2 - 3$, $a_5 = 6^2 - 3$. Looking at subscripts and values we see that $a_n = (n + 1)^2 - 3$ will work.

5. $a_1 = 2$, $a_2 = 3/4$, $a_3 = 4/9$, $a_4 = 5/16$, $a_5 = 6/25$.
    $a_n = ?$

Here we may note that $a_1 = \dfrac{1 + 1}{1^2}$, $a_2 = \dfrac{2 + 1}{2^2}$,

$a_3 = \dfrac{3 + 1}{3^2}$, $a_4 = \dfrac{4 + 1}{4^2}$, $a_5 = \dfrac{5 + 1}{5^2}$, so it appears

that $a_n = \dfrac{n + 1}{n^2}$.

Exercises

1. Find a consistent formula for a_n:

    (a) $a_1 = 2$, $a_2 = 4$, $a_3 = 6$, $a_4 = 8$, $a_5 = 10$;

    (b) $a_1 = 4$, $a_2 = 7$, $a_3 = 10$, $a_4 = 13$, $a_5 = 16$;

    (c) $a_1 = 1$, $a_2 = 8$, $a_3 = 27$, $a_4 = 64$, $a_5 = 125$;

    (d) $a_1 = 7$, $a_2 = 19$, $a_3 = 37$, $a_4 = 61$, $a_5 = 91$;

    (e) $a_1 = 1/2$, $a_2 = 2/3$, $a_3 = 3/4$, $a_4 = 4/5$, $a_5 = 5/6$;

    (f) $a_1 = 1/2$, $a_2 = 1$, $a_3 = 3/2$, $a_4 = 2$, $a_5 = 5/2$;

    (g) $a_1 = 9/2$, $a_2 = 19/4$, $a_3 = 29/6$, $a_4 = 39/8$,
        $a_5 = 49/10$;

    (h) $a_1 = 4$, $a_2 = 2$, $a_3 = 1$, $a_4 = 1/2$, $a_5 = 1/4$;

    (i) $a_1 = 1$, $a_2 = 4/3$, $a_3 = 5/3$, $a_4 = 2$, $a_5 = 7/3$.

2. Which of the sequences in Exercise 1 have finite ac-
    cumulation points? What are these accumulation points?

3. Graph the sequences in Exercise 1.

4. Why do $a_n = n^2$ and $b_n = n^2 + (n - 1)(n - 2)(n - 3)$
    $(n - 4)(n - 5)$ have the same values for $n = 1, 2, 3, 4,$
    5 but not $n = 6, 7, 8, \ldots$?

5. Give at least three different, nonequivalent formulas
    for a_n in the sequence in (a) Example 1, (b) Example 2,
    (c) Example 4, (d) Example 5. [Note: n^2 and n^3/n are
    different but equivalent, for example, while n^2 and
    $n^2 + (n^2 - 1)(n^2 - 4)(n^2 - 9)(n^2 - 16)(n^2 - 25)$ are
    different and nonequivalent i.e., two formulas are
    equivalent if for any positive integer n they have the
    same value.]

6. What do you call a yellowish, apple-shaped fruit grow-
    ing in a pot of ocean water? (Answer: A sea quince.)

● ●

*Objective 76. To explain what is meant by "The rational numbers are *dense* in the number line."

● ●

Here are two fairly common explanations of density in the mathematical sense: (a) A set *S* is *dense* in the number line if every point on the number line is an accumulation point of *S*. (b) A set *S* is *dense* in the number line if between every pair of points of the number line (no matter how close together) there is always a point of *S*. Thus the rational numbers are dense in the number line [using explanation (a)]:
Let *P* be any point on the number line:

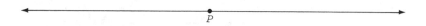

Are there infinitely many rational points arbitrarily close to *P*? Let's mark off a very short distance to the left and right of *P*:

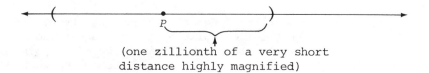

(one zillionth of a very short distance highly magnified)

Now let's consider the two integers between which *P* lies, say -17 and -18, and start bisecting (or trisecting, or whatever we want) the line segment joining them to locate other rational points:

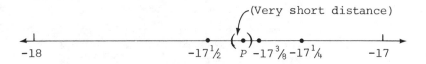

And of course we keep going until we get a rational number within the very short distance of *P* (in this case, -17 5/16 will do).

•••

To cite original examples (other than those given in the text of (a) unbounded, (b) bounded, infinite sets which are *not* dense in any segment of the number line.

•••

Examples 1. *Infinite set not dense in any segment of the number line and unbounded*: The integers.

The integers are not dense by explanation (a) of density because they have no accumulation point.

2. *Bounded infinite set not dense in any segment of the number line*:

$$\{x: x = \frac{1}{n + 1}, \quad n = 1,2,3, \ . \ . \ .\}.$$

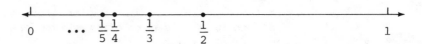

Here, although the point 0 on the number line is an accumulation point of the given set, no other point of the number line is an accumulation point of the set. The set *is* bounded, by 0 below and 1 above (also by -1 below and 2 above, or -1/8 and 3/4, or . . .).

Exercises 1. Show how the two explanations of density are equivalent: Show that if (a) holds, then so does (b), and that if (b) holds, then so does (a).

2. Explain how the rational numbers are dense in the number line according to (b).

3. Give at least three examples of disjoint, infinite, unbounded sets of rational numbers that are not dense in the number line.

4. Give at least three examples of disjoint, infinite, bounded sets of rational numbers that are not dense in the number line.

5. Give at least three examples of different subsets of the rational numbers which are themselves dense in the number line. (Hint: Exercise 3 on pages 210, 211.)

6. Why is a mathematical dunce like the set of rational numbers? (Answer: He's dense on the number line.)

CHAPTER 6

REAL NUMBERS AND EXTENSIONS

As you know, number systems are extended in order to solve more equations: -1 was invented to solve $x + 1 = 0$, 2/3 to solve $3x = 2$, -1/5 to solve $5x + 1 = 0$, etc. In this chapter we consider more extensions to solve still more equations. For example, $\sqrt{7}$ was invented to solve $x^2 - 7 = 0$ and i was invented to solve $x^2 + 1 = 0$ (that is, $i^2 = -1$). (This is the first instance in this book in which a square has turned out to be negative.) This last invention leads to the Everything-is-Nothing Problem, a "proof" that every number is 0:

$$i = i$$

$$\sqrt{-1} = \sqrt{-1}$$

$$\sqrt{\frac{-1}{1}} = \sqrt{\frac{1}{-1}}$$

$$\frac{\sqrt{-1}}{\sqrt{1}} = \frac{\sqrt{1}}{\sqrt{-1}}$$

$$\frac{i}{1} = \frac{1}{i}$$

So $i = -(-1)/i = -i^2/i = -i$. Dividing by i, $1 = -1$ or $2 = 0$. Dividing by 2, $1 = 0$. Since every number is a multiple of 1, then every number is a multiple of 0, and therefore by the Yul Brynner or Telly Savalas principle every number is 0.

In this chapter we will briefly discuss extensions of the field of rational numbers to the field of real numbers and beyond.

Challenges 1. Try to explain what's wrong with the preceding "proof" that every number is 0.

2. Is it true in any field that if $x + x = 0$, then $x = 0$? Explain your answer. (Hint: finite fields.)

ANOTHER
EXTENSION OF
NUMBER SYSTEMS

So far we have built up the field of rational numbers, which provides for solution of any equation of a form equivalent to $ax + b = 0$, where a and b are rational. But we have not yet discussed numbers which allow us to solve $x^2 - 3 = 0$, for example. Well, it develops that we can adjoin an irrational solution (i.e., the solution to $x^2 - 3 = 0$, which is not a rational number and is thus called *irrational*) of this equation to the rationals to form an extended field whose elements are numbers of the form $a + b\sqrt{3}$, where a and b are rational. (Note: At this point we are assuming $\sqrt{3}$ is irrational, i.e., not rational, but we haven't proved it. Yet!)

Student: What do you mean, these numbers form a field: What's the multiplicative inverse of $-4/3 + 1/2\sqrt{3}$, say? Author D. L.: Ah, a good question! Take a look at this:

$$\left(\frac{-48}{37} - \frac{18}{37}\sqrt{3}\right) \times \left(\frac{-4}{3} + \frac{1}{2}\sqrt{3}\right)$$

$$= \frac{192}{111} + \frac{24}{37}\sqrt{3} - \frac{24}{37}\sqrt{3} - \frac{27}{37}$$

$$= \frac{192}{111} - \frac{81}{111} = \frac{111}{111} = 1 . \quad \text{Ho, ho!}$$

Student: Hey! Whoa! Where did you get that inverse? D. L.: Calm down, now. We merely used that old high school rule of "rationalizing the denominator" by multiplying top and bottom by the "conjugate" of the denominator: The multiplicative inverse of $-4/3 + 1/2\sqrt{3}$ is

$$\frac{1}{\dfrac{-4}{3} + \dfrac{1}{2}\sqrt{3}}$$

$$= \left(\frac{1}{\dfrac{-4}{3} + \dfrac{1}{2}\sqrt{3}}\right)\left(\frac{\dfrac{-4}{3} - \dfrac{1}{2}\sqrt{3}}{\dfrac{-4}{3} - \dfrac{1}{2}\sqrt{3}}\right)$$

$$= \frac{\dfrac{-4}{3} - \dfrac{1}{2}\sqrt{3}}{\left(\dfrac{-4}{3}\right)^2 - \left(\dfrac{1}{2}\sqrt{3}\right)^2}$$

$$= \frac{-48}{37} - \frac{18}{37}\sqrt{3} .$$

Student: I get it; the inverse of $2 - 3\sqrt{3}$ is

$$\frac{1}{2 - 3\sqrt{3}} \cdot \frac{2 + 3\sqrt{3}}{2 + 3\sqrt{3}} ;$$

the inverse of $a + b\sqrt{3}$ is

$$\frac{1}{a + b\sqrt{3}} \cdot \frac{a - b\sqrt{3}}{a - b\sqrt{3}} ,$$

etc. (I probably could've figured this out by myself. . . .)

Exercises   1.   Show in detail that

$$\frac{\dfrac{-4}{3} - \dfrac{1}{2}\sqrt{3}}{\left(\dfrac{-4}{3}\right)^2 - \left(\dfrac{1}{2}\sqrt{3}\right)^2} = \frac{-48}{37} - \frac{18}{37}\sqrt{3} .$$

2. Compute the multiplicative inverses of: (a) $3 + 4\sqrt{3}$, (b) $3 - 4\sqrt{3}$, (c) $-3 + 4\sqrt{3}$, (d) $-3 - 4\sqrt{3}$, (e) $1/3 + 1/4\sqrt{3}$, (f) $1/3 - 1/4\sqrt{3}$.

3. Assuming the usual CAD laws for rationals, prove that $R(\sqrt{3}) = \{x: x = a + b\sqrt{3},\ a,\ b$ rational$\}$ forms a field under addition and multiplication.

4. (a) What is $R(\sqrt{2})$?

   (b) Is $R(\sqrt{2})$ a field? Why?

5. Is $R(\sqrt{5})$ a field? Why?

6. Is $R(\pi)$ a field? Why? (π, or "pi" is the ratio of the circumference of a circle to its diameter. It turns out that π is not rational and not even algebraic, i.e., it's not even the solution of a polynomial equation. See Chapter 9 for details on π.

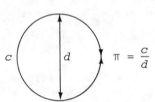

$$\pi = \frac{c}{d}$$

Let's identify the objective to which we are leading.

● ●

Objective 78. To draw a Venn diagram illustrating a development of the complex numbers from the cardinal numbers, giving in each superset an example of an element not in the preceding subset.

● ●

We'll content ourselves with telling you about some sets of numbers between the rationals and the complex numbers and give a partial example of what we want in the Venn diagram, but leave most of the details to you.

ALGEBRAIC
NUMBERS

Definition | *The __algebraic numbers__ are the numbers represented by points on the number line which are roots of equations of the form $a_1x^n + a_2x^{n-1} + a_3x^{n-2} + \cdots + a_{n+1} = 0$, where $a_1, a_2, a_3, \ldots, a_{n+1}$ are rational and n is a counting number.*

Examples 1. $\sqrt{3}$ is algebraic, since it is a root of $x^2 + 3 = 0$. On the number line it's about thus:

2. $1 + \sqrt[3]{7}$ is algebraic, since it is a root of

$x^3 - 3x^2 + 3x - 8 = 0$.

On the number line its
position is approximately:

3.   By way of contrast, π is *not* algebraic, because it is
not a root of any equation of the form $a_1 x^n + a_2 x^{n-1} +$
$\cdots + a_{n+1} = 0$.   (See Chapter 9, for more details of
π.)   Also i is *not* algebraic, because while it *is* a
root of $x^2 + 1 = 0$, it is *not representable on the
number line*.   (A reason for this is that if it were, it
would be either to the left of 0 or to the right of 0;
that is, either $i < 0$ or $i > 0$.   If $i < 0$, then $-i > 0$,
and $-i(i) < 0$, or $1 < 0$, an impossibility.   Similarly,
$i > 0$ leads to nonsense.)

The problem with algebraic numbers is that there exists
a possible ambiguity.   For example, when we're looking
at a solution of $x^2 - 3 = 0$, how do we know whether we
want $\sqrt{3}$ or $-\sqrt{3}$ (since both, when squared, give us 3)?
To avoid confusion, mathematicians have introduced the
concept of *principal root*.   We make it a convention to
take the *positive* root whenever there is a choice.
Thus for example $\sqrt[4]{16} = 2$, even though $(-2)^4 =$
$(-2)(-2)(-2)(-2) = 16$, and $\sqrt[4]{9} = \sqrt{3}$ rather than $-\sqrt{3}$.
In the case of odd roots, there's no ambiguity: $\sqrt[3]{-7} =$
$-\sqrt[3]{+7} = -\sqrt[3]{7}$.   Notice that this means that it's not always true that $\sqrt{x^2} = x$; for example, $\sqrt{(-2)^2} = \sqrt{4} =$
$2 \neq -2$.

Now that you know what algebraic numbers are, we can
look at a Venn diagram showing their relation to rational numbers:

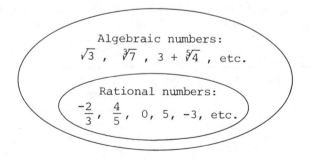

Algebraic numbers:
$\sqrt{3}$, $\sqrt[3]{7}$, $3 + \sqrt[5]{4}$, etc.

Rational numbers:
$\frac{-2}{3}$, $\frac{4}{5}$, 0, 5, -3, etc.

Exercises   1.   Which of the following numbers are algebraic?

(a) $\sqrt{17}$,   (b) $\sqrt{16}$,   (c) $\sqrt{-17}$,   (d) $\sqrt[3]{-17}$,   (e) -2,

(f) 0,　(g) $\sqrt[4]{1/16}$,　(h) $\sqrt[3]{-8/27}$,　(i) $\sqrt{\pi}$,　(j) $\sqrt[5]{2}$,
(k) $1 + \sqrt[5]{2}$,　(l) $\sqrt{2} + \pi$,　(m) 22/7,　(n) $\sqrt{6} + \sqrt[3]{7}$,
(o) $(\sqrt{7})^{\sqrt{7}}$,　(p) $1^{\sqrt{7}}$,　(q) $\sqrt{2} - \sqrt[3]{\pi}$,　(r) $\sqrt{2} - \sqrt[3]{22/7}$,
(s) $\sqrt{2} - \sqrt[3]{-22/7}$,　(t) $\sqrt{2} - \sqrt{-22/7}$.

2.　If possible, graph the numbers in Exercise 1 on the number line.

3.　Taking it as given that π is not algebraic, show that $R(\pi) = \{x: x = a + b\pi,\ a \text{ and } b \text{ rational}\}$ is *not* a field.

4.　(a) If $i < 0$, why does it follow that $-i > 0$?

　　(b) If $i < 0$ and $-i > 0$, why does it follow that $-i(i) < 0$?

　　(c) What is the value of $-i(i)$?

　　(d) Show that $i > 0$ is impossible.

5.　Find the principal values of the following:　(a) $\sqrt{4}$,　(b) $\sqrt[3]{8}$,　(c) $\sqrt[3]{-8}$,　(d) $\sqrt[4]{16}$,　(e) $\sqrt{1/4}$,　(f) $\sqrt[3]{8/27}$.

6.　(a) What is the principal value of the fourth root of 1?

　　(b) What are the *other* fourth roots of 1?

7.　Is it always true that $\sqrt{xy} = \sqrt{x}\sqrt{y}$?　Why?

8.　Is it always true that $\sqrt{x/y} = \sqrt{x}/\sqrt{y}$?　Why?

9.　Explain what's wrong in the Everything-is-Nothing Problem.

PROOF THAT A NUMBER IS IRRATIONAL

Now, let's back up for a minute and examine that word "irrational" and its meaning for numbers. First, "irrational" simply means "not rational," as we all know. So what is an irrational number? One which is not rational, obviously! To be more precise mathematically, we say:

Definition

An __irrational number__ is one which has no representation of the form a/b, where a and b are integers, b ≠ 0.

We have implied on the previous pages that $\sqrt{7}$, $\sqrt{3}$, π, and i are irrational. It's time we put our money where our mouth is (so to speak) with the next objective.

● ●

Objective 79.　To prove that $\sqrt{n}$ is irrational, for any nonsquare, nonnegative integer n.

● ●

Let's work with $\sqrt{3}$, since we have been assuming that it is irrational. However, the following proof is fairly general and so should show you all you need to know in order to attain this objective.

Proof that $\sqrt{3}$ is irrational: Here we'll use a standard method of proof in mathematics, an *indirect proof*, in which we assume the opposite of what we want and show that this assumption leads to a contradiction.

Suppose, then, that $\sqrt{3}$ is *rational*, contrary to all hopes. Let a/b be the *reduced* representative of $\sqrt{3}$. Then $b \neq 0$, and $b \neq 1$ (since otherwise 3 would be a perfect square). So we have

$$\frac{a}{b} = \sqrt{3} = \frac{3}{\sqrt{3}} = \frac{3}{\frac{a}{b}} = 3 \times \frac{b}{a} = \frac{3b}{a}.$$

Since a/b is the *reduced* representative of $\sqrt{3}$ = $\{a/b, 2a/2b, 3a/3b, \ldots\}$, it follows that $3b/a$ is identically na/nb, for some positive integer n; that is, $3b = na$ and $a = nb$. But if $a = nb$, then $a/b = nb/b = n/1$, which *contradicts* that a/b is reduced and $b \neq 1$. Since our original supposition that $\sqrt{3}$ is rational led to this contradiction, that supposition must be false, and its opposite must be true: $\sqrt{3}$ is irrational, QED.

Exercises

1. Prove that $\sqrt{3}$ is not a perfect square. (Hint: if $1^2 < 3 < 2^2$, then how are 1, 2, $\sqrt{3}$ related?)

2. Why is $\sqrt{3} = 3 \div \sqrt{3}$?

3. Why does $3 \div (a/b) = 3 \times (b/a)$?

4. Prove that $\sqrt{2}$ is irrational.

5. Prove that $\sqrt{2}$ is irrational a *second* way. (Hint: Use *indirect* reasoning again and consider oddness and evenness of the numbers involved.)

6. Prove that $\sqrt{5}$ is irrational.

7. Where does the proof break down if we try to prove that $\sqrt{4}$ is irrational using the proof that $\sqrt{3}$ is irrational as a pattern?

8. Prove that $\sqrt[3]{2}$ is irrational.

9. Prove that $\sqrt[4]{2}$ is irrational.

REALS ON THE NUMBER LINE

You have seen that not all numbers represented by points on the number line are rational. Even though the rationals are dense in the number line, there are many irrational algebraic numbers, for example, also on the number line. Well, it turns out that there are many more *non*algebraic numbers on the number line than there are algebraic numbers (which include the rational numbers). In fact, the situation is as follows: If we take a single point, say 0, out of the number line, its absence is not detectable because its "width" was zero anyway.

Complete number line	Number line with 0 missing

Similarly, the omission of any finite number of numbers from the number line is not detectable, and furthermore the omission of any *countable* set of numbers (i.e., any set in one-to-one correspondence with the positive integers) is not detectable.

Complete number line	Number line with all of the integers missing

It develops that the algebraic numbers are countable, so all of *them* may be thrown out with no detectable absence in the number line.

Complete number line	Number line with all of the algebraic numbers missing

(This fact is proved in books on *measure theory* dealing with how much "stuff"—area, volume, etc.—there is in a given set.)

Definition	*The* <u>*real*</u> <u>*numbers*</u> *are the numbers which are representable on the number line. Real numbers that are not algebraic are called* <u>*transcendental*</u>.

Our old pal π is an example of a transcendental real number. Another is e, the limit of $(1 + (1/n))^n$ as n gets infinitely large. There's a really amazing fact relating π, e, and i, discovered by the Swiss mathematician Leonard Euler in the eighteenth century:

$$e^{\pi i} + 1 = 0.$$

Exercises   1.   Show that the integers are countable by putting them in one-to-one correspondence with the counting numbers. (If you want an expression for the nth odd counting number, it's $2n - 1$, while of course the nth even counting number is $2n$.)

2. Look up an explanation of the fact that the rational numbers are countable.

3. Compute $\left(1 + (1/n)\right)^n$ for $n = 1, 2, 3, 4, 5$.

4. Between what two integers does e lie? Give a plausible explanation to support your answer.

5. Look up decimal approximations of π and e, and graph them on the number line.

6. What's the value of (a) $e^{2\pi i}$, (b) $e^{\pi i/2}$, (c) $e^{2\pi i} + 2e^{\pi i} + 1$? (Figure this last part out at least two ways.)

COMPLEX
NUMBERS

The real numbers do not constitute the ultimate, super system of numbers. They in turn are contained in the "complex numbers," which themselves may be extended to such exotic systems as "quaternions" and "octonions." We, however, will stop with the complex numbers, and even then mention them only very briefly.

The *complex numbers* are numbers of the form $a + bi$, where a and b are real numbers, which follow the usual rules for real numbers, with $i^2 = -1$. Numbers of the form bi, where $a = 0$, are called *imaginary numbers*.

Examples

1. $3 + 2i$ is a complex number; 3 is called the *real part* and $2i$ the *imaginary part*. The multiplicative inverse of $3 + 2i$ is

$$\frac{1}{3 + 2i} = \frac{1}{3 + 2i} \cdot \frac{3 - 2i}{3 - 2i}$$

$$= \frac{3 - 2i}{9 - 6i + 6i - 4i^2} = \frac{3 - 2i}{9 - 4(-1)}$$

$$= \frac{3 - 2i}{9 + 4} = \frac{3}{13} - \frac{2}{13}i .$$

What is its additive inverse? Yes, $-3 - 2i$.

2. Let's take the multiplicative inverse we found in Example 1 and check to see if it really is the inverse of $3 + 2i$. How? Well, the product of a number and its multiplicative inverse must equal the identity, 1.

$$\left(3 + 2i\right)\left(\frac{3}{13} - \frac{2}{13}i\right) = 3\left(\frac{3}{13} - \frac{2}{13}i\right) + 2i\left(\frac{3}{13} - \frac{2}{13}i\right)$$

$$= \frac{9}{13} - \frac{6}{13}i + \frac{6}{13}i - \frac{4}{13}(i)^2$$

$$= \frac{9}{13} - \frac{4}{13}(-1) = \frac{9 + 4}{13} = \frac{13}{13} = 1 .$$

Which CAD laws were used here?

3. Is π + *ei* a complex number? Look again at the defini-
    tion. All numbers of the form *a* + *bi* (yes) where *a*
    and *b* are real. Now, *a* = π and *b* = e. Are π and e
    real numbers? Yes! So π + *ei* is a complex number.

Exercises   1. Compute, in *a* + *bi* form, the multiplicative inverses
                of: (a) *i*, (b) 2 + 3*i*, (c) 1/2 + 3*i*, (d) 1/2 + 3*i*/5,
                (e) 1/2 - 3*i*/5.

            2. Use examples to show that the complex numbers form a
                field.

            3. Draw a Venn diagram illustrating a development of the
                complex numbers from the cardinal numbers, giving in
                each superset an example of an element not in the pre-
                ceding subset. The diagram should show the cardinal,
                rational, algebraic, real, and complex systems, as
                well as either the nonnegative rationals or the inte-
                gers.

DECIMAL
EXPANSIONS OF
REAL NUMBERS

● ●

Objective 80. To explain the difference between rational and irra-
                tional real numbers, as far as decimal expansions are
                concerned.

● ●

                Now that you know that the real numbers consist of ra-
                tional and irrational elements, it's natural to ask
                what the differences are between the two. One of these
                differences is in the decimal representation of the
                numbers. Instead of just telling you what this differ-
                ence is, we'll let you figure it out via exercises.

Exercises   1. Find the decimal expansion of 2/7, -5/37, and 5/19,
                fairly typical rational numbers.

            2. Looking at the results of Exercise 1, what conjecture
                do you make about the decimal expansion of *any* rational
                number?

            3. Prove your conjecture of Exercise 2. (Hint: In Exer-
                cise 1, how many positive integers are there less than
                7, 37, or 19? How many distinct remainders can we have
                in our division steps?)

4. Find a common fraction representation of $-2.\overline{3456}$, $.5\overline{64}$, and $3.2\overline{8}$, fairly typical repeating decimals.

5. On the basis of Exercise 4, what do you conjecture about any real number which has a repeating decimal expansion?

6. Prove your conjecture of Exercise 5.

7. Could any irrational real number have a repeating decimal? Why?

8. What is the decimal expansion difference between rational and irrational real numbers?

9. What mathematical term applies to a crazy cinematic dance production? (Answer: Irrational reel number.)

COMPUTATION OF
SQUARE ROOTS

With the abundance of electronic desk and hand calculators, the following procedure is becoming a lost art. But in the interest of both history and art let's look at the next objective.

● ●

*Objective 81. For a given nonsquare counting number n, to compute $\sqrt{n}$ to the nearest hundredth by (a) algorithm, (b) successive approximations, (c) Newton's method.

● ●

An algorithm, as we all remember, is a mechanical procedure for attaining some computational end. Here is the standard algorithm for computing square roots:

Step 1. Count off pairs of digits in both directions from the decimal point, going one pair more to the right than the number of decimal places desired (so we'll mark off *three* pairs because we want accuracy to the nearest hundredth or two decimal places):

$\sqrt{0563.000000}$

Step 2. Find the largest perfect square that is less than or equal to the number represented by the pair furthest to the left (in this case 4 is the largest square less than 05). Write the square root of that number above the first pair and the number itself below:

4

Step 3. Subtract the square (4 in this example) from the first pair and bring down the next pair:

$$
\begin{array}{r}
2\ \ .\quad\quad\quad\quad \\
\sqrt{0563.000000} \\
\underline{4} \\
163
\end{array}
$$

Step 4. Off to one side multiply the top number by 20:

$$
\begin{array}{r}
2\ \ .\quad\quad\quad\quad \\
\sqrt{0563.000000} \\
\underline{4} \\
163
\end{array}
\qquad
\begin{array}{r}
2 \\
\times\ 20 \\
\hline
40
\end{array}
$$

Step 5. Find a nice number such that the product of it plus the result in Step 4 is as close as possible and less than the number below (here 3 is the nice number to be found); write the nice number above the second pair:

$$
\begin{array}{r}
2\ 3.\quad\quad\quad\quad \\
\sqrt{0563.000000} \\
\underline{4} \\
163
\end{array}
\quad
\begin{array}{r}
2 \\
\times\ 20 \\
\hline
40
\end{array}
\quad
\begin{array}{r}
43 \\
\times\ 3 \\
\hline
129
\end{array}
\quad
\begin{array}{r}
\cancel{44} \\
\times\ \cancel{4} \\
\hline
\cancel{176}
\end{array}
$$

Step 6. Subtract the product in Step 5 (in our example, 129) from the number below (here, 163), and bring down the next pair:

$$
\begin{array}{r}
2\ 3.\quad\quad\quad\quad \\
\sqrt{0563.000000} \\
\underline{4} \\
163 \\
\underline{129} \\
3400
\end{array}
\quad
\begin{array}{r}
2 \\
\times\ 20 \\
\hline
40
\end{array}
\quad
\begin{array}{r}
43 \\
\times\ 3 \\
\hline
129
\end{array}
\quad
\begin{array}{r}
\cancel{44} \\
\times\ \cancel{4} \\
\hline
\cancel{176}
\end{array}
$$

Step 7. Repeat Steps 4, 5, and 6 until there is a number (technically, a *numeral* of a number) above each pair (of numerals):

$$
\begin{array}{r}
2\ 3.\ 7\ 2\ 7 \\
\sqrt{0563.000000} \\
\underline{4} \\
163 \\
\underline{129} \\
3400 \\
\underline{3269} \\
13100 \\
\underline{9484} \\
361600 \\
\underline{332129} \\
28471
\end{array}
$$

$$
\begin{array}{r}
2 \\
\times\ 20 \\
\hline
40
\end{array}
\quad
\begin{array}{r}
43 \\
\times\ 3 \\
\hline
129
\end{array}
\quad
\begin{array}{r}
\cancel{44} \\
\times\ \cancel{4} \\
\hline
\cancel{176}
\end{array}
$$

$$
\begin{array}{r}
23 \\
\times\ 20 \\
\hline
460
\end{array}
\quad
\begin{array}{r}
467 \\
\times\ 7 \\
\hline
3269
\end{array}
\quad
\begin{array}{r}
\cancel{468} \\
\times\ \cancel{8} \\
\hline
\cancel{3744}
\end{array}
$$

$$
\begin{array}{r}
237 \\
\times\ 20 \\
\hline
4740
\end{array}
\quad
\begin{array}{r}
4742 \\
\times\ 2 \\
\hline
9484
\end{array}
\quad
\begin{array}{r}
\cancel{4743} \\
\times\ \cancel{3} \\
\hline
\cancel{14229}
\end{array}
$$

$$
\begin{array}{r}
2372 \\
\times\ 20 \\
\hline
47440
\end{array}
\quad
\begin{array}{r}
47447 \\
\times\ 7 \\
\hline
332129
\end{array}
\quad
\begin{array}{r}
\cancel{47448} \\
\times\ \cancel{8} \\
\hline
\cancel{379584}
\end{array}
$$

Step 8. Round off the desired number of decimal places (2, for Objective 81):

$$\sqrt{563} \doteq 23.73, \text{ answer.}$$

($\doteq$ means "is approximately equal to.")

Here is the algorithm again with another number, 1823.2.

Step 1. $\sqrt{1823.20}$

Step 2.
$$\begin{array}{r} 4 \\ \sqrt{1823.20} \\ \underline{16} \end{array}$$
Want largest square less than 18.
Okay, 16.

Step 3.
$$\begin{array}{r} 4 \\ \sqrt{1823.20} \\ \underline{16} \\ 223 \end{array}$$
Now multiply 4 by 20:
$$\begin{array}{r} 4 \\ \underline{20} \\ 80 \end{array}$$

Step 4.
$$\begin{array}{r} 4 \\ \sqrt{1823.20} \\ \underline{16} \\ 223 \end{array}$$
Next, 8? × ? is less than 223. Well,
$$\begin{array}{rr} 82 & 8\!\!\!/3 \\ \underline{2} & \underline{3} \\ 164 & 2\!\!\!/4\!\!\!/9 \end{array}$$

Step 5.
$$\begin{array}{r} 4\ \ 2 \\ \sqrt{1823.20} \\ \underline{16} \\ 223 \\ \underline{164} \\ 5920 \end{array}$$
$$\begin{array}{rrr} 4 & 82 & 8\!\!\!/3 \\ \underline{20} & \underline{2} & \underline{3} \\ 80 & 164 & 2\!\!\!/4\!\!\!/9 \end{array}$$

Step 6.
$$\begin{array}{r} 4\ \ 2.\ \ 6 \\ \sqrt{1823.20} \\ \underline{16} \\ 223 \\ \underline{164} \\ 5920 \\ \underline{5076} \\ 844 \end{array}$$
$$\begin{array}{rrr} 4 & 82 & 8\!\!\!/3 \\ \underline{20} & \underline{2} & \underline{3} \\ 80 & 164 & 2\!\!\!/4\!\!\!/9 \\ \\ 42 & 84\!\!\!/5 & 846 & 84\!\!\!/7 \\ \underline{20} & \underline{5} & \underline{6} & \underline{7} \\ 840 & 4\!\!\!/2\!\!\!/2\!\!\!/5 & 5076 & 5\!\!\!/9\!\!\!/2\!\!\!/9 \end{array}$$

Okay, let's see how close we are, i.e., $(42.6)^2 + 8.44$ should equal 1823.20:

$(42.6)(42.6) + 8.44 = 1814.76 + 8.44 = 1823.20$

Eureka! So what happens if we start with a perfect square, say 169?

Step 1.
$$\begin{array}{r} 1\ \ . \\ \sqrt{0169.00} \\ \underline{01} \\ 69 \end{array}$$
This is obvious.

Step 2.
$$\begin{array}{r} 1\ \ 3. \\ \sqrt{0169.00} \\ \underline{01} \\ 69 \\ \underline{69} \end{array}$$
$$\begin{array}{rrr} 1 & 23 & 2\!\!\!/4 \\ \underline{20} & \underline{3} & \underline{4} \\ 20 & 69 & 9\!\!\!/6 \end{array}$$

Aha, yes! All is right with our world.

Exercises	1.	Use the algorithm to compute the following, to the nearest hundredth, and check your answers: (a) $\sqrt{2}$ ($= \sqrt{02.000000}$), (b) $\sqrt{34}$, (c) $\sqrt{.86}$ ($= \sqrt{00.860000}$), (d) $\sqrt{732.1}$, (e) $\sqrt{2209}$, (f) $\sqrt{9902}$.
	2.	Why do we multiply the number on top by 20 on every level?

For those who think algorithms should all go rhythmically home, here is a way to extract square roots via successive approximations ($\doteq$ means approximately equal to):

Step 1. 563 is between $400 = (20)^2$ and $625 = (25)^2$. (This information is just part of our recondite knowledge.) Therefore $20 < \sqrt{563} < 25$.

Step 2. Since 563 is closer to 625 than 400, let's try a number closer to 25 than 20, say 23: $(23)^2 = 529 < 563$. So we know $23 < \sqrt{563} < 25$, and $\sqrt{563}$ is much closer to 23 than to 25.

Step 3. Let's try 23.5: $(23.5)^2 \doteq 552 < 563$.

Step 4. Let's try 23.8, say: $(23.8)^2 \doteq 566 > 563$. So we now have $552 < 563 < 566$, and therefore we know that $23.5 < \sqrt{563} < 23.8$, with $\sqrt{563}$ closer to 23.8.

Step 5. Try 23.7: $(23.7)^2 \doteq 562$. So $\sqrt{563}$ is a little greater than 23.7.

Step 6. Try 23.72: $(23.72)^2 \doteq 562.6$, a little too small.

Step 7. Try 23.73: $(23.73)^2 \doteq 563.1$ So $23.72 < \sqrt{563} < 23.73$, and $\sqrt{563}$ is closer to 23.73, the answer.

Exercise	Use successive approximations to compute the following to the nearest hundredth: (a) $\sqrt{3}$, (b) $\sqrt{43}$, (c) $\sqrt{.68}$, (d) $\sqrt{237.5}$, (e) $\sqrt{6889}$, (f) $\sqrt{9886}$, (g) $\sqrt{3.86}$.

For you algebra nuts, here is another neat algorithm, Newton's method. We'll look at it in general, then take specific examples. Suppose we want to find $\sqrt{n}$. Proceed as follows:

Step 1. Let g_0 be any guess, no matter how bad.

Step 2. Now let $g_1 = n/g_0$. Look at this geometrically. If g_0 is smaller than $\sqrt{n}$, then $g_1 = n/g_0$ is larger than $\sqrt{n}$:

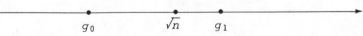

If g_0 is larger than $\sqrt{n}$, then g_1 is smaller than $\sqrt{n}$. In either case, $\sqrt{n}$ is caught between g_0 and g_1.

Step 3. Let $g_2 = (g_0 + g_1)/2$, the average of our original guess and our computed guess. Notice that g_2 will lie between g_0 and g_1.

Step 4. $g_3 = n/g_2$. And again $\sqrt{n}$ will lie between g_2 and g_3, which are closer bounds than were g_0 and g_1.

Continuing in this manner ($g_4 = (g_2 + g_3)/2$ and $g_5 = n/g_4$), we get better and better approximations for $\sqrt{n}$. We stop after our successive approximations get close enough together. I.e., if we want accuracy to the hundredth place we stop when two successive approximations agree to the hundredth.

Suppose $n = 274$, what is $\sqrt{274}$?

Step 1. Let $g_0 = 10$, since we know $10^2 = 100$ and $20^2 = 400$

Step 2. $g_1 = \dfrac{274}{10} = 27.40$, dividing into n

Step 3. $g_2 = \dfrac{27.40 + 10.00}{2} = \dfrac{37.40}{2} = 18.70$, averaging

Step 4. $g_3 = \dfrac{274}{18.70} \doteq 14.65$, dividing into n

Step 5. $g_4 = \dfrac{18.70 + 14.65}{2} = \dfrac{33.35}{2} \doteq 16.68$, averaging

Step 6. $g_5 = \dfrac{274.00}{16.68} \doteq 16.43$, dividing into n

Step 7. $g_6 = \dfrac{16.68 + 16.43}{2} = \dfrac{33.11}{2} \doteq 16.55$, averaging

Step 8. $g_7 = \dfrac{274.00}{16.55} \doteq 16.55$, answer.

So we can assume that this is the answer to two decimal places. Let's check: $(16.55)^2 = 273.9025$, so we are off by only $.0975$.

Another example? Okay, let $n = 8.32$. Since $2^2 = 4$ and $3^2 = 9$:

Step 1. Let $g_0 = 3.0000$.

Step 2. $g_1 = \dfrac{8.3200}{3.0000} \doteq 2.7733$, dividing into n

Step 3. $g_2 = \dfrac{3.0000 + 2.7733}{2} = \dfrac{5.7733}{2} \doteq 2.8867$. averaging

Step 4. $g_3 = \dfrac{8.3200}{2.8867} \doteq 2.8822$, dividing into n

Step 5. $g_4 = \dfrac{2.8867 + 2.8822}{2} = \dfrac{5.7689}{2} \doteq 2.8844$

averaging

Step 6. $g_5 = \dfrac{8.3200}{2.8844} \doteq 2.8845$, dividing into n

Step 7. $g_6 = \dfrac{2.8844 + 2.8845}{2} = 2.8844$, averaging.

So the answer to the fourth decimal place is 2.8844. Checking this, we see that $(2.8844)^2 = 8.31976336$, which is pretty close to 8.32.

Exercises

1. Use the averaging algorithm to compute the following to the nearest hundredth: (a) $\sqrt{3}$, (b) $\sqrt{43}$, (c) $\sqrt{.68}$, (d) $\sqrt{237.5}$, (e) $\sqrt{6889}$, (f) $\sqrt{9886}$.

2. What are the advantages and disadvantages of each of these methods relative to the other?

3. Find a fourth method for computing square roots.

4. What do you call a crew-cut carrot that likes to read *Reader's Digest*? (Answer: a square root.)

5. What do you call a crew-cut fan of an athletic team? (Answer: a square rooter.)

6. What do you call a road through middle America? (Answer: a square route.)

THE REAL NUMBERS AS A COMPLETE, ORDERED FIELD

It turns out that the real numbers may be perfectly described by the mathematical phrase, "a complete, ordered field."

● ●

*Objective 82. To explain what is meant by "The real numbers form a complete, ordered field."

● ●

We can attack this objective confidently, since we already know what a field is. An *ordered* field is merely one in which there is a "less than" relation—that is, there are negative, zero, and positive elements such that the sum of any two positive elements is positive, the product of any two positive elements is positive, and any given element x is either positive or zero itself or else $-x$ is positive. So "$a < b$" means $b - a$ is positive.

Exercises	1.	Prove that $a > 0$ if and only if a is positive. (That "if and only if" means that you are to prove two things: If $a > 0$, then a is positive, and if a is positive, then $a > 0$.)
	2.	Prove that $a < 0$ if and only if a is negative.
	3.	Prove that if a and b are any real numbers, then either $a < b$ or $a = b$ or $b > a$. (Use the statement in the explanation of ordered fields about x.)
	4.	Prove that any field (such as the complex numbers) containing i ($i^2 = -1$) is *not* ordered. (Hint: If we *could* order such a field, then we'd have either $i < 0$, $i = 0$, or $0 < i$ [why?]. Check out each of these possibilities.)
	5.	Explain why or why not $R(\sqrt{3}) = \{a + b\sqrt{3}:\ a$ and b rational$\}$ is an ordered field.
	6.	Explain why or why not the field of integers, mod 5, is an ordered field.

Let us now consider the property of completeness. Before we do that, we need to discuss the concept of a "least upper bound." According to the 1971 *Guinness Book of World Records*, the tallest woman on record is one of height 7 feet, $9\frac{1}{2}$ inches. Thus we can say that 8 feet is *an* upper bound for heights of women, or that $8\frac{1}{2}$ feet is *another* upper bound, or 100 feet, for that matter, is yet *another* upper bound. But 7 feet, $9\frac{1}{2}$ inches is the *least* possible upper bound, since any shorter height would not allow for the record holder.
We are now in a position to define the concept of "completeness."

Definition	*A set S is* <u>*complete*</u> *if and only if every bounded, non-empty subset* $B \subset S$ *has a least upper bound* $\ell \in S$.

Examples	1.	Let $S = \{a/b:\ a$ is an integer, b is a power of 2$\}$, and $B = \{c/d:\ c$ is a positive integer, d is a power of 2, $c/d \leq 1/3\}$. Then $B \subset S$. Furthermore, $B \neq \emptyset$, since $1/4 \in B$; and B is bounded, below by 0 (or -1, or -2, or . . .) and above by $1/3$ (or $1/2$, or 1, or 2, or . . .). Here the *least* upper bound $\ell = 1/3$, but $1/3 \notin S$. Therefore S is *not* complete.
	2.	Let $S = \{1, 2, 3, \ . \ . \ .\}$. Is S complete? Let B be any finite set of positive integers. Then the largest element of B is the least upper bound and the smallest element of B is the greatest lower bound; both bounds are in B and therefore in S. Furthermore, any subset B in S which is bounded must also be finite. Thus S is complete.

Exercises	1.	(a) What are some *lower* bounds of heights of adult (18 years or older) women?
		(b) What is the greatest lower bound? (Answer: 23.2 inches—1971 *Guinness Book of World Records*, p. 14.)
	2.	Prove that $1/3 \notin S$ in Example 1.
	3.	Give a logically equivalent alternative definition of "completeness," using lower bounds instead of upper bounds.
	4.	Why is the least upper bound of B in Example 2 always a member of B?
	5.	Why is any bounded set B in S of Example 2 always finite?
	6.	Explain, in ordinary language, what it means to say "The real numbers form a complete, ordered field." (This will probably take two or more paragraphs of explanation.)
	7.	Let a seventh grader read your explanation in Exercise 6 and see if he (or she) understands it. If not, rewrite until he does.
	8.	Organize a basketball team and call it "The Least Upper Rebounds."

● ●

*Objective 83.   To explain why the rational numbers do *not* form a complete, ordered field.

● ●

In attaining this objective it will be necessary to show that the rationals are either incomplete, or not ordered, or not a field.

Exercises	1.	Which of these will you show? Why?
	2.	To show that a field is incomplete, what do you have to produce?
	3.	What are some upper and lower bounds of $B = \{r: r \text{ is rational}, r^2 \leq 3\}$?
	4.	Name five elements which are in B of Exercise 3.
	5.	What is the least upper bound of B in Exercise 3?
	6.	Explain why the rational numbers do *not* form a complete, ordered field.

| GRAPHING SETS OF REAL NUMBERS | There is not much to add about graphing sets of real numbers that hasn't already been said about graphing cardinals and rationals. (The definition of absolute value extends naturally to real numbers, i.e., $\lvert x \rvert = x$ if $x \geq 0$, $-x$ if $x < 0$.) |

● ●

Objective 84.   To graph sets of real numbers (some of which may be defined in terms of absolute value).

● ●

Once again we plunge fearlessly into examples:

Examples   1. $\{x: \lvert x - 2 \rvert = 0\}$:

x is any number which is 0 units away from 2.

2. $\{x: \lvert x - 2 \rvert > 0\}$:

The distance x is from 2 is any positive number. (Note: distance is always positive.) So x is any number not equal to 2.

3. $\{x: \lvert x - 2 \rvert < 0\}$:

(Empty set)

x is any number whose distance from 2 is any negative number; therefore $\{x: \lvert x - 2 \rvert < 0\} = \emptyset$.

4. $\{x: \lvert x - 2 \rvert = 3\}$:

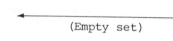

x is any number whose distance from 2 is 3 units.

5. $\{x: \lvert x - 2 \rvert \geq 3\}$:

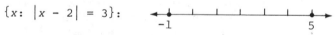

x is any number whose distance from 2 is 3 or more units.

6. $\{x: \lvert x - 2 \rvert < 3\}$

x is any number whose distance from 2 is less than 3 units.

7. $\{x: \lvert x - (n/2) \rvert < 1/8,\ n\ \text{an integer}\}$:

x is any number which is within one-eighth of a unit from n/2. Here we let n vary over the integers and find all possible values of x corresponding to each integer n.

Exercise	Graph the following: (a) $\{x: x^2 = 3\}$,

                    (b) $\{x: x^2 \leq 3\}$,   (c) $\{x: x^2 > 3\}$,   (d) $\{x: x^2 \leq -3\}$,

                    (e) $\{x: 1/x < 2\}$,   (f) $\{x: x = \sqrt{n}$, n = whole number$\}$,

                    (g) $\{x: x = \sqrt{-n}$, n = whole number$\}$,

                    (h) $\{x: x = \sqrt[3]{n}$, n = whole number$\}$,

                    (i) $\{x: |x^2 - 2| = 0\}$,   (j) $\{x: |x^2 + 2| = 0\}$,

                    (k) $\{x: |x^2 - 2| \geq 0\}$,   (l) $\{x: |3x^2 + 2| < 0\}$,

                    (m) $\{x: |3x + 2| = 1\}$,   (n) $\{x: |3x + 2| \geq 1\}$,

                    (o) $\{x: |3x + 2| < 1\}$,   (p) $\{x: |x - 2| > 5\}$,

                    (q) $\{x: |x - 2| \leq 3\}$,   (r) $\{x: |x - 2| = 2\}$,

                    (s) $\{x: |x - 2n| < 1/2$ or $|x - (2n + 1)| < 1/4$, n an

integer$\}$,   (t) $\{x: |x - n| \leq 1/2^n$, n a whole number$\}$.

SUMMARY OF OBJECTIVES	78.	To draw a Venn diagram illustrating a development of the complex numbers from the cardinal numbers, giving in each superset an example of an element not in the preceding subset (page 220).
	79.	To prove that $\sqrt{n}$ is *irrational, for any* nonsquare, nonnegative integer n (page 222).
	80.	To explain the difference between rational and irrational real numbers, as far as decimal expansions are concerned (page 226).
	*81.	For a given nonsquare counting number n, to compute $\sqrt{n}$ to the nearest hundredth by (a) algorithm, (b) successive approximations, (c) Newton's method (page 227).
	*82.	To explain what is meant by "The real numbers form a complete, ordered field" (page 232).
	*83.	To explain why the rational numbers do *not* form a complete, ordered field (page 234).
	84.	To graph sets of real numbers (some of which may be defined in terms of absolute value) (page 235).

WORDS TO KNOW	irrational number (page 218)	rationalize the denominator (page (219)
	conjugate (page 219)	

CHAPTER 7

RELATIONS, FUNCTIONS, AND GRAPHS

$$1 = \frac{3!}{3+3}$$

$$2 = 3 - \frac{3}{3}$$

$$3 = \sqrt{3 \cdot \sqrt{3} \cdot \sqrt{3}}$$

THE THREE 3s PROBLEM	On page 239 we have a pig who is inordinately proud of having expressed 1, 2, and 3 using exactly three 3s, but no other numerals. Of course, the classical three 3s problem is to express all of the integers from 0 through 33 using three 3s, no more, no less, and no other numerals, although any mathematical symbols other than numerals, such as +, -, ÷, $\sqrt{}$, !, etc. are okay.
	Many of these symbols, plus some others, will occur in our forthcoming discussion of relations and functions.

Challenge	Try to solve the Three 3s Problem.

RELATIONS AND FUNCTIONS

● ●

Objective 85. To define *relation*, *domain*, *range*, and *function*.

● ●

Without knowing any mathematics, you might guess that a relation is some sort of dependence or connection between mathematical objects—and you'd be very nearly correct.

Definition	*A relation is a rule which associates to each element of a set, called the domain of the relation, one or more specific elements of a set called the range of the relation.*

The rule describing a relation may be simply a list of ordered pairs, i.e., a formulated rule. The first element in the ordered pair is in the domain and the second element is in the range. So $\{(1,1),(1,-1),(4,2),(4,-2), \ldots\}$, $\{(1,1),(2,4),(3,6), \ldots\}$, and $\{(1,3),(2,2),(3,8),(4,-6)\}$ are all relations, although it would be hard to describe a rule for the third set.

Another relation is the rule $y^2 = x$, where x is an integer. Some of the ordered pairs for this relation are (2,4), (-2,4), (3,9), and (-3,9). We can express this relation as the set of ordered pairs $\{(x,y):$ $y^2 = x$ and x an integer$\}$. When describing a relation as a set of ordered pairs, the domain element is *always* the first element of the ordered pair.

Definition	A _function_ is a relation according to which each element of the domain is associated with one and only one element of the range.

Notationally, if x is an element of the domain of a relation f, the element of the range with which x is associated is denoted by $f(x)$. We call $\{y: y = f(x),\ x$ an element of the domain of $f\}$ the _image_ of f.

Examples	1.

f given by arrows:

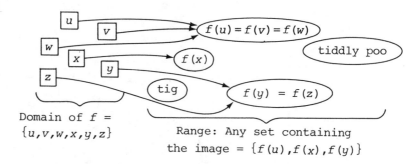

Domain of f = $\{u,v,w,x,y,z\}$

Range: Any set containing the image = $\{f(u),f(x),f(y)\}$

Here f is not only a relation but in fact a function, since each element of the domain goes into one and only one element of the range. The ordered pairs of this function are $(u,f(u))$, $(v,f(v))$, $(w,f(w))$, $(x,f(x))$, $(y,f(y))$, and $(z,f(z))$. Notice that the diagram tells more about this function than do the ordered pairs.

2.

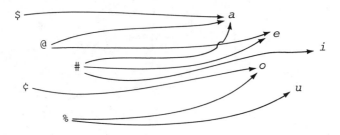

Here the rule is given by the arrows. This is a relation but not a function because $, @, #, and % all go into more than one element of the range. The domain is the set $\{\$,@,\#,¢,\%\}$ and the range is the set $\{a,e,i,o,u\}$.

3. Domain = {1,2,3,4}, range = {2,4,6,8}, and the rule is
    "x is related to y if and only if y is divisible by x."
    This is a relation but not a function since $x = 1$ is
    related to every element of the range. The ordered
    pairs here are: (1,2), (1,4), (1,6), (1,8), (2,2),
    (2,4), (2,6), (2,8), (3,6), (4,4), (4,8).

4. Domain and range are the same as in Example 3, but the
    rule is "x is related to y if and only if $y = 2x$."
    This is a function, as each x is related to one and
    only one y. The ordered pairs here are (1,2), (2,4),
    (3,6), (4,8).

5. The rule is "x is legally married to y in the USA,"
    with domain and range the set of all legally married
    people in the USA. This relation, an everyday rela-
    tion, is a function under our present laws since we may
    be legally married to only one person at one time.

6.

$D = \{x: x \text{ is a pig}\}$
$R = \{y: y \text{ is a cardinal number}\}$
$f: D \rightarrow R$ is defined by $f(x)$
    = the number of baths taken
      by x in a week.

Examples 2, 5, and 6 illustrate that either the domain D or the range R or both may be sets of elements other than numbers.

7. Let's look again at the notation for the rule of a function, f or $f(x)$. Suppose the rule for a function is $f(x) = 2x + 3$. Just what do we mean here? What is $f(2)$, $f(-3)$, $f(a)$, or $f(a + b)$? Well, the function $f(x) = 2x + 3$ is the set of ordered pairs of the form $(x, 2x + 3)$. That is, if d is in the domain of f then $2d + 3$ is in the range of f. So we can think of the function $f(x) = 2x + 3$ as a machine which takes an x, doubles it, and then adds 3. Therefore, $f(2) = 2 \cdot 2 + 3 = 7$, $f(-3) = 2(-3) + 3 = -3$, $f(a) = 2a + 3$, and $f(a + b) = 2(a + b) + 3$.

8. Try another one, say the function $f(x) = 2x^2 - 3x + 4$. Then $f(0) = 4$, $f(1) = 3$, $f(-3) = 2(-3)^2 - 3(-3) + 4 = 31$, $f(p) = 2p^2 - 3p + 4$, and $f(p + q) = 2(p + q)^2 - 3(p + q) + 4$.

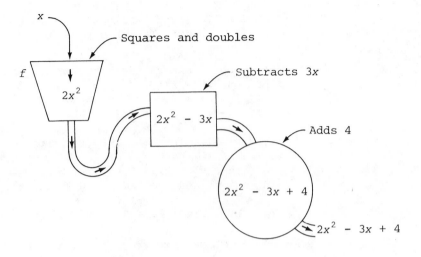

x

Squares and doubles

f

$2x^2$

Subtracts $3x$

$2x^2 - 3x$

Adds 4

$2x^2 - 3x + 4$

$2x^2 - 3x + 4$

Exercises   1.   Which of the following are functions?

(a) $y = \sqrt{x}$

(b) $y^2 = x$

(c) $\{(1,1),(1,2),(2,4),(3,6),(4,8)\}$

(d) $\{(1,1),(2,1),(3,1),\ .\ .\ .\}$

(e) $\{(-1,2),(3,4),(1,-1),(3,5)\}$

(f)

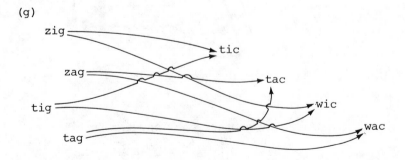

x

$f(u) = f(v)$

y

$f(x) = f(y)$

z

u

$f(z)$

v

(g)

zig

tic

zag

tac

tig

wic

tag

wac

(h)

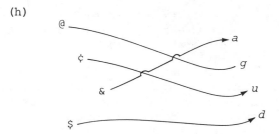

    (i) $y = |x + 3|$

2.   Find: (i) $f(0)$, (ii) $f(2)$, (iii) $f(1/2)$,
    (iv) $f(-1/2)$, (v) $f(p)$, (vi) $f(p + q)$,
    (vii) $f(p + q + 2)$ for each of the following functions:
    (a) $f(x) = -x + 2$, (b) $f(x) = x^2 + x + 5$,
    (c) $f(x) = |x|$, (d) $f(x) = |x + 3|$, (e) $f(x) = 1/x$.

3.   Is $f(p + q)$ necessarily equal to $f(p) + f(q)$? An example?

4.   Is $f(p^2)$ necessarily equal to $(f(p))^2$? An example?

● ●

Objective 86.   Given a situation, to cite a pertinent function,
                    stating its domain, range, and rule.

● ●

Of course, there is no single right answer for this objective. The bathtub situation cartoon of Example 6,
for example, might give rise to any of the following
pertinent functions:

(a) $D = \{x\colon x$ is a bathtub in Tigville$\}$

    $R = \{y\colon y$ is a real number, $y \geq 0\}$

    $f\colon D \to R$ is defined by $f(x)$ = volume in gallons of
    water in x at 12:30 AM on April 2, 1975.

(b) $D = \{x\colon x$ is any person who ever sat in a bathtub$\}$

    $R = \{y\colon y$ is any person who ever lived$\}$

    $f\colon D \to R$ is defined by $f(x) = x$'s mother.

(c) $D = \{x\colon x$ is a bathtub faucet$\}$

    $R = \{y\colon y$ is a cardinal number$\}$

    $f\colon D \to R$ is defined by $f(x)$ = the volume, to the
    nearest litre, of the water that has passed through
    x.

(d) $D = \{x\colon x$ is an actress who has made a single TV
    commercial in a bathtub$\}$

    $R = \{y\colon y$ is a nonnegative rational number$\}$

$f: D \to R$ is defined by $f(x) =$ (the number of products advertised in x's commercial) $\div$ (1 more than the number of people who have seen x's commercial on TV).

Exercises   1.   Make up five relations that are *not* functions, stating for each the domain, range, and rule. Express at least one rule as a formula.

2.   Make up five functions, stating for each the domain, range, and rule. Express at least one rule as a formula.

3.   Cite at least three different functions pertinent to this cartoon, stating for each the domain, range, and rule. Include at least one function in which neither the domain nor the range is a set of numbers.

As we have seen, any relation may be expressed as a set of ordered pairs (either finite or infinite), and since a function is a special relation, any function may also be expressed as a set of ordered pairs.

●●

Objective 87.   Given a function on a finite domain, to express it as
                  a set of ordered pairs.

●●

One more example should be ample:

$D = \{1, 2, 3, 4, 5\}$

$R = \{1, 1/2, 1/3, 1/4, 1/5\}$

$f: D \to R$ is defined by $f(x) = 1/x$.

Another way of defining f is to list the following set
of ordered pairs:

$\{(1,1), (2,1/2), (3,1/3), (4,1/4), (5,1/5)\}$,

in which each ordered pair is of the form $(x, f(x))$.

Exercises   Rewrite each of the following functions as a set of
                 ordered pairs:

1. $D = \{0,1,2,3\}$, $R = \{y: y$ is an integer$\}$, f $D \to R$
      is defined by $f(x) = 4 - 3x$.

2. $D = \{1,1/2,1/3,1/4\}$, $R = \{y: y$ is a cardinal number$\}$,
      $f: D \to R$ defined by $f(x) = 1/x^2$.

3. $D = \{p,i,g,s\}$, $R = \{y: y$ is a counting number $\leq 26\}$,
      $f: D \to R$ defined by $f(x) = x$'s position in the alphabet
      (so $f(a) = 1$, $f(b) = 2$, $f(c) = 3$, etc.).

●●

Objective 88.   Given several sets of ordered pairs, to state which are
                  functions.

●●

Here again, our motto is Example Ho!

Examples   1. $\{(1,-2),(2,-3),(3,-4)\}$ is a function because to each
                  first element one and only one second element is as-
                  sociated:

                  $1 \to -2$, $2 \to -3$, $3 \to -4$.

                  The domain is $\{1,2,3\}$ and the range any set including
                  $\{-2,-3,-4\}$. A possible rule is $f(x) = -(x + 1)$.

            2. $\{(1,1),(1,-1),(4,2),(4,-2)\}$ is not a function because
                  there is ambiguous assignment of elements of the do-
                  main:

                  A possible rule for this relation if $f(x) = \pm\sqrt{x}$.

RELATIONS, FUNCTIONS, AND GRAPHS   247

3. $\{(1,1),(-1,1),(2,4),(-2,4)\}$ is a function because each element of the domain is unambiguously assigned:

$1 \rightarrow 1, \ -1 \rightarrow 1, \ 2 \rightarrow 4, \ -2 \rightarrow 4.$

This function might have the rule $f(x) = x^2$.

Exercises

For each of the following sets of ordered pairs, write yes if it is a function, no if it is not; for each no, state specifically what's wrong.

1. $\{(1,1),(2,1),(3,1),(4,1),(5,2)\}$.
2. $\{(1,1),(1,2),(1,3),(1,4),(2,5)\}$.
3. $\{(1,1),(2,2),(3,3),(4,4),(5,6)\}$.
4. $\{(1,1),(2,2),(3,3),(4,4),(6,5)\}$.
5. $\{(1,2),(2,3),(3,2),(2,1)\}$.
6. $\{(a,b),(c,d),(e,f)\}$.
7. $\{(a,b),(c,v),(d,b)\}$.
8. $\{(b,a),(b,c),(b,d)\}$.
9. $\{(\text{pig, wolf}),(\text{pig, dog}),(\text{pig, pig})\}$.
10. $\{(\text{wolf, pig}),(\text{dog, pig}),(\text{pig, pig})\}$.

Some relations have special properties and thus special names. Consider the following examples:

Examples   1.

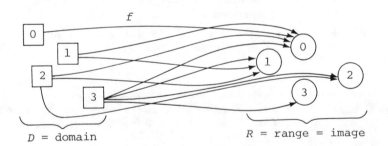

D = domain R = range = image

Here f is a relation but not a function, because 1, 2, and 3 all go into more than one element of the range. This example also shows that the domain and range of a relation may be the same set. It also shows that the image and range of a relation may be the same, in which case the relation is called *onto*. The ordered pairs here are $(0,0),(1,0),(1,1),(2,0),(2,1),(2,2),(3,0),$ $(3,1),(3,2),(3,3)$.

2. Rule: $f(x) = y$, where $y \leq x$ and y is a cardinal number.

>   Domain $= \{0,1,2,3\}$
>   Range $\;\;= \{0,1,2,3\}$.

This is just Example 1 again, stated differently. If we did not want an onto relation, we could have let the range be $\{0,1,2,3,4\}$, $\{0,1,2,3,4,5\}$, $\{0,1,2,3,a,b,c,$ . . .$\}$, or any other set which contains $\{0,1,2,3\}$ as a subset.

3. $D = \{0,1,2,3, \; . \; . \; .\}$ (the set of all cardinal numbers)

$R = \{0,1,2,3, \; . \; . \; .\}$ $(= D)$

Rule: $f: D \to R$ is defined by $f(n) = n!$ for each $n \in D$. Here we have the factorial function. It is not onto, but it is *one-to-one*: i.e., no two different elements of the domain D go into the same element of the range R. In ordered pair notation, this function is the set $\{(n,n!): n \in D\}$.

4. $D =$ the set of all real numbers
    $R =$ the set of all real numbers
    $f: D \to R$ is defined by $f(x) = x^3$ for each $x \in D$.

Here f is a function that is one-to-one and onto. Thus its *inverse function* $f^{-1}: R \to D$ is well defined, with $f^{-1}(y) = \sqrt[3]{y}$ for each $y \in R$.

The inverse of a function is more noticeable in ordered pair notation, as we just reverse the pair, letting the second element be first: (y,x) instead of (x,y). So if the function is $\{(x,y): x \in D\}$, then its inverse is $\{(y,x): x \in D\}$, or, as in Example 4, $(y,\sqrt[3]{x})$.

Exercises 1. Which of the following relations are onto? Which are one-to-one?

(a) $D = \{a,b,c\}$,
    $R = \{1,2,3\}$, and
    the rule is:

(b) $D = \{a,b,c\}$, R is the set of whole numbers, and a is related to any even number and b is related to any odd number while c is related to 0.

(c) D is the set of integers and R is the set of positive integers; the rule is $y = x^2$, $x \in D$.

(d) The domain and range are the set $\{1,2,3,4,5\}$, and the rule is $y = x + 1$ if $x < 5$ and where 5 is related to 1.

(e) The domain is $\{x: x = 1/n,\ n$ an integer$\}$, the range is the set of integers, and the rule is $y = 1/x$.

2. Find the inverse of each of the following functions:
(a) $y = x^2$;   (b) $y = x + 2$;   (c) $y = 3x - 4$;
(d) $\{(2,3),(3,4),(4,5),(5,6)\}$;   (e) $\{(2,3),(3,3),(4,3),(5,4),(6,4),(7,5)\}$.

3. Which of the inverses of Exercise 2 are themselves functions?

4. Which of the relations of Exercise 1 are functions?

Objective 88 is really easy to attain if you understand the definition of a function. The next one is not so easy, as it calls for ingenuity in discovering patterns.

● ●

*Objective 89.   Given a function represented by three or more ordered pairs, to give at least two nonequivalent function formulas which are consistent with the ordered pairs.

● ●

That is, you are supposed to identify a function's rule lurking behind ordered pairs. This is admittedly a guessing game (not an easy one), and there is no single correct answer. (In fact, no formulated rule need exist but the set of ordered pairs is nevertheless a function if every first element in the pairs is used once and only once.)

Examples   1. $\{(1,1),(2,4),(3,9),(4,16)\}$. You might say: that's easy, $f(x)$ must be x^2. Very good. $f(x) = x^2$ certainly *is* consistent with these ordered pairs. Now, how about *another* rule? Student: Okay, $f(x) = -x^2$? D. L.: Then the ordered pairs would be $\{(1,-1),(2,-4),(3,-9),(4,-16)\}$, which is not the same set as the original. Student: (Long pause.) This objective is impossible. There are no other answers. D. L.: How about $x^2 + (x - 1)(x - 2)(x - 3)(x - 4)(x - 5)$? Student: Ho! That won't work; try $x = 1$:

$$1^2 + (1 - 1)(1 - 2)(1 - 3)(1 - 4)(1 - 5) = 1 + 0 = 1.$$

Hm. Lucky! Try $x = 2$:

$$2^2 + (2 - 1)(2 - 2)(2 - 3)(2 - 4)(2 - 5) = 4 + 0 = 4.$$

Hm. Math teachers are sneaky.

2. $\{(-2,-1),(-1,0),(0,1),(1,2),(2,3)\}$.

Some possible consistent rules are: (a) $f(x) = x + 1 + x^2(x^2 - 1)(x^2 - 4)$,   (b) $f(x) = x + 1$,   (c)

$$f(x) = (x + 1)(1 + 5(x^2 - 1)(x^2)(x^2 - 4)), \quad \text{(d)} \ f(x) = (x + 1) + (\pi/3)x^2(x^2 - 1)(x^2 - 4).$$

Exercises

1. Compute $f(x) = x^2$, $g(x) = x^2 + (x - 1)(x - 2)(x - 3)(x - 4)(x - 5)$ for $x = 1, 2, 3, 4, 5, 6$.

2. How is the Yul Brynner principle (see page 218) used in $g(x)$ in Exercise 1?

3. Verify that each of the formulas in Example 2 is consistent with the given ordered pairs.

4. Compute $f(3)$ for each formula in Example 2.

5. Some people might write $f(x) = (2x + 2)/2$ as a fifth formula for Example 2, but that would not satisfy Objective 89 because $x + 1$ and $(2x + 2)/2$ are *equivalent* for all values of x. One way to ensure a nonequivalent formula is to give one that agrees for $x = 0, \pm 1, \pm 2$ (in Example 2) but disagrees for $x = 3$, say. Write at least two formulas nonequivalent to any of those given in Example 2, which disagree with each other and previous examples for $x = 3$.

6. Give at least two nonequivalent function formulas which are consistent for each of the following ordered pairs:

   (a) $\{(0,-2),(1,1),(2,4),(3,7),(4,10)\}$;

   (b) $\{(1,1),(2,8),(3,27),(4,64)\}$;

   (c) $\{(1,2),(2,6),(3,12),(4,20),(5,30)\}$;

   (d) $\{(2,1),(4,2),(6,3)\}$;

   (e) $\{(0,1),(1,1),(2,2),(3,6),(4,24)\}$;

   (f) $\{(1,0),(2,1),(3,1),(4,2),(5,2)\}$;

   (g) $\{(a,7a),(b,7b),(c,7c)\}$.

GRAPHS OF
RELATIONS

● ●

Objective 90. To graph given linear and quadratic relations, including inequalities and relations defined in terms of absolute value.

● ●

Basically, graphing a relation consists of tabulating corresponding elements of the domain and range, then plotting the domain elements along the x-axis and the range elements along the y-axis. Before looking at any

examples, let's review
graphing of points in the
xy-plane: (2,3) is plotted
by starting from the *origin* (intersection of *x*-
axis and *y*-axis) and going
over 2 to the right, up 3:

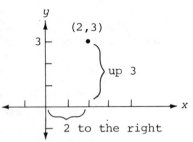

(-2,3) is located by going
over 2 to the *left*, up 3:

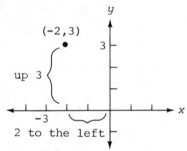

(-2,-3) is located by go-
ing over 2 to the left,
down 3:

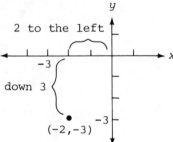

(2,-3) is located by go-
ing over 2 to the right,
down 3:

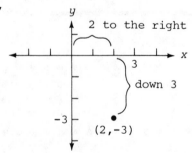

In general, (x,y) is plotted by going over x units
(to the right or left) and
up (or down) y units:

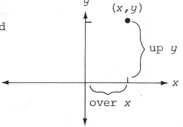

Let us now look at some examples of Objective 90.

Examples   1.   Graph $y = x^2$ (i.e., $\{(x,y): y = x^2\}$), where the domain
is all real numbers.
   The table at the right
uses only convenient ele-
ments of the domain, but
plotting these points will
give us a rough outline of
the relation. This rela-
tion is a function.

x	y
0	0
±1	1
±2	4
±3	9

2.   Graph $y^2 = x$, where x is any positive real number.
   The table at the right
demonstrates that this is
not a function, since the
domain elements, with the
exception of 0, are each
related to two range ele-
ments.

x	y
0	0
1	±1
4	±2

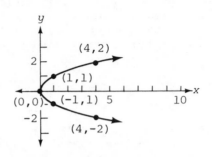

3. Graph $x^2 + y^2 = 4$ (i.e., $\{(x,y): x^2 + y^2 = 4\}$).

In order to tabulate corresponding values of x and y, let's first solve for y in terms of x:

$$y^2 = 4 - x^2$$
$$y = \pm\sqrt{4 - x^2}$$

Before filling in the table, we might comment on that algebraic solution for y. First of all, that $\pm$ in front of the square root sign ("radical") shows that our relation is not a function, because it assigns *two* values of y to a single value of x (except when $x^2 = 4$). Second, what shall we do about the complex numbers that result if $x^2 > 4$? The answer is that no graph is drawn for these values of x. Thus the domain for this relation is $\{x: x^2 \leq 4\}$. Finally, let's fill in the table and plot the graph:

x	$y = \pm\sqrt{4 - x^2}$
-2	0
-1	$\pm\sqrt{3} \doteq \pm 1.7$
0	± 2
1	$\pm\sqrt{3} \doteq \pm 1.7$
2	0

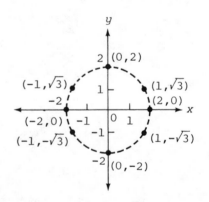

(The dotted curve—in this case a circle—represents all the points of the graph between the plotted points, which were chosen for computational convenience.)

4. Graph $x + 2y < 3$.

In investigating inequalities, it's often a good idea to look at more familiar equalities first. Accordingly, let's look at $x + 2y = 3$:

x	$y = \frac{1}{2}(3 - x)$
-2	$5/2 = 2\text{-}1/2$
-1	2
0	$3/2 = 1\text{-}1/2$
1	1
2	1/2
3	0

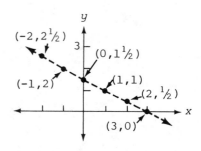

Next, the reasoning is that if this is the graph of $x + 2y = 3$, then one side of it is the graph of $x + 2y < 3$, and the other side is the graph of $x + 2y > 3$. Let's plot some more points, chosen again for computational convenience:

x	y	$x + 2y$
0	0	$0 < 3$
-1	1	$1 < 3$
-2	2	$2 < 3$
1	2	$5 > 3$
2	1	$4 > 3$

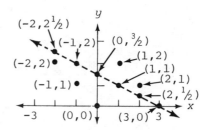

From this array of dots we conclude that the graph of the given relation is that portion of the xy-plane *below* the graph of $x + 2y = 3$:

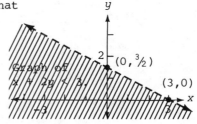

5.　Graph $2y = |3 - x|$.

　　Here the important thing to remember is that absolute value is always nonnegative; hence nothing will appear below the x-axis ($2y = |3 - x|$ is the same as the two equations $2y = 3 - x$ if $3 - x \geq 0$ and $2y = -(3 - x)$ if $3 - x < 0$, put together.)

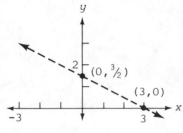

Graph of $2y = 3 - x$

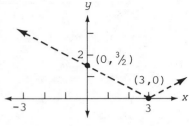

Graph of $2y = |3 - x|$

This last graph is a function, since there is one and only one value of y corresponding to each value of x.

6. Graph $|x + 2y| = 3$.

Recall that this absolute value equation breaks down into two more familiar equations: $x + 2y = 3$ where $x + 2y \geq 0$, and $x + 2y = -3$ where $x + 2y < 0$. We know all about the first already, so let's look at the second:

x	$y = \frac{1}{2}(-3 - x)$
-3	0
-2	$-1/2$
-1	-1
0	$-1\ 1/2$
1	-2
2	$-2\ 1/2$

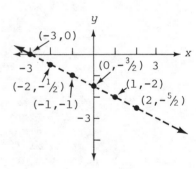

Thus the graph of $|x + 2y| = 3$ looks like

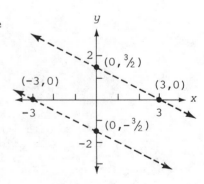

Exercises   Graph the relations determined by:

1. $x + 2y = 3$

2. $3x - 4y < 5$

3. $x = y^2 + 2$ (a *parabola*)

4. $x \geq y^2 + 2$

5. $x < y^2 + 2$

6. $x^2 - y^2 = 4$ (a *hyperbola*)

7. $y^2 - x^2 = 4$

8. $y^2 - x^2 \leq 4$

9. $|3x - 4y| = 5$

10. $|x| = y^2$

11. $|x^2 - y^2| = 4$

12. $|x - y| = 4$

13. $|x + y| = 4$

14. Can you look at a graph of a relation and determine if it is a function? Why?

GRAPHS OF
FUNCTIONS

● ●

Objective 91. To graph given polynomial functions and the absolute value of polynomial functions.

● ●

Many people tend to think linearly: If the cost of living previously went up 3% and a student got an increase in his allowance from 40¢ to 45¢, then when the cost of living goes up another 6% the allowance should go up to 55¢. If Swisher McTig scores 18 points in the first half of a basketball game, then he should score 36 points in the whole game. If J. Pompons Stickington wins 1,000,000 votes with a $500,000 campaign fund, then he would have won 1,500,000 votes with a $750,000 fund. If an increase of 1 in x results in an increase of 3 in y, then an increase of 4 in x should result in an increase of 12 in y. It turns out that most functions in life are *not* linear. However, many are, and linear functions are among the simplest functions, so we start with them.

Examples 1. $y = 3x - 2$ (also written $f(x) = 3x - 2$). Here, every time x increases by 1, y increases by 3. If you think about it, you'll probably realize that this means the graph of the function is a straight line (hence the

name "linear function"). We can check this out by
graphing a few points:

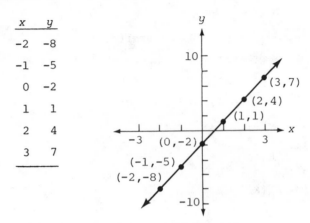

x	y
-2	-8
-1	-5
0	-2
1	1
2	4
3	7

2. $y = -2x + 4$. Once you realize that the graph of a function of the form $f(x) = mx + b$ (m and b constants) is a straight line, if you remember that two points determine a straight line you can save yourself some calculations:

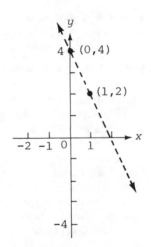

x	y
0	4
1	2

Exercises
1. Graph $f(x) = $: (a) $3x - 1$, (b) $3x$, (c) $3x + 1$, (d) $3x + 2$.

2. If $f(x) = mx + b$, what influence does b have on the graph of this function?

3. Graph $f(x) = $: (a) $2x - 1$, (b) $x - 1$, (c) -1, (d) $-x -1$, (e) $-2x - 1$, (f) $-3x - 1$.

4. If $f(x) = mx + b$, what influence does m have on the graph of this function?

5. Graph $f(x) = :$ (a) $|3x - 1|$, (b) $|-2x + 4|$,
    (c) $|3x| - 1$, (d) $|-2x| + 4$, (e) $-2|x| + 4$.

___

We now look at higher-order, nonlinear polynomial functions.

___

Examples 1. $y = 3x^2 - 2$
    Let's check a few values and see what happens here
    when we increase x one unit at a time:

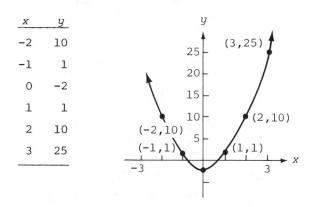

x	y
-2	10
-1	1
0	-2
1	1
2	10
3	25

Here the change in y varies, increasing as we move
further (in this case) from $x = 0$. The curve that is
generated is a *parabola*.

2. $y = -3x^2 + 2x + 4$

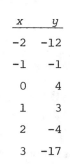

x	y
-2	-12
-1	-1
0	4
1	3
2	-4
3	-17

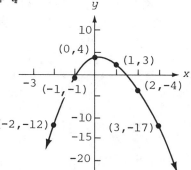

3. $y = \left| -3x^2 + 2x + 4 \right|$

x	y
-2	12
-1	1
0	4
1	3
2	4
3	17

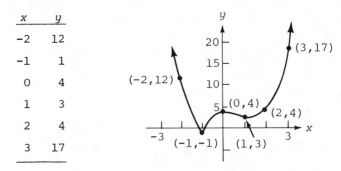

Exercises

1. Graph $f(x) = :$ (a) $-2x^2 + 2x + 4$,   (b) $-x^2 + 2x + 4$,
    (c) $2x + 4$,   (d) $x^2 + 2x + 4$,   (e) $2x^2 + 2x + 4$,
    (f) $3x^2 + 2x + 4$.

2. If $f(x) = ax^2 + bx + c$, what influence does a have on
    the graph of the function?

3. Graph $f(x) = :$ (a) $-3x^2 - 2x + 4$,   (b) $-3x^2 - x + 4$,
    (c) $-3x^2 + 4$,   (d) $-3x^2 + x + 4$,   (e) $-3x^2 + 3x + 4$.

4. If $f(x) = ax^2 + bx + c$, what influence does b have on
    the graph of this function?

5. Graph $f(x) = :$ (a) $-3x^2 - 2x + 3$,   (b) $-3x^2 - 2x + 2$,
    (c) $-3x^2 - 2x + 1$,   (d) $-3x^2 - 2x$,   (e) $-3x^2 - 2x - 1$.

6. If $f(x) = ax^2 + bx + c$, what influence does c have on
    the graph of this function?

7. If you slip your math professor \$10, what influence
    does that have on your grade?

8. Which of $3x^2$, $-2x$, or 1 is the most dominant term of
    $f(x) = 3x^2 - 2x + 1$, if (a) $x = 0$,   (b) $x = 1$,
    (c) $x = 10$,   (d) $x = 100$,   (e) $x = 1000$,   (f) $x = -1$,
    (g) $x = -10$,   (h) $x = -100$,   (i) $x = -1000$?

9. Graph $f(x) = :$ (a) $3x^2 - 2x + 1$,   (b) $-3x^2 - 2x + 1$,
    (c) $-3x^2 + 2x - 1$,   (d) $-3x^2 + 2x + 1$.

10. What is the difference between the graphs of $f(x) =$
    $3x^2 - 2x + 1$ and $f(x) = -3x^2 + 2x - 1$?

POLYNOMIAL
FUNCTIONS

Let us now pass from parabolas to graphs of general
polynomial functions

$$f(x) = a_n x^n + a_{n-1} x^{n-1} + a_{n-2} x^{n-2} + \cdot \cdot \cdot + a_1 x + a_0.$$

For largish values of x, the most dominant term is the one with the highest powers of x. Consider $f(x) = 4x^3 - 2x^2$: When $x = 1,000,000$, then $x^3 = 1,000,000, 000,000,000,000$, while x^2 is a relatively insignificant $1,000,000,000,000$ (only one-millionth of x^3); so overall $4x^3$ is the principal determiner of the shape of the graph.

Now we'll classify polynomials according to their highest terms. The notation $f(x) = (\text{pos})x^{(\text{even})} + \cdots +$ will stand for a polynomial whose *coefficient* of the highest power of x is *positive* and whose highest *exponent* is *even*. Thus an illustration of $f(x) = (\text{pos})x^{(\text{even})} + \cdots$ is $f(x) = 3x^4 - 2x^3 + x^2 + 3x - 5$. Similarly, an example of $f(x) = (\text{neg})x^{(\text{even})} + \cdots$ is $f(x) = -3x^2 + 2x - 1$; an example of $f(x) = (\text{neg})x^{(\text{odd})} + \cdots$ is $f(x) = -3x^5 + 4x^3 + 2x - 1$; and an illustration of $f(x) = (\text{pos})x^{(\text{odd})} + \cdots$ is $f(x) = 3x^3 + 2$.

Let's look at $f(x) = (\text{pos})x^{(\text{even})} + \cdots$. When x is large in absolute value (say, ± 1000), then $x^{(\text{even})}$ is positive (e.g., $(\pm 10,000)^2$ is positive) and $(\text{pos})x^{(\text{even})}$ is still positive. Thus the graph of $(\text{pos})x^{(\text{even})} + \cdots$ looks like a W:

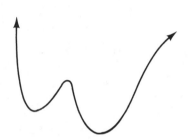

where the precise number and nature of the wiggles in the middle depends on the particular values of n, a_n, a_{n-1}, etc.

Reasoning similarly, the graph of $(\text{neg})x^{(\text{even})} + \cdots$ looks like an M:

The graph of $(\text{neg})x^{(\text{odd})} + \cdots$ looks like an S:

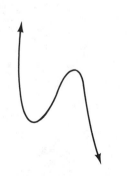

And the graph of (pos) $x^{(odd)} + \cdots$ looks like an N:

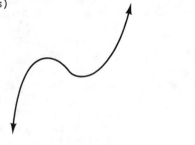

Consider $y = -3x^5 + 25x^3 - 60x + 38$

First, we recognize this as a (neg) $x^{(odd)} + \cdots$ case. Hence we know the graph will look basically like an S, give or take some wrinkles in the middle.

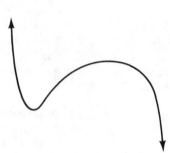

So we tabulate and plot points until a shape of this sort emerges:

x	y
-3	272
-2	54
-1	76
0	38
1	0
2	22
3	-196

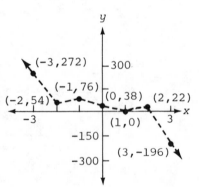

Exercises
1. Convince yourself of the W, M, S, N classification system by graphing the following polynomials.

(a) $-2x$ and $2x$,

(b) $-3x^2 + 6x$ and $3x^2 - 6x$,

(c) $-x^3 + 3x$ and $x^3 - 3x$,

(d) $-x^4 + 8x^2$ and $x^4 - 8x^2$,

(e) $-x^5 + 5x^3 - 10x$ and $x^5 - 5x^3 + 10x$.

2. Classify each of the following according to its graph as W, M, S, or N: (a) $-3x^3 + 2x$, (b) $4x^4 + 6x^2 - 10$,

(c) $-4x^2 + 6x - 2$,   (d) $4x^5 - 2x^3 + 3x - 5$,   (e) x^3,
(f) $-x^4$,   (g) $-x^5$,   (h) x^6.

3. Graph $f(x)$ = :   (a) $-2x^3 + 8x$,   (b) $-2x^4 + 8x$,
(c) $2x^4 + 8x$,   (d) $2x^3 + 8x$.

4. Graph the absolute value of the functions in
Exercise 1.

GREATEST
INTEGER
FUNCTION

● ●

*Objective 92.   To graph given greatest integer functions and the abso-
lute value of greatest integer functions.

● ●

Every time we use postage for mailing we are using an
"almost linear" function. Thus to mail a 4-oz letter
costs about twice as much as a 2-oz letter, a 6-oz letter about three times as much as a 2-oz letter, etc.
The nonlinear complication comes in when we mail a
letter that weighs, say, somewhere *between* 2 oz and
3 oz.

"Postage stamp" or step functions are all variants
of the *greatest integer function* $f(x) = [x]$.

Definition   *It x is any real number, then the <u>greatest integer</u> [x]
<u>of</u> x is defined to be the greatest lower bound of the
set $\{n: n \leq x, n \text{ an integer}\}$.*

So $[x]$ is the first integer to the left of x on the
number line, or the largest integer less than x. Be
careful when encountering negative x: -3 is the first
integer to the left of $-2\ 1/2$, so $[-2\ 1/2] = -3$.

Examples

1. $\left[3\frac{1}{2}\right] = \left[3\frac{1}{10}\right] = \left[3\frac{7}{8}\right] = \left[3\frac{99}{100}\right] = [3] = [\pi] = 3$

$\left[-2\frac{1}{2}\right] = \left[-2\frac{1}{10}\right] = \left[-2\frac{9}{10}\right] = [-3] = -3.$

On the number line:

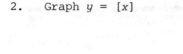

all have −3	all have 3
as the greatest	as the greatest
integer.	integer.

2. Graph $y = [x]$

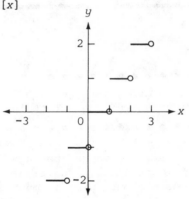

(Note: hollow dot means the point is not included in the graph.)

3. Graph $y = [3x - 2]$

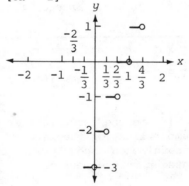

Exercise Graph $f(x) = :$ (a) $[2x]$, (b) $[-2x]$, (c) $[x + 2]$,
(d) $[x - 2]$, (e) $[1/2x]$, (f) $[2x - 1]$,
(g) $[1/2x - 1]$, (h) $[x + 2/3]$, (i) $[|x|]$,
(j) $[2|x| - 1]$, (k) $|[1/2x - 2/3]|$.

HINTS ON THE THREE 3s PROBLEM	The greatest integer function, together with factorials, square roots, and other less esoteric operations, gives us lots of ammunition in attacking the three 3s and related problems.

● ●

*Objective 93.	To express a given set of integers in terms of exactly a given number of a certain numeral and using no other numerals.

● ●

Let's try to express 10 using exactly three 3s and no other numerals (3^0, for example, not allowed).

3! = 6 gets us pretty close.

3 + 3! = 3 + 6 = 9 gets us even closer.

So, we have 3 + 3! = 9.

Challenge	Try to get that 1 with a single 3 without peeking ahead.

How about this?

$3 + 3! + [\sqrt{3}] = 3 + 3! + [1.7321] = 3 + 3! + 1 = 10.$

Exercises	1.	Solve the three 3s problem.
	2.	Solve the four 4s problem: Express each integer from 0 through 44 in terms of exactly four 4s.
	3.	Solve the two 2s problem; 0 through 22.
	4.	Express the integers 0 through 15 in terms of exactly (a) two 3s, (b) three 2s, (c) two 3s and a 4.
	5.	Explain why for a suitable number of $\sqrt{}$ signs $\left[\sqrt{\cdot \cdot \cdot \sqrt{n}}\right] = 1$ for any positive integer n.
	6.	Explain the value of a goal like Objective 93.

SUMMARY OF OBJECTIVES	85.	To define *relation*, *domain*, *range*, and *function* (page 240).
	86.	Given a situation, to cite a pertinent function, stating its domain, range, and rule (page 245).
	87.	Given a function on a finite domain, to express it as a set of ordered pairs (page 247).

88. Given several sets of ordered pairs, to state which are functions (page 247).

*89. Given a function represented by three or more ordered pairs, to give at least two nonequivalent function formulas which are consistent with the ordered pairs (page 250).

90. To graph given linear and quadratic relations, including inequalities and relations defined in terms of absolute value (page 251).

91. To graph given polynomial functions and the absolute value of polynomial functions (page 257).

*92. To graph given greatest integer functions and the absolute value of greatest integer functions (page 263).

*93. To express a given set of integers in terms of exactly a given number of a certain numeral and using no other numerals (page 265).

WORDS TO KNOW

domain (page 240)
range (page 240)
relation (page 240)
relation rule (page 240)
function (page 241)
image (page 241)
function rule (page 242)
inverse function (page 249)
one-to-one relation (page 249)
onto relation (page 249)
linear relation (page 251)

quadratic relation (page 251)
hyperbola (page 257)
linear function (page 258)
parbola (page 259)
polynomial function (page 259)
greatest integer function (page 263)
postage stamp function (page 263)
step function (page 263)

CHAPTER 8

STATISTICS AND PROBABILITY

Thirty ecstatic piglets were playing musical chairs around Ziggy's birthday cake, with a jumbo-size piece of cake as the prize. When the lucky winner had consumed the last crumb of his cake, they got to comparing birth dates (same day and month, although not necessarily same year). What is the probability that at least two of the pigs had the same birth dates?

Challenges 1. Check the birth dates of a set of thirty people and see if any two have the same birthdate.

2. Check another set of thirty people.

3. Check a set of twenty people.

4. Check a set of forty people.

5. Check the set of US presidents.

6. Guess the probability that at least two of a set of thirty people have the same birth date.

7. Try to compute the probability that at least two of a set of thirty people have the same birth date. (You're not expected to get this—yet.)

In the Birth Date Problem we assume that we know all about the total population of pigs and try to deduce the probability of a certain event in a small sample of this population. This is, to our complete nonsurprise, a *probability* problem. If we change our assumption, and suppose that we know all about a sample and from that try to induce a property of the whole population, we are involved in a *statistics* problem. This chapter provides a brief introduction to the study of these two types of problems.

DESCRIPTIVE
STATISTICS
Statisticians divide their subject into two domains; *descriptive* and *inferential* statistics. Descriptive statistics deals with collection, organization, and presentation of data, while inferential statistics deals with the (sometimes sophisticated) inference of properties of a total population from a study of a sample subset of that population. Statistical experience in elementary schools is limited pretty much to descriptive statistics, so we'll begin by attacking an objective that deals with organization and presentation of data.

● ●

Objective 94. Given a set of scores, to construct (a) an ungrouped
frequency distribution, (b) a grouped frequency distribution, (c) a histogram of (b), (d) a frequency
polygon of (b).

● ●

Let us work an example and point out the value of the
objective as we move along.

Examples   1.   Consider the following set of scholastic ineptitude
test scores. (The SIT scores are used to get to the
bottom of student troubles. They are also used occa-
sionally to assess aptitude for chairmanship.)

77, 51, 30, 38, 20, 86, 86, 42, 99, 1, 68, 41, 48,
27, 74, 51, 90, 81, 39, 80, 72, 89, 35, 55, 7, 19,
50, 23, 71, 74, 69, 97, 92, 2, 88, 55, 21, 2, 97, 73.

Now, after having looked at these scores, cover them
up with a card or your hand. (A pause here, while you
cover them.) Now, without peeking, can you say what the
range of the scores is? (I.e., what was the highest
and what was the lowest?) What score is nearest to the
average? What score appeared most often? What score
was in the middle, with as many scores above it as below it? Were the scores mostly low, or mostly high, or
mostly in the middle? Unless you have an unusual mem-
ory, or you cheated and peeked, you probably could not
answer these questions very accurately. Thus the
scores did not communicate much information to you.
Let's go on to see if Objective 94 helps improve the
communication.

First, let's construct an *ungrouped frequency distribution* (sometimes called a "tally sheet.") Here we
list all cardinal numbers from the lowest on the list
to the highest and make a dot, dash, or other mark next
to each number as it occurs in the list of scores; a
score that occurs more than once will have more than
one mark next to it.

99*	86**	73*
98	85	72*
97**	84	71*
96	83	70
95	82	69*
94	81*	68*
93	80*	67
92*	79	66
91	78	65
90*	77*	64
89*	76	63
88*	75	62
87	74**	61

60	40	20*
59	39*	19*
58	38*	18
57	37	17
56	36	16
55**	35*	15
54	34	14
53	33	13
52	32	12
51**	31	11
50*	30*	10
49	29	9
48*	28	8
47	27*	7*
46	26	6
45	25	5
44	24	4
43	23*	3
42*	22	2**
41*	21*	1*

Ungrouped frequency distribution of SIT scores

Now we can tell at a glance that 99 is the top score, 1 is the bottom score, that several scores occurred twice (97, 86, 74, 55, 51, 2), that some score in the low 70s or high 60s was in the middle, and that most scores were toward the high end. Thus the organization of the data has improved communication.

The preceding frequency distribution could just as well have been laid out horizontally instead of vertically, so that the dots were strung out above numbers 1 through 99 listed on the x- axis. This would have looked like:

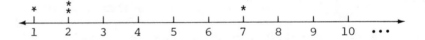

The trouble here is that without a very wide piece of paper it's difficult to squeeze all the data into a tidy space. This difficulty can easily be overcome by using a *grouped* frequency distribution. We choose a congenial sort of interval length, say 10, and group the scores according to these intervals. (There is nothing magic about 10; we could just as well have chosen 5 or 7 or 15 or whatever suited our fancy.) We take the first interval to be 1 to 10, the next from 11 to 20, then 21 to 30, until we end up with 91 to 100. The resulting grouped frequency distribution improves communication, since it is easier to take it in at a single glance. Of course, we lose something, too: We no longer know precisely what the original scores were. Nevertheless, our new frequency distribution probably conveys a more meaningful summary of the situation, and certainly a more concise and digestable one.

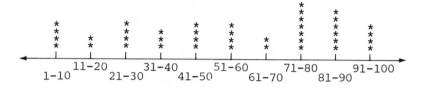

Grouped frequency distribution

A histogram (alias "bar graph") of the grouped SIT scores is drawn as shown in the following steps. The result is a more graphic representation of the grouped frequency distribution.

Step 1. We start with a number line marked in multiples of 10 to establish intervals.

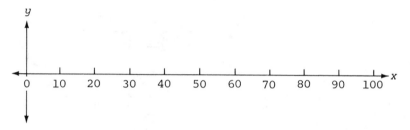

Step 2. (These intervals are from .5 to 10.5, 10.5 to 20.5, 20.5 to 30.5, etc., so that we won't have to go into any big fret in deciding which intervals 10, 20, 30, etc. belong to.

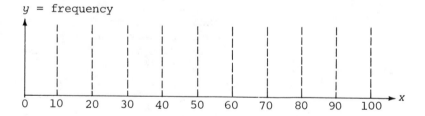

Step 3. Next draw horizontal lines across these intervals corresponding to the number of scores falling within the interval (forming a rectangle).

y = frequency

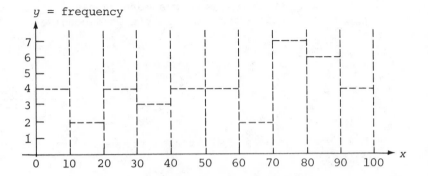

Step 4. Finally, join the horizontal and vertical
lines as shown.

y = frequency rectangle

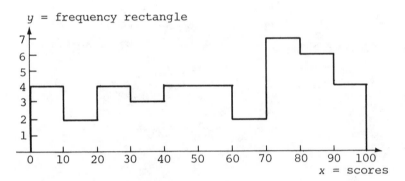

Histogram of SIT scores

If we want a *frequency polygon* of the SIT scores,
grouped into these same intervals, we construct it as
follows, going back to Step 3 of the histogram.

Step 3. Place dots at the midpoints of the tops of
the bars. Add two extra intervals, one at
each end, representing empty intervals, with
dots at their midpoints. Now join the midpoint dots with straight lines, forming a
frequency polygon.

y = frequency

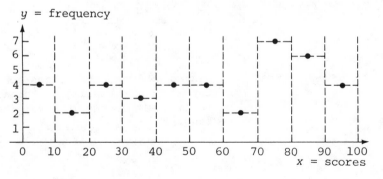

Step 4.

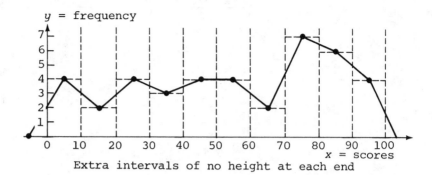

y = frequency

Extra intervals of no height at each end

Step 5.

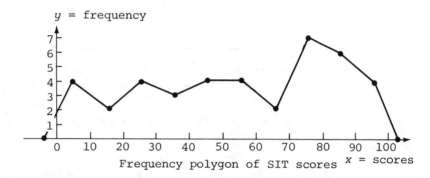

y = frequency

Frequency polygon of SIT scores   x = scores

2.   (Rated X—shocking and explicit!) Let your mind dwell
      on the following set of monthly electricity bills:
      $19.86, $22.43, $31.13, $38.60, $45.05, $44.69, $43.52,
      $27.20, $22.32, $20.38, $19.00, $17.96, $17.08, $31,62,
      $29.62, $31.77, $45.49, $50.22, $43.83, $36.51, $24.82,
      $14.45, $21.30, $43.88, $40.18.

      (a) Ungrouped frequency distribution (to the nearest
          dollar):

$50*	$37*	$25*
49	36	24
48	35	23
47	34	22**
46	33	21*
45***	32**	20**
44***	31*	19*
43	30*	18*
42	29	17*
41	28	16
40*	27*	15
39*	26	14*
38		

Alternative form (more common, but less graphic):

Amount	Frequency		Amount	Frequency
$50	1		$31	1
49			30	1
48			29	
47			28	
46			27	1
45	3		26	
44	3		25	1
43			24	
42			23	
41			22	2
40	1		21	1
39	1		20	2
38			19	1
37	1		18	1
36			17	1
35			16	
34			15	
33			14	1

(It's understood that a blank in the "Frequency" column opposite an amount means that the amount did not occur.)

(b) Grouped frequency distribution (to the nearest dollar):

Amount Interval	Frequency	or	Amount Interval	Frequency
$46-$50	1		$46-$50	1
$41-$45	~~TTTT~~ 1		$41-$45	6
$36-$40	111		$36-$40	3
$31-$35	111		$31-$35	3
$26-$30	11		$26-$30	2
$21-$25	1111		$21-$25	4
$16-$20	~~TTTT~~		$16-$20	5
$11-$15	1		$11-$15	1

(c) Histogram [of grouped frequency distribution in (b)]:

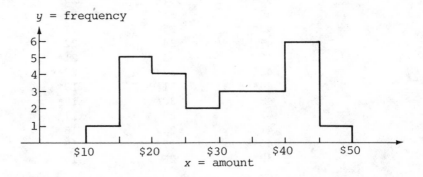

(d) Frequency polygon [of distribution in (b)]:

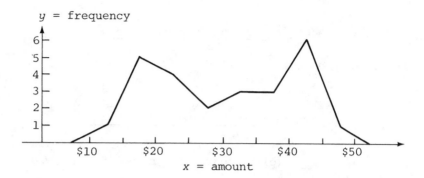

We might reflect upon this last polygon and ask what information it communicates to us. As before, we quickly note that the electric bills range between $10 and $50. We also see (considering the area enclosed by the polygon and the number line) that about as many bills are above $30 as are below it. We also discern two humps, one at around $20, the other around $40. This we shrewdly analyze to mean that a lot of warm-weather bills are about $20 and a lot of cold-weather bills are about $40.

3. Heights in inches of students enrolled in a course in mathematics for elementary teachers: 62, 65, 66, 72, 65, 63, 62, 62, 71, 68, 69, 62, 60, 59, 63, 64, 61, 68, 60, 70, 72, 75, 62, 61, 60, 65, 64, 63, 70, 61, 62, 71, 64, 62, 66, 63, 68.

(a) Ungrouped frequency distribution

Height	Frequency
75	1
74	
73	
72	2
71	2
70	2
69	1
68	3
67	
66	2
65	3
64	3
63	4
62	7
61	3
60	3
59	1

(b) Grouped frequency distribution (three-inch intervals)

Height Interval	Frequency
73-75	1
70-72	6
67-69	4
64-66	8
61-63	14
58-60	4

(c) Histogram of grouped frequency distribution

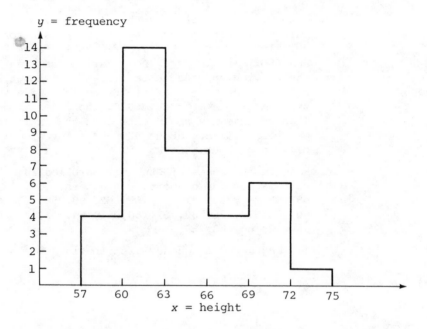

(d) Frequency polygon of grouped distribution

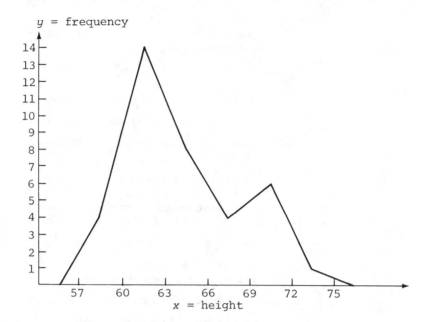

In this frequency polygon we again notice two peaks. On reflection, this is as it should be, one peak (the higher one) probably for the most frequent female height, the other peak for the most frequent male height. As usual in such courses, the female forces outnumber those of the male.

Exercises   1. Preachers entered in the most recent sermon handicap scored as follows (in minutes) last Sunday: 36, 29, 37, 38, 41, 35, 35, 26, 31, 26, 36, 10 (sermon called off early due to a fit of hiccups), 30, 38, 20, 45, 45, 42, 17, 27.

(a) Construct an ungrouped frequency distribution of these sermon lengths (i) using dots, (ii) using numerals only.

(b) Construct a grouped frequency distribution using five-minute intervals starting with 6-10 (i) using dots, (ii) using numerals only.

(c) Construct a histogram of the distribution in (b).

(d) Construct a frequency polygon of the distribution in (b).

2. Twenty mathematics education professors registered the following numbers of gripes in reaction to the first draft of this textbook: 31, 75, 15, 72, 60, 68, 98,

53, 39, 15, 47, 4 (he gets several complimentary copies!), 83, 55, 88, 65, 12, 25, 96, 31.

(a) Construct an ungrouped frequency distribution of these scores (i) using dots or hash marks, (ii) using numerals only.

(b) Construct a grouped frequency distribution with the first interval 0-9 (i) using dots or hash marks, (ii) using numerals only.

(c) Construct a histogram of the distribution in (b).

(d) Construct a frequency polygon of the distribution in (b).

3. On his last 15 outings with the paste pot, little Teddy the kindergartner spilled the following amounts of paste (measured in tablespoonfuls) on the floor: 2, 3, 1, 5, 3, 2, 4, 2, 3, 2, 1, 7, 5, 2, 4.

(a) Construct an ungrouped frequency distribution.

(b) Construct a grouped frequency distribution with 0-1 as the first interval.

(c) Construct a histogram of the distribution in (b).

(d) Construct a frequency polygon of the distribution in (b).

4. How does the area of a histogram of a grouped frequency distribution compare with the area of a frequency polygon for the same distribution?

5. Why is or is not a histogram a graph of a function?

6. Why is or is not a frequency polygon a graph of a function?

7. "Frequency polygon" is the reply to what question? (Answer: "Where is the parrot who wants to let Quincy out of jail?")

MEAN, MODE,
MEDIAN,
STANDARD
DEVIATION

Frequency distributions, histograms, and frequency polygons all have the drawback that, like movie stars, they require a lot of space on the printed page. They also are open to some visual interpretation that may vary from individual to individual. By resorting to more concise and precise numbers we can dodge some of these drawbacks.

● ●

Objective 95.   Given a set of scores, to compute to the nearest hundredth the mean, mode, median, and standard deviation.

● ●

Let's look at an example in which we'll define these terms as well as compute them.

Examples   1.   For this purpose we'll take a small set of small numbers, so that we can concentrate on statistical concepts rather than arithmetic manipulation: 1, 3, 5, 4, 3. The *mean* (alias "average") of a set of scores is merely the number obtained by adding the scores in that set and dividing the sum by the cardinality of the set. So here the mean Mn is given by:

$$Mn = \frac{1 + 3 + 5 + 4 + 3}{5} = \frac{16}{5} = 3.20.$$

The *mode* Mo of a set of scores is the score that occurs most frequently (i.e., the score on the x-axis beneath the highest peak of a histogram or frequency polygon). In our example, 3 occurs twice, while 1, 4, and 5 occur only once, so

Mo = 3.00.

The *median* Md of a set of scores is the score which has as many scores below it as above it, or geometrically, the score which divides the area of the histogram into two equal areas. If we had had 1, 2, 3, 4, 5 as our original set of scores, the median would have been 3, which has two scores (1 and 2) below it and two (4 and 5) above it. Unfortunately our set of scores is such that no whole number can be the median. What we do, then, is take our chunk of 3s and cut it up so that some of it is on one side of the decimal fractional median with the 1 and the rest is on the other side with the 4 and 5. This will be achieved if we put one of the 3s in with the 1 and divide the other 3 into halves to be distributed on the lower and upper sides evenly. Thus we want three-fourths of the 3s associated with the lower end of the scores and one-fourth associated with the upper end.

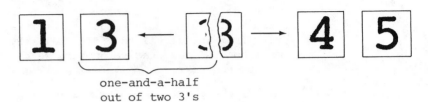

one-and-a-half
out of two 3's

Hence, since 3 begins at $2\frac{1}{2}$ and ends at $3\frac{1}{2}$, roundoff-wise, we move three-quarters of the way from $2\frac{1}{2}$ to $3\frac{1}{2}$:

$$Md = 2\frac{1}{2} + \frac{3}{4} = 3\frac{1}{4} = 3.25.$$

Let's look at the mean, mode, and median on a histogram of this distribution:

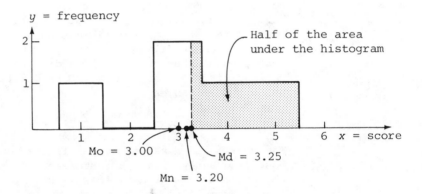

2.   Let's try that median bit again with another set of numbers, say 1, 2, 4, 4, 5, 8, 9. Again, there is no cardinal number that has as many numbers below it as above it, so we put one 4 with the numbers 1 and 2, grouping the 5, 8, and 9 above. The second 4 we divide and give half to the upper set and half to the lower set. So the median is 3 1/2 + 3/4 = 14/4 + 3/4 = 17/4 = 4.25. We will see more medians later, so even if this process seems unclear now, keep reading and light will come.

    Median, mode, and mean are "measures of central tendency"—that is, they tell us where, in one sense or another, most of the scores are. Standard deviation, on the other hand, tells us how spread out the scores are. The (sample) *standard deviation S* is the square root of the average square of the differences between the scores and the mean. Of course, this means nothing to you, as is usually the case when mathematical formulas are described in words. Here, then, is the standard deviation for this example:

$$S = \sqrt{\frac{(1-3.20)^2+(3-3.20)^2+(5-3.20)^2+(4-3.20)^2+(3-3.20)^2}{5}}$$

$$= \sqrt{\frac{(-2.20)^2 + (-.20)^2 + (1.80)^2 + (.80)^2 + (-.20)^2}{5}}$$

$$= \sqrt{\frac{4.8400 + .0400 + 3.2400 + .6400 + .0400}{5}}$$

$$= \sqrt{\frac{8.8000}{5}} = \sqrt{1.7600} \doteq 1.33. \quad (\text{"}\doteq\text{" means "approximately equal")}$$

The general formula for standard deviation is

$$S = \sqrt{\frac{(x_1-Mn)^2 + (x_2-Mn)^2 + (x_3-Mn)^2 + \cdots + (x_N-Mn)^2}{N}}$$

where $\{x_1, x_2, x_3, \ldots, x_N\}$ is the given set of N scores.

The meaning of this standard deviation will become clear as we see more examples.

3. Professor Dr. Hippopippo has a fit every time his students are, to his mind, insufficiently reverent (as when they smack him heartily on the back and yell, "What ho, Hip, old pip!"). In direct reaction to such irreverences Prof. Dr. H. had the following numbers of fits per day over the last seven days: 3, 6, 2, 5, 4, 2, 5. Let us (sympathetically) apply the apparatus of Objective 95.

$$Mn = \frac{3 + 6 + 2 + 5 + 4 + 2 + 5}{7} = \frac{27}{7} \doteq 3.86.$$

The modes Mo_1 and Mo_2 are 2.00 and 5.00. (Thus we have a "bimodal" distribution. Multimodal distributions are perfectly okay.)

If we arrange these daily fit figures in ascending order, 2, 2, 3, 4, 5, 5, 6, we see that 4 is in the middle position. Hence the median Md is 4.00.

The standard deviation $S =$

$$\sqrt{\frac{(3-3.86)^2+(6-3.86)^2+(2-3.86)^2+(5-3.86)^2+(4-3.86)^2+(2-3.86)^2+(5-3.86)^2}{7}}$$

$$= \sqrt{\frac{(-.86)^2 + (2.14)^2 + (-1.86)^2 + (1.14)^2 + (.14)^2 + (-1.86)^2 + (1.14)^2}{7}}$$

$$= \sqrt{\frac{.7396 + 4.5796 + 3.4596 + 1.2996 + .0196 + 3.4596 + 1.2996}{7}}$$

$$= \sqrt{\frac{14.8572}{7}} \doteq \sqrt{\frac{2.1225}{1}} = 1.46$$

4. During each week of last summer session, Elton McTig found that his dormitory pals had deposited toads in his bedclothes. The weekly toad totals were as follows: 1, 3, 10 (counting adolescent tadpoles), 4, 3. Let's hop to the computation of the Objective 95 statistics: $Mn = (1 + 3 + 10 + 4 + 3)/5 = 21/5 = 4.20$; $Mo = 3.00$; $Md = 3.25$. (Rearranged, the numbers are 1, 3, 3, 4, 10. So we divide the 3 as in Example 1.) The standard deviation $S =$

$$\sqrt{\frac{(1-4.20)^2+(3-4.20)^2+(10-4.20)^2+(4-4.20)^2+(3-4.20)^2}{5}}$$

$$=\sqrt{\frac{(-3.20)^2 + (-1.20)^2 + (5.80)^2 + (-.20)^2 + (-1.20)^2}{5}}$$

$$=\sqrt{\frac{10.2400 + 1.4400 + 33.6400 + .0400 + 1.4400}{5}}$$

$$=\sqrt{\frac{46.8000}{5}} = \sqrt{9.3600} \doteq 3.06.$$

The standard deviations in Examples 1 and 4 were computed from scores of 1, 3, 5, 4, 3 and 1, 3, 10, 4, 3, respectively. Notice that by replacing 5 with 10 we spread the scores out more. This spreading is reflected by the standard deviation changing from the original 1.33 to 3.06. Thus the higher the standard deviation, the more spread in the scores (and vice versa).

5. We look at more modes:

    (a) The mode of $\{2,3,1,5,1,3,5,1,4,2\}$ is 1; 2, 3, and 5 are not modes because they do not occur as often as 1.

    (b) The modes of $\{2,3,1,5,1,3,5,1,4,2,2,5\}$ are 1, 2, and 5, each of which occurs three times.

6. We ogle more medians:

    (a) The median of $\{1,1,1,2,2,3,3,4,5,5\}$ is 2.50, which is midway between 2 (the highest number in $\{1,1,1, 2,2\}$) and 3 (the lowest number in $\{3,3,4,5,5\}$. Notice that since we have an even number of elements in the set, they regroup into two sets easily, making the median obvious.

    (b) The median of $\{1,1,1,2,2,3,4,4,5,5,6\}$ is 3, the middle score. Here we have an odd number of elements with an obvious middle element.

    (c) The median of $\{-1000,1,1,2,2,3,4,4,5,5,700\}$ is also 3.

(d) The median of $\{1,1,1,2,2,2,3,3,4,5,5\}$ is figured as
follows:

   (i) Without using any of the 2s, line up the
       left- and right-hand sides:

       1, 1, 1   3, 3, 4, 5, 5

  (ii) Balance the left-hand side by putting in two
       of the 2s:

       1, 1, 1, 2, 2   3, 3, 4, 5, 5

 (iii) Split the remaining 2 between the two sides:

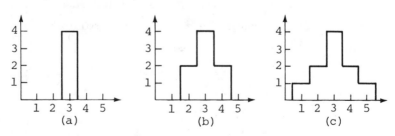

1, 1, 1, 2, 2,————→ 3, 3, 4, 5, 5

two-and-a-half
out of three 2's

So we have 6/2 2s, of which $2\frac{1}{2}$ of them go
with the lower set.
So the median is $2\frac{1}{2}/3 = 5/6$ of the way from
$1\frac{1}{2}$ to $2\frac{1}{2}$:

$$Md = 1\frac{1}{2} + \frac{5}{6} = 2\frac{1}{3} = 2.33 \ .$$

(e) The median of $\{1,1,1,2,3,3,3,3,4,5,5\}$:

   (i) 1, 1, 1, 2   4, 5, 5
  (ii) 1, 1, 1, 2, 3   3, 3, 4, 5, 5
 (iii) 1, 1, 1, 2, 3 ←————→ 3, 3, 4, 5, 5

So here the median is $1\frac{1}{2}/4 = 3/8$ of the way
from $2\frac{1}{2}$ to $3\frac{1}{2}$:

$$Md = 2\frac{1}{2} + \frac{3}{8} = 2\frac{7}{8} = 2.88 \ .$$

7. Let us look at the standard deviations of distributions
   with the following histograms:

Notice that because of symmetry the means, modes, and medians all coincide (and equal 3) in these distributions, but the distributions spread as we go from (a) to (c). Let's follow the concomitant drama of the standard deviation:

(a) The scores here are 3,3,3,3. Thus, the standard deviation is

$$S = \sqrt{\frac{(3-3)^2 + (3-3)^2 + (3-3)^2 + (3-3)^2}{4}} = .00.$$

(b) The scores are 2,2,3,3,3,3,4,4.

$$S = \sqrt{\frac{(2-3)^2+(2-3)^2+(3-3)^2+(3-3)^2+(3-3)^2+(3-3)^2+(4-3)^2+(4-3)^2}{8}}$$

$$= \sqrt{\frac{1 + 1 + 1 + 1}{8}} = \sqrt{.5000} \doteq .71.$$

(c) The scores are 1,2,2,3,3,3,3,4,4,5.

$$S = \sqrt{\frac{(1-3)^2+(2-3)^2+(2-3)^2+(4-3)^2+(4-3)^2+(5-3)^2}{10}}$$

$$= \sqrt{\frac{4 + 1 + 1 + 1 + 1 + 4}{10}} = \sqrt{1.20} \doteq 1.10.$$

Exercises

1. Compute to the nearest hundredth the means of the following sets of scores:

   (a) 2, 5, 3;

   (b) 2, 5, 8 (what's the message here?);

   (c) 2, 5, 3, 4, 2;

   (d) 2, 5, 8, 11, 14 (what's the message here?);

   (e) 2, 5, 8, 3, 22;

   (f) 12, 15, 18, 13, 32 (what's the message here?)

   (g) 14, 17, 20, 15, 34 (message?);

   (h) 28, 34, 40, 30, 68 (message?).

2. Compute the modes of the following sets of scores:

   (a) 2, 2, 5, 3;

   (b) 2, 2, 5, 3, 3;

   (c) 2, 2, 5, 5, 3, 3;

   (d) 2, 5, 3;

   (e) 2, 2, 5, 3, 3, 4, 1, 4, 4,

   (f) 2, 2, 5, 3, 2, 3, 4, 1, 4, 4.

3. Compute to the nearest hundredth the medians of the following sets of scores:

(a) 2, 5, 3, 2, 6;

(b) 0, 5, 3, 2, 20 (what's the message?);

(c) 2, 5, 3, 2, 6, 5;

(d) 12, 9, 6, 10, 15, 2, 0, 6;

(e) 12, 9, 9, 10, 15, 2, 0, 6;

(f) 12, 9, 9, 10, 9, 15, 2, 0, 6;

(g) 1, 2, 3, 4, 4, 5, 6;

(h) 1, 2, 3, 4, 4, 4, 5, 6;

(i) 1, 2, 3, 4, 4, 4, 4, 5, 6;

(j) 1, 2, 3, 4, 4, 4, 4, 4, 5, 6;

(k) 1, 2, 3, $\underbrace{4, 4, \ldots, 4}_{n\ 4s}$, 5, 6.

4. Draw histograms and compute the standard deviations of each of the following sets of scores:

(a) 1,2,3,4,4,5,5,6,6,6,7,7,8,8,9,10,11;

(b) 2,2,2,3,3,4,4,5,6,7,8,8,9,9,10,10,10;

(c) 1,1,2,2,3,4,8,9,10,10,11,11;

(d) 5,6,6,6,6,7;

(e) 0,0,1,1,1,2,2,2,3,18,20,22;

(f) 0,0,1,1,2,2,3,15,17,19;

(g) 0,0,1,2,3,12,14,16;

(h) 10,10,11,12,13,22,24,26. What's the message in (g) and (h)?

5. For algebra enthusiasts. By definition,

$$S = \sqrt{\frac{(x_1 - Mn)^2 + (x_2 - Mn)^2 + \cdots + (x_N - Mn)^2}{N}}.$$

Another, more easily calculable formula is

$$S = \sqrt{\frac{x_1^2 + x_2^2 + \cdots + x_N^2}{N}}.$$

(a) Verify that both of these formulas give the same answer for $x_1 = 1$, $x_2 = 3$, $x_3 = 5$, $N = 3$.

(b) Prove that these two formulas give the same answer for $N = 3$; $x_1 = a$, $x_2 = b$, $x_3 = c$.

(c) Prove that these two formulas give the same answer for any N.

6. Sometimes the Greek letter μ (mu, pronounced "mew") is used to denote the mean, especially when the set of scores under discussion represents an entire population. Why is such a set of scores like a fierce cat? (Answer: they both have a mean μ.)

STATISTICAL   So far we have dealt with computation of statistics.
INTERPRETATION   Let's turn now to interpretation of statistics.

● ●

Objective 96.   Given the means and standard deviations of two sets of scores, (a) to explain which set of scores represents a more predictable situation and why, (b) to draw a mathematically reasonable inference about each of the two situations.

● ●

Examples   1. Iggy McTig perspires nervously at the thought of flunking a required psychology course. He therefore chooses carefully between the two sections of the course that are offered, seeking that section in which he is less likely to receive an extremely low grade. From previous final exams, Iggy has determined that the mean in Professor Lowe's classes is 36.72 (out of 100 possible points) with a standard deviation of 2.06, while the mean in Professor Hye's classes is 63.0 (again out of 100), with a standard deviation of 12.30. In which section should Iggy enroll?

If you don't know how to advise Iggy in this situation, what would you suggest if the standard deviation in Prof. Lowe's class were 0.00? This would mean that every student in the class received 36.72 on the final exam. Since it's unlikely that Prof. Lowe would give either all As or all Fs, you'd probably guess that he'd give all Cs and thus recommend his section to Iggy. Now $2.06 \neq 0.00$, but 2.06 is closer to 0.00 than 12.30 is. Therefore in the present situation Iggy should enroll in Lowe's section in order to receive an unlow grade.

2. In the situation in Example 1, because of the difference in standard deviations, i.e., in the "spreads," we might reasonably infer that there are relatively few As and Fs in Lowe's section, a lot more in Hye's section.

3. The mean IQ in Mrs. Mean's fifth grade class is 102.34, and the standard deviation is 20.16. The mean IQ in Mrs. Nice's fifth grade class is 101.58 and the

standard deviation is 12.07. If we grab a kid at random from each class and the size of the classes is the same, which of the two kids is probably closer to 102 in IQ?

The answer is the kid from Mrs. Nice's class, because the standard deviation in that class is so much less than in Mrs. Mean's class.

4. We might reasonably infer that Mrs. Mean has to work harder than Mrs. Nice, in that she has more individual differences with which to deal.

Exercises   1. Tiggy McGoo and Toogy McGee took a ten-word spelling test every day in Mr. Fauxnetique's third grade class. At the end of the first grading period, each student averaged (i.e., "had a mean of") 6.88. Tiggy's standard deviation was 2.96, while Toogy's was .98.

(a) Which student was more consistent?

(b) Assuming that all other factors are essentially the same but that one of the student's parents squabble a lot, which pair of parents would you suspect?

2. The mean annual income in Tigville is $11,906.52, with a standard deviation of $3012.75, while the mean in Wartburg is $10,988.95 and the standard deviation there is $1543.33.

(a) In which town would you expect sharper contrast between neighborhoods?

(b) Which town probably has the richer rich?

(c) Does one have to have a big income to be rich?

3. Last year Moe mowed his lawn on alternate Saturdays, averaging Mn = 83.25 minutes, with a standard deviation of S = 29.38 minutes. Moe's brother Bo mowed the lawn on the remaining Saturdays, with Mn = 61.08 minutes and S = 5.76 minutes.

(a) If you had to guess how long it would take one of the boys to mow the lawn on a given Saturday, with which boy would it be easier to guess?

(b) Which boy is more likely to take about 51 minutes to mow the lawn?

MATHEMATICAL   Let's now switch our attention from observation to pre-
PROBABILITY   diction, from statistics to probability. The first
               thing we have to do is decide what we mean by proba-
               bility. To this end, we launch into some more exam-
               ples.

Examples   1.   We (Kelly and Logothetti) are conducting an experiment, dropping a thumbtack headfirst into a shoe box three feet below (Plink! Plink! Plink! . . .), and we consider each drop a success if the tack lands point up. (We're after what is sometimes referred to as "a sharp result"; such results are often taxing to the experimenters, but we go to any lengths to help our students get the point.)   If s represents the number of successes and t represents the total number of trials, then we get (. . . Plink! Plink! Plink! . . .):

At the end of 10 trials, $\dfrac{s}{t} = \dfrac{8}{10} = .80$

At the end of 50 trials, $\dfrac{s}{t} = \dfrac{25}{50} = .50$

At the end of 100 trials, $\dfrac{s}{t} = \dfrac{52}{100} = .52$

At the end of 150 trials, $\dfrac{s}{t} = \dfrac{77}{150} \doteq .51$

At the end of 200 trials, $\dfrac{s}{t} = \dfrac{106}{200} = .53$

At the end of 250 trials, $\dfrac{s}{t} = \dfrac{138}{250} \doteq .55$

At the end of 300 trials, $\dfrac{s}{t} = \dfrac{167}{300} \doteq .55$

At the end of 350 trials, $\dfrac{s}{t} = \dfrac{200}{350} \doteq .57$

At the end of 400 trials, $\dfrac{s}{t} = \dfrac{233}{400} \doteq .58$

At the end of 450 trials, $\dfrac{s}{t} = \dfrac{264}{450} \doteq .59$

At the end of 500 trials, $\dfrac{s}{t} = \dfrac{297}{500} \doteq .59$.

Excitedly, we now graph s/t as a function of t:

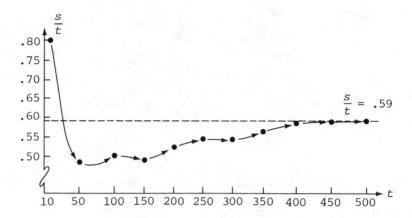

Thus we see that after some preliminary downward and upward movement s/t eventually settles in at .59. We are led to believe (although certainly not through any mathematical proof) that s/t approaches the limit .59 as t gets increasingly larger (i.e., as t gets larger, s/t gets closer and closer to .59), and we say that .59 is the probability of dropping a "point-up" on a single drop.

2. Often we can profit from previous human experience and avoid going through tedious experiments to determine a probability.

   For instance, we have found out by experience that if we drop a die (half a pair of dice) the probability of getting a 1, say, is $1/6 \doteq .17$. This is also the probability of getting a 2, or of getting a 3, or a 4, or a 5, or a 6. Thus we say that each outcome is "equiprobable." When equiprobability is either known or generally assumed, then the probability of our outcome (here, getting a one) is computed by letting s be the number of successful outcomes of our trial (here, dropping a die) and t being the total number of outcomes of our event:

   $$p(1) = \frac{s}{t} = \frac{1}{6}$$

   where $p(A)$ denotes the probability of A.

3. Suppose we pull a card at random from a standard poker deck of 13 clubs, 13 diamonds, 13 hearts, and 13 spades, and we want to figure out the probability of pulling a spade. Here the selection of any particular card is equiprobable. Then $s = 13$, the number of "successful" spade cards, and $t = 52$, the total number of cards in the deck. Hence,

$$p(\text{spade}) = \frac{s}{t} = \frac{13}{52} = \frac{1}{4} = .25.$$

4. Consider the same situation as in Example 3, only this time we want to figure the probability of pulling a face card (i.e., jack, queen, or king of any suit).

    Here $s = 4 \times 3 = 12$, and $t = 52$ again.

    (for the num-   (the number of face
    ber of suits)   cards in each suit)

    Thus, $p(\text{face card}) = \frac{12}{52} = \frac{3}{13} \doteq .23.$

PROBABILITY
OF AN EVENT

With the preceding examples as background we now boldly summarize in general terms.

Definition

The probability of an event E is defined to be the limit of s/t as t increases without bound, where s is the number of times E occurs in a total of t trials:

$p(E)$ = limit of s/t, as t increases indefinitely.

If $E_1, E_2, \ldots, E_n$ are all the possible events, or outcomes, of a trial, and $p(E_1) = p(E_2) = p(E_3) = \cdots = p(E_n)$, then $E_1, E_2, E_3, \ldots, E_n$ are equiprobable, and

$$p(E_i) = \frac{1}{n}, \text{ for } i = 1,2,3, \ldots, n.$$

In a trial with equiprobable outcomes, with s ways of an event E occurring out of a total of t possible outcomes,

$$p(E) = \frac{s}{t}.$$

These results enable us to attack the following objective.

●●●

Objective 97.

Given an outcome of a coin, card, or dice experiment, (a) to conduct 100 trials, graphing ratio of number of successes to number of trials as a function of the number of trials, and (b) to compute the probability of the outcome.

●●●

Examples 1. A die is thrown, and a card is pulled at random from a poker deck. What is the probability that we get a total of 4 (counting an ace as 1)?

Let's compute t first, as it's easier. How many ways may the die turn up? Six. And for each of those six outcomes of the die, how many outcomes are there in pulling a card? Fifty-two, one for each card of the deck. Thus $t = 6 \times 52 = 312$. Now let's struggle with s. First of all, how many ways are there to get a total of 4 from the die and a card? We'll list them:

Die	Card
1	3
2	2
3	1

The die can come up 1, say, in only one way. But the accompanying card can come up four ways (a 3 in each of the four suits). So, if we expand our table, we get:

Die	Card	Number of Ways
1	3	4
2	2	4
3	1	4

Hence $s = 4 + 4 + 4 = 12$, and

$$p(4) = \frac{12}{312} = \frac{1}{26} \doteq .038.$$

2. A coin is flipped and a card is randomly drawn from a poker deck. What is the probability that we get heads and a heart? (Sounds like transplant time at the Stanford Medical Center!) Here the coin can come up two ways, and for each of those ways there are 52 possible ways that the card can come out, so $t = 2 \times 52 = 104$. To figure out s, we note that heads can come up only one way, but the heart can come up 13 ways, so $s = 1 \times 13 = 13$. Therefore,

$$p(\text{head and heart}) = \frac{13}{104} = \frac{1}{8} = .125.$$

3. Let's take the same experiment as in Example 2, but ask after the probability of getting heads *or* a heart (or both). Now t is still 104. Let's make a chart to figure the number of successes:

Coin	Card	Number of Ways
Heads	Any-thing	52
Tails	Heart	13

Thus $s = 52 + 13 = 65$. Hence,

$$p(\text{head } or \text{ heart}) = \frac{65}{104} = .625.$$

4. We flip a coin. What is the probability that it comes up heads *and* tails? Here $t = 2$, but $s = 0$, since there are zero ways in which a coin can come up simultaneously heads and tails. Hence

$$p(\text{heads and tails}) = \frac{0}{2} = 0.$$

The probability of any impossible event is zero.

5. This time we draw a card at random from our poker deck and inquire into the probability of drawing either a club or a diamond or a heart or a spade. Here $t = 52$, and s is the number of cards which are clubs or diamonds or hearts or spades: $s = 13 + 13 + 13 + 13 = 52$. Therefore

$$p(\text{club, diamond, heart, or spade}) = \frac{52}{52} = 1.$$

Here we recognize that *the probability of any "sure thing" is 1*. And since nothing is more probable than a sure thing, no probability can turn out to be greater than 1.

6. Once again we randomly draw a card from the poker deck. What is the probability that the card either has face value less than 9 (ace counts as 1) or is in a red suit (i.e., is a diamond or a heart)? Of course, t is 52. How many cards have face value less than 9? Eight cards in each of the four suits: $8 \times 4 = 32$. How many cards are red? Twenty-six, half of the total. Hence we might say $p(\text{less than 9 or red}) = (32 + 26)/52 = 58/52 = 29/26 \doteq 1.12$. Oops! There is some mistake! *Probabilities cannot be greater than 1.* Evidently, in counting s we counted some cards more than once. Of course! After counting the 36 cards of face value less than 9, some of which are already red, we need only count the remainder of the red cards, that is, the 9, 10, J, Q, K of diamonds and hearts. There are $2 \times 5 = 10$ of these. Thus the correct probability is

$$p(\text{less than 9 or red}) = \frac{36 + 10}{52} = \frac{46}{52} \doteq .88.$$

7. What is the probability of throwing a 1 upon rolling a die? What is the probability of throwing a number greater than 1?

$$p(1) = \frac{1}{6} \doteq .167$$

$$p(>1) = p(2 \text{ or } 3 \text{ or } 4 \text{ or } 5 \text{ or } 6)$$

$$= \frac{1 + 1 + 1 + 1 + 1}{6} = \frac{5}{6} \doteq .833.$$

Notice that $p(1)$ and $p(>1)$ are mutually exclusive and exhaust all possibilities (i.e., if E_1 is the event of getting a 1 and E_2 is the event of getting a number greater than 1, then no outcome is in both E_1 and E_2 but every outcome is in one of E_1 or E_2), and $p(1) + p(>1) = 1$. In general, *if $E_1, E_2, \ldots, E_n$ are mutually exclusive events that exhaust all possible outcomes of a trial, then $p(E_1) + (E_2) + \cdot \cdot \cdot + p(E_n) = 1$.*

8. Suppose Goofus McToofus becomes involved in a simple game using one die. His friend wins whenever he can roll a number larger than 3 and Goofus wins if he (the friend) rolls a number less than or equal to 3. Goofus is losing steadily and finally tackles his friend to look at this die. He soon finds the problem. The die is weighted in such a way that the 6 is six times as likely to turn up as the 1, the 5 is five times as likely as the 1, the 4, four times as likely as the 1, etc. What is the probability of any face turning up, and what is the probability that Goofus wins?
    First let's let $p(1) = a$ (some number). Then

    $p(2) = 2a$
    $p(3) = 3a$
    $p(4) = 4a$
    $p(5) = 5a$
    $p(6) = 6a$

    From Example 7 we know $p(1) + p(2) + p(3) + p(4) + p(5) + p(6) = 1$. So $a + 2a + 3a + 4a + 5a + 6a = 1$. Then $21a = 1$, so $a = p(1) = 1/21$, and $p(2) = 2/21$, $p(3) = 3/21$, $p(4) = 4/21$, $p(5) = 5/21$, and finally $p(6) = 6/21$. Therefore the probability that good old Goofus wins is $(1 + 2 + 3)/21 = 6/21 \doteq .286$.

Exercises   1. Conduct 100 trials of each of the following experiments and graph s/t as a function of t. Check s/t for $t = 10, 20, 30, 40, 50, 60, 70, 80, 90, 100$.

(a) Drop a thumbtack head down from a height of one foot onto a flat, smooth surface and see if it lands point up.

(b) Drop a thumbtack head down on a rug from a height of three feet and see if it lands point up.

(c) Drop a coin, edge down, on a flat, smooth surface and see if it comes up tails.

(d) Drop a die, 1-face down, from a height of three feet onto a flat, smooth surface and see if it comes up 1.

(e) Drop a die, 1-face down, from a height of three feet onto a flat, smooth surface and see if it comes up 6.

(f) Drop a die, 1-face down, from a height of three feet onto a flat, smooth surface and see if it comes up 4.

(g) Drop an unopened pack of gum, end down, from a height of three feet onto a flat, smooth surface and see if it lands with one of its biggest faces up.

(h) Drop two dice, 1-faces down, from a height of three feet onto a flat, smooth surface and see if they come up totaling 7.

(i) Drop two dice, 2-faces down, from a height of three feet onto a flat, smooth surface and see if they come up totaling 7.

(j) Shuffle a standard 52-card poker deck five or six times, look at the tenth card from the top, and see if it is a face card.

(k) Same as (j) but see if it is a spade.

(l) Same as (j) but see if it is a red card.

(m) Shuffle a standard 52-card poker deck five or six times, look at the cards tenth from the top and tenth from the bottom, and see if they are both the same color.

(n) Same as (m) but see if they both are hearts.

(o) Same as (m) but see if one or both of them is a spade.

(p) Plant five beans in the ground and see if any of them grows up into the sky overnight.

2. Compute the mathematical probability of the following events.

(a) A coin is flipped and comes up tails.

(b) Two coins are flipped and both come up tails.

(c) Two coins are flipped and just one comes up tails.

(d) Three coins are flipped and all come up tails.

(e) Three coins are flipped and exactly two come up tails.

(f) Three coins are flipped and just one comes up tails.

(g) A die is rolled and comes up an even number.

(h) A die is rolled and comes up a multiple of 3.

(i) A die is rolled and comes up a multiple of 4.

(j) A die is rolled and comes up a multiple of 1.

(k) A die is rolled and comes up a multiple of 7.

(l) A die is rolled and comes up a multiple of 6.

(m) A die is rolled and comes up a factor of 6.

(n) A die is rolled and comes up a prime factor of 6.

(o) A die is rolled and comes up a prime number.

(p) Two dice are rolled and come up totaling 1.

(q) Two dice are rolled and come up totaling 2.

(r) Two dice are rolled, and both come up with the same numbers.

(s) Two dice are rolled and come up with one a 2 and the other a 3.

(t) Two dice are rolled and come up with one or both of them a 2 or 3.

(u) A card is drawn at random from a poker deck and is a face card.

(v) A card is drawn at random from a poker deck and is a spade.

(w) A card is drawn at random from a poker deck and is a red card.

(x) Two cards are drawn at random from a poker deck and they both are the same color.

(y) Two cards are drawn at random from a poker deck and are both hearts.

(z) Two cards are drawn at random from a poker deck and one or both of them is a spade.

3. If two dates of a 365-day year are chosen at random, what is the probability that they are (a) the same, (b) different? (c) What is the sum of the answers in (a) and (b)?

4. If three dates of a 365-day year are chosen at random, what is the probability that

    (a) they are all the same,

    (b) exactly two of them are the same,

    (c) none of them are the same?

    (d) What is the sum of the answers in (a), (b), (c)?

5. A die is weighted so that the 1, 3, and 6 are twice as heavy as the 2, 4, and 5. Answer parts (g) through (o) of Exercise 2.

6. A die is weighted so that the 1 is twice as heavy as the 6, the 2 is three times as heavy as the 5, and the 3 is 4 times as heavy as the 4, but the 4, 5, and 6 are all equally likely. Answer parts (g) through (o) of Exercise 2.

7. At Nag Downs Racing Park in Tigville, Nellie has three times the probability to win that Mollie has. But

Mollie is four times as likely to win as Pete is. It's a small race track so these are the only three horses racing.

(a) What is the probability that Nellie wins?

(b) What is the probability that Mollie wins?

(c) What is the probability that Pete wins?

(d) What is the probability that either Nellie or Mollie wins?

(e) What is the probability that Pete loses?

ODDS

● ●

Objective   98.   To convert given probabilities to odds, and vice versa.

● ●

In daily life it is more common to hear about odds than about probabilities, even though odds may be less meaningful. Thus, when Secretariat was going into the Belmont Stakes of the horse racing Triple Crown, we heard that the odds in favor of his winning were 3 to 2, rather than that the probability of his winning was 60%. Let's examine some examples to see how odds and probabilities are related.

CHANGING FROM ODDS TO PROBABILITY	Suppose the odds for an event E are given as s to f. This means there are s chances of winning for every f chances of losing. The total number of possibilities then must be $s + f$, the chances of winning plus the chances of losing. So $t = s + f$. The number of times event E occurs is the number s of chances of winning. Therefore the probability of event E is $p(E) = s/t = s/(s + f)$.

Examples	1.	Odds of 3 to 2 in favor of an event E mean that there are three chances of winning for every two chances of losing, a total of $t = 3 + 2 = 5$ in all. Since $s = 3$,

$p(E) = 3/5 = .60 = 60\%.$

Notice that these same odds could have been given as 6 to 4, or 15 to 10, or 150 to 100, or 375 to 250, or most generally $3n$ to $2n$, since |

$$\frac{6}{6 + 4} = \frac{15}{15 + 10} = \frac{150}{150 + 100} = \frac{375}{375 + 250} = \frac{2n}{3n + 2n}$$

$$= \frac{3}{5} = 60\%.$$

2. Similarly, odds of 5 to 8 in favor of event E mean that the probability of event E is $5/(5 + 8) = 5/13 \doteq .38$.

3. When Citation went into the Belmont Stakes on his way to the Triple Crown, the odds were 5 to 1 that he'd win. What was the probability that he'd win?

$$p(\text{win}) = \frac{5}{5 + 1} = \frac{5}{6} \doteq .83 = 83\%.$$

CHANGING FROM PROBABILITY TO ODDS FOR AN EVENT E	If $p(E) = s/t$, then the chances of winning are s, and there are $f = t - s$ chances of losing, the remaining part. So the odds are s to $t - s$, or s to f.

Examples

1. A certain weather forecaster said that there was a 20% chance of rain for the Belmont Stakes. What were the odds for rain?
   Here $s/t = 20\% = .20 = 1/5 = 1/(1 + 4)$, so the odds were 1 to 4. Why not 4 to 1? Well, probability of 20% is pretty low (i.e., indicating that the event is not very likely to occur.) Hence there is less chance of rain than not rain.

2. The probability of rolling a sum of 7 with 2 dice is $6/36 = 1/6$. (The total number of outcomes possible is $6 \times 6 = 36$, and the ways to obtain success are $\{(1,6),(2,5),(3,4),(4,3),(5,2),(6,1)\}$. So the number of successes is 6.) Hence the odds in favor of rolling a sum of 7 are 1 to 5.

3. The probability of rolling a sum of 7 or 11 on 2 dice is $1/6 + 2/36 = 6/36 + 2/36 = 8/36 = 2/9$. So the odds in favor of rolling a sum of either 7 or 11 are 2 to 7.

CHANGING FROM
PROBABILITY TO
ODDS AGAINST

Examples

1. Suppose that the official probability of the Big Bad Wolf catching a pig this week is 37%. What are the odds *against* the wolf's catching a pig?

Here, if we take $t = 100$, then $s = 37$. Hence out of 100 trials the wolf should be unsuccessful $100 - 37 = 63$ times. Thus there would be 63 noncatches to 37 catches, and so the odds against catching a pig are 63 to 27.

2. The probability of Goofus Letoofus passing history is only 55%. What are the odds against him to pass history? Since $100 - 55 = 45$, we see that Goofus has only a 45% chance of failing. So the odds against passing history for Goofus are 45 to 55 or 9 to 11.

In general,

(a) If the odds in favor of E are s to f, then

$$p(e) = \frac{s}{s + f};$$

(b) If the odds against E are f to s, then

$$p(E) = \frac{s}{s + f};$$

(c) If $p(E) = x\%$, then the odds in favor of E are x to $(100 - x)$;

(d) If $p(E) = x\%$, then the odds against E are $(100 - x)$ to x.

Exercises
1. The odds against the New Pork Yankees winning the Hamerican League title are 100 to 1.

   (a) What are the odds in favor of New Pork winning?

   (b) What is the probability of New Pork winning?

   (c) What is the probability of New Pork coming in second or worse?

2. The odds in favor of the Los Angeles Hams winning the National Football Peague title are 8 to 5.

   (a) What are the odds against their winning?

   (b) What is the probability of their winning?

   (c) What is the probability of their not coming in first?

3. If there's a 40% chance of rain tomorrow, (a) What is the probability that it'll rain? (b) What is the probability that it won't rain? (c) What are the odds against rain? (d) What are the odds in favor of rain?

4. If there's a 57% chance that this book receives sour reviews from college professors, what are the odds for a good review?

5. If the odds for a bad review of this book from college students are 1 to 7 what is the probability of a good review?

6. The next time a thug peeks out of an alley and says (Psst! Hey, Buddy! I offer even money that (etc.), calculate (a) the odds, (b) the probability if the given event really is "even money" (i.e., bet x dollars against his x dollars).

PROBABILITY AND NORMAL DISTRIBUTION

Besides "odds," another term that frequently arises in everyday conversation is "the law of averages." When most people use this phrase they are probably really thinking of a situation representing the so-called *normal distribution*, illustrated by the following bell-shaped curve:

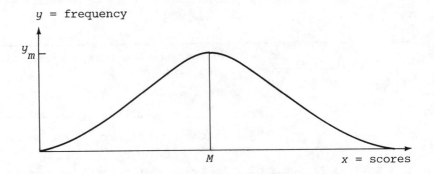

Here, the mean, mode, and median are all $x = M$
("average"), and the frequencies of the scores steadily
decrease as the scores become extremely high or extremely low. This normal distribution is the kind of
distribution we usually expect when we have a vast number of scores on some examination, say, with the test
takers randomly chosen.

Suppose we give a test of informal geometry (TIG for
short) and get a normal distribution of scores thus:

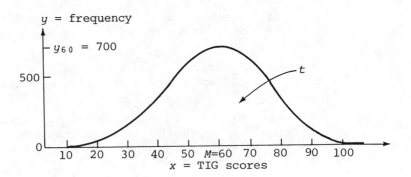

Suppose further that we wanted on the basis of this
distribution to figure out the probability of a randomly chosen person scoring 75 or higher. Then what we
can do is let t = area under the whole curve and s =
(area under the curve and at or to the right of 75:

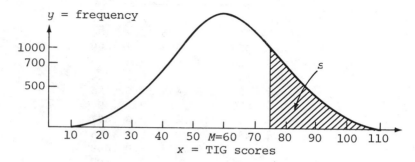

Then $p(\geq 75) = \dfrac{s}{t} = \dfrac{\text{shaded area}}{\text{total area}}$.

The problem now is to figure out these two areas, s and t. It turns out that areas under a normal curve have been tabulated (using integral calculus), and there are lots and lots of normal curves possible. Are they all tabulated? The answer is no. Mathematicians have tabulated areas for a certain normal curve and adapt other curves to it via what are called "standard scores."

Before looking at standard scores, let us look at some of the properties of the official normal distribution.

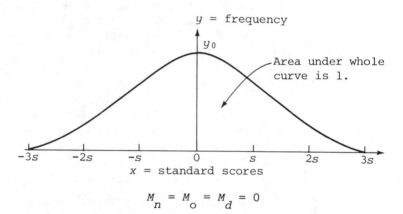

$$M_n = M_o = M_d = 0$$

The area under the whole curve is taken to be 1. The mean, mode, and median all concur at 0. The length of the base is essentially $6s$, i.e., 6 standard deviations; three of these are to the left of the mean and three are to the right. Actually, 68% of the total area is between s and $-s$, 95% between $2s$ and $-2s$, and 99.7% between $3s$ and $-3s$. The following brief table gives the area from the mean to the given score z in standard deviations, also known as the *standard score*.

z	Area	z	Area	z	Area
0.0	.000	1.1	.364	2.1	.482
0.1	.040	1.2	.385	2.2	.486
0.2	.079	1.3	.403	2.3	.489
0.3	.118	1.4	.419	2.4	.492
0.4	.155	1.5	.433	2.5	.494
0.5	.192	1.6	.445	2.6	.495
0.6	.226	1.7	.455	2.7	.497
0.7	.258	1.8	.464	2.8	.497
0.8	.288	1.9	.471	2.9	.498
0.9	.316	2.0	.477	3.0	.499
1.0	.341			3.1	.499

Table gives this area

Mn   Z

Exercises

1. Roll two dice 500 times and make (a) a histogram, (b) a frequency polygon of the numbers of times that 2, 3, 4, 5, 6, 7, 8, 9, 10, 11, 12 come up. How do your figures compare with a normal distribution?

2. Toss 5 coins 500 times (or 50 coins 50 times, or 2500 coins once, or one coin 2500 times, or . . .) and make (a) a histogram, (b) a frequency polygon of the numbers of times the coins come up 0, 1, 2, 3, 4, or 5 heads. How do your figures compare with a normal distribution?

3. Ask 100 college students to pick a cardinal number less than 10 and make (a) a histogram, (b) a frequency polygon of the results. How do your figures compare with a normal distribution?

4. Ask 100 college students their heights and classify the answers as less than 4'5", 4'5" to 4'11", 5'0" to 5'4", 5'5" to 5'11", 6'0" to 6'4", 6'5" to 6'11", greater than 6'11", and make (a) a histogram, (b) a frequency polygon of the data. How do your figures compare with a normal distribution?

5. Same as Exercise 4, except ask only women. How and why do the results in Exercise 4 and 5 differ?

6. Same as Exercise 5, except ask weights instead of heights and classify the replies as less than 90 lbs, 91-100 lbs, 101-110 lbs, 111-120 lbs, 121-130 lbs, 131-140 lbs, 141-150 lbs, 151-160 lbs, greater than 160 lbs.

7. Use the table of areas under a normal curve to graph the listed area as a function of z, $-3s \leq z \leq 3s$. How is the resulting graph related to the normal curve?

8. Use the table of areas to graph (1 - area) as a function of z, $-3s \leq z \leq 3s$. How is this graph related to the normal curve?

9. How is a slider related to the normal curve? How about a knuckler? Fastball? Spitball?

Let's now consider the problem of adapting an arbitrary normal distribution to the official normal distribution just tabulated. This table involves standard scores which are measured from the mean in standard deviation units. So if we had the following distribution:

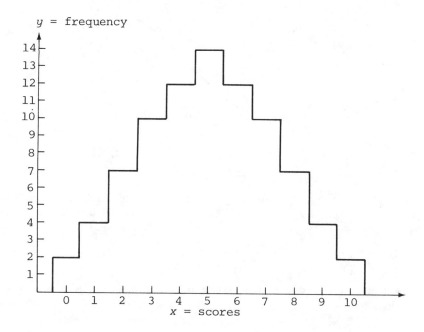

we'd have to first figure out the mean and standard deviation. We can see at a glance that Mn = 5. The standard deviation is given by

$$S = \sqrt{\frac{\begin{array}{l} (2(0-5)^2 + 4(1-5)^2 + 7(2-5)^2 + 10(3-5)^2 \\ + 13(4-5)^2 + 14(5-5)^2 + 13(6-5)^2 \\ + 10(7-5)^2 + 7(8-5)^2 + 4(9-5)^2 + 2(10-5)^2) \end{array}}{86}}$$

$$= \sqrt{\frac{460}{86}} = \sqrt{\frac{230}{43}} \doteq \sqrt{5.3488} \doteq 2.31.$$

So to get the standard score corresponding, say, to $x = 3$, we first measure from the mean,

$$3 - 5 = -2,$$

then put in standard deviation units:

$$z = \frac{3-5}{2.31} = \frac{-2}{2.31} \doteq -.866 \doteq -.9.$$

Here, then, the "raw" (or original) score of 3 corresponds to the standard score of -.9.

So if we substitute a normal curve for the preceding histogram, we have the following situation:

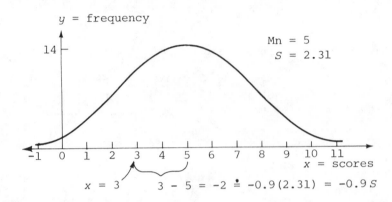

In general, to convert a raw score x from a normal distribution with mean Mn and standard deviation S into a standard score z, we compute

$$z = \frac{x - Mn}{S} \ .$$

●●

*Objective 99.   To compute z-scores of given x-scores, given the mean and standard deviation of normally distributed xs.

●●

Examples   Assuming that IQ scores are normally distributed, with Mn = 100, s = 16, change the following IQs to standard scores:

1.   IQ = 70.   If x = 70, then

$$z = \frac{x - Mn}{S} = \frac{70 - 100}{16} = \frac{-30}{16} = \frac{-15}{8} = -1.875 \doteq -1.9$$

2.   IQ = 125.   If x = 125, then

$$z = \frac{x - Mn}{S} = \frac{125 - 100}{16} = \frac{25}{16} \doteq 1.562 \doteq 1.6$$

3.   IQ = 100.   If x = 100, then

$$z = \frac{x - Mn}{S} = \frac{100 - 100}{16} = \frac{0}{16} = 0.$$

The z-score of the mean is always 0.

Exercises   1.   Why can we see at a glance that Mn = 5 for the histogram given in the last section of the text?

2. Change the following IQs to standard scores: (a) 54,
    (b) 90,   (c) 110,   (d) 146,   (e) 180,   (f) 200.

3. There's a message hidden in the selection of the IQs
    in Exercise 2(a)-(d). What is it?

4. Let us assume that SAT (Scholastic Aptitude Test)
    scores are normally distributed, with Mn = 500, S =
    100. Compute the standard scores of the following
    SATS: (a) 360,   (b) 480,   (c) 540,   (d) 720,   (e) 800.

5. Is an SAT score an SIT score that's resting on its
    laurels?

6. Take TIG scores to be normally distributed, with Mn =
    60, S = 17. Change the following TIGs to zs: (a) 26,
    (b) 43,   (c) 60,   (d) 77,   (e) 94.

We are now in a position to attack the next objective.

● ●

*Objective 100.   To compute the probability of falling within a speci-
fied range of a normal distribution.

● ●

Examples   1.   Compute the probability of a randomly selected person's
IQ being between 90 and 120, using the assumptions
found in the examples following Objective 99.

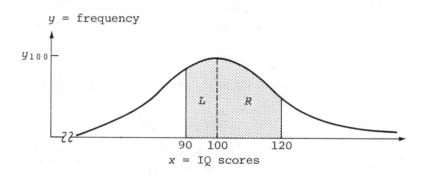

Here, we're interested in the area of the shaded region
in the diagram. We have to split this region into L
and R, as our table only gives us information about regions whose bases extend out from the mean. First,
let's look at L: If x = 90, then

$$z = \frac{90 - 100}{16} = \frac{-10}{16} = \frac{-5}{8} = -.625 \doteq -0.6.$$

Consulting the table, we find that .226 of the area
is in L. (Note: We ignore the sign on -0.6; since the
M_n on the table is 0, -.6 and +.6 give the same area.)

Now for R. If $x = 120$, then

$$z = \frac{120 - 100}{16} = \frac{20}{16} = \frac{5}{4} = 1.25 \doteq 1.3.$$

Looking at the table again, we find that .403 of the area is in R.

Thus $p(90 \leq IQ \leq 120) = .226 + .403 = .629.$

2. Suppose Randy Dumb is randomly chosen. What is the probability that Randy's IQ is higher than 140? If $x = 140$, $z = (140 - 100)/16 = 40/16 = 5/2 = 2.5$. For $z = 2.5$, the table gives .494. The trouble is, we have

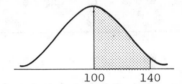

and we want

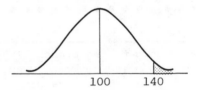

How do we get this? Merely by subtracting the tabulated entry from half of the total area, .500:

$p(\geq 140) = .500 - .494 = .006.$

3. What is the probability of an IQ being as far from the mean as Randy Dumb's? How does this differ from Example 2?

We answer the second question first. In Example 2 we wanted only the high extremity

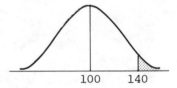

whereas in Example 3 we want both extremities:

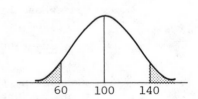

Since 60 is as far below the mean 100 as 140 is above it, we want the area to the left of 60 as well as to the right of 140. By the symmetry of the normal distribution these two areas are the same, so

$$p(IQ \leq 60 \text{ or } \geq 140) = 2 \times (.006) = .012.$$

Exercises 1. Compute the probability of randomly chosen IQs falling in the following ranges: (a) 84 to 116, (b) 68 to 132, (c) 52 to 148, (d) 84 to 132, (e) less than 68, (f) further from 100 than 68, (g) within 10 points of the mean, (h) from 100 to 110, (i) exactly 110 (careful!).

2. Making the same assumptions as in Exercise 4, page 305, what is the probability of a randomly chosen SAT score being (a) from 400 to 600? (b) less than 350? (c) greater than 720? (d) within 150 points of 500? (e) more than 200 points from 500?

3. What SAT scores account for (a) the middle 50% of all scores? (b) the top 10%? (c) the bottom 25%?

4. Draw a graph of the normal distribution of SAT scores, labeling the x-axis carefully. (Never mind about the y-axis.)

5. Draw a cartoon of Norman Distribution.

| SOLUTION OF THE BIRTH DATE PROBLEM | We end this chapter with a problem solving technique and its application to the Birth Date Problem. |

Sherlock Hams, the great detective

This technique was described by Sir Arthur Conan Doyle in 1908: "When you have eliminated all that is possible, whatever remains, however improbable, must be the solution."

| Example | What is the probability of rolling two dice and not getting a pair (such as "snake-eyes," two 1s)? Here we know that $t = 6 \times 6 = 36$, and we could figure out s by counting all nonpairs. But Doyle's idea is much simpler: We'll figure out the probability that we do get a pair, then subtract this probability from 1 to get the answer to our original equation. |

$$p(\text{pair}) = \frac{6}{36} = \frac{1}{6}.$$

(We could get two 1s, two 2s, two 3s, two 4s, two 5s, or two 6s, in all, six ways of getting a pair.) Hence

$$p(\text{not a pair}) = 1 - \frac{1}{6} = \frac{5}{6}.$$

We can generalize Doyle's hint as applied to probability:

$$p(E) = 1 - p(\text{not } E).$$

● ●

Objective 101.   To compute a given coin, card, or dice probability two ways: (a) directly, (b) by subtracting from 1.

● ●

Examples   1.   Compute in two ways the probability of throwing five coins and getting at least one head.

(a) Direct computation:

First, each coin can come up two ways, so five coins can come up $2 \times 2 \times 2 \times 2 \times 2 = 2^5 = 32$ ways. Thus $t = 32$.
To figure s, we count the number of ways of getting exactly one head, two heads, etc.

One head: HTTTT, or THTTT, or TTHTT, or TTTHT, or TTTTH, five ways in all.
Two heads: HHTTT, or HTHTT, or HTTHT, or HTTTH, or THHTT, or THTHT, or THTTH, or TTHHT, or TTHTH, or TTTHH, ten ways in all.
Three heads = two tails: ten ways.
Four heads = one tail: five ways
Five heads: one way.

So $s = 5 + 10 + 10 + 5 + 1 = 31$.
And so $p(\geq 1H) = 31/32 \doteq .97$.

(b) Subtracting from 1:

There is only one way of not getting at least one head, and that is to get all tails. There is only one way to get all five tails.

Therefore, $p(\text{five tails}) = 1/32$.
Hence $p(\geq 1H) = 1 - p(\text{no } H) = 1 - p(5T)$
$= 1 - (1/32) = 31/32$.

2.   Compute the probability that at least two of 30 randomly chosen pigs have the same birth date (taking 365 days per year).

Let E be the event that at least two pigs have the same birth date, and let us compute $p(\text{not } E)$. If no two pigs have the same birth date, then all have different dates.

The total number of birth dates is $t = 365 \times 365 \times \cdots \times 365 = 365^{30}$, since each pig has 365 possible days for its birth date.

How many ways can each pig have a different birth date? Well, the first pig can have any of 365 days for its birth date, but the second pig cannot have the same date as the first pig so it has only 364 possible birth dates. The third pig has only 363 possible dates, as it must be different from the first two, etc. So the number of ways their birth dates can all be different is

$$\frac{365 \times 364 \times 363 \times \cdots \times 336}{365^{30}} \doteq .29$$

Hence, however improbable it may seem,

$p(\geq$ two pigs have same birthday)
$= 1 - p$(no two pigs have same birthday)
$\doteq 1 - .29 = .71$

Exercises

Compute the following probabilities two ways: (a) directly, (b) by subtracting from 1.

1. Five coins are flipped and more than two come up heads.

2. Six coins are flipped and at least one comes up heads.

3. Six coins are flipped and at least two come up heads.

4. Six pigs are flipped and at least one comes up squealing.

5. One die is rolled and no primes come up.

6. Two dice are rolled and no primes come up in the total.

7. Three dice are rolled and no primes come up in the total.

8. Three dice are rolled and we get no triples (such as all three 5s).

9. A card is pulled at random from a poker deck and is a club, spade, or heart.

10. A card is pulled at random from a poker deck and is neither a spade nor a queen.

11. A card is pulled at random from a poker deck and is not a face card.

12. Some two of five pigs have the same birthday (pigs randomly chosen).

13. Some three of five pigs have the same birthday (pigs randomly chosen).

SUMMARY OF
OBJECTIVES

94. Given a set of scores, to construct (a) an ungrouped frequency distribution, (b) a grouped

frequency distribution, (c) a histogram of (b), (d) a frequency polygon of (b) (page 269).

95. Given a set of scores, to compute to the nearest hundredth the mean, mode, median, and standard deviation (page 279).

96. Given the means and standard deviations of two sets of scores, (a) to explain which set of scores represents a more predictable situation and why, (b) to draw a mathematically reasonable inference about each of the two situations (page 286).

97. Given an outcome of a coin, card, or dice experiment, (a) to conduct 100 trials, graphing ratio of number of successes to number of trials as a function of the number of trials, and (b) to compute the probability of the outcome (page 290).

98. To convert given probabilities to odds, and vice versa (page 296).

*99. To compute z-scores of given x-scores, given the mean and standard deviation of normally distributed xs (page 304).

*100. To compute the probability of falling within a specified range of a normal distribution (page 305).

101. To compute a given coin, card, or dice probability two ways: (a) directly, (b) by subtracting from 1 (page 309).

WORDS TO KNOW

descriptive statistics (page 268)
inferential statistics (page 268)
probability (page 268)
statistics (page 268)
frequency (page 269)
tally sheet (page 269)
ungrouped frequency distribution (page 269)
grouped frequency distribution (page 270)
bar graph (page 271
histogram (page 271)
frequency polygon (page 272)
average (page 279)
mean (page 279)
median (page 279)

mode (page 279)
measure of central tendency (page 280)
standard deviation (page 281)
spread (page 282)
trial (page 289)
equiprobable (page 289)
outcome (page 289)
equiprobability (page 290)
event (page 290)
probability of impossible event (page 292)
probability of sure thing (page 292)
mutually exclusive events (page 293)
odds (page 296)

CHAPTER 9

GEOMETRY AND MEASUREMENT

The pig on the right side of the drawing on page 313
can be drawn with a single stroke, with the stroke beginning anywhere on the drawing. Can the pig on the
left also be drawn with a single stroke? If so, where
should the stroke begin, and where should it end?

Challenges 1. Draw the right-hand pig twice, each time with a single
stroke, starting at two different points. Where do
each of the drawings end?

2. Try to draw the left-hand pig with a single stroke. If
you do, where do you start and where do you end?

POINTS, LINES,
CURVES, AND
PLANES
All drawings represent combinations of points, lines,
and curves, and most drawings are done on planes. So
drawings are not only attractive to children; they are
also loaded with mathematical concepts. This section
of the book deals with an informal and intuitive,
rather than axiomatic, treatment of some of the key
ideas of geometry. We begin with basic terminology.

● ●

Objective 102. To explain what each of the following geometric objects
is and draw a sketch of it: (a) point, (b) line,
(c) curve, (d) closed curve, (e) simple curve,
(f) half-line, (g) ray, (h) line segment, (i) vertex,
(j) edge, (k) plane, (l) half-plane, (m) parallel lines.

● ●

Excitedly, we charge right into this objective.

(a) *Point*. Geometrically a point has no dimen-
sion. It can be conceived
of as merely a location,   Sketch of a point
perhaps as the intersec-
tion of two shadows. If you took an unsanforized speck
of dust and washed and shrank it six sextillion times,
it would still be infinitely larger than a mathematical
point. Of course, our sketch is necessarily inaccu-
rate; it would, however, be useless if we could not see
the point at all.

(b) *Line*. By "line" we mean a connected (side by
side, or joined) set of points running off along a
straight line infinitely in both directions, never
turning. (This is not a definition, remember, just an

explanation. If it were
supposed to be a defini-
tion, it would be a poor
one, as it uses the term
it is explaining in the
explanation. See Chap-
ter 1 for comments on the
impossibility of defining
every term of a mathematical system.)

Sketch of a line

(c) *Curve*. Curves are
connected sets of points
(so a line is a special
case of a curve), not necessarily straight, either
finite or infinite in ex-
tent.

Sketches of curves

(d) *Closed Curve*. A
closed curve is a curve
that can be drawn with a
single stroke starting and
finishing at the same
point. Thus, it has no
"loose tails" sticking
out.

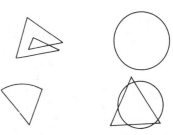

Sketches of closed curves

(e) *Simple Curve*. Sim-
ple curves that do not
intersect themselves, ex-
cept possibly at some
"starting point" that is
also a "finishing point."
Thus if they are drawn, no
point is covered twice except maybe the start-
finish. Simple curves may
or may not be closed.

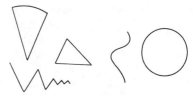

Sketches of simple curves

(f) *Half-line*. If we
drop a point out of a
line, then take one of the
two resulting pieces ex-
cluding the omitted point
or "endpoint," we get a
half-line.

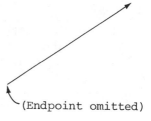

(Endpoint omitted)

Sketch of a half-line

(g) *Ray.* A ray is the union of a half-line and its endpoint.

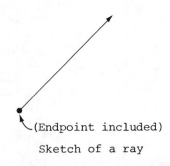

(Endpoint included)

Sketch of a ray

(h) *Line segment.* A line segment is a connected subset of a line and consists of two endpoints and all points between these endpoints.

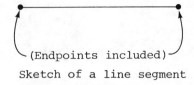

(Endpoints included)

Sketch of a line segment

(i) *Vertex* (plural: vertices). A vertex is a point of intersection of two or more curves. Usually it is at a "corner" of some sort. Of course, the curves may be straight lines.

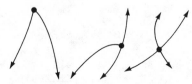

Sketches of three different kinds of vertices

(j) *Edge.* An edge is a curve that either connects two vertices (finite edge) or extends infinitely from a single vertex (infinite edge). Many finite edges are line segments, and many infinite edges are rays.

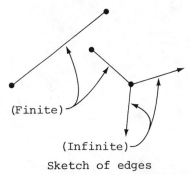

(Finite)

(Infinite)

Sketch of edges

(k) *Plane.* A plane is a flat set of points extending infinitely in all directions. Through any point of a plane infinitely many lines may be drawn.

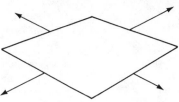

Sketch of a plane

(1) *Half-plane.* If we
drop a line out of a
plane, then take one of
the two resulting pieces
excluding the omitted line
or "endline," we get a
half-plane.

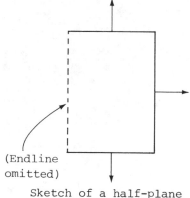

(Endline
omitted)

Sketch of a half-plane

(m) *Parallel lines.* Two
lines in a plane that do
not intersect are paral-
lel. (Intersecting lines
have one and only one
point in common.)

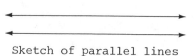

Sketch of parallel lines

Exercises   1.   Draw, if possible, some curves that are: (a) closed,
linear (i.e., composed of line segments), and simple;
(b) closed, linear, and not simple; (c) simple,
linear, and not closed; (d) closed, simple, and not
linear; (e) simple and finite; (f) simple and infinite; (g) closed and finite; (h) closed and infinite.

            2.   Classify each of the capital letters of our alphabet
as closed or not closed, simple or not simple, linear
or not linear. (If any part of a curve is not linear
then the curve is not linear.)

NETWORKS,
TRAVERSABILITY,
AND THE
DRAWING
PROBLEM
SOLUTION

A batch of definitions like the preceding ones, taken
by itself constitutes pretty dull stuff that is often
quickly forgotten. But if we use these definitions in
interesting problems they take on more vital meanings
and are learned (and frequently retained) naturally.
The following objective provides an opportunity to use
some of these definitions in this way.

● ●

*Objective 103.   Given two-dimensional connected networks, (a) to state
whether or not they're traversable, and (b) to explain
the logic behind these decisions.

● ●

A *network* is really just a mathematical idealization of a line drawing ("line" not used in the technical sense); that is, it is a union of vertices and edges. A network is *traversable* if a midget bug can traverse its entirety, passing through each vertex as many times as it pleases but over each edge only once.

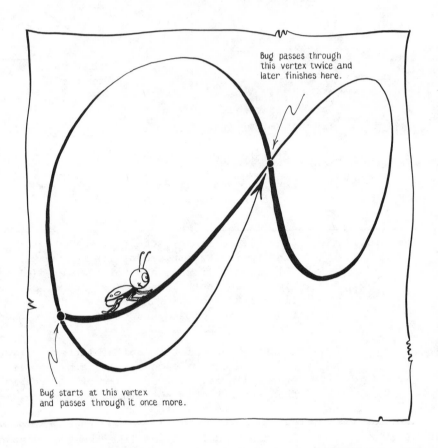

Bug passes through this vertex twice and later finishes here.

Bug starts at this vertex and passes through it once more.

Since the crucial elements of this objective are vertices *and* edges, we'll emphasize the vertices by making them look knobby:

Knobby vertices on a traversable pig

Now that definitions and drawing conventions are established, we are ready to begin empirical spadework for solution of the Drawing Problem.

Exercises 1. Determine, by trial and error if necessary, which of the following networks are traversable:

(a)   (b)   (c)   (d)

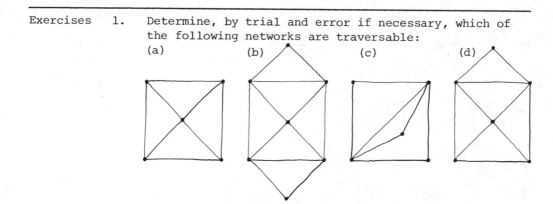

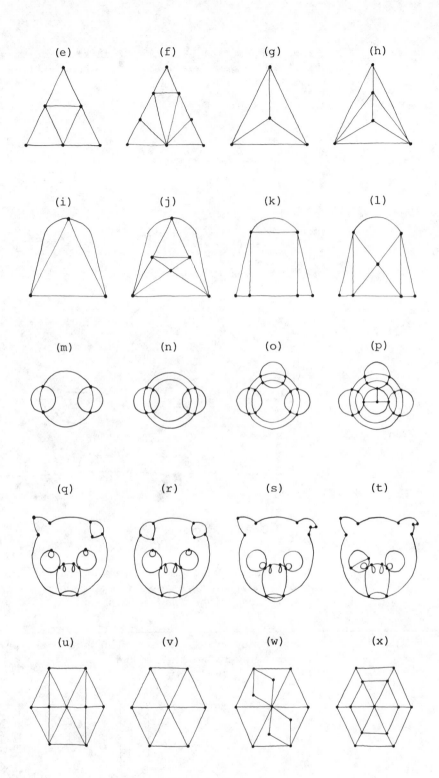

2. Of those networks in Exercise 1 that are traversable,
    (a) from which vertices can you begin, (b) at which
    vertices can you end?

A vertex is called *odd* if it is the intersection of an
odd number of edges and *even* if it is the intersection
of an even number of edges.

Odd vertices   Even vertices

It turns out that, besides the obvious property of con-
nectedness, the properties of oddness and evenness of
vertices are crucial to the Drawing Problem. Moreover,
these properties are considered relative to another
dichotomy of vertices in a network: Some vertices are
definitely *end vertices*, i.e., either starts or finishes but not both, while the others are *through vertices*—vertices that the midget bug always passes
through but at which it never starts or stops its trip
unless it both starts and stops there. By definition,
a *connected network* may be drawn in a single stroke if
and only if it has exactly two end vertices, or no
vertices (such as the circle).

Exercises   1. How many odd vertices are there in each network of Ex-
                 ercise 1 on page 319?

             2. If an odd vertex occurs in a network, (a) when is it
                 an end vertex, (b) when is it a through vertex?

             3. If an even vertex occurs in a network, (a) when is it
                 an end vertex, (b) when is it a through vertex?

             4. In order to be traversable, a network can have a maxi-
                 mum of how many (a) odd vertices, (b) even vertices?

             5. If a traversable network has all even vertices,
                 (a) at which vertices can we begin our stroke? (b) at
                 which vertices can we end our stroke?

             6. Explain how to determine whether or not a network is
                 traversable.

             7. Draw the left-hand pig at the beginning of the chapter
                 in a single stroke. Where can you begin the stroke?
                 Where do you end the stroke?

             8. Run through the previous and this set of exercises with
                 an elementary school child (in words at his or her

level). At the end ask the child what a "vertex" is
and see if the answer is correct.

COUNTING PARTS   Of course, we can do more with points and lines than
                  draw pictures with them. It's also pretty natural to
                  count them.

● ●

Objective 104.   To compute the number of points, lines, line segments,
                  planes, etc. determined by a given set of points,
                  lines, line segments, etc.

● ●

Examples   1.   Two points determine (among other things)

            (a) a line,   (b) a line segment,   (c) two rays.

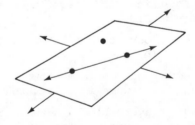 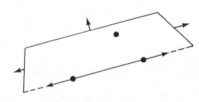

            2.   A point and a line determine

                  (a) a plane,   (b) a half-plane.

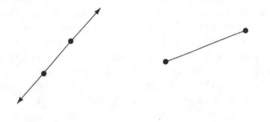 

            3.   Two lines determine

                  (a) a point,   (b) a plane,   (c) and maybe
                      maybe,   maybe,   not

                                                  (Lines in
                                                  space may miss
                                                  each other.)

322   CHAPTER 9

4.   A line and a plane determine

(a) a point, maybe,   (b) and maybe not:

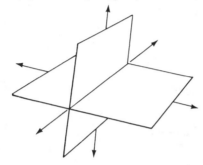   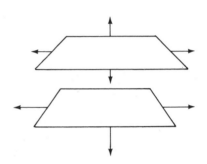

5.   Two planes determine

(a) a line, maybe,   (b) and maybe not:

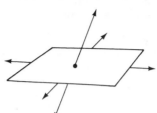   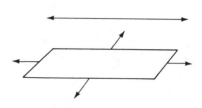

6.   A plane and a point determine a half-space (defined
     analogously to "half-line," where "space" is ordinary
     three-dimensional space), if the point is not on the
     plane, otherwise merely a point on the plane.

7.   Consider a simple, nonclosed curve and its endpoints.

(a) With no additional points (vertices) given, one
    curve segment is determined (a curve segment is a
    subset of a curve consisting of two points and that
    part of the curve between the two points).

(b) With one additional
    point on the curve,
    two segments are de-
    termined.

(c) With two additional
    points on the curve,
    three segments are
    determined.

(d) With three additional
    points on the curve,
    four segments are de-
    termined.

(e) with n additional points on the curve, $n + 1$ segments are determined.

8. Consider a plane and some lines in it, every pair of lines intersecting somewhere, but no three intersecting anywhere.

(a) One of the lines splits the plane into two regions:

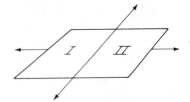

(b) Two of the lines split the plane into four regions:

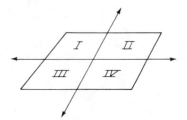

(c) Three of the lines split the plane into seven regions:

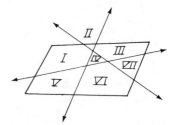

(d) Four of the lines split the plane into 11 regions:

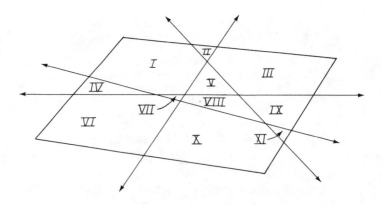

(e) n of the lines split the plane into how many regions? We'll probably just get mixed up if we try to draw more pictures, so let's see if our

arithmetic intuition can step in where our geometric insight might break down. Let's tabulate
what we've found so far:

No. of Lines	Regions Determined
1	2
2	4
3	7
4	11
. . .	. . .
n	?

Now the question is, what is the pattern in 2, 4,
7, 11, . . .?

If nonplussed, let's look at the first element in
this sequence: What is 2? Well, it's certainly
1 + 1. How about 4? It's 1 + 3, and 7 = 1 + 6,
and 11 = 1 + 10. Some of us may recognize the sequence 1, 3, 6, 10, . . . , and some may not. We
can try again, this time relating each element to
its predecessor:

No. of Lines	Regions Determined
1	2 = 1 + 1
2	4 = 1 + 1 + 2
3	7 = 1 + 1 + 2 + 3
4	11 = 1 + 1 + 2 + 3 + 4
. . .	. . .
n	?

We see it now! For n lines there are 1 + 1 + 2
+ 3 + • • • + n regions!

Exercises 1. (a) How many line-segment
edges are in Figure 1?

Figure 1

(b) How many line-segment
edges are in Figure 2?

Figure 2

(c) How many line-segment
edges are in Figure 3?

Figure 3

(d) How many line-segment edges are in Figure n?

2. Consider a plane and some lines in it, every pair intersecting somewhere, all possibly intersecting at the same point. What is the minimum number of regions that could be determined by

(a) one of these lines,

(b) two of these lines,

(c) three of these lines,

(d) four of these lines,

(e) n of these lines?

3. (a) Three points in a plane, not collinear ("collinear" = all on the same line), determine how many lines?

(b) Four points, no three collinear, determine how many lines?

(c) Five points, no three collinear, determine how many lines?

(d) Six points, no three collinear, determine how many lines?

(e) n points, no three collinear, determine how many lines?

4. (a) Two collinear points determine how many half-lines? (By "determine" we mean here that one point is an endpoint of the half-line and the other is on the half-line.)

(b) Two collinear points determine how many rays?

(c) Three collinear points determine how many rays?

(d) Four collinear points determine how many rays?

(e) n collinear points determine how many rays?

5. Consider all of the following to be set within a single plane. How many regions are determined by a network with (a) one vertex and one edge, (b) one vertex and two edges, (c) one vertex and three edges, (d) one vertex and four edges, (e) one vertex and n edges?

6. (Continuation of Exercise 5) No isolated vertices or infinite edges allowed in the following exercises:

(a) two vertices and one edge,

(b) two vertices and two edges,

(c) two vertices and three edges,

(d) two vertices and four edges,

(e) two vertices and n edges?

7. (Continuation)

(a) three vertices and two edges,

(b) three vertices and three edges,

(c) three vertices and four edges,

(d) three vertices and five edges,

(e) three vertices and *n* edges?

8. (Continuation)

(a) four vertices and three edges,

(b) four vertices and four edges,

(c) four vertices and five edges,

(d) four vertices and six edges,

(e) four vertices and *n* edges?

9. (Continuation) *m* vertices and *n* edges?

10. Make three-dimensional models illustrating Examples 3(c), 4(a), 4(b), 5(a), 5(b).

11. A bunch of lines in a plane are parallel in pairs (i.e., every pair is a pair of parallel lines). How many different pairs of parallel lines are there if in that bunch there are (a) 2, (b) 3, (c) 4, (d) 5, (e) *n* lines?

MEASURING IN METRIC UNITS

So far we've considered drawing and counting curves and curve segments. Another common pastime with these figures is measuring. While you're certainly familiar with such units of measurement as inches, feet, yards, and miles, you're probably not so proficient with metric units of length. It appears that the United States will adopt the international metric system and so fall in step with most of the rest of the countries of the world. This is really no big deal, as it merely means that we'll measure things just as we did before, except with different rulers and different measuring cups. If we do adopt this system, then the school kids will learn the metric units only, just as they now learn English units only. They will come to think naturally in terms of metres, litres, etc. and hence rarely need to convert to or otherwise use our present English units. But you *teachers* will need to know how to convert from the units on which you were reared to the new ones, hence the following treatment of metric units of length.

● ●

Objective 105. To measure the length of given curves to the nearest given metric unit.

● ●

The basic metric unit of
linear measure is the
metre (this is the international spelling), ab-
breviated m, which is
approximately 39.37 inches
long. Thus it's a little
longer than a yard.

This is not a convenient unit for measuring shorter,
more intimate lengths. Therefore, the *centimetre*
(abbreviated cm) is also used. It is one-hundredth
of a metre and about .39 inches long. Another way of
thinking of this is that an inch is approximately 2.54
centimetres long.

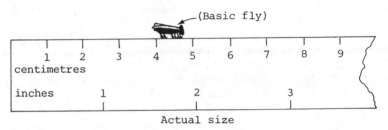

Actual size

For really tiny measurements the *millimetre* (mm) is
used; it is one-thousandth of a metre, therefore a
tenth of a centimetre. It's about one twenty-fourth
of an inch.

If we go to the other extreme and measure large distances, the appropriate metric unit is the *kilometre*
(km), which is a thousand metres, or about 3281 feet.
(Compare this to the mile, which is 5280 feet.)

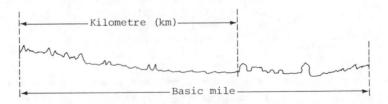

Examples   1.   Measure the length ℓ of the following rectilinear curve
to the nearest centimetre. ("Rectilinear" means "made
up of straight line segments.")

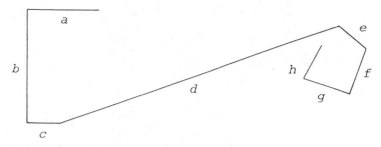

Upon measuring, you'll find that

$\ell = a + b + c + d + e + f + g + h$

$= (2 + 3 + 1 + 8 + 1 + 1.5 + 1.5 + 1)$ cm

$= 19$ cm.

2. Measure, to the nearest metre and centimetre, the length of the following rectilinear curve.

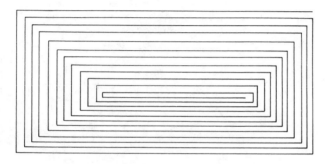

Answer: 192.5 cm, which we'll round off to 193 cm. This is 1.93 m, or 1 m, 93 cm (one metre, 93 centimetres).   Thus this curve is about 5 ft., 3 in. long.

3. Measure the length of the following curve to the nearest centimetre.

    This, of course, presents a slight complication.   The curve is not rectilinear, but rulers usually are.   One way to measure this curve (aside from using a tape measure) is to use ever more accurate rectilinear approximations to the original curly curve:

(a) Rough approximation: $4.6 + 3.0 + 3.4 \doteq 11$ cm.

(b) Better approximation: 3.3 + 2.2 + 1.5 + 1.8 + 2.2
    ≐ 11 cm. Since this latter approximation did not
    increase our estimate to the nearest centimetre,
    we are already close enough. Answer: 15 cm.

This last technique may seem naive to you, but it is
actually the basis for the mathematical definition of
the length of a curve. If the limit of the lengths of
increasingly accurate rectilinear approximations exists,
then that limit is defined to be the length of the
original curve.

Exercises   1.   Measure the length of each of the following curves to
                  the nearest centimetre, or metre and centimetre, which-
                  ever is more appropriate:

(a)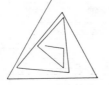

(b)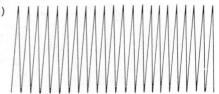

(c)

(d)

          2.   A quick way of adding 1 + 2 + 3 + • • • + 98 + 99 + 100
               is to add it twice and divide by 2:

$$
\begin{array}{rcrcrcccccrcrcr}
s &=& 1 &+& 2 &+& 3 &+& \cdots &+& 98 &+& 99 &+& 100 \\
s &=& 100 &+& 99 &+& 98 &+& \cdots &+& 3 &+& 2 &+& 1 \\
\hline
2s &=& 101 &+& 101 &+& 101 &+& \cdots &+& 101 &+& 101 &+& 101
\end{array}
$$

                        100 of these

                  = 10,100. So s = 10,100/2 = 5050.

               Use this trick (twice) to find quickly the length of
               the rectilinear curve in Example 2. (See also
               Example 2, page 371).

3. Find, to the nearest centimetre, the length of the following rectilinear spiral, assuming it never ceases winding in toward the center:

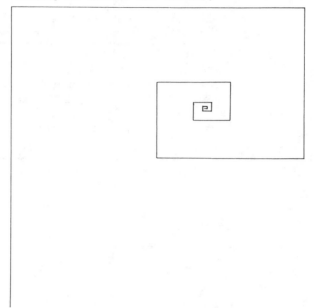

4. (a) What is $8 + 4 + 2 + 1 + \frac{1}{2} + \frac{1}{4} + \cdot \cdot \cdot$?

   (b) How is this sum related to Exercise 3?

5. Why did the metrically inclined boy send his girl friend to the north pole? (Answer: He wanted to see a Santa-meet-her.)

CONVERSION

Because both English units (inches, feet, yards, miles) and metric units are still commonly used throughout the world today, it's nice to know how to switch from one to the other.

● ●

Objective 106. To convert English units of linear measure to metric units and vice versa, given that one metre is approximately 39.37 inches.

● ●

Examples

1. How long is an inch in centimetres? We reason as follows:

$$1 \text{ in.} = \frac{1}{39.37} \text{ m} = \frac{100}{39.37} \text{ cm} = 2.54 \text{ cm.}$$

2. How many feet are in (a) one metre, (b) one kilometre?

   (a) $1 \text{ m} = 39.37 \text{ in.} = \frac{39.37}{12} \text{ ft.} \doteq 3.281 \text{ ft.}$

   (b) $1 \text{ km} = 1000 \text{ m} = 1000 \ (3.281) \text{ ft.} = 3281 \text{ ft.}$

3. How many metres in one mile?

$$1 \text{ mi.} = 5280 \text{ ft.} = 5280(12) \text{ in.} = 63,360 \text{ in.}$$

$$= \frac{63360}{39.37} \text{m} \doteq 1609 \text{ m}.$$

Notice how much more congenial it is to switch from metres to centimetres or kilometres (by merely multiplying by 100 or dividing by 1000) than it is to switch from feet to inches or miles. This is perhaps the chief reason for the popularity of the metric system.

Exercises
1. Do 2.54 push-ups and 39.37 jumping jacks.

2. Complete the following chart:

English Unit	cm	m	km
1 in.	2.54		
1 ft.			
1 yd.			
1 mi.		1609	

3. Complete this exciting chart:

Metric Unit	in.	ft.	yd.	mi.
1 cm	.39			
1 m	39.37	3.28		
1 km		3281		

4. According to the *Guinness Book of World Records*, the smallest waist of a normal-sized person measures 13 inches. Rewrite this in centimetres.

5. *Guinness* again: The tallest recorded man was 8 ft., 11 in. in height. Change this to metres and centimetres.

6. The so-called metric mile, a running event in international track meets, is over a distance of 1500 metres. Rewrite this in (a) feet, (b) yards, (c) miles.

ANGLES

In addition to lengths of curves (especially straight ones), people have devoted some attention to certain relationships between curves, namely the angles between them.

An angle   A "wrecked-angle"

● ●

Objective 107.   To explain what each of the following geometric items
is and draw a sketch of it: (a) plane angle, (b)
measure of an angle, (c) degree, (d) bisector of an
angle, (e) perpendicular lines.

● ●

(a) An *angle* (or *plane angle*) is a geometric figure
formed by two rays with a common endpoint.

(b) The *measure of an
angle* tells us how many
unit angles are in the
given angle. The measure
of the illustrated angle
is about $4\frac{1}{2}$ units. Theoretically, unit angles may
be chosen arbitrarily.

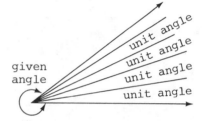

(c) A *degree* is the measure of a standard unit angle.
If we start with a certain (relatively small) angle and
"open it up" until the two rays coincide, the resulting
angle has a measure of 360 degrees (360°):

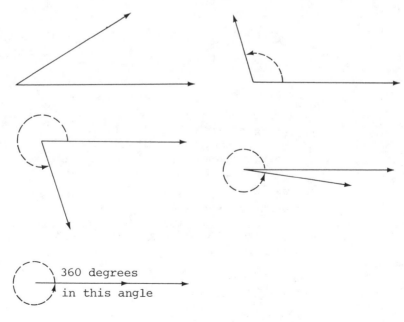

360 degrees
in this angle

(d) A *bisector* of an angle is a ray (or a piece of that ray) that divides the angle into two angles of equal measure. For example, a bisector of a 60° angle divides that angle into two 30° angles.

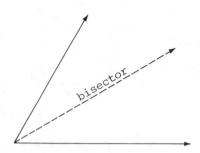

(e) *Perpendicular* lines are lines that intersect to form 90° angles (called *right angles*).

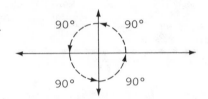

Exercises 1. Using a protractor (not a compass), draw angles of the following measures:

(a) 0°, (b) 30°, (c) 45°,

(d) 60°, (e) 90°,

(f) 135°, (g) 150°,

(h) 180°, (i) 240°,

(j) 270°, (k) 300°,

(l) 315°, (m) 360°,

(n) 420°, (o) 540°,

(p) 630°, (q) 750°.

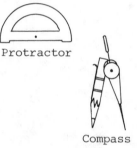

Protractor

Compass

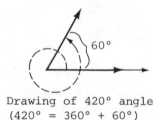

Drawing of 420° angle
(420° = 360° + 60°)

2. If we repeatedly bisect (i.e., bisect, then bisect each of the resulting angles, then bisect again each of the resulting angles, etc.) a 128° angle, we eventually get many 1° angles. Explain arithmetically why this is so.

3. Which of the following angles, if repeatedly bisected, eventually yield a 1° angle? (a) 400°, (b) 384°, (c) 256°, (d) 160°, (e) 96°, (f) 32°, (g) 320°, (h) 16°? (i) What do the angles selected from (a)-(h) have in common?

4. If we repeatedly bisect:

(a) a 1504° angle, do we eventually get a 47° angle?

(b) a 168° angle, do we eventually get a 4° angle?

(c) a 724° angle, do we eventually get a 3° angle?

(d) a 723° angle, do we eventually get a 3° angle?

(e) a 768° angle, do we eventually get a 3° angle?

(f) a 777° angle, do we eventually get a 3° angle?

(g) How can we tell if repeated bisection of an $n°$ angle will eventually yield a 3° angle?

5. For each of the following, (i) draw angle ABC (symbolized ∢ ABC) for the given measure, (ii) draw the bisector b of ∢ ABC, (iii) draw line ℓ perpendicular to b, through B, with a point P on ℓ, *(iv)* measure angles PBA and DBP.

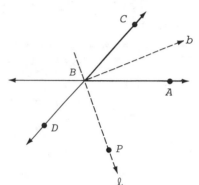

(a) m(∢ ABC) = 30° (read, "Measure of angle ABC equals thirty degrees"),

(b) m(∢ ABC) = 44°, (c) m(∢ ABC) = 50°, (d) m(∢ ABC) = 86°. (e) What rule is suggested by (a)-(d)?

6. (a) Case 1: How many different acute angles are formed by an acute angle and its bisector? (An *acute* angle is an angle of measure less than 90°.)

(b) Case 2: How many different acute angles are formed by an acute angle, its bisector, and the bisectors of its half-angles, as illustrated?

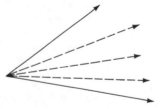

(c) Case 3: How many different acute angles if each angle in Case 2 is bisected?

(d) How many different acute angles are there in Case 4?

(e) How many different acute angles are there in Case n?

7. (a) Explain what the *trisectors* of an angle are.

(b) Draw each of the following size angles and its trisectors: (i) 30°, (ii) 45°, (iii) 60°, (iv) 90°, (v) 135°, (vi) 180°.

8. Write a better poem about angles than this one, "The Last Tangle":

Two rays of an angle
Started to tangle
Over a vertex, or maybe a joint.

They continued to wrangle
And mutually mangle
But neither ever really got the point.

Marlon Brandothetti, 1973

RECTANGLES

Besides points and lines, the geometric figure perhaps most often encountered is the rectangle, and its special case, the square. First, we try to appease your mad hunger for terminology:

● ●

Objective 108.

To explain what each of the following is and draw a sketch of it: (a) quadrilateral, (b) rectangle, (c) square, (d) similar rectangles, (e) diagonals of a rectangle.

● ●

(a) *Quadrilateral*. The Latin roots probably lead you to guess that a quadrilateral is a four-sided figure. Technically, it's a simple, closed, rectilinear figure formed by the union of four line segments.

Sketch of a quadrilateral

(b) *Rectangle*. A rectangle is a quadrilateral with four 90° angles (or right angles).

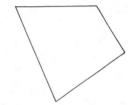

Sketch of a rectangle

(c) *Square*. A square is a rectangle with all sides of equal length.

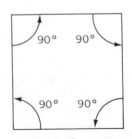

Sketch of a square

(d) *Similar rectangles.*
Two rectangles are similar
if they are of the same
shape; this is so if the
ratio of the height to
width of one rectangle is
equal to the ratio of the
height to width of the
other rectangle. Two
squares are always similar,
since $h/w = 1$ every time.

$$\frac{h}{w} = \frac{4}{8} = \frac{1}{2}$$

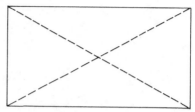

$$\frac{h}{w} = \frac{2}{4} = \frac{1}{2}$$

Sketch of similar rec-
tangles

(e) *Diagonals of a rec-
tangle.* The diagonals of
a rectangle are the two
line segments that are (i)
determined by the vertices
and (ii) not sides.

Sketch of diagonals of
a rectangle

Exercises 1. A *complete quadrilateral* is defined to be four lines
that intersect at six points.

(a) Draw at least three differently shaped complete
quadrilaterals.

(b) Is a complete quadrilateral (i) simple,
(ii) closed, (iii) rectilinear?

2. Draw a *nonsimple*, closed rectilinear figure formed by
the union of four line segments.

3. (a) Draw a Venn diagram indicating the set relationships between the set of quadrilaterals, the set
of rectangles, and the set of squares.

(b) What is another set that "fits in between" the set
of quadrilaterals and the set of rectangles?

4. (a) Cut out of paper a
rectangle which when
folded in two yields a
rectangle similar to
the original rectangle.

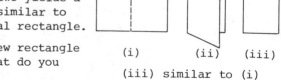

(i)   (ii)   (iii)

(iii) similar to (i)

(b) Fold the new rectangle
in two; what do you
notice?

(c) Fold the rectangle in (b) in two; what rule do you
see emerging?

5. Compute the exact (as opposed to decimal approximation)
height and width of a rectangle which when "folded in
two" yields a rectangle similar to the original one.

(Hint: Let the original height be y, the width be x, and use algebra.)

6. (a) Draw at least three differently shaped rectangles and measure their diagonals to the nearest millimetre (tenth of a centimetre).

   (b) How do the lengths of the diagonals of a rectangle compare?

   (c) Draw a quadrilateral that is *not* a rectangle, but where diagonals have the property in (b).

7. (a) Draw at least three differently shaped rectangles and measure the distances from the vertices of the rectangle to the intersection of the diagonals (to the nearest millimetre).

   (b) How do the diagonals of a rectangle cut each other?

   (c) Draw a quadrilateral that is not a rectangle, but whose diagonals have the property in (b).

8. Compare and contrast "rectangle" and "wrecked angle."

COUNTING Of course, nothing excites us like counting squares and rectangles.

● ●

Objective 109. Given a figure or sequence of figures composed of rectangles, to count specified rectangles, vertices of rectangles, diagonals, etc. in either particular or general cases.

● ●

Examples 1. (a) Case 1: How many squares are there of all sizes? Just one.

   (b) Case 2: How many squares are there of all sizes? We might systematically start by counting first the number of 1-by-1 squares: 4. Next 2-by-2: 1. Sum: $4 + 1 = 5$.

   (c) Case 3: How many squares are there of all sizes?
   1-by-1: 9
   2-by-2: 4 (one in each corner)
   3-by-3: 1. $9 + 4 + 1 = 14$.

(d) Case 4: How many
squares are there of
all sizes?
1-by-1: 16
2-by-2:   9 (three in
  each 2-by-4 row)
3-by-3:   4 (one in
  each corner)
4-by-4:   1. 16 + 9 + 4 + 1 = 30.

(e) Case n: How many squares are there of all sizes?
We look, of course, for a pattern here. What kind
of a sum is 16 + 9 + 4 + 1? What kind of numbers
are 16, 9, 4, 1? With a little thought we see that
they're all squares!
So, we have

Case 1: $1 = 1^2$
Case 2: $1 + 4 = 1^2 + 2^2$
Case 3: $1 + 4 + 9 = 1^2 + 2^2 + 3^2$
Case 4: $1 + 4 + 9 + 16 = 1^2 + 2^2 + 3^2 + 4^2$.

Hence, we strongly suspect (but surely haven't
proved) that in Case n there are $1^2 + 2^2 + 3^2 +$
$\cdots + (n - 1)^2 + n$ squares.

2. How many squares are there
of all sizes? Here we are
dealing with two types
(both in many different
sizes) of squares, "up-

right" $\lfloor$ ' and "teetering"

$\diamondsuit$. How can we use the solution in Example 1?
Well, we note that it counted all of the upright
squares, so in Case 3 there are 14 of them. Let's now
restrict our attention to part of the problem, counting the teetering squares, and to this end let's *systematically count special cases*. (Note: each italicized phrase is a useful procedure in solving any problem, not just this one. You might try these behaviors
in solving problems on your own.)

Number of teetering 1-by-1 squares: 12
Number of teetering 2-by-2 squares: 5
Total number of teetering squares: 17
Hence, grand total: 14 + 17 = 31.

3. In the figure of Example 2, how many different diagonals of squares are there?
We could laboriously count (probably incorrectly on
the first try), or we could ask ourselves, "How can we
use previously solved Example 2?" There we found out
that there were 31 distinct squares. Now distinct
squares have distinct diagonals, and there are two
diagonals per square. Thus, there are 31 × 2 = 62 different diagonals.

4. In an n-by-$2n$ rectangle, there are how many smaller rectangles similar to and in the same orientation as the given rectangle?

Let's systematically count special cases:

No smaller similar rectangles: 0. $n = 1$: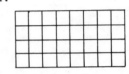

In this 2-by-4 rectangle the smaller similar rectangles are the 1-by-2 rectangles, and there are six of them (three in each row): 6. $n = 2$:

Here the smaller similar rectangles are 1-by-2 and 2-by-4, of which there are 15 and six, respectively: 15 + 6 = 21. $n = 3$:

In this case the smaller similar rectangles are 1-by-2, 2-by-4, 3-by-6, of which there are 28, 15, six, respectively: 28 + 15 + 6 = 49. $n = 4$:

Now, what kind of numbers are 0, 6, 21, 49? Let's see:

   $6 = 1 + 2 + 3.$
   $21 = 6 + 15 = (1 + 2 + 3) + (1 + 2 + 3 + 4 + 5).$
   $49 = 6 + 15 + 28 = (1 + 2 + 3) + (1 + 2 + 3 + 4 + 5)$
       $+ (1 + 2 + 3 + 4 + 5 + 6 + 7).$

So for $n = 5$ we would expect $(1 + 2 + 3) + (1 + 2 + 3 + 4 + 5) + (1 + 2 + 3 + 4 + 5 + 6 + 7) + (1 + 2 + 3 + 4 + 5 + 6 + 7 + 8 + 9)$. The crucial numbers here are those last odd numbers:

Case	Last Odd Number
1	—
2	$3 = 2(2) - 1$
3	$5 = 2(3) - 1$
4	$7 = 2(4) - 1$
5	$9 = 2(5) - 1$

So in Case n we expect the last odd number to be $2n - 1$ (which is, "oddly" enough, the nth odd number).

Hence the answer appears to be (but hasn't been proved to be) $(1 + 2 + 3) + (1 + 2 + 3 + 4 + 5) + \cdots + (1 + 2 + 3 + 4 + 5 + \cdots + (2n - 1))$.

Exercises   1.   (a) How many rectangles
                       of all sizes in this
                       figure?

             (b) How many rectangles
                 in this figure?

             (c) How many in this
                 figure?

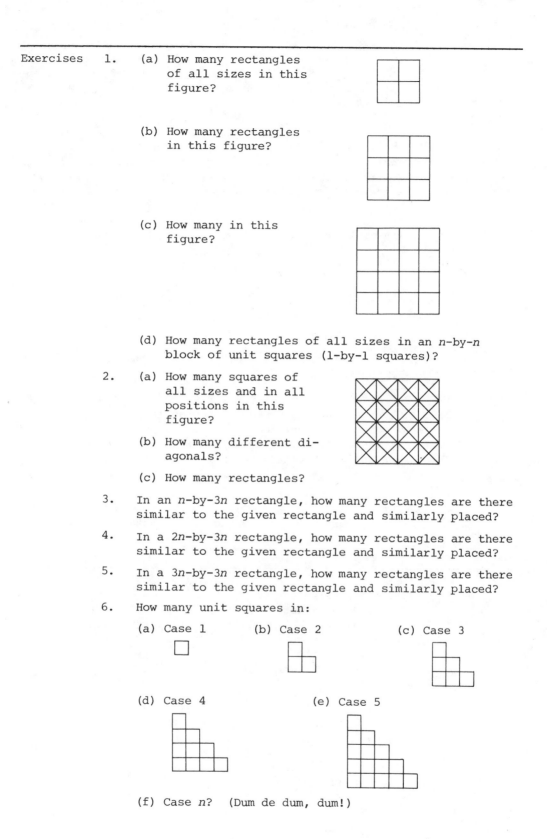

             (d) How many rectangles of all sizes in an *n*-by-*n*
                 block of unit squares (1-by-1 squares)?

        2.   (a) How many squares of
                 all sizes and in all
                 positions in this
                 figure?

             (b) How many different di-
                 agonals?

             (c) How many rectangles?

        3.   In an *n*-by-3*n* rectangle, how many rectangles are there
             similar to the given rectangle and similarly placed?

        4.   In a 2*n*-by-3*n* rectangle, how many rectangles are there
             similar to the given rectangle and similarly placed?

        5.   In a 3*n*-by-3*n* rectangle, how many rectangles are there
             similar to the given rectangle and similarly placed?

        6.   How many unit squares in:

             (a) Case 1   (b) Case 2   (c) Case 3

             (d) Case 4   (e) Case 5

             (f) Case *n*?   (Dum de dum, dum!)

7. How many squares of all sizes in Case n for Exercise 6?

8. How many vertices in:

(a) Case 1:   (b) Case 2   (c) Case 3

COMPUTING
AREAS

We turn next to the areas of rectangles. The *area* of a figure is the (real) number of unit squares that can be fit into the region bounded by that figure. A *unit square* is a square of edge-length one unit. Here are some pictures, actual size, of some unit squares:

1 square cm
(symbol: 1 cm^2)

1 square inch
(symbol: 1 $in.^2$)

● ●

Objective 110. Given a figure composed of rectangles, with their dimensions in specified units, to compute the area of the figure in given units (not necessarily the same as the originally specified units).

● ●

Hungry to attack Objective 110, we lust after a formula for the area of a rectangle. For those of you who have forgotten it, *regardez*:

Examples 1. Compute the area of a rectangle 2 cm wide and 3 cm long. Here we have one square centimeter corresponding to row 1, column 1, another to row 1, column 2, etc. So there are as many square centimetres as there are ordered pairs of rows and columns. Thus the area A, in square centimetres, is the cardinal number of $\{1,2\} \otimes \{1,2,3\}$, which is $2 \times 3 = 6$. Answer: 6 cm^2.

Another, less formal, way of looking at this is to note that we have two rows of three square centimetres each, thus $2 \times 3 = 6$ cm^2.

2. Compute the area of a rectangle 3 cm wide and 5 cm long (each square represents 1 cm^2):

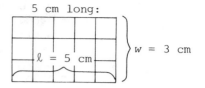

5 cm long:

$\ell = 5$ cm

$w = 3$ cm

$A = 3 \times 5 = 15$ cm^2

Notice that we may think of "cm" as an algebraic symbol, just like u (for "unit"). Just as

$$(3u) \times (2u) = \big((3u) \times 2\big) \times u \text{ (associative law)}$$

$$= \big(3 \times (u \times 2)\big) \times u \text{ (associative law again)}$$

$$= \big(3 \times (2 \times u)\big) \times u \text{ (commutative law)}$$

$$= \big((3 \times 2) \times u\big) \times u \text{ (associative law)}$$

$$= (6 \times u) \times u \text{ (renaming)}$$

$$= 6 \times (u \times u) \text{ (associative law)}$$

$$= 6u^2 \text{ (definition of } u^2\text{)},$$

so we may write

$$(3 \text{ cm}) \times (2 \text{ cm}) = 6(\text{cm} \times \text{cm}) = 6 \text{ cm}^2.$$

In general, if the width of a rectangle is w units (w not necessarily a whole number) and the length is ℓ units, then the area A is given by

$$A = (\ell \text{ units}) \times (w \text{ units}) = (\ell \times w) \text{ square units.}$$

3. You can use the dimension of units to help check your work. For example, suppose that in haste on a quiz you wrote that the area of a 2 cm by 3 cm rectangle was 2 cm + 3 cm = 5 cm. Then you could say to yourself, "Ho! The answer I have here is in linear centimetres, while it *should* be in areal square centimetres. What's wrong? Ha! I added instead of multiplying. The answer really is 2 cm × 3 cm = 6 cm^2."

4. What is the area in square inches of a rectangle 2 cm by 3 cm?

We know from the past (Exercise 3, page 332) that 1 cm $\doteq$ .39 in. So

$$A = (2 \text{ cm}) \times (3 \text{ cm}) = 2(.39 \text{ in.}) \times 3(.39) \text{ in.}$$

$$= 6 \times (.39)^2 \text{ in.}^2 = 6 \times .1521 \text{ in.}^2 = .9126 \text{ in.}^2$$

$$\doteq .91 \text{ in.}^2, \text{ to the nearest hundredth.}$$

5. Compute the area of the following figure in acres, if it is known that 1 acre = 43,560 ft^2.

One bother here is that the figure is not a rectangle. *How can we use previous problems here?*

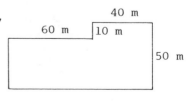

40 m

60 m   10 m

50 m

Let's break the figure up
into good old familiar
rectangles, for example,
like this:

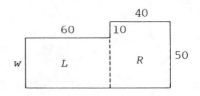

Then we readily see that
the area R is given by

$$R = 40 \text{ m} \times 50 \text{ m} = 2000 \text{ m}^2$$

We have the length of L, but not the width. How can we
use what is given to get what we want? Aha! $w + 10$
$= 50$, since the opposite edges of a rectangle are
equal. So $w = 40$, and

$$L = 40 \text{ m} \times 60 \text{ m} = 2400 \text{ m}^2$$

Thus $A = L + R = (2000 + 2400)\text{m}^2 = 4400 \text{ m}^2$

The new latest bother is that this last answer is in
square metres, while we want it in acres. The units
that we know about and that connect metres and acres
are feet. From the past, 1 m $\doteq$ 3.28 ft. Therefore,

$$A = 2400 \text{ m}^2 \doteq 2400(3.28 \text{ ft.})^2 = 2400(3.28)^2 \text{ ft.}^2$$

$$= 2400(10.7584) \text{ ft.}^2 = 25820.16 \text{ ft.}^2$$

$$= \frac{25820.16}{43,560} \text{ acres} \doteq .59 \text{ acres, to the nearest}$$

hundredth.

Exercises 1. Compute the areas of rectangles of the given dimensions
in the specified square units:

(a) 42 cm by 5 cm, in sq. in.

(b) 42 in. by 5 in., in sq. cm.

(c) 42 in. by 5 in., in sq. m.

(d) 2 m by 5 m, in sq. in.

(e) 2 m by 5 m, in sq. ft.

(f) 210 m by 200 m, in acres.

(g) 210 ft. by 200 ft., in acres.

(h) 2 mi. by 3 mi., in sq. km.

(i) 2 km by 3 km, in sq. mi.

2. Complete the chart:

English Unit	sq. cm	sq. m	sq. km
1 sq. in.	6.45		
1 sq. ft.			
1 sq. yd.			
1 sq. mi.			
1 acre			

3. Complete the chart:

Metric Unit	sq. in.	sq. ft.	sq. yd.	sq. mi.
1 sq. cm	.15			
1 sq. m				
1 sq. km				
1 acre		43,560		

4. Which of the two charts do you prefer completing? Why?

5. (a) What is the area of the "before" rectangle?

   (b) What is the area of the "after" rectangle?

   (c) How can we gain a unit of area by merely rearranging pieces of a square?

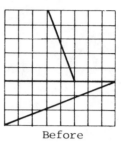
Before

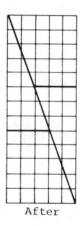
After

6. Devise a paradox similar to that in Exercise 5, based on the fact that 64 = 63 + 1.

7. Compute the areas of the following figures in sq. cm, if the given dimensions are in cm (assume symmetry where applicable).

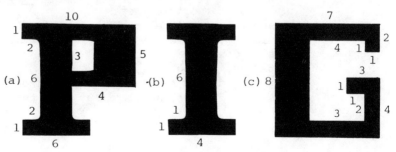

8. (a) What is the area of
    this figure?

    (b) What is the area of half of the rectangle in (a)?

    (c) What is the area of
    this figure?

    (d) What is the area of half (part A) of the rectangle
    in (e)?

    (e) What is the area of
    this figure?

    (f) What is the area of half (part A) of the rectangle
    in (e)?

    (g) What is the area of
    this figure?

    (h) What is the area of half (part A) of the rectangle
    in (g)?

    (i) What sums are represented by the indicated half-
    rectangles in (a), (c), (e), (g)?

    (j) Half of what rectangle would represent the sum
    $1 + 2 + 3 + \cdots + (n - 2) + (n - 1) + n$?

    (k) Derive a short formula (no ellipsis dots allowed)
    for the sum $1 + 2 + 3 + \cdots + (n - 2) + (n - 1)$
    $+ n$.

TRIANGLES

What do two men in love with the same woman, civil de-
fense, and change, all have in common? They are all
symbolized by a triangle.
The Star of David is com-
posed of two triangles
superimposed, one "right-
side up," the other "up-
side down." Next to rec-
tangles and squares,
triangles may be the most familiar of the closed rectilinear figures, and it is at them that we next look.

Objective 111.   To explain what each of the following is and draw a
                  sketch of it: (a) triangle, (b) isosceles triangle,
                  (c) equilateral triangle, (d) similar triangles,
                  (e) right triangle, (f) hypotenuse.

•••

(a) *Triangle.* This
sounds like a three-angled
figure, and that's just
about right. The official
definition of a triangle
is "a simple, closed rec-
tilinear figure formed by
the union of three line
segments."

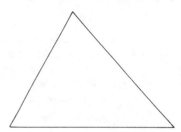

Sketch of a triangle

(b) *Isosceles triangle.*
An isosceles triangle is a
triangle with two of its
sides equal in length.

Sketches of isosceles
triangles

(c) *Equilateral triangle.*
An equilateral triangle is
a triangle that has all of
its laterals equal; that
is, all sides of the same
length.

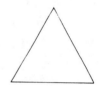

Sketch of equilateral
triangle

(d) *Similar triangles.*
Two triangles are similar
if they have the same
shape; this is so if the
measures of the angles of
the first triangle are
equal to the measures of
the angles of the second
triangle.

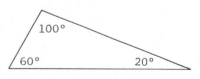

Sketch of similar
triangles

(e) *Right triangles*. A triangle is a right triangle if one of its angles is a right angle (i.e., has 90° measure).

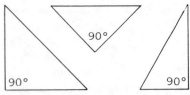
Sketches of right triangles

(f) *Hypotenuse*. The hypotenuse of a right triangle is the side opposite the right angle. It is also the longest side of the triangle.

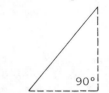
Sketch of the hypotenuse

Exercises   1.   Draw appropriate pictures and answer each of the following true or false:

(a) Every triangle is isosceles.

(b) Every isosceles triangle is equilateral.

(c) Every equilateral triangle is isosceles.

(d) Any two isosceles triangles are similar.

(e) Any two equilateral triangles are similar.

(f) Any two similar triangles are isosceles.

(g) Any two right triangles are similar.

(h) A right triangle may be isosceles.

(i) A right triangle may be equilateral.

(j) A right triangle may have two 90° angles.

(k) A right triangle may have two 45° angles.

(l) A right triangle may have two 30° angles.

(m) An equilateral triangle may have two 45° angles.

(n) An equilateral triangle may have two 60° angles.

(o) An isosceles triangle may have two 45° angles.

(p) An isosceles triangle may have two 120° angles.

(q) Two triangles are similar if the sum of the angle measures of one triangle is equal to the sum of the angle measures of the other triangle.

(r) If two triangles are similar, then the sum of the angle measures of one triangle is equal to the sum of the angle measures of the other triangle.

2. In the movie "The Wizard of Oz," what was incorrect about the proposition ("In an isosceles triangle the square of the hypotenuse equals the sum of the squares of the sides.") announced by the Scarecrow upon receipt of his diploma?

3. Draw a Venn diagram indicating the relationships between the following sets: the set of all triangles, the set of all isosceles triangles, the set of all equilateral triangles, the set of all right triangles.

COUNTING PARTS Objective 109 sets the stage for more.

● ●

Objective 112. Given a figure or sequence of figures composed of triangles, to count specified elements (e.g., vertices, triangles, right triangles, triangles similar to a given triangle, etc.) in either particular or general cases.

● ●

Examples 1. How many of the smallest triangles are there in Case n?

Case 1   Case 2   Case 3   Case 4

Let's *look for a pattern* and solve this problem by *systematically counting special cases*.

Case	No. "Upright" Triangles	No. "Upside Down" Triangles	Total No. of Triangles
1	1	0	1
2	3	1	4
3	6	3	9
4	10	6	16
· · ·	· · ·	· · ·	· · ·
n			?

Since $1 = 1^2$, $4 = 2^2$, $9 = 3^2$, and $16 = 4^2$, we therefore guess that in Case n there are n^2 triangles.

2. In Case 4 of Example 1, how many triangles are similar to the largest triangle?

First of all, there are all of the smallest ("size 1") triangles counted in Example 1, or $4^2 = 16$.

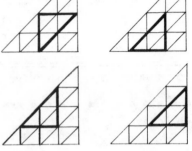

Next, let's count all of the next smallest ("size 2") triangles similar to the largest triangle. These are outlined in heavy line segments in the accompanying figures. There are a total of seven of these, six "upright" and one "upside down."

If we count the "size 3" triangles, there are three "uprights" and zero "up-side-downs," a total of 3.

Finally, there is just one "size 4" triangle, the largest one. Hence the total number of triangles similar to (and including) the largest triangle is $16 + 7 + 3 + 1 = 27$.

3. How many vertices are there in Case n of Example 1?

Case	No. of Vertices
1	$3 = 1 + 2$
2	$6 = 1 + 2 + 3$
3	$10 = 1 + 2 + 3 + 4$
4	$15 = 1 + 2 + 3 + 4 + 5$
$\cdots$	$\cdots$
n	?

Again, after tabulation it appears fairly readily that in Case n there are $1 + 2 + 3 + \cdots + n + \dfrac{n(n+1)}{2}$ vertices.

Exercises 1. How many (a) "upright," (b) "upside-down" triangles are there in Case n of Example 1?

2. How many triangles in Example 2 are *not* similar to the largest ("size 4") triangle?

3. Use a figure like those in Examples 1 and 2 to demonstrate that $(n + 1)^2 = n^2 + 2n + 1$.

4. Draw Case 5 of Example 1. How many triangles are there of all sizes?

5. How many vertices are there in Case *n* of Example 2?

6.

Case 1   Case 2   Case 3

   (a) Draw Case 4.

   (b) How many of the smallest triangles are in Case *n*?

   (c) How many triangles of all sizes in Case *n*?

   (d) How many equilateral triangles in Case *n*?

   (e) How many isosceles triangles in Case *n*?

   (f) How many right triangles in Case *n*?

   (g) How many vertices in Case *n*?   (⌐ indicates a
                                                right angle.)

7.

Case 1   Case 2   Case 3   Case 4

   (a) Draw Cases 5 and 6.

   (b) How many right triangles in Case 2?

   (c) How many right triangles in Case 3?

   (d) How many right triangles in Case *n*?

   (e) How many triangles in Case *n* are similar to the triangle in Case 1?

8.
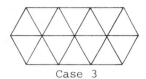
(Although not in general, ⊿ here indicates a 60° angle.)

  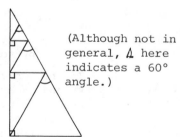
Case 1   Case 2   Case 3

(a) Draw a large picture of Case 4.

(b) How many right triangles in Case 1?

(c) How many right triangles in Case 2?

(d) How many right triangles in Case *n*?

(e) How many triangles in Case *n* are similar to the largest triangle in Case *n*?

(f) How many wrong triangles in Case *n*?

We concentrate now on the measures of the angles of a triangle.

● ●

Objective 113. (a) To state the sum of the angle measures of a triangle and (b) to demonstrate the truth of this statement.

● ●

We leap immediately into some exercises.

Exercises   1. Cut out at least five triangular regions of different sizes and shapes. Then tear each of these regions into three parts, with one vertex per part. Reassemble the parts with the vertices fitted together as illustrated.

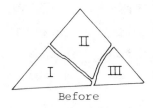

Before

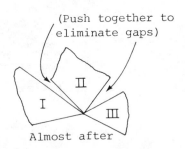

(Push together to eliminate gaps)

Almost after

For each triangle record the measure of the angle formed by the juxtaposition of the three torn pieces.

2. In the accompanying figure, ℓ_1 and ℓ_2 are parallel, and ℓ_2 coincides with the bottom edge (alias *base*) of the triangle.

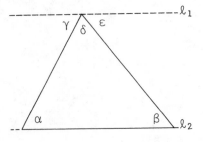

(a) How do the measures of α and γ compare?

(b) How do the measures of β and ε compare?

(c) What is the sum of the measures of γ, δ, ε?

(d) What is the sum of the measures of α, β, δ?

3. What is the sum of the measures of the angle of a triangle?

4. Compute, if possible, the measures of each of the three angles of the following triangles:

   (a) isosceles triangle,

   (b) isosceles right triangle,

   (c) equilateral triangle,

   (d) right triangle with a 30° angle,

   (e) isosceles triangle with two 30° angles,

   (f) equilateral triangle with 45° angle.

5. Draw at least five different kinds of quadrilaterals and one diagonal in each. Find the sum of the angle measures of each of the quadrilaterals.

6. In *spherical geometry* (i.e., geometry on a sphere) we can have two right angles in a triangle, as illustrated in the figure.

   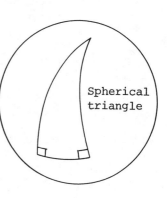

   Spherical triangle

   (a) Draw a spherical triangle with three right angles.

   (b) What is the minimum sum of angle measures of a spherical triangle?

   (c) What is the maximum?

CURRY TRIANGLE PARADOX

The Curry Triangle Paradox, it turns out, involves not the angle measures of a triangle, but the area of a triangle. Before charging into this paradox we'll need to brace ourselves with a formula for the area of a triangle.

In hunting down this formula let us use some of our problem-solving techniques. *What is given?* A triangle; here it is:

How can we use a previously solved problem? The only related previously solved problem was that of finding the area of a rectangle. How can we adapt a rectangle to our triangle?

Well, we can fit one around (in technical language, *circumscribe*) the triangle, thus:

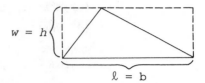

$w = h$

$\ell = b$

The width w of the rectangle is the same as the height h of the triangle, and the length ℓ of the rectangle is the same as the length of the base b of the triangle. We know that the area of the rectangle is $A = w \times \ell$. Now the question is, how is the area of the triangle related to that of the rectangle? Perhaps an additional, *auxiliary line* will help; if so, where is a natural place to put it? We might try inserting one to represent the distance from the peak of the triangle to its base:

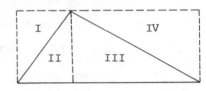

I   IV

II   III

Ha! We now spot the fact that triangle I is the same size and shape as (technically, *congruent to*) triangle II, and triangle III is the same size and shape as triangle IV. Thus the area A of the original triangle is half the area of the circumscribed rectangle (II and III constitute half of I, II, III, and IV), so

$A = \frac{1}{2} \times h \times b$.

Examples   1.

  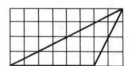

$A = \frac{1}{2}(4)(6) = 12$ sq. units for all three of these triangles.

2. $A = \frac{1}{2}(7 \text{ cm})(5 \text{ cm})$
$= 35/2 \text{ cm}^2 = 17.5 \text{ cm}^2$.

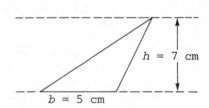

$h = 7$ cm

$b = 5$ cm

Exercises   Compute the areas of the following triangles:

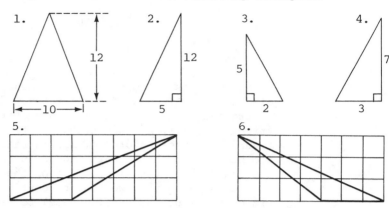

●●●

*Objective 114.   (a) To state the Curry triangle paradox, (b) to explain
                    the fallacy of this "paradox."

●●

In order to attack this objective you have to know
what the "paradox" is, so here you are: We start with
the large triangle below left and cut it up along the
heavy lines.

We then reassemble the parts as in the figure on the
right.

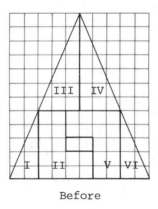

Before   After

Student: "Hey! What happened to that little two-unit
rectangle?" This is the right question. How can we
take all but two square units of a 60-square-unit triangle and completely fill up another 60-square-unit
triangle? This is the Curry triangle paradox (named
after Paul Curry).

The next task is to explain the fallacy in this "paradox." Now *if* the left edge of the largest triangle is
a straight line segment, then triangles I and III are

similar. Let us look at the height-to-base ratio for each of the triangles:

Triangle   I: $\dfrac{h}{b} = \dfrac{5}{2} = 2.50$

Triangle III: $\dfrac{h}{b} = \dfrac{7}{3} = 2.33.$

These ratios are not the same! Hence the left (and also the right) edge of the largest "triangle" is not a straight line segment. The large "triangle" is no triangle at all, but a pentagon—a five-sided (edged) figure. So the "before" figure is really a little too bulgy, and the "after" figure is really a little too caved in at the sides. One of the lessons to be learned here is that we must be cautious in attributing properties (such as straightness) to geometric figures.

Exercises   1.   Compute the areas of figures I, II, III, IV, V, and VI, assuming that the left edge of the largest "triangle" passes through the lattice point (2,5), if we bring in a coordinate system with the origin at the lower left-hand vertex of that "triangle."

2.   This time assume that the overall figure really *is* bounded by a triangle.

(a) Does the left edge of this largest triangle pass above or below (2,5)?

(b) What is the true height of triangle I, if its base is 2 cm long? (Hint: If the left edge is straight, then all of the three triangles in the figure at the right are similar. Use some algebra on the ratios.)

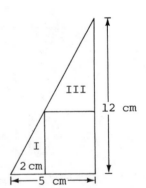

(c) What is the area of triangle I?

(d) What is the true height of triangle III, if its true base is 3 cm long?

(e) What is the true area of triangle III?

(f) How can you partially check your answers to (c) and (e)?

3.   Answer true or false whether it's possible for:

(a) the upper vertex of triangle I to be at (2,5) and also the upper vertex of triangle III to be at (5,12),

(b) the upper vertex of triangle I to be at (2,5) and also the left edge of the largest figure to be straight,

(c) the upper vertex of triangle III to be at (5,12) and also the left edge of the largest figure to be straight,

(d) the upper vertex of triangle I to be at (2,5), the upper vertex of triangle III to be at (5,12), and also the left edge of the largest triangle to be straight.

4.   Carefully draw and cut up a Curry triangle with base length 10 in. and height 12 in., preferably on transparent plastic marked with a permanent black marker so you can use it with an overhead projector when teaching. (A plastic report cover is good for this purpose.)

PYTHAGOREAN
THEOREM

Before putting your scissors away, try this cutting exercise: Draw a right triangle with its hypotenuse forming the edge of an adjacent square, as in the drawing. With the midpoint of *each* side of the square as an endpoint, draw rays parallel to an edge of the right triangle; in the drawing, for example, ray r_1 is parallel to e_1, r_2 parallel to e_2.

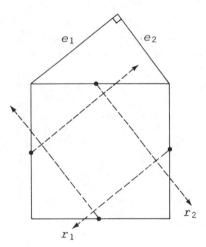

Next cut off the square along the hypotenuse, and cut along parts of the rays, as indicated by the heavy lines in the sketch with the regions numbered. Finally, reassemble quadrilaterals I, II, III, IV, and V to form squares on edges e_1 and e_2 of the original triangle:

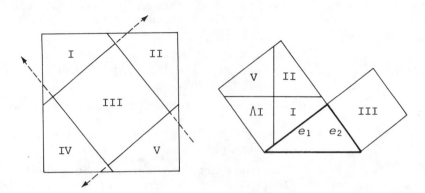

The preceding dissection exercise demonstrates the famous *Pythagorean Theorem*: The area of the square on the hypotenuse of a right triangle is equal to the sum of the areas of the squares on the other two sides. This theorem can also be stated more algebraically: If a, b, c are the lengths of the sides of a right triangle, with c the length of the hypotenuse, then $c^2 = a^2 + b^2$.

Before plowing further, let us state the next objective.

● ●

Objective 115. (a) To state the Pythagorean Theorem, (b) to illustrate it with dissections, (c) to prove it via computation of areas.

● ●

The preceding scissors-and-paper exercise and paragraph take care of (a) and (b), so we need only show you how to take care of part (c). Before we do this, we need to develop a formula for the area of a quadrilateral called a *trapezoid*, two opposite sides of which are parallel.

Trapezoids with top and bottom sides parallel

How can we *use a previously solved problem*? Let's try again circumscribing a rectangle about a trapezoid:

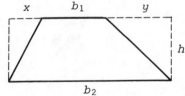

This does't suggest much, so let's *add some auxiliary lines*.

We see some things now: Triangles I and II have the same area, and so do triangles III and IV. So we can write:

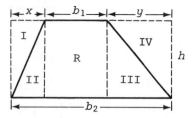

Area of trapezoid = area of large rectangle - areas of I and IV

$$= h \cdot (b_2) - \left(\left(\frac{1}{2} \cdot h \cdot x\right) + \left(\frac{1}{2} \cdot h \cdot y\right)\right)$$

$$= b_2 h - \frac{1}{2} h (x + y)$$

$$= b_2 h - \frac{1}{2} h (b_2 - b_1)$$

$$= b_2 h - \frac{b_2 h}{2} + \frac{b_1 h}{2}$$

$$= \frac{b_2 h}{2} + \frac{b_1 h}{2} = h \frac{b_1 + b_2}{2} .$$

So for a trapezoid we have that the area equals the product of the height and the average (mean) of the two parallel sides:

$$A = h \times \frac{1}{2}(b_1 + b_2)$$

Examples 1.

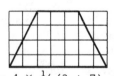

$$A = 4 \times \frac{1}{2} (3 + 7) = 20$$

2.

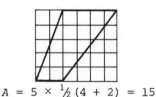

$$A = 5 \times \frac{1}{2} (4 + 2) = 15$$

3.

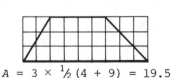

$$A = 3 \times \frac{1}{2} (4 + 9) = 19.5$$

1.   Compute the areas of the following trapezoids:

(a)   (b)   (c)

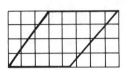

2.   (a) What does a trapezoid become if we let the upper
          parallel side shrink down to a point?

      (b) Is the formula for a trapezoid consistent if we
          let the upper parallel side shrink down to a point?
          Why?

3.   Derive the formula for the area of a trapezoid in a
      different way from that in the text, starting with this
      figure:

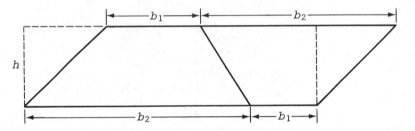

4.   Use algebra and similar triangles to derive the formula
      for the area of a trapezoid in a different way from the
      text or Exercise 3, starting with these ideas: By sim-
      ilar triangles, $(h + y)/b_2 = y/b_1$. y can be found as a
      function of b_1, b_2, and h.

      Area of small triangle = $\frac{1}{2} y b_1$

      Area of large triangle = $\frac{1}{2} (h + y) b_2$.

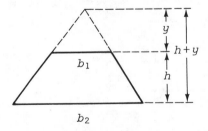

5.   Derive the formula for the
      area of a trapezoid using
      this figure:

6. Make up and construct out of heavy posterboard a dissection puzzle that illustrates the formula for the area of a trapezoid.

7. (a) Trap a trapezoid.

    (b) Wreck a rectangle.

Now that we have a formula for the area of a trapezoid, we can give a neat proof of the Pythagorean Theorem, a proof derived by President James A. Garfield. The proof begins by adding auxiliary lines to the figure.

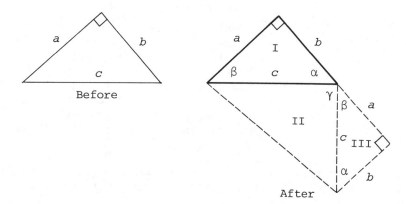

Before   After

The resulting large quadrilateral is a trapezoid with parallel sides of lengths a and b, height $a + b$. Of the constituent triangles, I and III have the same area, since III is just a copy of I. Triangle II turns out to be what it looks like, an isosceles right triangle. It's isosceles, by definition. Consider the angle measures α, β, γ. In triangle I, $\alpha + \beta + 90° = 180°$, so $\alpha + \beta = (180 - 90)° = 90°$. Now $\alpha + \beta + \gamma = 180°$, by arrangement. So $\gamma = 180° - (\alpha + \beta) = 180° - 90° = 90°$. So now we set the area of the trapezoid equal to the sum of the areas of I, II, and III, and let algebra do the rest:

$$(a + b) \times \tfrac{1}{2}(a + b) = \tfrac{1}{2}ab + \tfrac{1}{2}c^2 + \tfrac{1}{2}ab, \text{ or}$$

$$(a + b)^2 = ab + c^2 + ab, \text{ or}$$

$$a^2 + 2ab + b^2 = 2ab + c^2, \text{ or}$$

$$a^2 + b^2 = c^2, \text{ QED.}$$

Exercises   1. In the above proof,   (a) Why does $\alpha + \beta + 90° = 180°$?
(b) How do we go from the first line of the algebra to the second?   (c) Show that $(a + b)^2 = a^2 + 2ab + b^2$.

2. Prove the Pythagorean The-
    orem another way, starting
    from these facts: All
    three triangles in this
    figure are similar:
    $a/b = x/h = h/y$. Area of
    large triangle equals the
    sum of the areas of the
    smaller triangles:
    $\frac{1}{2}ab = \frac{1}{2}hx + \frac{1}{2}hy$.
    (Hint: Show that $c^2 = (ab/h)(x + y) = a^2 + b^2$.)

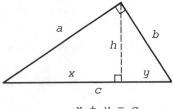

$$x + y = c$$

3. Look up *The Pythagorean Proposition** in which are pub-
    lished 370 different proofs of this theorem.

4. Try to write a better pun than the following:
       Three Native American women were sitting around sing-
    ing, one on a hippopotamus, one on a deerskin, and one
    on a bearskin. If the first woman took as long to sing
    her song as it took both of the others to sing theirs,
    one after the other, then the whole scene was virtually
    the Pythagorean Theorem: The aria of the squaw on the
    hippopotamus is equal to the sum of the arias of the
    squaws on the other two hides.

APPLICATIONS   The next objective deals with using the Pythagorean
OF THE   Theorem.
PYTHAGOREAN
THEOREM

● ●

Objective 116.   Given, either directly or indirectly, the lengths of
                 two sides of a right triangle, to compute the length
                 of the third side.

● ●

Examples   1.   The two legs (i.e., nonhypotenuses) of a right tri-
                 angle are 3 cm and 4 cm long. What is the length of
                 the hypotenuse?
                    By the Pythagorean Theorem,

                 $$c^2 = (3 \text{ cm})^2 + (4 \text{ cm})^2 = 25 \text{ cm}^2.$$

                 If we take the square root
                 of both ends of this chain
                 of equations, we get
                 $c = 5$ cm.

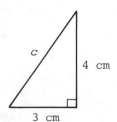

*Elisha Scott Loomis, Ralston, Virginia: National Council of Teachers of
Mathematics, 1968.

2. One leg of a right triangle is 3 in. long, and the hypotenuse is 4 in. long. How long is the other leg? Again, by the Pythagorean Theorem,

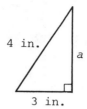

$$(4 \text{ in.})^2 = (3 \text{ in.})^2 + a^2, \text{ or}$$

$$a^2 = (4 \text{ in.})^2 - (3 \text{ in.})^2 = 7 \text{ in.}^2, \text{ so}$$

$$a = \sqrt{7} \text{ in.}$$

3. What is the height of an equilateral triangle whose edge is 2 cm long?
   First we draw a figure, sketching in the altitude of the triangle (the length of the altitude is the height of the triangle). Next we apply the Pythagorean Theorem to one of the two right triangles formed:

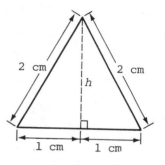

$$(2 \text{ cm})^2 = (1 \text{ cm})^2 + h^2, \text{ or}$$

$$h^2 = (2 \text{ cm})^2 - (1 \text{ cm})^2 = 3 \text{ cm}^2, \text{ so}$$

$$h = \sqrt{3} \text{ cm.}$$

The triangle we have been dealing with is the well-known 30°-60° right triangle; its sides are in the ratio $a:c:b = 1:2:\sqrt{3}$ (notice the order $a:c:b$, not $a:b:c$).

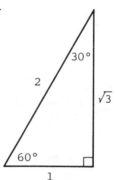

4.

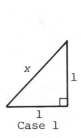 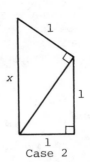 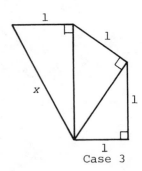

Case 1   Case 2   Case 3

(a) How long is x in Case 1?
As usual, we "Pythagorate" all over the place:

$$x^2 = 1^2 + 1^2 = 2, \text{ so } x = \sqrt{2}.$$

(b) How long is x in Case 2?
We use the results of previous part (a):

$$x^2 = (\sqrt{2})^2 + (1)^2 = 3, \text{ so } x = \sqrt{3}.$$

(c) How long is x in Case 3?

$$x^2 = (\sqrt{3})^2 + 1^2 = 4, \text{ so } x = \sqrt{4} = 2.$$

(d) How long is x in Case n?
Let us look for a pattern.

Case	x
1	$\sqrt{2}$
2	$\sqrt{3}$
3	$\sqrt{4}$
. . . .	
n	?

Thus we are led to say that in Case n, $x = \sqrt{n+1}$.
(But we have not *proved* that this guess is correct!)

Exercises   1.   Compute the length of the missing side for each of the
following right triangles:

(a)

(b)

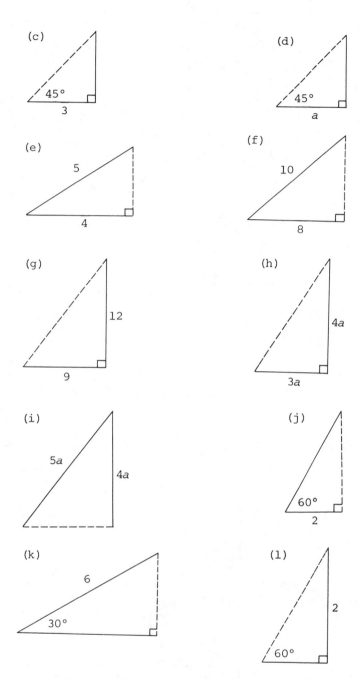

(c) 45° 3

(d) 45° a

(e) 5 4

(f) 10 8

(g) 12 9

(h) $4a$ $3a$

(i) $5a$ $4a$

(j) 60° 2

(k) 6 30°

(l) 2 60°

(Hint: What kind of right triangle is this?)

2. How long is the hypotenuse of a right triangle if the lengths of the two legs are:

(a) $3 = 2^2 - 1$ and $4 = 2 \times 2$,

(b) $8 = 3^2 - 1$ and $6 = 2 \times 3$,

(c) $15 = 4^2 - 1$ and $8 = 2 \times 4$,

(d) $24 = 5^2 - 1$ and $10 = 2 \times 5$,

(e) $x^2 - 1$ and $2x$,

(f) $x^2 - 4$ and $4x$,

(g) $x^2 - 9$ and $6x$,

(h) $x^2 - 16$ and $8x$,

(i) $x^2 - y^2$ and $2xy$?

3. Calculate the lengths of the indicated altitudes of the following isosceles triangles:

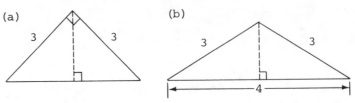

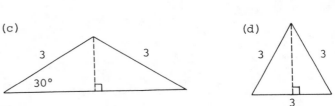

4.

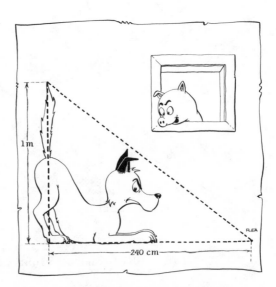

How far is it from the flea to the tip of the wolf's tail?

5.

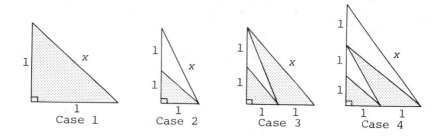

Case 1   Case 2   Case 3   Case 4

What is the length of x in (a) Case 1, (b) Case 2,
(c) Case 3, (d) Case 4, (e) Case 5, (f) Case 6,
(g) Case 7, (h) Case n, if n is odd, (i) Case n, if
n is even?

6. (a) What is the shaded area of Case n in Exercise 5 if
       n is odd?

    (b) What is the shaded area of Case n in Exercise 5 if
       n is even?

OTHER POLYGONS   Rectangles and triangles are special cases of certain
                  rectilinear figures called "polygons," upon which the
                  next batch of objectives is based.

● ●

Objective 117.   To explain what each of the following is and draw a
                  sketch of it: (a) polygon, (b) regular polygon,
                  (c) similar polygons, (d) diagonal of a polygon,
                  (e) perimeter of a polygon, (f) convex polygon.

● ●

     (a) *Polygon*. Just as it
sounds, a polygon is a
many-sided figure. Offi-
cially, it's "a simple,
closed rectilinear figure
formed by the union of
three or more line seg-
ments."

Sketches of polygons

(b) *Regular polygon.* A polygon is regular if (i) its sides are all of the same length, and (ii) its angles are all of the same measure.

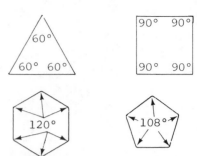

Sketches of regular polygons

(c) *Similar polygons.* Two polygons are similar if they have the same shape. This is the case if (i) corresponding angles are of equal measure, and (ii) corresponding sides are in a constant ratio. For example, in the figure, 4:2 = 6:3 or 4/2 = 6/3.

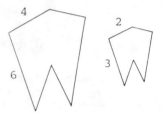

Sketch of similar polygons

(d) *Diagonals of a polygon.* The diagonals of a polygon are the line segments that are (i) determined by vertices, and (ii) not sides.

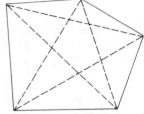

Sketch of diagonals of a polygon

(e) *Perimeter of a polygon.* The perimeter of a polygon is the sum of the lengths of the sides of the polygon. In the figure, the perimeter $p = 2 + 2 + 3 + 4 + 1 + 3 = 15$.

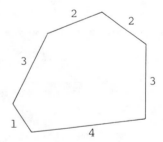

Sketch of a polygon with perimeter 15

(f) *Convex polygon*. A polygon (or any geometric figure, for that matter) is *convex* if it has no "dents" in it. Mathematically, this means that if we select any two points in the interior of the polygon, then the line segment joining them lies entirely within the polygon. (*Concave* means "not convex.")

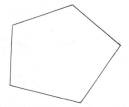

Sketch of a convex polygon

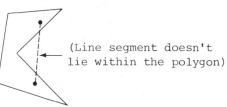

(Line segment doesn't lie within the polygon)

Sketch of nonconvex (concave) polygon

Exercises

1. Carefully draw each of the following regular polygons, each of edge length 1 in., using a ruler and protractor: (a) triangle, (b) quadrilateral, (c) pentagon (five-sided polygon), (d) hexagon (six-sided polygon), (e) octagon (eight-sided polygon), (f) nonagon (nine-sided), (g) decagon (10-sided), (h) dodecagon (12-sided).

2. A *rhombus* (looks like a "squashed square") is a quadrilateral with opposite sides parallel and all sides of equal length. Is a rhombus necessarily regular? Why?

3. Draw the following nonregular, equilateral (i.e., all sides of equal length) polygons if possible: (a) triangle, (b) quadrilateral, (c) pentagon, (d) hexagon, (e) octagon.

4. Draw the following nonregular, equiangular (i.e., all angles of equal measure) polygons, if possible: (a) triangle, (b) quadrilateral, (c) pentagon, (d) hexagon, (e) octagon.

5. The two illustrated polygons are given to be similar.

   (a) If $a = 3$, $b = 2$, $c = 4$, what is d?

   (b) If $i = 6$, $j = 3$, $k = 10$, what is l?

   (c) If $a = 4$, $k = 16$, $l = 12$, what is b?

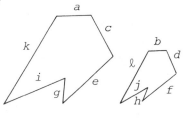

   If $a = 3$, $c = 4$, $e = 7$, $g = 3$, $i = 6$, $k = 10$, $l = 7$, what, to the nearest tenth, is: (d) b, (e) d, (f) f, (g) h, (h) j?

6. Draw an example of each of the following nonregular
    polygons, complete with all of its diagonals:
    (a) triangle, (b) quadrilateral, (c) pentagon,
    (d) hexagon, (e) heptagon (seven-sided polygon).

7. Compute the perimeters of each of the following poly-
    gons: (a) triangle of side lengths 2, 3, 4; (b) equi-
    lateral triangle of side length 2; (c) rectangle of
    width 3, length 4; (d) square of side length 3;
    (e) pentagon of side lengths 1, 2, 3, 4, 5.

8. Draw, if possible, each of the following nonconvex
    polygons: (a) triangle, (b) quadrilateral,
    (c) pentagon, (d) hexagon, (e) heptagon.

9. Go (a) try a triangle, (b) get pent up about a penta-
    gon, (c) put a hex on a hexagon, (d) get hep over a
    heptagon, (e) deck a decagon.

COUNTING PARTS   With all of these juicy things around just waiting to
                  be counted, you must have expected the following objec-
                  tive.

● ●

Objective 118.   Given a figure or sequence of figures composed of poly-
                  gons, to count specified elements (e.g., vertices,
                  edges, diagonals), in either particular or general
                  cases.

● ●

Examples   1.   How many different poly-
                  gons appear in the figure
                  to the right? Some
                  triangles, of course.

                  Two types of quadrilater-
                  als: and

                  Heptagons:

                  Hexagons:

Let's count special cases systematically:

Type of Polygon	Number
Triangle	6
Quadrilateral	12
Pentagon	0
Hexagon	7
Heptagon	6
Total	31

2. How many different convex polygons in the figure of Example 1?

   Only the heptagons and all but one hexagon above are nonconvex polygons. Hence the total number of convex polygons is 31 - (6 + 6) = 19.

3. How many diagonals are there in an n-sided polygon? Again, let's count special cases systematically and look for a pattern.

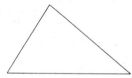

Triangle: zero diagonals

Quadrilateral: two diagonals

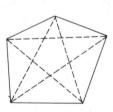

Pentagon: five diagonals

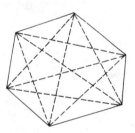

Hexagon: nine diagonals

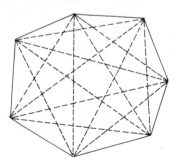

Heptagon: 14 diagonals

Number of Sides	Number of Diagonals
3	0
4	$2 = 0 + 2$
5	$5 = 0 + 2 + 3$
6	$9 = 0 + 2 + 3 + 4$
7	$14 = 0 + 2 + 3 + 4 + 5$
$\cdot\ \cdot\ \cdot$	$\cdot\ \cdot\ \cdot$
n	?

Here, thanks to the idea of relating each entry in the right column to its predecessor, it appears that for an n-agon the number of diagonals is $2 + 3 + 4 + \cdot\ \cdot\ \cdot\ + (n - 2)$.

We can use a certain standard trick to get this sum in a shorter form:

Let $s = 2 + 3 + 4 + \cdot\ \cdot\ \cdot + (n - 2).$

Then $s = (n - 2) + (n - 3) + (n - 4) + \cdot\ \cdot\ \cdot + 2,$

and $2s = \underbrace{n + n + n + \cdot\ \cdot\ \cdot + n}_{n\ -\ 3\ \text{of these}}$

$= n(n - 3),$

and so $s = \dfrac{n(n - 3)}{2}$.

Exercises
1. Use the trick of Example 3 to find short answers to the following sums:

(a) $1 + 2 + 3 + 4 + 5$,

(b) $1 + 2 + 3 + \cdot\ \cdot\ \cdot + 98 + 99 + 100$,

(c) $1 + 2 + 3 + \cdot\ \cdot\ \cdot + 999$,

(d) $1 + 2 + 3 + \cdot\ \cdot\ \cdot + n$,

(e) $6 + 8 + 10 + \cdot\ \cdot\ \cdot + 2n$,

(f) $6 + 9 + 12 + \cdot\ \cdot\ \cdot + 3n$.

2. Look up the boyhood of the great mathematician Carl Friedrich Gauss in *Men of Mathematics** and see how he used the trick of Example 3.

3. How many different poly-gons appear in the accom-panying figure?

4. How many different convex polygons appear in this figure?

---

*E. T. Bell, New York: Simon & Schuster, 1937.

5. (a) In how many points do the diagonals of a square intersect?

    (b) In how many points do the diagonals of a regular pentagon intersect?

    (c) In how many points do the diagonals of a regular hexagon intersect?

    (d) In how many points do the diagonals of a regular heptagon intersect?

6. What is the sum of the measures of the angles of:
    (a) a triangle, (b) a quadrilateral, (c) a pentagon,
    (d) a hexagon, (e) a heptagon, (f) an *n*-agon?

MAXIMIZING
AREA

We've done a lot of counting, but so far we haven't (no doubt to your extreme consternation) calculated the areas of general polygons. We hasten to remedy this with the following objective.

● ●

*Objective 119.   Given a type of polygon and its perimeter, to determine, if possible, the size and shape which maximize the area of the polygon.

● ●

Examples   1.   Determine the isosceles triangle of maximum area which has perimeter 15 cm. What is that area?
         Although there are exact and routine methods of solving such problems in calculus, the aim here and in the elementary schools is to solve these problems empirically, i.e., by observing a lot of special cases. One way of proceeding is to tie a string or thin wire into a closed loop 15 cm in perimeter and then form this loop into a variety of isosceles triangles. It's probably a good idea to do this systematically, rather than at random; a pattern and conclusion are more likely to emerge.

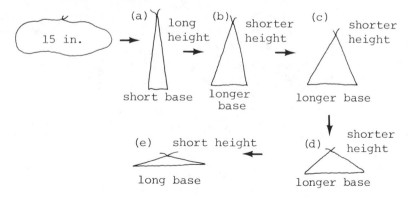

Let us now superimpose this sample of isosceles triangles on a sheet of graph paper, with each small square representing 1 cm by 1 cm, and hence with area 1 sq. cm. (This is pedagogically apt, as it emphasizes that an area is a number of square units.)

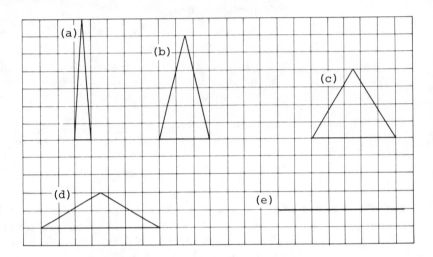

We tabulate the approximate areas, by counting squares: We count squares of which half or more are included in the triangle, ignore the rest. (We might also have measured the bases and altitudes and used our formula for areas of triangles.)

Case	Approximate Area in cm^2
a	4
b	9
c	10
d	5
e	0 (exact)

Thus it appears that an equilateral triangle of edge length 5 cm has the maximum area, which is approximately 10 cm^2.

2. Determine the rectangle of unequal height and width and perimeter 16 cm which has maximum area.

Here we don't actually have to use a loop of string to get our data because once we select a width w, the corresponding length ℓ, is easily computed:

$$16 = \ell + w + \ell + w = 2(\ell + w)$$

$$8 = \ell + w$$

$$\ell = 8 - w.$$

Length in cm	Width in cm	Area in cm^2
1	7	7
2	6	12
3	5	15
4	4	16
5	3	15
6	2	12
7	1	7

(Notice the systematic choices of lengths.) Thus it seems that in order to get maximum area we need to take $\ell = w = 4$ cm. However, the problem asks for the rectangle of *unequal* height and width. Since we can make ℓ as close to 4 cm as we wish (but not equal to 4 cm), it is impossible to find the desired rectangle.

3. Determine the equilateral hexagon with perimeter 36 cm and maximum area. What is this area?

To attack this problem we need to know how to compute the area of a hexagon. In general, any polygon's area may be found by dividing that polygon into triangles and then computing the areas of those triangles:

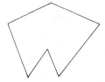

Before triangulation   After

In our problem here we will not want any nonconvex hexagons, since a nonconvex polygon can immediately be made into a convex polygon with the same perimeter and greater area by "flipping" the concave part outward:

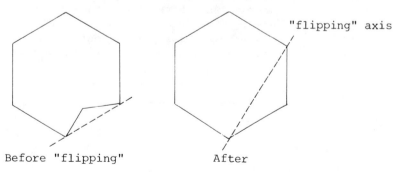

Before "flipping"   After   "flipping" axis

So for our empirical data in this problem, let's systematically concentrate on convex equilateral hexagons, again superimposed on graph paper where each square represents 1 cm^2.

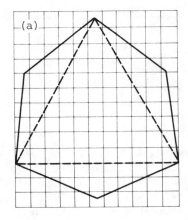

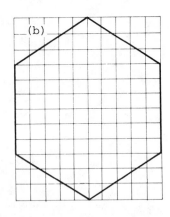

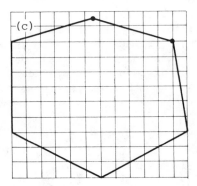

Here we try to *use a previously attacked problem*: In
(a) we make an equilateral triangle of edge length 11
cm (why not 12 cm?) and then glue isosceles triangles
onto it to build it out to a hexagon. In (b) we try a
regular hexagon, for comparison. It looks pretty good,
so in (c) we fix four of the vertices and wiggle the
other two (marked with small circles) around to see
what chance there is of squeezing out a little more
area. The upshot is, as seen in the following table,
that the regular polygon once again appears to be the
polygon of maximum area (if the perimeter is fixed.)

Case	Approximate Area in cm^2
a	92
b	96
c	94

Even with string and thumbtacks, making all of those
figures for gathering empirical data can be depressing.
However, in the special cases, when edge lengths are
fixed (in particular, in equilateral cases), you can

quickly and easily make a sturdy model out of tongue depressors (available, 500 per box, from drug stores) as illustrated below. Not only is the model Quickly and Easily Done (QED!), it is also QEF (Quite Educationally Fun) to play with, especially when laid on a piece of graph paper.

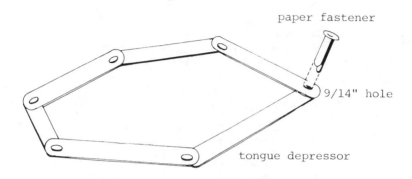

paper fastener

9/14" hole

tongue depressor

Exercises   1.   Use string figures with pins or thumbtacks at the vertices over graph paper with a fine grid (i.e., small squares) to determine if possible the *shape* (relative orientation of sides) of the following polygons with maximum area: (a) triangle, perimeter 6 in.;   (b) right triangle, perimeter 10 cm;   (c) equilateral triangle, perimeter 18 cm;   (d) *scalene* triangle (non-isosceles), perimeter 10 in.;   (e) equilateral quadrilateral, perimeter 20 cm;   (f) equilateral pentagon, perimeter 20 cm;   (g) pentagon, perimeter 20 cm;   (h) hexagon, perimeter 30 cm;   (i) heptagon, perimeter 28 cm;   (j) octagon, perimeter 40 cm;   (k) *parallelogram* (quadrilateral with opposite sides parallel), perimeter 40 cm; (l) trapezoid, perimeter 40 cm; (m) triangle, perimeter 6 in., with one edge 2 in. long;   (n) rectangle, perimeter 24 cm, with one edge 10 cm long;   (o) pentagon, perimeter 24 cm, with one edge 4 cm long.

2.   Compute the area of an equilateral triangle of edge length 1 (a) to exact form (using $\sqrt{3}$),   (b) in decimal approximation to the nearest tenth.

3.   Measure, to the nearest millimetre, the heights and base lengths of each of the triangles in Example 1, and compute the areas using our formula for the area of triangles.

4.   Compute the area of a regular hexagon of edge length 1 (a) in exact form,   (b) in decimal approximation to the nearest tenth.

5.   Triangulate each of the hexagons in Example 3. Then measure the heights and base lengths and compute the areas via formula.

6. Compute the area of a regular octagon of edge length 1 (a) in exact form, (b) in decimal approximation to the nearest tenth. (Hint: Obtain the octagon by chopping off the corners of a certain square.)

7. (For people who like the quadratic formula.) Compute the area of a regular decagon of edge length 1 (a) in exact form, (b) in decimal approximation to the nearest tenth. (Hint: Use the figure at the right. There are two similar triangles in this figure. Set corresponding ratios equal to each other.)

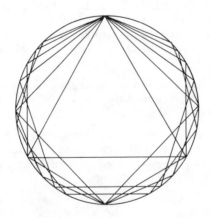

8. Compute to the nearest tenth the maximum areas of each of the polygons in Exercise 1.

9. Construct the following equilateral polygons out of tongue depressors and paper fasteners: (a) triangle, (b) quadrilateral, (c) pentagon, (d) hexagon, (e) heptagon, (f) octagon.

10. Look up *Flatland** and note the criteria for social status.

11. Compose an aria about area beginning, "Oh, the geometer sure looked funny with his two square feet. . . ."

CIRCLES

*E. A. Abbott, New York: Dover Publ., 1932.

In the preceding figures, as *n* gets larger and larger, the regular *n*-agon looks more and more like a circle. Whether or not a circle is considered to be the limiting case of regular polygons, it certainly has occupied the thoughts of both professional mathematicians and laymen for as far back as history has been recorded. Hence we ought to study it, if for no other than cultural reasons. We begin this study by establishing terminology.

● ●

Objective 120. To explain what each of the following is and draw a sketch of it: (a) circle, (b) diameter, (c) radius, (d) circumference, (e) circular arc, (f) chord, (g) circular sector, (h) circular segment.

● ●

(a) *Circle*. A circle is a set of all points in a plane a constant distance from a fixed point. This fixed point, called the *center* of the circle, is not part of the circle.

Sketch of a circle and its center

(b) *Diameter*. A diameter of a circle is a line segment through the center of the circle with its endpoints on the circle. *The* diameter of a circle is the length of any diameter. By the definition of "circle," all diameters are of the same length.

Sketch of a diameter

(c) *Radius*. A radius of a circle is a line segment with one endpoint at the center and the other on the circle. *The* radius is the length of any radius. All radii (plural of radius) are of equal length.

Sketch of a radius

(d) *Circumference*. The circumference of a circle is the length of a curve starting at a point on the circle, going once around the circle, and ending at the starting point. In less precise language, it's the distance around the circle.

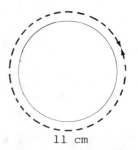

Sketch of a circle with an 11-cm circumference

(e) *Circular arc*. A circular arc (usually re-ferred to merely as "arc") is a connected subset of a circle and consists of two endpoints and all points on the circle be-tween these two points. (When you say "between" you really have to say more, for in the drawing to the right we could just as well say "*C* is between *A* and *B*" as "*D* is between *A* and *B*." The terms "smaller arc" or "larger arc" help clarify the situation.)

Sketch of a circular arc

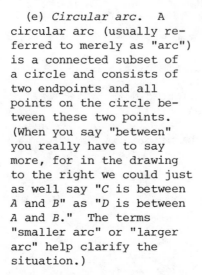

(f) *Chord*. A chord is a line segment joining two points of a circle. A diameter is a chord through the center of the circle.

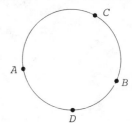

Sketch of a chord

(g) *Circular sector*. A sector of a circle is a region bounded by an arc of the circle and two radii drawn to the end-points of the arc. It looks like a piece of pie.

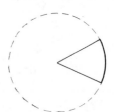

Sketch of a sector

(h) *Circular segment.* A segment of a circle is a region bounded by an arc of the circle and the chord joining the endpoints of the arc. It looks like one view of a slice of orange.

Sketch of a segment

Exercises

1. Look up "circle" in an unabridged dictionary and note how it is steeped in humanism.

2. Tie a pin or thumbtack to one end of a string and a pencil to the other and use this "compass" to draw a circle. How is the definition of circle applied here?

3.

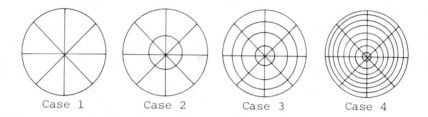

Case 1   Case 2   Case 3   Case 4

(a) How many circles are there in Case n?

(b) There are four different diameters in Case 1 and eight in Case 2. How many different diameters are there in Case n?

(c) How many different radii are there in Case n?

(d) If the radius of the largest circle is 1 cm, what is the radius of the smallest circle in Case n?

(e) If the circumference of the largest circle is 6.4 cm, what is the circumference of the smallest circle in Case n?

(f) There are 56 different arcs in Case 1. Explain how this figure is arrived at. (Hint: Two vertices on a circle determine two arcs.)

(g) How many different arcs are there in Case n?

(h) How many different chords are there in Case n?

(i) How many different sectors are there in Case n? (Hint: Two vertices on a circle determine two sectors, one like this,

and one like this.)

(j) How many different segments are there in Case *n*?

4. Two points on a circle determine two different arcs. Three points on a circle determine three nonoverlapping arcs and six arcs altogether (not counting full circular arcs determined by single points). Then *n* points on a circle determine how many: (a) nonoverlapping arcs, (b) arcs altogether?

5. How many different chords are determined by *n* points on a circle?

6. Why did the landlord send a knight to collect money from his tenants? Answer: He wanted to see a Sir-come-for-rents.

PI

If you're still with us, it's time for you to get your just desserts, in this case a piece of pi.

● ●

Objective 121.   (a) To explain what pi is, (b) to explain in detail how to estimate it using calculations with a regular octagon.

● ●

(a) Pi, symbolized π, is the ratio of the circumference of a circle to the diameter. It is constant from circle to circle and has the approximate value of 3.14159. (Some people approximate π with $3\frac{1}{7}$, and some nonmathematicians have even tried to simplify the approximation to just 3; in fact, a midwestern state legislator once introduced a bill to make π actually equal to 3. This is rather like legislating steers to be all prime rib; it would be nice, but just isn't so.)

(b) A polygon is inscribed in a circle if all of its vertices lie on the circle.

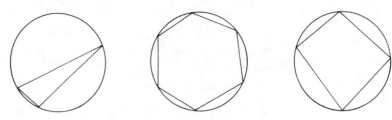

Sketches of polygons inscribed in circles

As we can see from the drawing at the beginning of this section on circles, regular *n*-agons become increasingly more accurate approximations of the circle in which they are inscribed as *n* gets increasingly larger. This fact can be used to approximate pi (details investigated in the next set of exercises):

$$\pi = \frac{c}{d} \doteq \frac{4\left(\dfrac{d}{\sqrt{2}}\right)}{d} = \frac{4}{\sqrt{2}} = \frac{2\sqrt{2}\sqrt{2}}{\sqrt{2}} = 2\sqrt{2} \qquad \text{(see figures below)}$$

$$\doteq 2(1.414) = 2.828, \text{ a very rough approximation.}$$

$$\pi = \frac{c}{d} = \frac{c}{2r} \doteq \frac{6r}{2r} = 3.000, \text{ a better approximation.}$$

$$\pi = \frac{c}{d} = \frac{c}{s\sqrt{4 + 2\sqrt{2}}} \doteq \frac{8s}{s\sqrt{4 + 2\sqrt{2}}}$$

$$= \frac{8}{\sqrt{4 + 2\sqrt{2}}} \doteq \frac{8}{\sqrt{4 + 2(1.414)}} = \frac{8}{\sqrt{6.828}}$$

$$\doteq \frac{8}{2.613} \doteq 3.0617, \text{ even better.}$$

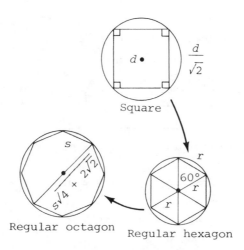

Square

Regular octagon   Regular hexagon

Exercises   1.   (a) Draw circles of radius (i) 5 cm,   (ii) 10 cm, (iii) 15 cm.

(b) Use a piece of string and a ruler to measure the circumference of each of these circles.

(c) Divide the diameter of each circle into its circumference.

2.   (a) Compute $3\frac{1}{7}$ in decimal form to five decimal places (i.e., the nearest hundred-thousandth.)

(b) How does $3\frac{1}{7}$ compare to π?

(c) Compute 3 10/71 in decimal form, to five places.

(d) How does 3 10/71 compare to π?

3. Look up the historical development of the symbol π for the ratio of circumference to diameter in *A History of Mathematical Notations*, Volume II*. (Apparently the first person to use the symbol thus was a guy named Bill Jones!)

4. If the diagonal of a square is of length d, why is each side of length $d/\sqrt{2}$?

5. If a regular hexagon is inscribed in a circle of radius r, why is each side of length r?

6. The figure to the right shows how a regular octagon may be considered to be a square with its corners clipped.

   (a) Compute e in terms of s.

   (b) Compute w in terms of s.

   (c) Compute d in terms of s.

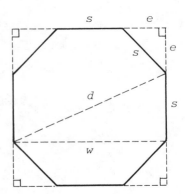

7. Explain what Exercise 6 has to do with approximating the value of π.

8. In the illustrated regular decagon:

   (a) What is the measure of α?

   (b) What is the measure of β?

   (c) What is the measure of γ?

   (d) Why is the dotted line segment of length s, if it is given that the decagon is of edge length s?

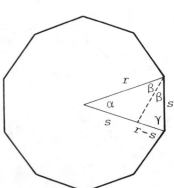

   (e) Why is the line segment joining the center of the circle and the end of the dotted line of length s?

   (f) Why is $r/s = s/(r - s)$?

   (g) Compute r in terms of s.

   (h) Estimate the value of π using calculations with a regular decagon.

*Florian Cajori, La Salle, Ill.: Open Court Publ. Co., 1929.

9. Write a better poem about π than this one, "Catcher in the π":

    3.14159,
    That's the number
    For which I pine.

    If you hear me sadly sigh,
    I won't want cake;
    I will want π.

                    J. D. Logothettinger, 1973

AREAS

It turns out that π is crucial not only to the computation of the circumference of a circle but also to the computation of its area, hence our next objective.

• •

Objective 122.

To give a plausible informal argument for the validity of the formula $A = \pi r^2$ for the area of a circle.

• •

Our clue as to how to proceed comes from the previous work in estimating π. Instead of a circle we substitute an inscribed regular polygon, as illustrated in the following diagrams.

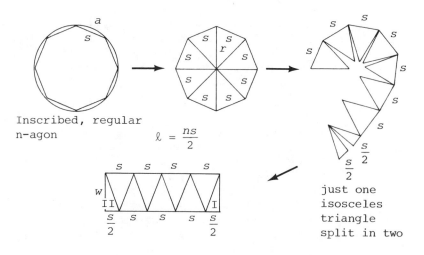

Inscribed, regular n-agon

$$\ell = \frac{ns}{2}$$

just one isosceles triangle split in two

The area of this resulting rectangle is approximately the area of the circle, and the approximation becomes better as the number n of sides of the regular polygon increases. Moreover, w gets closer to r and $n \cdot s$ closer to c as n gets larger and the sectors get smaller. Now, recall that $c = \pi d = 2\pi r$, and check the following:

$$A \doteq w \times \ell = w \times \frac{ns}{2} \doteq r \times \frac{ns}{2} \doteq r \times \frac{c}{2} = r \times \frac{2\pi r}{2} = \pi r^2 .$$

Exercises 1. Carefully draw a circle of radius 10 cm and an in-scribed, regular dodecagon (12 sides). Then cut up the circle as illustrated on page 385, except do not cut off the small circular segments. Rearrange the re-sulting circular sectors to form an almost rectangle. Save these pieces for when you teach areas of circles.

2. Using $\pi = 3.14$, $\sqrt{2} = 1.41$, $\sqrt{6.83} = 2.61$, compute to the nearest hundredth the difference between the area of a unit circle (circle of radius 1) and each of the fol-lowing inscribed, regular polygons: (a) triangle, (b) square, (c) hexagon, (d) octagon.

3. Why should consideration of units of measure restrain us from confusing the two formulas $A = \pi r^2$ and $C = 2\pi r$?

Now that we have this neat formula at our disposal, let's use it to calculate some areas.

● ●

Objective 123. To compute to the nearest hundredth the area of a given circle, circular sector, or circular segment.

● ●

Examples 1. What is the area of a circle of diameter 10 cm? First we carefully note that if $d = 10$ cm, then $r = 5$ cm. Hence $A = \pi r^2 \doteq (3.1415)(5 \text{ cm})^2 = 3.1416 \times 25 \text{ cm}^2 = 78.54 \text{ cm}^2$.

2. The central angle of a circular sector measures 30°. If the radius of the circle is 2 in., what is the area of the sector?

Unfortunately, we do not have a formula for the area of a circular sector, so we must be clever. *How can we use a previously solved problem?* We know how to compute the area of a whole circle; how can we  use that area to find this part? Well, there are 360° "around" the center of the circle, of which we want only 30°. Hence the area of the sector is

$$\frac{30°}{360°}\left(\pi r^2\right) = \frac{1}{12}\left(3.1416\right)(4 \text{ in.})^2 \doteq .2618(16 \text{ cm}^2)$$

$$\doteq 4.19 \text{ cm}^2 .$$

3. Compute the area of the
    illustrated circular seg-
    ment.

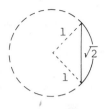

Again, *how can we use a
previously solved problem*?
We clip off a triangle
from a circular sector and
thus we are left with a circular segment. Let's look
at the triangle first. What is special about the given
triangle? Ho! $1^2 + 1^2 = (\sqrt{2})^2$, so it's a right triangle. Thus we can take $h = b = 1$; the area of the
triangle is $\frac{1}{2} \times 1 \times 1 = \frac{1}{2}$. We can use the "right-
ness" of the triangle again to get the area of the
sector:

$$\frac{90°}{360°}\left(\pi \cdot 1^2\right) = \frac{1}{4}\left(\pi\right).$$

Hence the area of the segment is given by

$$A = \frac{\pi}{4} - \frac{1}{2} \doteq \frac{3.1416}{4} - .50$$

$$= .7854 - .50 \doteq .29 \text{ sq. units.}$$

4.

| Case 1 | Case 2 | Case 3 | Case 4 |

What is the ratio of the area of the circle in Case *n*
to the area of the circle in Case 1?

Let us *look for a pattern by systematically investigating special cases.*

Case	Area of Circle	Ratio of Area to Area of Case 1
1	$\pi(1)^2 = \pi$	$\pi/\pi = 1$
2	$\pi(1/2)^2 = \pi/4$	$(\pi/4)/\pi = 1/4$
3	$\pi(1/4)^2 = \pi/16$	$(\pi/16)/\pi = 1/16$
4	$\pi(1/8)^2 = \pi/64$	$(\pi/64)/\pi = 1/64$
. . .	. . .	. . .
n		?

Now, what kind of numbers are 1, 1/4, 1/16, 1/64,
. . .? Yes! They're all powers of 1/4: $1 = (1/4)^0$,
$1/4 = (1/4)^1$, $1/16 = (1/4)^2$, $1/64 = (1/4)^3$. Now if we
inspect an abbreviated table:

Case	Ratio
1	$(1/4)^0$
2	$(1/4)^1$
3	$(1/4)^2$
4	$(1/4)^3$
. . .	. . .
n	?

it isn't too hard to see that in Case n the ratio is $(1/4)^{n-1}$.

Exercises

1. Compute to the nearest hundredth the areas of the circles with the following radii: (a) 3 cm, (b) 9 cm, (c) 27 cm, (d) 1/3 in., (e) 1/9 in.

2. Compute to the nearest hundredth the areas of the circles with the following diameters: (a) 2 in., (b) 4 in., (c) 16 in., (d) 256 in.

3. Compute the areas of the sectors of a circle of radius 4 cm if the central angles have the following measures: (a) 60°, (b) 90°, (c) 135°, (d) 270°, (e) 300°.

4. Compute the areas of the circular segments formed by "snipping away the triangles" from the sectors of Exercise 3.

5.

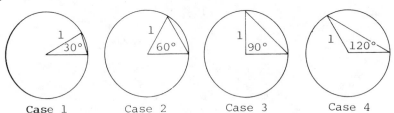

Case 1　　　　Case 2　　　　Case 3　　　　Case 4

(a) Compute the area of the sector in Case 1.

(b) Compute the area of the sector in Case 2.

(c) Compute the area of the sector in Case 3.

(d) Compute the area of the sector in Case n (careful!).

(e) Compute the area of the segment in Case 1.

(f) Compute the area of the segment in Case 2.

(g) Compute the area of the segment in Case 6.

(h) Compute the area of the segment in Case $6n$.

(i) Compute the area of the segment in Case 7.

(j) Compute the area of the segment in Case $(6n + 1)$.

6. In the sequence of figures of Example 4:

   (a) What is the ratio of the area of the circle of Case n to the area of the circle in Case $n - 1$?

   (b) What is the ratio of the area of the circle in Case n to the area of the circle in Case $n - 2$?

   (c) What is the ratio of the area of the circle in Case n to the area of the circle in Case $n - 3$?

   (d) What is the ratio of the area of the circle in Case n to the area of the circle in Case $n - k$?

7. When is a religious group's rowing implement like a piece of pie?   (Answer: When it's a sect-oar.)

BOXES

===

DEFINITIONS   The geometric figures we have considered so far have been two-dimensional. We turn now to three dimensions and civilization's perhaps most common three-dimensional figure, the box.

• •

Objective 124.   To explain what each of the following is and draw a sketch of it: (a) prism, (b) rectangular prism, (c) cube, (d) face diagonal of a prism, (e) body diagonal of a prism.

• •

(a) *Prism*. A prism consists of several planar faces, two of which (the *ends*) are parallel and of the same size and shape (which shape determines the name of the prism); the rest of the faces are all bounded by parallelograms.

Triangular   Pentagonal

Sketches of prisms

(b) *Rectangular prism.* A rectangular prism is just an unopened box. In more technical language, it's a prism all of whose faces are rectangular.

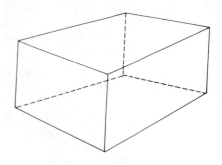

Sketch of a rectangular prism

(c) *Cube.* A cube is a rectangular prism all of whose faces are square. Thus a sugar cube is really a cube, but a "cube" of butter is not.

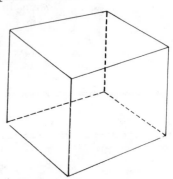

Sketch of a cube

(d) *Face diagonal of a prism.* This is just what it sounds like: a diagonal of a polygon bounding one of the faces of the prism.

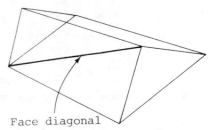

Face diagonal

Sketch of a face diagonal of a prism

(e) *Body diagonal of a prism.* A body diagonal of a prism is a line segment that is (i) determined by the vertices of the prism, (ii) not an edge, (iii) not a face diagonal. Thus a body diagonal does not lie within any of the faces.

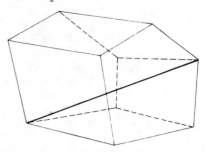

Sketch of a body diagonal of a prism

Exercises   1.   Draw a Venn diagram illustrating the relationships between the sets of all prisms, all rectangular prisms, and all cubes.

2. Draw sketches of the following types of prisms: (a) "parallelogramular," (b) hexagonal, (c) heptagonal.

3. How many face diagonals are there on a: (a) triangular prism, (b) quadrilateral prism, (c) pentagonal prism, (d) hexagonal prism, (e) n-agonal prism?

4. How many body diagonals are there in a: (a) triangular prism, (b) quadrilateral prism, (c) pentagonal prism, (d) hexagonal prism, (e) n-agonal prism?

5. (a) *What kind of triangle* is the heavy dotted triangle in the accompanying drawing of a cube?

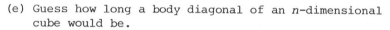

   (b) If each edge is of length 1, how long is the face diagonal?

   (c) How long is each body diagonal?

   (d) Guess how long a body diagonal of a four-dimensional cube would be.

   (e) Guess how long a body diagonal of an n-dimensional cube would be.

   (f) Try to draw a picture of a four-dimensional cube.

6. Compute the length of a body diagonal of a rectangular prism measuring 3 cm by 4 cm by 12 cm.

7. Construct each of the following geometric objects, leaving one face hinged so that it can be opened and closed like a door. On each face draw at least one face diagonal (if possible) and use string to construct at least two different body diagonals.

   (a) a cube,

   (b) a noncubic rectangular prism,

   (c) three different nonrectangular prisms.

VOLUMES   We now deal with volumes, sweetly.

● ●

*Objective 125. Given a figure formed from stacked sugar cubes and painted black on the outside, to deduce the number of sugar cubes with a given number of faces painted black.

● ●

Examples	1.	Compute the number of cubes with either zero, one, two, or three faces painted black if the cubes form a 3-by-4-by-5 rectangular prism.

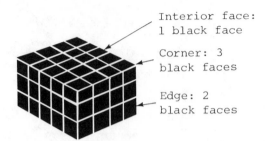

Interior face:
1 black face

Corner: 3
black faces

Edge: 2
black faces

Interior: 0 black faces

Since every cube in the rectangular prism has either zero, one, two, or three black faces, all we really want here is the volume of the big block. There are three layers, each layer with 4×5 cubes, so the total volume (i.e., number of cubes) is $3 \times 4 \times 5 = 60$.

2. How many cubes altogether in a 2-by-3-by-15 rectangular prism?

Using the same reasoning as in Example 1, we get

$V = 2 \times 3 \times 15 = 90$ cubic units.

(Here the cubic unit is a sugar cube.)

3. What is the volume of a rectangular prism measuring 6 cm by 7 cm by 10 cm?

$V = (6 \text{ cm}) \times (7 \text{ cm}) \times (10 \text{ cm}) = 420 \text{ cm}^3.$

4. Answer the question in Example 1 a different way, counting cubes with zero, one, two, three black faces separately.

There are   8 corner cubes
            24 edge cubes
            22 interior face cubes
            <u>6</u> interior cubes
            60 cubes altogether.

Exercises	1.	Compute the volumes of the following rectangular prisms (alias "boxes"): (a) 2 cm by 8 cm by 25 cm, (b) 4 ft. by 47 ft. by 25 ft., (c) 8 mm by 253 mm by 125 mm.

2. Consider a cube made up of 1,000,000 sugar cubes. How many cubes have exactly: (a) zero faces black, (b) one face black, (c) two faces black, (d) three faces black, (e) four faces black, (f) five faces black, (g) six faces black?

3. Consider the pile of cubes
   in the accompanying figure
   (with no nasty surprises
   on the three sides you
   can't see). How many
   cubes have exactly
   (a) zero faces black,
   (b) one face black,
   (c) two faces black,
   (d) three faces black,
   (e) four faces black,
   (f) five faces black,
   (g) six faces black?

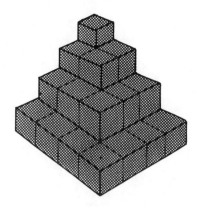

4. How many cubes in a figure like that of Exercise 3 if
   there are (a) one, (b) two, (c) three, (d) four,
   (e) five, (f) *n* layers?

5. How many cubic cubits are in a box measuring 1 m by 2 m
   by 3 m, if one cubit is 46 cm?

1 cubit
46 cm

OTHER   Just as quadrilaterals may be generalized to polygons,
POLYHEDRA   so may prisms be generalized to what are called poly-
               hedra (or polyhedrons).

● ●

Objective 126. To explain what a polyhedron is, draw a sketch of one,
                and construct the five regular polyhedra and at least
                one other polyhedron.

● ●

Roughly speaking, a polyhedron is a three-dimensional
figure composed of flat faces (hedrons) like an unopened box. In official mathematical language, it's
a simple, closed surface formed by the union of plane
regions, each region bounded by a single polygon.
Thus, ring-shaped faces are not allowed.

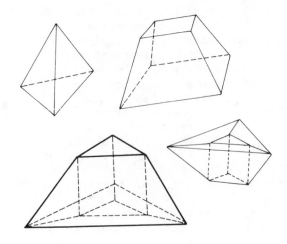

Sketches of polyhedra

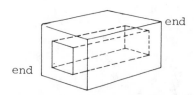

The above surface is not
a polyhedron because the
two ends are ring-shaped
(each bounded by *two* polygons, in this case, two
squares).

Some more familiar polyhedra are cubes, boxes, and
other prisms, pyramids,* and truncated pyramids
(pyramids with their tops chopped off).

REGULAR
POLYHEDRA

Like polygons, polyhedra may be regular. A regular
polyhedron is one all of whose faces are regular and of
the same size and same shape, and all of whose vertices
are endpoints of the same number of edges.

*A pyramid has as its base a plane triangle, rectangle, or other poly-
gon, and as its sides several triangles with a common vertex and with
their bases forming the sides of the pyramid's base.

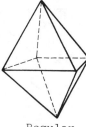

Regular   Irregular

It turns out that there are five regular polyhedra: the
octahedron (eight faces) drawn above, the cube, and the
three below.

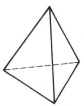

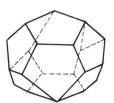

Regular   Regular   Regular
tetrahedron   dodecahedron   icosahedron
(4 faces)   (12 faces)   (20 faces)

To construct one of these polyhedra we need to start
in our mind's eye with a completed polyhedron, cut it
along the edges (still in the mind's eye), and then assemble the faces into a convenient chain that will require a minimum amount of tabs and gluing in the actual
building of the model. Let's illustrate with the
dodecahedron:

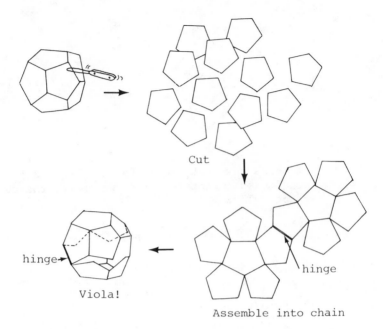

Cut

hinge→

Viola!

hinge

Assemble into chain

Exercises 1. Are the following figures polyhedra? Why?

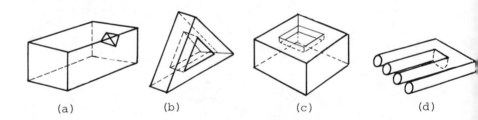

(a)   (b)   (c)   (d)

2. "Polyhedron" is a reply to what question? (Answer: "Is the parrot paying attention to Ron?")

3. Draw sketches of at least five polyhedra other than those illustrated in the text. Draw at least one with a tunnel through it. (Be careful that no faces are ring-shaped!)

4. Construct the five regular polyhedra (also called "Platonic solids"). Make your models at least 20 cm in "diameter."

5. Construct an irregular polyhedron all of whose faces are bounded by equilateral triangles.

6. Construct a polyhedron with a tunnel through it.

7. The polyhedron in the accompanying figure is the small (as opposed to great) stellated dodecahedron. Look up how to make it in *Polyhedron Models** or *Mathematical Models*†, then make it.

8. Weave together two strips of equilateral triangles (as below) to form a regular tetrahedron.

9. Look up "Mathematical Games" in the September 1971 issue of *Scientific American* and learn how Jean J. Pedersen weaves polyhedra from adding machine tape. Make at least one model other than the regular tetrahedron.

10. Show how a regular tetrahedron may be nested in a cube so that all vertices of the tetrahedron lie on vertices of the cube.

11. Go out and buy a nested polyhedra kit (Products of Behavioral Sciences, Inc., 1140 Dell Ave., Campbell, CA 95008) and construct a "nest" of all five of the regular polyhedra, as in Exercise 10.

EULER'S FORMULA

There are other things we can do with polyhedra besides constructing them, notably counting such parts as vertices, edges, and faces. As a matter of fact, a good way to introduce the terms "vertices" and "edges" is to count them on polyhedra; the kids quickly learn what a vertex or edge is when they start counting them. They can also discover a remarkable property which is the basis for the next objective.

*M. J. Wenninger, Ralston, Va.: National Council of Teachers of Mathematics, 1966.
†H. M. Cundy and A. P. Rollett, London: Cambridge Univ. Press, 1951.

•••

*Objective 127.   (a) To state Euler's formula for convex polyhedra,
                   (b) to illustrate it with the five regular polyhedra,
                   and (c) to sketch a polyhedron for which Euler's formu-
                   la does not hold.

•••

To discover Euler's formula let's count the vertices
v, edges e, and faces f of the following convex polyhedra:

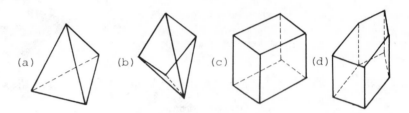

Polyhedron	v	e	f
(a)	4	6	4
(b)	5	8	5
(c)	8	12	6
(d)	10	15	7

Can we see any relationship between v, e, f? Well,
$v + f$ is almost equal to e. In Case (a), their difference is 2; in Case (b) it's 2; in Case (c) it's 2
again! Hm; it always seems to be 2. So Euler's formula must be

$$v + f = e + 2$$

Exercises   1.   Comment on the pun: "Euler was pretty slick."

            2.   Verify Euler's formula for each of the five regular
                 polyhedra.

            3.   Define "convex polyhedron." (See "convex polygon" for
                 a hint.)

            4.   For which of the polyhedra sketched on page 394 does
                 Euler's formula hold?

            5.   Draw a sketch, different from any in the text, of a
                 polyhedron for which Euler's formula does not hold.

We need to heed surfaces other than polyhedra. Hence
the next objective.

● ●

Objective 128.　To explain what each of the following is and draw a
sketch of it: (a) cylinder, (b) right circular cylinder, (c) cone, (d) right circular cone, (e) sphere,
(f) hemisphere.

● ●

(a) *Cylinder*. A cylin-
der is a surface generated
by moving a line segment
parallel to itself.

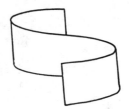

Sketch of a cylinder

(b) *Right circular
cylinder*. A right circu-
lar cylinder is a cylinder
of which one endpoint of
the generating line seg-
ment traces a circle on a
plane perpendicular to the
generating line.

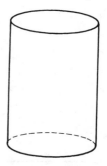

Sketch of a right circular
cylinder

(c) *Cone*. A cone is
generated by a line seg-
ment through a fixed end-
point (the vertex) moving
along some base curve.

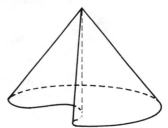

Sketch of a cone

(d) *Right circular cone.*
A right circular cone is a
cone with its vertex di-
rectly over the center of
its circular base curve.

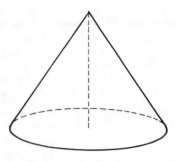

Sketch of right circular
cone

(e) *Sphere.* A sphere is
just a ball: a set of all
points in three-dimensional space which are a fixed
distance from a fixed
point (the *center* of the
sphere).

Sketch of a sphere

(f) *Hemisphere.* A hemi-
sphere is half of a sphere,
formed by slicing the
sphere with a plane
through its center.

Sketch of a hemisphere
lying on its slicing plane

Exercises   1.   Draw a nonright circular cylinder standing on a plane.

2.   Draw a noncircular right cylinder standing on a plane.

3.   Draw a nonright circular cone.

4.   Draw (a) a sphere, (b) a hemisphere inscribed in a
     cone.

5.   Draw (a) a sphere, (b) a cone inscribed in a hemi-
     sphere.

6.   Who said, "The only thing we have to fear is the sphere
     itself!"?   (Answer: The geometry teacher who couldn't
     draw.)

7.   Who was buried on Boot Hill?   (Answer: Same as in
     Exercise 6 above.)

SUMMARY OF
OBJECTIVES

102. To explain what each of the following geometric
objects is and draw a sketch of it: (a) point,
(b) line, (c) curve, (d) closed curve, (e) simple
curve, (f) half-line, (g) ray, (h) line segment,
(i) vertex, (j) edge, (k) plane, (l) half-plane,
(m) parallel lines (page 314).

*103. Given two-dimensional connected networks, (a) to
state whether or not they're traversable, and
(b) to explain the logic behind these decisions
(page 317).

104. To compute the number of points, lines, line segments, planes, etc. determined by a given set of
points, lines, line segments, etc. (page 322).

105. To measure the length of given curves to the
nearest given metric unit (page 327).

106. To convert English units of linear measure to
metric units and vice versa, given that one metre
is approximately 39.37 inches (page 331).

107. To explain what each of the following geometric items is and draw a sketch of it: (a) plane angle, (b) measure of an angle, (c) degree, (d) bisector of an angle, (e) perpendicular lines (page 333).

108. To explain what each of the following is and draw a sketch of it: (a) quadrilateral, (b) rectangle, (c) square, (d) similar rectangles, (e) diagonals of a rectangle (page 336).

109. Given a figure or sequence of figures composed of rectangles, to count specified rectangles, vertices of rectangles, diagonals, etc. in either particular or general cases (page 338).

110. Given a figure composed of rectangles, with their dimensions in specified units, to compute the area of the figure in given units (not necessarily the same as the originally specified units) (page 342).

111. To explain what each of the following is and draw a sketch of it: (a) triangle, (b) isosceles triangle, (c) equilateral triangle, (d) similar triangles, (e) right triangle, (f) hypotenuse (page 347).

112. Given a figure or sequence of figures composed of triangles, to count specified elements (e.g., vertices, triangles, right triangles, triangles similar to given triangle, etc.) in either particular or general cases (page 349).

113. (a) To state the sum of the angle measures of a triangle and (b) to demonstrate the truth of this statement (page 352).

*114. (a) To state the Curry triangle paradox, (b) to explain the fallacy in this "paradox" (page 355).

115. (a) To state the Pythagorean Theorem, (b) to illustrate it with dissections, (c) to prove it via computation of areas (page 358).

116. Given, either directly or indirectly, the lengths of two sides of a right triangle, to compute the length of the third side (page 362).

117. To explain what each of the following is and draw a sketch of it: (a) polygon, (b) regular polygon, (c) similar polygons, (d) diagonal of a polygon, (e) perimeter of a polygon, (f) convex polygon (page 367).

118. Given a figure or sequence of figures composed of polygons, to count specified elements (e.g., vertices, edges, diagonals), in either particular or general cases (page 370).

*119. Given a type of polygon and its perimeter, to
       determine, if possible, the size and shape which
       maximize the area of the polygon (page 373).

120.   To explain what each of the following is and draw
       a sketch of it: (a) circle, (b) diameter,
       (c) radius, (d) circumference, (e) circular arc,
       (f) chord, (g) circular sector, (h) circular
       segment (page 379).

121.   (a) To explain what pi is, (b) to explain in de-
       tail how to estimate it using calculations with
       a regular octagon (page 382).

122.   To give a plausible informal argument for the
       validity of the formula $A = \pi r^2$ for the area of
       a circle (page 385).

123.   To compute to the nearest hundredth the area of a
       given circle, circular sector, or circular seg-
       ment (page 386).

124.   To explain what each of the following is and draw
       a sketch of it: (a) prism, (b) rectangular prism,
       (c) cube, (d) face diagonal of a prism, (e) body
       diagonal of a prism (page 389).

*125. Given a figure formed from stacked sugar cubes
       painted black on the outside, to deduce the num-
       ber of sugar cubes with a given number of faces
       painted black (page 391).

126.   To explain what a polyhedron is, draw a sketch of
       one, and construct the five regular polyhedra and
       at least one other polyhedron (page 393).

*127. (a) To state Euler's formula for convex polyhedra,
       (b) to illustrate it with the five regular poly-
       hedra, and (c) to sketch a polyhedron for which
       Euler's formula does not hold (page 398).

128.   To explain what each of the following is and draw
       a sketch of it: (a) cylinder, (b) right circular
       cylinder, (c) cone, (d) right circular cone,
       (e) sphere, (f) hemisphere (page 399).

WORDS TO KNOW

line (page 314)   plane (page 316)
point (page 314)   ray (page 316)
curve (page 315)   vertex (page 316)
closed curve (page 315)   connected network (page
endpoint (page 315)   317)
half-line (page 315)   endline (page 317)
simple curve (page 315)   half-plane (page 317)
edge (page 316)   linear (page 317)
line segment (page 316)   parallel lines (page 317)

TO EXERCISES AND CHALLENGES

Pages 8-9 1.   The following are additional examples. However, you should give three other examples.

(a) $\{a,b,c\}$: Consider the set A of all even prime numbers; then $A = \{2\}$.

(b) $\{x: x$ has a certain property$\}$: Let $A = \{x: x^2 - 4x + 4 = 0\}$; then $A = \{2\}$.

(c) $a \in A$: Let A be the set of world spices and a be rosemary.

(d) $a \notin A$: Let A be the set of four-legged animals and a be you.

(e) U: If two proud parents are comparing babies then $U = \{x: x$ is a human child under two years of age$\}$.

(f) $\emptyset$: Let $A = \{x: x^2 + 1 = 0$ and x is a real number$\}$ or $B = \{x: x$ has one brother and no siblings$\}$.

(g) $a \subset B$: Let $A = \{a,b,c\}$ and $B = \{a,b,c,d,e,f,g\}$.

(h) $A = B$: $A = \{x: x$ is an even counting number$\}$ and $B = \{2,4,6, \ldots\}$.

2.   (a) $3 \times 2 \times 1 = 6$

(b) $4 \times 3 \times 2 \times 1 = 24$

(c) $5 \times 4 \times 3 \times 2 \times 1 = 120$

(d) $n \times (n - 1) \times (n - 2) \times \bullet \bullet \bullet \times 3 \times 2 \times 1 = n!$

3.   (a) $\{0,3,6,9,12, \ldots\}$ (b) $\{3,6,9,12, \ldots\}$

(c) $\{2,7,12,17,22, \ldots\}$ (e) $\{2\}$

4.   (a) $\{x: x$ is a multiple of 2 and is between 2 and 10 inclusive$\}$

(b) $\{x: x$ is a multiple of 2 larger than 0$\}$

(c) Same as (a)

(d) $\{x: x = 2^n, n = 1,2,3, \ldots\}$

(e) $\{x: x = 7m, m = 1,2,3, \ldots\}$

(f) $\{x: x = 7n, n = \pm 1, \pm 2, \pm 3, \ldots\}$

(g) $\{x: x$ is a president of the US before 1974$\}$

(h) $\{x: x$ is a baby animal$\}$

5.   (a) $\emptyset, \{a\}$; 2

(b) $\emptyset, \{a\}, \{b\}, \{a,b\}$; 4

(c) $\emptyset, \{a\}, \{b\}, \{c\}, \{a,b\}, \{a,c\}, \{b,c\}, \{a,b,c\}$; 8

(d) $\emptyset$, $\{a\}$, $\{b\}$, $\{c\}$, $\{d\}$, $\{a,b\}$, $\{a,c\}$, $\{a,d\}$, $\{b,c\}$,
$\{b,d\}$, $\{c,d\}$, $\{a,b,c\}$, $\{a,b,d\}$, $\{a,c,d\}$, $\{b,c,d\}$,
$\{a,b,c,d\}$; 16

(e) 2^n

Pages
12 - 13

1. The following are additional examples. However, you
should give three other examples.

(a) $A \cap B$: Let $A = \{x: x^2 - 1 = 0\}$ and
$B = \{x: 2x - 2 = 0\}$; then $A \cap B = \{1\}$

(b) $A \cap B = \emptyset$: Let $A = \{h,a,p,p,y\}$ and $B = \{f,r,o,w,n\}$

(c) $A \cup B$: Let $A = \{x: x \text{ is lucky}\}$ and
$B = \{x: x \text{ is a square}\}$; then $A \cup B$ is the set of
all things which are either lucky or square, or both.

(d) $A \sim B$: Let $A = \{2,3,6,8,10,12, \ldots\}$ and
$B = \{3,6,9,12,18,111\}$; then
$A \sim B = \{2,8,10,14,16,20,22,24,26, \ldots\}$.

(e) $\sim A$: Let $U = \{x: x \text{ is a male}\}$ and $A = \{x: x \text{ is over}$
6 ft. tall$\}$; then $\sim A = \{x: x \text{ is a male 6 ft. or}$
shorter in height$\}$.

(f) $A \otimes B$: Let $A = \{2,*,o\}$ and $B = \{p,q\}$; then
$A \otimes B = \{(2,p),(2,q),(*,p),(*,q),(o,p),(o,q)\}$
and $B \otimes A = \{(p,2),(q,2),(p,*),(q,*),(p,o),(q,o)\}$.

2. (a) A (b) U (c) $\emptyset$ (d) $\emptyset$ (e) $A \otimes U$ (f) $\emptyset$ (g) A
(h) A (i) U (j) $\emptyset$

3. (a) $3 \times 4 = 12$; $4 \times 3 = 12$

(b) $23 \times 5 = 115$; $5 \times 23 = 115$

(c) $m \times n$; $n \times m$

4. (a) $\{1,2,3,4,6,8\}$ (b) $\{2,4\}$ (c) $\{6,8\}$ (d) $\{6,8\}$
(e) $\{1,3,5,6,7,8,9,10\}$ (f) $\{5,7,9,10\}$ (g) $\{5,7,9,10\}$
(h) $\{1,3,5,6,7,8,9,10\}$
(i) $\{(2,1)(2,2)(2,3)(2,4)(4,1)(4,2)(4,3)(4,4)(6,1)(6,2)$
$(6,3)(6,4)(8,1)(8,2)(8,3)(8,4)\}$
(j) $\{(1,2)(1,4)(1,6)(1,8)(2,2)(2,4)(2,6)(2,8)(3,2)(3,4)$
$(3,6)(3,8)(4,2)(4,4)(4,6)(4,8)\}$

5. (a) $\{x: x \text{ is a male or a student or both}\}$

(b) $\{x: x \text{ is a male student or a beauty or both}\}$

(c) $\{x: x \text{ is a female and not a student}\}$

(d) $\{x: x \text{ is not a male and not a student}\}$

(e) $\{x: x \text{ is not a male or not a student}\}$

(f) $\{x: x \text{ is not a male or not a student}\}$

(g) $\{x: x \text{ is an ugly male}\}$

(h) $\{x: x \text{ is a nonstudent male}\}$

(i) $\{x: x \text{ is a beauty but not a student}\}$.

1.

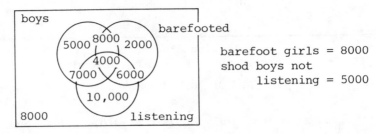

barefoot girls = 8000
shod boys not
       listening = 5000

2.   6000

3.   28

4.   5, 10, 76

5.   Three involving one condition, one involving three con-
      ditions, three involving two conditions, one involving
      zero conditions

6.   Here is one more example (be sure to write three more).
         In a recent journey to the park, Joey counted 25
      squirrels, 18 brown animals, and 15 animals munching
      lunch. Six of those eating were grey (not brown)
      squirrels and only eight squirrels were eating. Joey
      was delighted to see five brown animals eating and ten
      brown squirrels. If Joey counted exactly 38 animals,
      how many nonbrown nonsquirrels were eating? (Answer:
      4.)

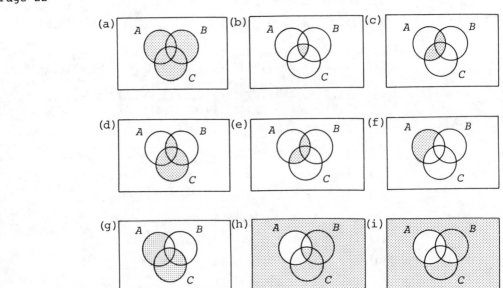

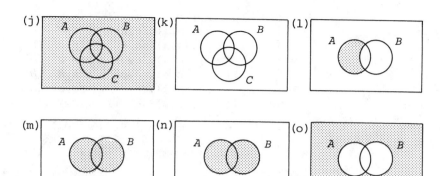

Page 23		Valid:	$A \cap B = B \cap A$
			$A \cup B = B \cup A$
		Invalid:	$A \otimes B = B \otimes A$

Page 23   Valid: $A \cap (B \cap C) = (A \cap B) \cap C$
                                $A \cup (B \cup C) = (A \cup B) \cup C$
         Invalid: $A \otimes (B \otimes C) = (A \otimes B) \otimes C$

Page 23   Valid: $A \cup (B \cap C) = (A \cup B) \cap (A \cup C)$
                              $A \cap (B \cup C) = (A \cap B) \cup (A \cap C)$
                              $A \otimes (B \cap C) = (A \otimes B) \cap (A \otimes C)$
                              $A \otimes (B \cup C) = (A \otimes B) \cup (A \otimes C)$
       Invalid: $A \cap (B \otimes C) = (A \cap B) \otimes (A \cap C)$
                              $A \cup (B \otimes C) = (A \cup B) \otimes (A \cup C)$

Page 24   1. 3×2

                2. 4×3

                3. $n \times (n - 1)$

Page 27   1. $A \otimes B$ matches every element of A to every element of B, whereas a one-to-one correspondence matches an element of A to an element of B. For example, if $A = \{1,2\}$, $B = \{a,b\}$, then $A \otimes B = \{(1,a),(1,b),(2,a),(2,b)\}$ and $A \leftrightarrow B$ is $\{(1,a),(2,b)\}$.

                2.   (a) $\{(c,f),(a,u),(d,n)\}$, $\{(c,f),(a,n),(d,u)\}$, $\{(c,u),(a,f),(d,n)\}$, $\{(c,n),(a,f),(d,u)\}$, $\{(c,n),(a,u),(d,f)\}$, $\{(c,u),(a,n),(d,f)\}$

                           (b) $\{(s,s),(h,o),(o,c),(e,k)\}$, $\{(s,s),(h,o),(o,k),(e,c)\}$, $\{(s,s),(h,c),(o,o),(e,k)\}$, $\{(s,s),(h,c),(o,k),(e,o)\}$, $\{(s,s),(h,k),(o,o),(e,c)\}$, $\{(s,s),(h,k),(o,c),(e,o)\}$, $\{(s,o),(h,s),(o,c),(e,k)\}$, $\{(s,o),(h,s),(o,k),(e,c)\}$, $\{(s,o),(h,c),(o,s),(e,k)\}$, $\{(s,o),(h,c),(o,k),(e,s)\}$,

$\{(s,o),(h,k),(o,s),(e,c)\}, \{(s,o),(h,k),(o,c),(e,s)\},$
$\{(s,c),(h,s),(o,o),(e,k)\}, \{(s,c),(h,s),(o,k),(e,o)\},$
$\{(s,c),(h,o),(o,s),(e,k)\}, \{(s,c),(h,o),(o,k),(e,s)\},$
$\{(s,c),(h,k),(o,s),(e,o)\}, \{(s,c),(h,k),(o,o),(e,s)\},$
$\{(s,k),(h,s),(o,o),(e,c)\}, \{(s,k),(h,s),(o,c),(e,o)\},$
$\{(s,k),(h,o),(o,s),(e,c)\}, \{(s,k),(h,o),(o,c),(e,s)\},$
$\{(s,k),(h,c),(o,s),(e,k)\}, \{(s,k),(h,c),(o,o),(e,s)\}$

3. (a) 1   (b) $2 = 2 \times 1$ (c) $6 = 3 \times 2 \times 1$ (d) $24 = 4 \times 3 \times 2 \times 1$ (e) $120 = 5 \times 4 \times 3 \times 2 \times 1$
    (f) $n(n - 1)(n - 2) \cdot \cdot \cdot 3 \times 2 \times 1 = n!$

4. (a) 720   (b) 120   (c) 6   (d) 720   (e) n (f) $(n + 1)!$

5. Yes; no

6. $0! \times 1 = 1! = 1.$ Therefore $0! = 1.$

7. The number of one-to-one correspondences between two equivalent sets with n elements is $n!$

8. (a) 3   (b) 4   (c) 6   (d) Impossible: $8! \neq 1,000$ (e) 0

Page 32   1.   25

           2.   253

           3.   3121

           4.   46651

Page 33   1.   (a) 5   (b) 4   (c) 3   (d) 2   (e) 1   (f) 0   (g) 1   (h) 24
                (i) 2   (j) 7   (k) 2   (1) 4

Page 35   1.   All fingers on one hand and two on the other

           2.   All your fingers and two toes, or all toes and two fingers

           3.   No fingers

Page 35 $\emptyset$; $\emptyset$

Page 37   1. A: 13, 14, 15 B: 32, 33, 34 C: $= \neq$, $= \#$, $\# \bullet$
                D: ∩∩////, ∩∩/////, ∩∩////// E: +-++, ++--, ++-+
                F: $\underline{**}$, $\underline{***}$, $\underline{****}$ G: XIII, XIV, XV

           2.   (a) 100, 144, $\# \bullet \bullet$, ∩∩∩∩∩∩∩∩∩∩ , ++--+-- , $\underline{\underline{\vdots}}$} 20, C

                (b) 64, 100, ==#, ∩∩∩∩∩∩////, +------, $\overset{****}{\underline{\underline{\vdots}}}$}12 lines, LXIV

                (c) 25, 31, -.., ∩∩/////, ++--+ , $\overline{\overline{}}$, XXV

                (d) 4, 4, #, ////, +--, ****, IV

412   ANSWER SECTION

(e) 1000, 1750, $-\neq$..., $\underbrace{\cap\cap\cap\cdots\cap}_{100}$, +++++-+--- ,

$\overline{\vdots}\}$ 200 bars, M

(f) 512, 1000, #-==, $\underbrace{\cap\cap\cap\cdots\cap}_{51}$// , +--------- ,

$\overset{**}{\overline{\vdots}}\Big)$ 102 bars, CCCCCXII

(g) 125, 175, -..., $\cap\cap\cap\cap\cap\cap\cap\cap\cap\cap\cap\cap\cap$///// , +++++-+,

$\overline{\vdots}\}$ 25 bars, CXXV

(h) 8, 10, $-\neq$, //////// , +--- , $\underline{***}$, VIII

3.   A: 10,   B: 8,   C: 5,   D: 2,   E: 2,   F: 2,   G: 6

4.   (a) a, b, c, ax, aa, ab, ac, bx, ba, bb, . . .

(b) Using a different symbol for each number with no base

Page 39

Let $A = \{a,b\}$ and B $\{c,d\}$. Then 2 + 2 is the cardinal number of the set $A \cup B = \{a,b,c,d\}$, but $\{a,b,c,d\}$ is equivalent to $\{1,2,3,4\}$, which has cardinal number 4. So 2 + 2 = 4.

Page 39

The paradox occurs since $A \cap B \neq \emptyset$, where A and B are sets with cardinal number 2.

Page 40   1.   See exercise on page 39
for one way.

2.   Let $A = \{a\}$ and $B = \{b\}$ then $A \cup B = \{a,b\}$,
            $\updownarrow$ $\updownarrow$ $\updownarrow\ \updownarrow$
           $\{1\}$ $\{1\}$ $\{1,2\}$

which has cardinal num-
ber 2.

3.   Let $A = \{a,b\}$ and $B = \{c\}$.   Then $A \cup B = \{a,b,c\}$
      $\{a,b\} \cup \{c\} = \{a,b,c\}$
      $\updownarrow\ \updownarrow$ $\updownarrow$ $\updownarrow\ \updownarrow\ \updownarrow$
      $\{1,2\}$ $\{1\}$ $\{1,2,3\}$

4. $A \cup B = B \cup A$; see Exercise 3.

6. $\{a,b,c\}$ and $\{d,e,f\}$ have the same cardinal number, i.e., are in one-to-one correspondence.

1. Let $A = \{a,b,c\}$. Since $A \cup \emptyset = A$, we have

$$\{1,2,3\}$$

    $A \cup \emptyset = \{a,b,c\}$. Thus $3 + 0 = 3$.

$$\{1,2,3\}$$

2. $A \cup \emptyset = \emptyset \cup A$; see Exercise 1.

3. Let N be a set representing n. Since $N \cup \emptyset = \emptyset \cup N$, see proof on page 41.

---

1. (a) $\{1\}$ $\{1,2\}$ $\{1,2\}$

$$(\{a\} \cup \{b,c\}) \cup \{d,e\} = \{a,b,c\} \cup \{d,e\} = \{a,b,c,d,e\}$$
$$= \{a\} \cup \{b,c,d,e\}$$
$$= \{a\} \cup (\{b,c\} \cup \{d,e\})$$

$$\{1\}\quad\{1,2\}\quad\{1,2\}$$

    (b)

$$((\bigcirc) \cup (\bullet\,\bullet)) \cup (\bullet\,\bullet) = (\bigcirc\,\bullet\,\bullet) \cup (\bullet\,\bullet)$$
$$= (\bigcirc\,\bullet\,\bullet\,\bullet\,\bullet) = (\bigcirc) \cup (\bullet\,\bullet\,\bullet\,\bullet) = (\bigcirc) \cup ((\bullet\,\bullet) \cup (\bullet\,\bullet))$$

2. (a) $\{1,2,3\}$ $\{1\}$ $\{1\}$
$$(\{a,b,c\} \cup \{d\}) \cup \{e\} = \{a,b,c,d\} \cup \{e\}$$
$$= \{a,b,c,d,e\} = \{a,b,c\} \cup \{d,e\}$$
$$= \{a,b,c\} \cup (\{d\} \cup \{e\})$$

$$\{1,2,3\}\quad\{1\}\quad\{1\}$$

    (b)

$$(\bigcirc\,\bigcirc\,\bigcirc) \cup (\bullet) \cup (\bullet) = (\bigcirc\,\bigcirc\,\bigcirc\,\bullet) \cup (\bullet)$$
$$(\bigcirc\,\bigcirc\,\bigcirc\,\bullet\,\bullet) = (\bigcirc\,\bigcirc\,\bigcirc) \cup (\bullet\,\bullet) = (\bigcirc\,\bigcirc\,\bigcirc) \cup (\bullet) \cup (\bullet)$$

3. Here again you should give three original examples and use the following for further clarification of the concepts.

    Pete is playing Yatze. He has three fours, four twos, and three fives. $(12 + 8) + 15$ is easy, while $(2 + (8 + 15))$ is not so easy.

1. (a) $\{a,b\} \cup \{c,d,e\} = \{a,b,c,d,e\} = \{a,b,c\} \cup \{d,e\}$

    $\{1,2\}$ $\{1,2,3\}$ $\{1,2,3\}$ $\{1,2\}$

    (b)

    $(\bigcirc\bigcirc) \cup (\bullet\bullet\bullet) = (\bigcirc\bigcirc\bullet\bullet\bullet) = (\bullet\bullet\bullet) \cup (\bigcirc\bigcirc)$

2. (a) $\{a,b,c\} \cup \{d\} = \{a,b,c,d\} = \{a\} \cup \{b,c,d\}$

    $\{1,2,3\}$ $\{1\}$ $\{1\}$ $\{1,2,3\}$

    (b)

    $(\bigcirc\bigcirc\bigcirc) \cup (\bullet) = (\bigcirc\bigcirc\bigcirc\bullet) = (\bullet) \cup (\bigcirc\bigcirc\bigcirc)$

3. Examples: 8 + 13 + 2 is hard but 8 + 2 + 13 is easy;
    25 + 64 + 75 is hard but 64 + 25 + 75 is easy.

1. (a) $36 = 3 \times 10^1 + 1 \times 10^0$

    (b) $752 = 7 \times 10^2 + 5 \times 10^1 + 2 \times 10^0$

    (c) $8406 = 8 \times 10^3 + 4 \times 10^2 + 0 \times 10^1 + 6 \times 10^0$

    (d) $3100 = 3 \times 10^3 + 1 \times 10^2 + 0 \times 10^1 + 0 \times 10^0$

    (e) $2.71 = 2 \times 10^0 + 7 \times 10^{-1} + 1 \times 10^{-2}$

    (f) $26.58 = 2 \times 10^1 + 6 \times 10^0 + 5 \times 10^{-1} + 8 \times 10^{-2}$

    (g) $2.005 = 2 \times 10^0 + 0 \times 10^{-1} + 0 \times 10^{-2} + 5 \times 10^{-3}$

    (h) $.006302 = 0 \times 10^{-1} + 0 \times 10^{-2} + 6 \times 10^{-3} +$
    $3 \times 10^{-4} + 0 \times 10^{-5} + 2 \times 10^{-6}$

1. (a) 1, 10, 11, 100, 101, 110, 111, 1000, 1001, 1010,
    1011, 1100, 1101, 1110, 1111, 10,000, 10,001,
    10,010, 10,011, 10,100, 10,101, 10,110, 10,111,
    11,000, 11,001, 11,010, 11,011, 11,100, 11,101,
    11,110

    (b) 1, 2, 10, 11, 12, 20, 21, 22, 100, 101, 102, 110,
    111, 112, 120, 121, 122, 200, 201, 202, 210, 211,
    212, 220, 221, 222, 1000, 1001, 1002, 1010

    (c) 1, 2, 3, 4, 10, 11, 12, 13, 14, 20, 21, 22, 23, 24,
    30, 31, 32, 33, 34, 40, 41, 42, 43, 44, 100, 101,
    102, 103, 104, 110

    (d) 1, 2, 3, 4, 5, 6, 7, 10, 11, 12, 13, 14, 15, 16, 17,
    20, 21, 22, 23, 24, 25, 26, 27, 30, 31, 32, 33, 34,
    35, 36

(e) 1, 2, 3, 4, 5, 6, 7, 8, 9, *T*, *E*, 10, 11, 12, 13, 14, 15, 16, 17, 18, 19, 1*T*, 1*E*, 20, 21, 22, 23, 24, 25, 26

2. 0, 00, 000, etc. Base one can have only the symbol 0, thus really can't exist. Or since 0 is the only numeral, we could use the stroke /, resulting in the earliest counting system—stroke marks.

3. (a) 14, 20, 21, 22

    (b) 21, 22, 100, 101

    (c) 101, 110, 111, 1000

    (d) 1111, 10,000, 10,001, 10,010

    (e) 23, 24, 30, 31

    (f) 444, 1000, 1001, 1002

    (g) 565, 566, 600, 601

    (h) 2066, 2100, 2101, 2102

    (i) 39, 3*T*, 3*E*, 40

    (j) 100*T*, 100*E*, 1010, 1011

    (k) *TTT*, *TTE*, *TE*1, *TE*2

    (l) *EEEE*, 10,000, 10,001, 10,002

4. (a) 0, 1, 2, 3

    (b) 0, 1

    (c) 0, 1, 2

    (d) 0, 1, 2, 3

    (e) 0, 1, 2, 3, 4, 5, 6, 7

    (f) 0, 1, 2, 3, 4, 5, 6, 7, 8, 9, *T*, *E*

    (g) 0, 1, 2, 3, 4, 5, 6, 7, 8, 9, *T*, *E*, *F* (*F* or any symbol not previously used)

5. We need as many symbols as the base number, i.e., base *n* needs *n* symbols.

6. (a) 13 (b) 37 (c) 1873 (d) 38 (e) 83 (f) 171
    (g) Cannot exist—no 5 or 6 allowed.
    (h) Cannot exist—no 6 allowed.

    (i) 237

7. (a) 27 (b) 21 (c) 17 (d) 11 (e) Cannot exist
    (f) Cannot exist

8. (a) 3625 (b) 1558 (c) 750 (d) 153 (e) 70 (f) Cannot exist

9. (a) 269,713 (b) 65,692 (c) 19,258 (d) 1297 (e) 334
    (f) 53

10. (a) *E*7 (b) 213 (c) 1024 (d) 12,011 (e) 10,001,011

Page 48		One system (not very original) is counting, a, b, c, d, e, f, g, h, ba, bb, bc, bd, be, bf, bg, bh, ca, cb, . . . ch, . . . , ha, . . . , hh, baa, ...

Page 48	1.	(a) $\neq$ (b) -- (c) $\not\neq$ (d) -=- (e) $\neq$ ⊕ $\neq$ (f) -$\not\neq$- (Hint: This system is easy if you just count the strokes, i.e., 1 is one stroke -, 2 is two strokes =, three is three strokes $\neq$, . . . , and 6 is 6 strokes ⊕; etc.)
	2.	(a) 29 (b) 37 (c) 329 (d) 2050 (e) 63 (f) 601 (g) 512 (base 10)

Page 50	1.	(a) 1062 (b) 56 (c) 17,634 (d) 23,221
	2.	(a) 111,011 (b) 10,100,110 (c) No such number base 8 (d) 11,100,101
	3.	(a) 66 (b) 6 (c) 72 (d) 21
	4.	(a) 60 (b) 483 (c) 3866 (d) 917
	5.	(a) 6 (b) 13 (c) 45 (d) 109
	6.	(a) 1,000,001 (b) 1,010,010,010 (c) 11,101,000 (d) 10,000,000,010

Pages 51 - 52	1.	Number the cards from 0 up. If the answer is yes on card n add 2^n; if the answer is no add 0.
	3.	0, 2, 4, 8, 16
	4.	All are powers of 2.
	5.	Base 2
	6.	If this is difficult, review pages 49-50.

Pages 52 - 53	1.	The binary system needs only two symbols.
	2.	Card 1: units; card 2: twos; card 3: twos squared; card 4: twos cubed; card 5: twos to the fourth power. $31 = 2^4 + 2^3 + 2^2 + 2^1 + 2^0$
	3.	See answer to Exercise 2.
	4.	63, 127
	5.	Base 3
	6.	If this is difficult, review pages 49-50.
	7.	$26 + 1 = 27 = 3^3$
	8.	4
	10.	Good luck!

11. Answer yes if the mystery number is on the card, maybe if the mystery number is on the card with parentheses around it, and no otherwise.

12. "Yes" means the mystery number has one 3^n in its expanded notation and "maybe" means the mystery number has 2×3^n in its expanded notation, answer no otherwise where n refers to the card. Add these multiples of powers of 3 and you have the mystery number.

13. Base 4: You will need colors for 1×4^n, 2×4^n, and 3×4^n, or three colors.

Pages 57 - 58

1. (a) 10,000 (b) 10,100 (c) 10,000 (d) 11,001

2. (a) 3343 (b) 4210 (c) 10,000 (d) 2330

3. (a) 8766 (b) 10,224 (c) 10,000 (d) 4228

4. (a) $T64T$ (b) $ET67$ (c) 10,000 (d) 5138

5. (a) ⊕$\overline{⊕}$ ≠ $\overline{\overline{⊕}}$ (b) ⊕ - ⊕$\overline{⊕}$ (c) -.... (d) -=•≠

6. (a) Base three or any larger base

(b) Base eight

(c) Base eight or any larger base

(d) Base three or any larger base

(e) No base works

(f) Base eleven

(g) No base works

(h) Base seven

7. (a) 12, 13, 14, 15, 20

(b) 15, 18, 1E, 22

(c) $x = 5$; 20, 23, 26, 30

(d)

3	7	12
5	4	11
7	1	10
11	7	20
30	23	53

4	1	5
10	3	13
15	5	1T
20	7	27
26	9	34
74	23	97

Sum of bottom row entries must equal sum of last column entries.

(f)

(g) if the base is 6:

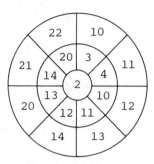

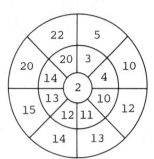

Note: this is not the
only possible answer.

8. (a)

11	10	22
100	12	1
2	21	20

(b)

20	1	13	6
7	11	4	16
2	17	5	14
11	11	16	2

(c)

15	20	1	8	13
1E	5	7	12	14
4	6	11	18	1T
T	10	17	19	3
E	16	21	2	9

Page 60   1. (a) $2 - 1 = 1$ (b) $3 - 1 = 2$ (c) $5 - 2 = 3$
                (d) $8 - 3 = 5$ (e) $5 - 5 = 0$

           2. (a) $4 = 1 + 3$ (b) $9 = 4 + 5$ (c) $16 = 9 + 7$
                (d) $25 = 16 + 9$ (e) $9 = 0 + 9$

           4. $13 = 5 + 8$

           5. $36 - 25 = 11$; $(n + 1)^2 - n^2 = 2n + 1$

Page 62   1. (a) 63   (b) 802   (c) 2   (d) 7302   (e) 6124   (f) 6109

         2.,3. If you find these difficult, review the previous sec-
                tion and examples.

           4. Suppose $m - n = p$. Then $(m + 10^n) - (n + 10^n) =$
                $m + 10^n - n - 10^n = m - n + 10^n - 10^n = m - n = p$.

           5. Suppose $a - b = c$. Let n be a positive whole number,
                where $10^n > b > 10^{n-1}$. Then $a + (10^n - b) = a - b$
                $+ 10^n = c + 10^n$.

Page 65   1. The answer is in ordered pairs, where $(a,b) \neq (b,a)$.

           2. Either way we will get the same number of ordered
                pairs.

3. Same as Exercise 2.

4.,5. If this is difficult, review the examples.

6. (a) Any sets of three and five elements work.

   (b) No

Page 1.,2.,3. If you find these difficult, review the previous sec-
67 tion.

Page 68   1. Sets must be disjoint for addition.

2.,3. If you find these difficult, review the examples.

4. Let sets A, B, and C represent the cardinal numbers
   a, b, and c, respectively, where $B \cap C = \emptyset$. Then
   $A \otimes (B \cup C) = (A \otimes B) \cup (A \otimes C)$. Therefore
   $a \times (b + c) = (a \times b) + (a \times c)$.

Pages   1. No, it is not.

68 - 69 2. One counterexample; for instance, $2 + (3 \times 4) \neq$
   $(2 + 3) \times (2 + 4)$.

3. One of a, b, or c may be 1 and the rest 0; $a = 0$,
   $b = 1 = c$; or all 0.

Pages   1. If this is difficult, review the previous examples.

70 - 71 2. $25 \times 375 \times 4 = 25 \times (375 \times 4)$
   $= 25 \times (4 \times 375)$ commutativity
   $= (25 \times 4) \times 375$ associativity
   $= 25 \times 4 \times 375$

3. If this is difficult, review the previous examples.

4. Additive commutativity; multiplicative commutativity.

5. Additive associativity and commutativity; e.g., the 7
   is repeatedly associated with the number above it, then
   they are commuted until it is associated with the 3,
   then they are added.

6. Look in mathematics teacher journals.

7. $(a + b)^2 = (a + b)(a + b)$
   $= (a + b)a + (a + b)b$ distributivity
   $= a \times a + b \times a + a \times b + b \times b$ distributivity
   $= a^2 + a \times b + a \times b + b^2$ multiplicative com-
   $= a^2 + 2ab + b^2$ mutativity

Page 72   1. $7 \times 21 = 7 \times (2 \times 10 + 1)$ expanded notation

$= 7 \times (2 \times 10) + 7 \times 1$ distributivity

$= (7 \times 2) \times 10 + 7$ multiplicative associativity

$= 14 \times 10 + 7$ multiplication tables

$= (10 + 4) \times 10 + 7$ expanded notation

$= 10 \times 10 + 4 \times 10 + 7$ distributivity

$= 10^2 + 4 \times 10 + 7$

$= 147$ base ten notation

2. $49 \times 3 = (4 \times 10 + 9) \times 3$ expanded notation

$= 4 \times 10 \times 3 + 9 \times 3$ distributivity

$= 4 \times 3 \times 10 + 9 \times 3$ multiplicative commutativity

$= 12 \times 10 + 27$ multiplication tables

$= (10 + 2) \times 10 + (2 \times 10 + 7)$ expanded notation

$= (10^2 + 2 \times 10) + (2 \times 10 + 7)$ distributivity

$= 10^2 + \left(2 \times 10 + (2 \times 10 + 7)\right)$ additive associativity

$= 10^2 + \left((2 \times 10 + 2 \times 10) + 7\right)$ additive associativity

$= 10^2 + \left((2 + 2) \times 10\right) + 7)$ distributivity

$= 10^2 + 4 \times 10 + 7$ addition tables

$= 147$

Page 73   1.   (a)

```
  268        268        268        268        268        268
   ↘          ↕          ↘          ↘          ↗          ↕
   73  →      73  →      73  →      73  →      73  →      73
  ─────      ─────      ─────      ─────      ─────      ─────
   14         146        146        1468       1468       14684
              0          02         02         026        026
                         4          41         41         412
                                               5          5
                                                         ─────
                                                         19564
```

(b)

```
     8          8          8
    ↗          ↗          ↕
  735   →    735   →    735
 ─────      ─────      ─────
   56         564        5640
              2          24
                        ─────
                         5880
```

(c)

```
  29         29         29         29
  ↕          ↘          ↗          ↕
  86   →     86   →     86   →     86
 ────       ────       ────       ────
  16         162        162        1624
             1          12         12
                        7          75
                                  ─────
                                   2494
```

2.   Similarities: positioning is vital, zeros omitted

Differences: multiply larger numbers first

3.
```
  73      multiplicative commutativity and associativity
  ↖
   5  →
 ────
  35
```

```
  73      distributivity and additive associativity
  ↕
   5
 ────
 355      addition tables
   1
 ────
 365
```

Page 74   1.   (a)

Answer: 2494

(b)

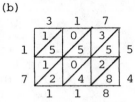

Answer: 17,118

(c)

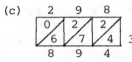

Answer: 894

2. The division of the boxes
    and adding along diagonals
    places like multiples of
    10s together; e.g., the 40
    from 8×5 and the 40 from
    8×30 are along the same
    diagonal while the 200
    from 8×30 is in the
    above diagonal.

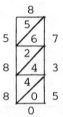

3. Advantages: Need only know multiplication to 9×9 and
    the rest is addition with no worrying about positions.
    Disadvantages: Answer is both vertical and horizontal;
    drawing the grid is a nuisance.
        You may find more advantages and disadvantages as you
    work on.

4.   (a)

$0x^3$ | 6 | 4 | 2
$6x^2$ | 3 | 2 | 1
  | $7x^1$ | $2x^0$

Answer:
$6x^2 + 7x + 2$

(b)

$0x^4$ | 6 | 4 | 8 | 2
$6x^3$ | 3 | 2 | 4 | 1
  | $7x^2$ | $10x$ | 4

Answer:
$6x^3 + 7x^2 + 10x + 4$

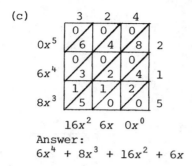

(c)

	3	2	4	
$0x^5$	0/6	0/4	0/8	2
$6x^4$	0/3	0/2	0/4	1
$8x^3$	1/5	1/0	2/0	5
	$16x^2$	$6x$	$0x^0$	

Answer:
$6x^4 + 8x^3 + 16x^2 + 6x$

Page 76   2.   (a)

174

232
2494

(b)

1268

1585
17118

(c)

894

(d)

3535

zero-
bone

(e)

707

3535
3535
389557

3. 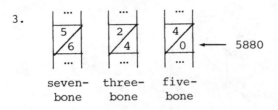 ← 5880

seven-   three-   five-
bone   bone   bone

Compare with grating: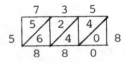

4. Advantages: Same as grating
    Disadvantages: Must remember positioning; always need
    bones

---

1. (a) 86 × 1 =   86
        ~~86 × 2 = 172~~
        86 × 4 = 344
        86 × 8 = 688
        86 × 16 = 1376
                  ‾‾‾‾
                  2494

    (b) ~~317 × 1 = 317~~
        317 × 2 =   634
        317 × 4 = 1268
        ~~317 × 8 = 2536~~
        317 × 16 = 5072
        317 × 32 = 10144
                   ‾‾‾‾‾
                   17118

    (c) 298 × 1 = 298
        298 × 2 = 596
                  ‾‾‾
                  894

    (d) 707 × 1 = 707
        ~~707 × 2 = 1414~~
        707 × 4 = 2828
                  ‾‾‾‾
                  3535

    (e) 707 ×   1 =   707
        707 ×   2 =   1414
        707 ×   4 =   2828
        ~~707 × 8 = 5656~~
        ~~707 × 16 = 11312~~
        707 × 32 = 22624
        ~~707 × 64 = 45248~~
        ~~707 × 128 = 90496~~
        ~~707 × 256 = 180992~~
        707 × 512 = 361984
                    ‾‾‾‾‾‾
                    389557

2. 45 × 73 $45 = 32 + 8 + 4 + 1 = 2^5 + 2^3 + 2^2 + 2^0$

    $73 × 2^0 = 73$
    ~~$73 × 2^1 = 146$~~   Same as $73 × (2^5 + 2^3 + 2^2 + 2^0)$
    $73 × 2^2 = 292$
    $73 × 2^3 = 584$
    ~~$73 × 2^4 = 1168$~~   Most important CAD law here is
    $73 × 2^5 = 2336$ distributivity.

3. Largest. Doesn't matter, just shortens process.
    Either number may be written in expanded base two no-
    tation.

4. Advantages: Need only know multiplication by 2 and addition.
   Disadvantages: It is a lengthy process.

5. (a) $86 \times 1 = 86$
   ~~$86 \times 2 = 172$~~
   ~~$86 \times 4 = 344$~~
   $86 \times 8 = 688$
   ~~$86 \times 10 = 860$~~
   $86 \times 20 = \underline{1720}$
   2494

   (b) ~~$317 \times 1 = 317$~~
   ~~$317 \times 2 = 634$~~
   $317 \times 4 = 1268$
   ~~$317 \times 8 = 2536$~~
   $317 \times 10 = 3170$
   ~~$317 \times 20 = 6340$~~
   $317 \times 40 = \underline{12680}$
   17118

   (c) $298 \times 1 = 298$
   $298 \times 2 = \underline{596}$
   894

   (d) $707 \times 1 = 707$
   ~~$707 \times 2 = 1414$~~
   $707 \times 4 = \underline{2828}$
   3535

   (e) $707 \times 1 = 707$
   ~~$707 \times 2 = 1414$~~
   ~~$707 \times 4 = 2828$~~
   ~~$707 \times 8 = 5656$~~
   $707 \times 10 = 7070$
   ~~$707 \times 20 = 14140$~~
   $707 \times 40 = 28280$
   ~~$707 \times 80 = 56560$~~
   $707 \times 100 = 70700$
   ~~$707 \times 200 = 141400$~~
   $707 \times 400 = \underline{282800}$
   389557

6. Any number can be written in expanded notation in the form $2^0 + 2^1 + 2^2 + 2^3 + 10 \times 2^0 + 10 \times 2^1 + 10 \times 2^2 + 10 \times 2^3 + 10^2 + 2^0 \cdots$.

7. $abcd \times 10 = (1000a + 100b + 10c + d) \times 10$
   $= (10^3 a + 10^2 b + 10c + d) \times 10$
   $= 10^4 a + 10^3 b + 10^2 c + 10d + 0 \times 10$
   $= abcd0$

Page 78   1. Check yourself by multiplying using any algorithm.

2. 45×73:
   5×3 gives the only units position.
   4×7 and 5×3 plus the carry give the tens position.
   4×7 plus the carry of 4 give the hundreds and thousands position.

3. 312×45: Think   Write
   2×5 0
   $1 \times 5 + 2 \times 4 + 1$ 4
   $4 \times 1 + 3 \times 5 + 1$ 0
   $3 \times 4 + 2$ 14 Answer: $14,040$

1.

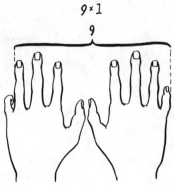

etc.

2. (a) 24 × 9 = 216   (b) 78 × 9 = 702

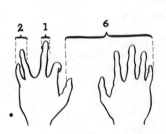   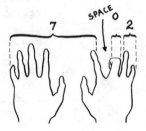

(c) 69 × 9 = 621   (d) 56 × 9 = 504

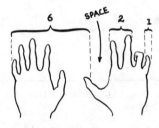   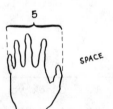 

3. Consider $n \times 9$, where n is less than 10: $n - 1$ is the tens digit and $10 - n$ is the units digit, i.e., $(n - 1)10 + (10 - n) = 10n - 10 + 10 - n = 9n = 9 \times n$.

4. And $ab \times 9$ where ab is any two-digit number with $a < b$. The hundreds digit is a, the tens digit is $(b - 1) - a$, and the units digit is $10 - b$, i.e., $a100 + (b - 1 - a)10 + (10 - b) = 100a + 10b - 10 - 10a + 10 - b = 90a + 9b = 9(10a + b) = 9 \times ab$.

Page 82   1.   (a) 30 + 12 = 42   (b) 7 × 7

$4 \times 3 = 12$

etc.

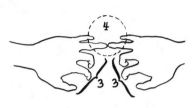

40 + 3 × 3 = 49

2.   (a) Does $(5 + 1)(5 + 2) = (1 + 2)10 + (5 - 1)(5 - 2)$?
Left-hand side:
$$6 \times 7 = (5 + 1)(5 + 2)$$
$$= 5^2 + 5 + 2 \times 5 + 2$$
$$= 5^2 + 3 \times 5 + 2$$
Right-hand side:
$$(1 + 2)10 + 4 \times 3 = (1 + 2)10 + (5 - 1)(5 - 2)$$
$$= 3 \times 10 + 5^2 - 5 - 2 \times 5 + 2$$
$$= 3(10) + 5^2 - 3(5) + 2$$
$$= 3(10 - 5) + 5^2 + 2$$
$$= 5^2 + 3 \times 5 + 2$$

(b) 8×9: Does $(5 + 3)(5 + 4)$
$$= (3 + 4)10 + (5 - 3)(5 - 4)?$$
Left-hand side:
$$(5 + 3)(5 + 4) = 5^2 + 3 \times 5 + 4 \times 5 + 3 \times 4$$
$$= 5^2 + 7 \times 5 + 12$$
Right-hand side:
$$(3 + 4)10 + (5 - 3)(5 - 4)$$
$$= 7 \times 10 + 5^2 - 3 \times 5 - 4 \times 5 + 3 \times 4$$
$$= 7 \times 10 + 5^2 - 7 \times 5 + 3 \times 4$$
$$= 5^2 + 7(10 - 5) + 3 \times 4$$
$$= 5^2 + 7 \times 5 + 12$$

3. $(m + n)10 + (5 - m)(5 - n)$

4. $(5 + m)(5 + n) = 5^2 + 5(m + n) + m \times n$
and
$(m + n)10 + (5 - m)(5 - n)$
$$= (m + n)10 + 5^2 - 5m - 5n + m \times n$$
$$= (m + n)10 + 5^2 - 5(m + n) + m \times n$$
$$= 5^2 + (m + n)(10 - 5) + m \times n$$
$$= 5^2 + 5(m + n) + m \times n$$

Page 83   1.   Consider the product $(100 - m)(100 - n)$.
The tens and units position in the LLT 100 method is
$m \times n$ and the higher positions are $(100 - m) - n$. So
our answer is $\big((100 - m) - n\big)100 + m \times n = 100^2 - 100m$
$- 100n + m \times n = (100 - m)(100 - n)$.

2.   (a)   96
            96
          9216
           ⌣ ⌣
           ↑   ↓
              4 × 4
         96 − 4

         (b)   82   18 × 4 = 72
                96   96 − 18 = 78
              7872

     (c)   94   27 × 6 = 162   (d)   98   2 × 13 = 26
            73   94 − 27 = 67   87   98 − 13 = 85
           162   8526
            67
          6862

     (e)   75   25 × 5 = 125
            95   95 − 25 = 70
           125
            70
          7125

3.   Same as above only use the 200s complements.

4.   Same as above only use the 1000s complements.

Page 84   1.   Method is the same as the LLT 100, only we use the dif-
                 ference of 100 and the number (i.e., a "negative com-
                 plement").

           2.   (a)   105   (b)   111   (c)   106
                       103   102   106
                     10815   11322   11236
                     ⌣ ⌣   ⌣ ⌣   ⌣ ⌣

                (d)   111   (e)   102   (f)   106
                       111   108   113
                       121   11016   11978
                       122   ⌣ ⌣   ⌣ ⌣
                     12321
                     ⌣ ⌣

           3.   Same as above, only use the "negative 300s complement."

           4.   Same as above, only use the "negative 2000s comple-
                ment."

Pages   1.   (a)   1011
85 − 86   110
                       10110
                        1011
                      1000010

                ~~1011 × 1 = 1011~~
                1011 × 10 =   10110
                1011 × 100 = 101100
                              1000010

Multiplying by
2, base 2, is
the same as
multiplying by
10

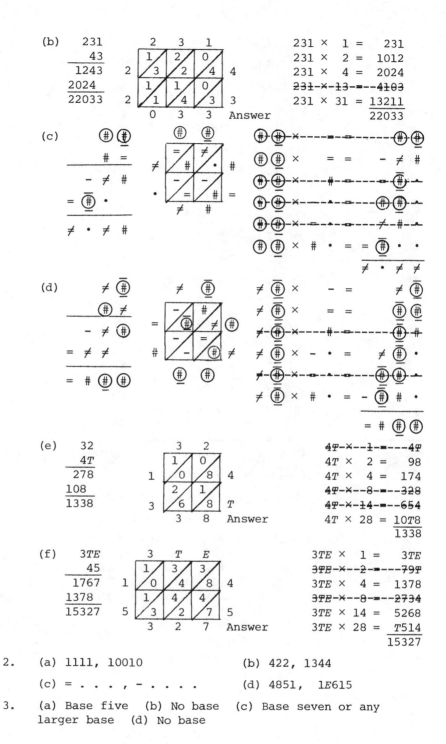

(b)
```
  231          2   3   1          231 ×  1 =    231
   43        1/  2/  0/           231 ×  2 =   1012
 1243    2  /3  /2  /4  4         231 ×  4 =   2024
 2024        1/  1/  0/           231 × 13 = 4103
22033    2  /1  /4  /3  3         231 × 31 = 13211
             0   3   3  Answer              22033
```

(c)

(d)

(e)
```
  32          3   2              4T × 1 = 4T
  4T        1/  0/               4T ×  2 =   98
 278     1  /0  /8  4            4T ×  4 =  174
 108        2/  1/               4T × 8 = 328
1338     3  /6  /8  T            4T × 14 = 654
             3   8  Answer       4T × 28 = 10T8
                                          1338
```

(f)
```
 3TE          3   T   E          3TE × 1 =   3TE
  45        1/  3/  3/           3TE × 2 = 79T
1767     1  /0  /4  /8  4        3TE × 4 =  1378
1378        1/  4/  4/           3TE × 8 = 2734
15327    5  /3  /2  /7  5        3TE × 14 = 5268
             3   2   7  Answer   3TE × 28 = T514
                                          15327
```

2.   (a) 1111, 10010   (b) 422, 1344

     (c) = . . . , - . . . .   (d) 4851, $1E615$

3.   (a) Base five (b) No base (c) Base seven or any larger base (d) No base

---

Page 87   1.   (a) $10 = (11 \times 0) + 10$

          (b) $100 = 11 \times 9 + 1$

          (c) $1000 = 11 \times 90 + 10$

(d) $10,000 = 11 \times 909 + 1$

(e) $100,000 = 11 \times 9090 + 10$

(f) $11 = 3 \times 3 + 2$

(g) $111 = 3 \times 37 + 0$

(h) $1111 = 3 \times 370 + 1$

(i) $11,111 = 3 \times 3703 + 2$

(j) $111,111 = 3 \times 37,037 + 0$

(k) $102 = 3 \times 34 + 0$

(l) $120 = 3 \times 67 + 0$

(m) $210 = 3 \times 70 + 0$

2. (a) $234 \div 3 = 78$

(b) $236 \div 3 = 78$ R 2

(c) $237 \div 3 = 79$

(d) $273 \div 3 = 91$

(e) $327 \div 3 = 109$

(f) $372 \div 3 = 124$

(g) $723 \div 3 = 241$

(h) $732 \div 3 = 244$

Page 89   1. If this is difficult, review the above example.

2. See answer to Exercise 3.

3. Canceling $(a - b)$ is the same as dividing by 0.

4. Review Exercise 3 if this is difficult.

5. 1; 1; undefined.

Page 91   1. We will do only the standard long division algorithm—you should be able to adapt this to the other methods.

(a)
```
      12 R 11
21)263
   21
   ──
    53
    42
    ──
    11
```

(b)
```
        2020 R 248
324)654728
    648
    ───
     672
     648
     ───
     248
```

(c)   11323 R 500
   729)8254967
       729
       ‾‾‾
       964
       729
       ‾‾‾
       2359
       2187
       ‾‾‾‾
       1726
       1458
       ‾‾‾‾
       2687
       2187
       ‾‾‾‾
        500
        ‾‾‾

2. Advantages: Any multiple guess works if it isn't too
    large.
    Disadvantages: Takes longer to write.

3. (a)   567   (b)   219
       567)321489   13)2847

    (c)   929   (d)   407
       929)863041   1365)555555

    Are these the only possible answers? No!

Page 93   1. (a) 1, 3 (b) 1,5 (c) 1,7 (d) 1, 3, 9 (e) 1, 11
              (f) 1, 13 (g) 1, 3, 5, 15 (h) 1, 17 (i) 1, 19
              (j) 1, 3, 7, 21 (k) 1, 23 (l) 1, 5, 25

          2. (a) 1, 2, 5, 10 (b) 1, 2, 3, 4, 6, 12 (c) 1, 2, 7, 14
              (d) 1, 2, 4, 8, 16 (e) 1, 2, 3, 6, 9, 18 (f) 1, 2, 4,
              5, 10, 20 (g) 1, 2, 11, 22 (h) 1, 2, 3, 4, 6, 8, 12,
              24

          3. (a) 2 (b) 3 (c) 4 (d) 5 (e) $n + 1$

          4. (a) 3 (b) 5 (c) 7 (d) 9 (e) $2n + 1$

          5. (a) 1200 (b) 2223 (c) 1333 (d) 393 (e) 10

          6. (a) 1201 (b) 600 (c) 400 (d) 300 (e) 240 (f) 200
              (g) 171 (h) 150 (i) 133 (j) 120 (k) 109 (l) 9
              (m) 5

          7. (a) 6 (b) 2 (c) 24 (d) 120 (e) 6

          8. (a) 0 (b) 3 (c) 33

          9. (a) 10 (b) 103 (c) 1033

         10. In Exercise 8 we are asking how many numbers have
              $2 \times 3 \times 5 = 30$ as a factor. In Exercise 9 we look for
              the numbers with 2 as a factor plus the numbers with 3
              as a factor plus the numbers with 5 as a factor.

1. (a) 3 (b) 5 (c) 7 (d) 3 (e) 11 (f) 13 (g) 3, 5
(h) 17 (i) 19 (j) 3, 7 (k) 23 (1) 5

2. (a) 2 (b) 2, 5 (c) 3, 2 (d) 2,7 (e) 2 (f) 2, 3
(g) 2, 5 (h) 2, 11 (i) 2, 3

3. (a) 2, 127 (b) 3, 5, 17 (c) 2

4. The fifteen smallest pairs are: 2,3; 5,7; 11,13; 17,19;
29,31; 41,43; 59,61; 71,73; 101,103; 107,109; 137,139;
149,151; 179,181; 191,193; 197,199; 227,229.

5. (a) 53, 59, 61, 67, 71, 73, 79, 83, 89, 97

(b) 101, 103, 107, 109, 113, 127, 131, 137, 139, 149

(c) 151, 157, 163, 167, 173, 179, 181, 191, 193, 197,
199

(d) 211, 223, 227, 229, 233, 239, 241

(e) 251, 257, 263, 269, 271, 277, 281, 283, 293

6. (a) 7 (b) 11 (c) 13 (d) 13 (e) 17 (f) largest
prime less than $\sqrt{n}$ where n is the larger of the two
numbers.

7. $(2 - 1) = 1$ and $1 \times n = n$ for all n.

8. 5, 17, 37, 101, 197, 257, 401, 577, 677

9. 7

10. 2

11. None

12. 2, 17, 257

13. 31

14. None

1. (a) 2 divides 10^n for any n; look at the expanded form
of any number, say $abcd = a10^3 + b10^2 + c10 + d$.
Thus 2 divides $abcd$ if and only if 2 divides d.

(b) 4 divides 10^k if $k \geq 2$. Again, look at the expanded form of the number.

(c) Consider the number $abcd = a \times 1000 + b \times 100 + c
\times 10 + d = 999a + 99b + 9c + (a + b + c + d)$.
Clearly 3 divides $(999a + 99b + 9c)$, so 3 divides
$abcd$ if and only if 3 divides $(a + b + c + d)$.
From part (a), 2 divides $abcd$ if $abcd$ is even.

(d) 8 divides 10^n if $n \geq 3$. See parts (a) and (b).

(e) See the answer to part (c).

(f) Obvious

2. Example (1): see the answer to 1(c).

    Example (2): $5 \div 10^n$ for any $n \geq 1$, see 1(a).

    Example (3): $10 = 11 - 1$, $100 = 9 \times 11 + 1$, $1000 = 91 \times 11 - 1$, $10^4 = 909 \times 11 + 1$, etc. So $abcd = 1000a + 100b + 10c + d = 11a(91) + 11b(9) + 11c + (d - c + b - a)$. Exercise 1, see above.

Pages
98 - 99

1. (a) GCF = 1, LCM = 110

    (b) 1, 110

    (c) 4, $2^2 \times 5^3 \times 11 = 5500$

    (d) $5 \times 3 \times 2 = 30$, $2^3 \times 3^2 \times 5^2 \times 7^2 = 88,200$

    (e) 1, $2^3 \times 3^2 \times 5^2 \times 7^2 \times 13 = 1,146,600$

2. (a) $2^3 \times 3^3 \times 5^2 \times 7^2 = 264,600$, $2^2 \times 5 \times 7 = 140$

    (b) 37,044,000

    (c) 37,044,000

    (d) They are equal. In the LCM the largest power of each prime is used and in the GCF the smallest power of each prime is used. Thus we have multiplied the two numbers together, i.e., used both powers.

3. Suppose p^n divides a and p^m divides b, where p is a prime number and n and m are whole numbers. Then $p^n p^m = p^{n+m}$ which divides $a \times b$. If $n \geq m$, then p^n divides LCM(a,b) and p^m divides GCF(a,b). So p^{n+m} divides LCM$(a,b) \times$ GCF(a,b). Since this is true for all p and no p that is not in a or b appears in either the GCF or the LCM, we have our theorem.

4. Not equal. Consider 2, 8, and 16. The GCF is 2 and the LCM is 16. $2 \times 16 = 32 \neq 2 \times 8 \times 16$. Not all powers of 2 are used in the product of the LCM and GCF, just the largest and smallest.

5. GCF needs less multiplying

6. No

7. Suppose $m = a \times b \times c$ and $m = d \times e \times f$. Then $a \times b \times c = d \times e \times f$, so a divides $d \times e \times f$. But if d, e, f are primes, then a must equal one of d, e, and f, and similarly for b and c. Thus $\{a,b,c\} = \{d,e,f\}$.

Pages
100 - 101

1. (a)

(b) Same as (a)

(c)

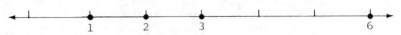

(d)

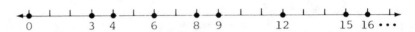

(e)

(f)

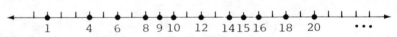

(g)

(h)

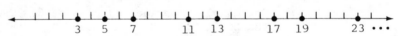

(i)

(j)

(k) ∅

(l)

(m)

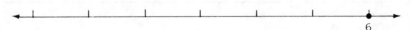

(n)

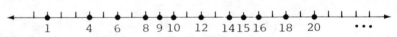

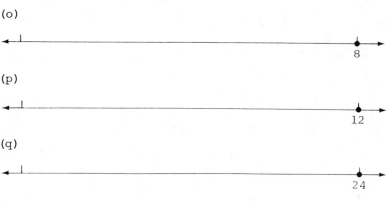

(o)

8

(p)

12

(q)

24

(r) ∅

(s) ∅

(t) ∅

2. (a) No; no. 14 − 5 = 11 and 11 is not a multiple of 6.
        792 − 5 = 787, again not a multiple of 6.

    (b) No. 279954 − 23 is not a multiple of 6.

    (c) 144

    (d) Infinitely many: $m \times n$, $2 \times m \times n$, $3 \times m \times n$, etc.

    (e) 2, 1

Page 102 $\{0,1,2, \ldots\} \otimes \{0,1,2,3, \ldots\} = \{(0,0),(0,1),$
           $(0,2), \ldots (1,0),(1,1),(1,2), \ldots (n,0),(n,1),$
           $(n,2), \ldots\}$. Each subset $\{(n,0),(n,1),(n,2), \ldots\}$
           can be thought of as a vertical number line, while each
           subset $\{(0,n),(1,n),(2,n), \ldots\}$ can be thought of
           as a horizontal number line.

Page 106   1.   (a)   (b)

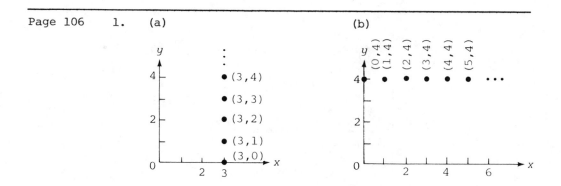

(c)

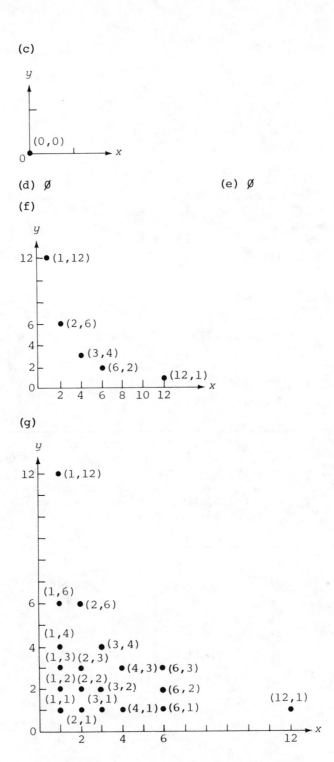

(d) Ø   (e) Ø

(f)

(g)

(h)

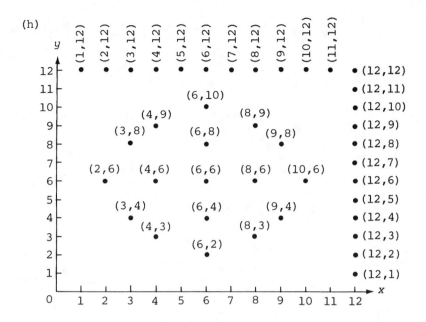

(i)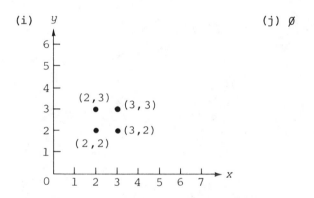

(j) ∅

(k)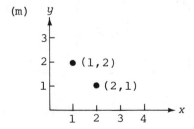

(l)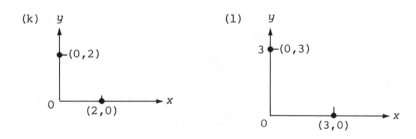

(m)

(n)

(o)

(p)

(q)

(r)

(s)

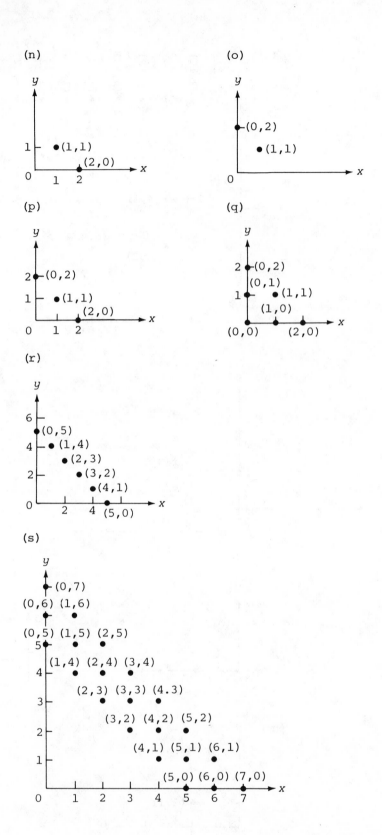

2. (a) No, 182 is not a multiple of 3.

    (b) Yes, 2006 - 6 is a multiple of 2 and 3001 - 1 is
        a multiple of 3; they are the same multiple, i.e.,
        1000 times. No, 4001 - 1 is not a multiple of 3.

    (c) Never

    (d) The 3,4-couple starts at the origin while the 2,3-
        couple starts at (102,102), and they meet after 102
        moves.

    (e) The 3,4-couple starts at (2,164) while the 2,3-
        couple starts at (59,221), and they meet after 57
        moves.

Page 110

Try $b = 4$ with $w = 1,2,3,4$; then try $w = 3$ with
$b = 8,9,10,11$.

Page 111

It should be -1.

Page 111

1. $A = \frac{1}{2}b + w - 1$

2. $\frac{1}{2}(12) + 6 - 1 = 11$

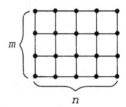

4. Proof for some rectangles:
   Consider an m-by-n rec-
   tangle with edges parallel
   to the x- and y-axes.
   Then we know the area is
   $A = (m - 1)(n - 1) =$
   $mn - m - n + 1$. Now
   $b = n + 2(m - 1) + (n - 2)$
   $= 2(m + n - 2)$, while $w =$
   $(m - 2)(n - 2) = mn - 2m - 2n + 4$. Then $\frac{1}{2}b + w - 1 =$
   $m + n - 2 + mn - 2m - 2n + 4 - 1 = mn - m - n + 1$.
   Harder: Try a rectangle not parallel to the axes.

Page 113

(a) $\{a, b, c\}$
     ↕ ↕ ↕↘
     $\{a, b, c, d\}$

(b) $\{a, b, c\} \cup \{d\}$
     ↕ ↕ ↕↘   ↕↘
     $\{a, e, i, o, u, y\}$

(c) $\{c, a, t\} \cup \{m, i, c, e\}$
     ↖ ↖ ↖   ↗ ↗ ↗ ↗
     $\{f, i, g, h, t, e, s\}$

(d) $\{y, o, u, r\}$
       ↘ ↓↗ ↗
        $\{i\}$

(e) $\{1,\ a,\ t,\ e\}$

$\{a\} \cup \{n,\ i,\ p\}$

(f) $\{u,\ n,\ c,\ l,\ e\} \cup \{m,\ o\}$

$\{g,\ o,\ t\} \cup \{h,\ i,\ m\}$

Pages
113 - 114

(a) 3 lies to the left of 4.

(b) 3 + 1 lies to the left of 6.

(c) 3 + 4 lies on 7.

(d) 4 lies to the right of 1.

(e) 4 lies on 1 + 3.

(f) 5 + 2 lies to the right of 3 + 3.

Page
115

2.,3.,4. Review the examples if this is difficult.

5. For any three numbers a,b,c, exactly one of the following occurs:

(i) $a < b < c$ (ii) $a = b < c$ (iii) $a < b = c$ (iv) $a = b = c$ (v) $b < a < c$ (vi) $b < a = c$ (vii) $b < c < a$ (viii) $b = c < a$ (ix) $b < c = a$ (x) $a < c < b$ (xi) $a = c < b$ (xii) $c < a < b$ (xiii) $c < a = b$ (xiv) $c < b < a$ 14 cases; no.

7. At most $n!$, but many will be duplications.

8. What did Mrs. Cot say when her son Try came home with a black eye? Answer: "Try Cot, Oh me!"

Pages
116 - 117

1. (a) $x = 0 = y$ (b) $\emptyset$ (c) $x = 1$, $y = 0$ (d) $\emptyset$ (e) $(7.0),(5,1)(3,2),(1,3)$ (f) $(3m + 1,\ 5m + 1)$, m any cardinal (g) $\emptyset$

2. (a) $(1,2)$ (b) $(0,1)$, $(1,2),(2,3)$ (c) $(2,0)$ (d) $\emptyset$ (e) $(0,0,0) = (x,y,z)$

3. (a) 157 (b) 2 (c) 23 (d) $\emptyset$ (e) 3

Page 119

1. $$\frac{256v + 175}{27} = (9v + 6) + \frac{13v + 13}{27}$$

Where $9v + 6$ is a whole number for any cardinal number v.

2. $27 = 3^3$

3. $4v + 4 = 4(v + 1)$, 9 does not divide 4, and they have no common factors.

4. 25

5. 250

1. (a) 5 (b) ∅ (c) 2 (d) 4 (e) 5 (f) ∅

2. (a) Odd (b) Even

---

1. (a) 23 (b) 3113 (c) 46,646 (d) 247 (e) 3121

2. One example: If it is 5 o'clock now, what time will it be in 18 hours. Now find other less trivial examples.

3. Let x be the number of coconuts, m the number of monkeys, and s the number of sailors. Then after the first sailor divides, we have

$$x = sq_1 + m \quad \text{for some positive integer } q_1.$$

After the second sailor we have

$$(s - 1)q_1 = sq_2 + m \quad \text{for some positive integer } q_2.$$

After the third sailor we have

$$(s - 1)q_2 = sq_3 + m \quad \text{for some positive integer } q_3.$$

$\cdot \ \cdot \ \cdot$

After the last sailor we have

$$(s - 1)q_{s-1} = sq_s + m.$$

Solving for x in terms of q_s we get

$$x = sq_1 + m = \frac{s(sq_2 + m)}{s - 1} + m$$

$$= \frac{s^2}{s - 1}q_2 + \frac{s}{s - 1}m + m$$

$$= \frac{s^2}{s - 1}\left(\frac{sq_3 + m}{s - 1}\right) + \frac{s}{s - 1}m + m$$

$$= \frac{s^3}{(s - 1)^2}q_3 + \left(\frac{s^2}{(s - 1)^2} + \frac{s}{s - 1} + 1\right)m = \cdots$$

$$= \frac{s^s q_s}{(s - 1)^{s-1}} + \left(\frac{s}{s - 1}\right)^{s-1} m + \left(\frac{s}{s - 1}\right)^{s-2} m + \cdots$$

$$+ \frac{s}{s - 1}m + m$$

$$= \frac{s^s q_s}{(s - 1)^{s-1}} + \left[\frac{1 - \left(\frac{s}{s - 1}\right)^{s-1}}{1 - \frac{s}{s - 1}}\right]m$$

$$\equiv \left[\frac{1 - \left(\frac{s}{s - 1}\right)^{s-1}}{1 - \frac{s}{s - 1}}\right]m \quad (\bmod \ s^s)$$

$$= \left[\frac{-(s-1)^{s-1} + s^{s-1}}{(s-1)^{s-2}} \right] m$$

$$= \left[-(s-1) + \frac{s^s}{s(s-1)^{s-2}} \right] m$$

$$\equiv -(s-1)m \quad (\text{mod } s^s).$$

So finally we have

$$x \equiv s^s - (s-1)m \quad (\text{mod } s^s).$$

Page 128 $265/505 = .\overline{5247}$

Page 129   1.   (a) 6/8, 9/12, 12/16, etc.   (b) 8/6, 12/9, 16/12, etc.
                   (c) 4/3, 8/6, 12/9, etc.   (d) 5/3, 10/6, 20/12, etc.
                   (e) 2/1, 4/2, 6/3, etc.   (f) 5/1, 10/2, 15/3, etc.
                   (g) 2/1, 4/2, 6/3, etc.   (h) 0/1, 0/2, 0/3, etc.
                   (i) 0/1, 0/2, 0/3, etc.

            2.   If $b \neq 0 \neq n$, then $nab = nab$.

            3.   To avoid confusion with Cartesian product and points in the plane of previous chapters

            4.   (a) 17/45   (b) 64/18   (c) 3/2   (d) 3/11

            5.   (a)   (b)

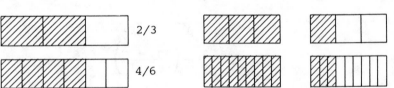

                (c)-(e) Similar

            6.   Cutting circles, sectioning spheres (oranges), etc.

Page 131   1.   (a) $1 \leftrightarrow \{1/1\} = \{1/1, 2/2, 3/3, \ldots\}$
                   (b) $2 \leftrightarrow \{2/1\} = \{2/1, 4/2, 6/3, \ldots\}$
                   (c) $0 \leftrightarrow \{0/1\} = \{0/80, 0/90, 0/100, \ldots\}$

            2. $a/1 = b/1$ if and only if $a \times 1 = 1 \times b \Rightarrow a = b$

Pages	1.	If this is difficult, review the examples.
133 - 134	2.	Reciprocal of 7/5 is 5/7—study Example 3.

3.   (a) 4/12 = 1/3 or 7/24 (b) 2/3 or 3/4 (c) 1/2 or 5/8
    (d) 7/8 or 5/6 (e) 1/3 or 3/12

4.   (a) 1/2, 1/2, 1/2, 2/2, 0/2

    (b) 1/3, 2/3, 2/3, 2/3, 1/3

    (c) 2/5, 4/5, 3/5, 4/5, 2/5

    (d) 3/10, 8/10, 5/10, 8/10, 4/10

5.   (a) 11/3, 22/6, 33/9, 44/12

    (b) 2/21, 4/42, 6/63, 8/84

    (c) 8/4, 2/1, 6/3, 4/2

    (d) 1/3, 2/6, 3/9, 4/12

    (e) 7/3, 14/6, 21/9, 28/12

    (f) 2/5, 4/10, 6/15, 8/20

Page 135   1. (a) $2 \times 3 \leftrightarrow 4/2 \times 6/2 = 24/2 = 6$

    (b) $1 \times 4 \leftrightarrow 2/2 \times 12/3 = 24/6 = 4$

    (c) $0 \times 5 \leftrightarrow 0/1 \times 10/2 = 0/2 = 0$

    (d) $2 \times 3 \times 5 \leftrightarrow 2/1 \times 6/2 \times 15/3 = 180/6 = 30$
                                     Associativity

2.   (a) 6/44 (b) 48/16 (c) 16/8 (d) 35/44 (e) 36/24

Page 137   1. If this is difficult, review the examples.

             2. See *Arithmetic Teacher* magazines.

Page 139   1. If this is difficult, review the examples.

             2. 0 has no multiplicative inverse.

             3. Let p, q and r be counting numbers. Then

    (a) $p \times q$ is a counting number, so it is closed.

    (b) $p \times (q \times r) = (p \times q) \times r$, so associativity holds.

    (c) $1 \times p = p$ for any p.

    (d) No inverses; so we do not have a group.

Page 140

    (a) $\dfrac{2}{3}x = \dfrac{3}{5}$

        $\dfrac{3}{2} \cdot \dfrac{2}{3}x = \dfrac{3}{5} \cdot \dfrac{3}{5}$ Inverses and closure

$$\frac{6}{6}x = \frac{9}{10} \qquad \text{Identity on left, associativity}$$

$$x = \frac{9}{10} \qquad \text{Closure}$$

(b) $\quad \dfrac{2}{3}\left(\dfrac{4}{5}x\right) = \dfrac{7}{8}$

$$\frac{8}{15}x = \frac{7}{8} \qquad \text{Associativity}$$

$$\frac{15}{8} \cdot \frac{8}{15}x = \frac{15}{8} \cdot \frac{7}{8} \qquad \text{Inverses}$$

$$\frac{120}{120}x = \frac{105}{64} \qquad \text{Associativity, identity}$$

$$x = \frac{105}{64}$$

only the answers for 3-7 are given. You can use 1 and 2 as examples for the work needed to solve them.

(c) $x = 0$

(d) $x = 3/2$

(e) x any number

(f) $x = 0$

(g) $x = 1$

Pages
141 - 142

1. Integers with + as the operation, 0 as the identity

2.
+	0	1	2	3
0	0	1	2	3
1	1	2	3	0
2	2	3	0	1
3	3	0	1	2

the operation of addition $(a + b)$ means start at a and proceed on b units.

3. (a) $R \;(\!f\!)\; R = R^2$ (b) I (c) I (d) A_1 (e) A (f) I
    (g) I

4. $\{I, A_1\}$, $A_1 \;(\!f\!)\; A_1 = I$, $I \;(\!f\!)\; I = I$.

So all inverses are present and the identity equals I: $A_1 \;(\!f\!)\; I = A_1 = I \;(\!f\!)\; A_1$. We also have closure, as we can see from the above operations.
   Finally, $(A_1 \;(\!f\!)\; I) \;(\!f\!)\; A_1 = A_1 \;(\!f\!)\; (I \;(\!f\!)\; A_1)$, so we have associativity.

5. $\{I, A_2\}$, $\{I, A_3\}$, $\{I, R\}$ or $\{I, A_1, A_2, A_3, R, R^2\}$

6. No. I must be in every group.

7. R_i—rotate about that dotted line. S revolves the square through 90°, S^2 revolves the square through 180°, and S^3 revolves through 270°; I remains fixed. Operation: $\widehat{f}$ means perform movement on left of $\widehat{f}$ followed by movement on right.

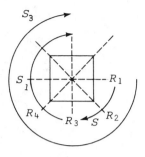

8. If this is difficult, make yourself a model and number all corners on all faces.

9. Yes

10. The line may be fixed, I, or rotated 180°, R. This group is the same as the group $A = \{0,1\}$, operation $+$, only with different names and symbols.

11. Try symmetries of a rectangle, or a table system as in Exercise 10.

Page 143

(a) $\{5/2, 10/4, 15/6, 20/8, 25/10, 30/12, 35/14, \ldots\}$
$\{3/7, 6/14, 12/28, \ldots\}$ $35/14 + 6/14 = 41/14$

(b) $31/20$

(c) $10/3$

(d) 1

(e) $83/56$

(f) $23/24$

Page 144

1. No, $b \times d = 0$ if and only if either $b = 0$ or $d = 0$.

2. $\dfrac{na}{nb} + \dfrac{mc}{md} = \dfrac{na \times md + nb \times mc}{nb \times md} = \dfrac{nm \times \big((a \times d) + (b \times c)\big)}{nm(b \times d)}$

$= \dfrac{(a \times d) + (b \times c)}{(b \times d)}$

3. (a) $9/10$ (b) $25/8$ (c) $42/36$ (d) $146/55$ (e) $66/8$

4. See Exercise 2 if in doubt.

Page 145

(a) $3 + 5 \leftrightarrow 3/1 + 5/1 = (3 + 5)/1 = 8/1 \leftrightarrow 8$

(b),(c) Use Exercise 1 as an example.

(d) Associativity

Page 145

1. Definition of addition

2. Commutativity and distributive

3.   Definition of multiplication

4.   Multiplication by a form of the identity

Page 149   1.   (a) 5/6 + 1/2 = 5/6 + 3/6 = 8/6, where 1/2 = {1/2, 2/4, 3/6, 4/8, . . .}

$$\frac{5}{6} + \frac{1}{2} = \frac{5 \times 2 + 6 \times 1}{6 \times 2} = \frac{10 + 6}{12} = \frac{16}{12}$$

	1 / 2		
5	+	10	16
6	6	12	12

(b) 5/6 + 1/2 + 3/4 = 10/12 + 6/12 + 9/12 = 25/12

$$\left(\frac{5}{6} + \frac{1}{2}\right) + \frac{3}{4} = \left(\frac{10 + 6}{12}\right) + \frac{3}{4} = \frac{16}{12} + \frac{3}{4} = \frac{16 \times 4 + 3 \times 12}{12 \times 4}$$

$$= \frac{64 + 36}{48} = \frac{100}{48}$$

	1 / 2			3 / 4		
5	+	10	16	+	64	100
6	6	12	12	36	48	48

(c) 1/2 + 1/3 + 1/4 + 1/5 = 30/60 + 20/60 + 15/60 + 12/60

$$= 77/60$$

$$\left(\frac{1}{2} + \frac{1}{3}\right) + \frac{1}{4} + \frac{1}{5} = \left(\frac{3 + 2}{6}\right) + \frac{1}{4} + \frac{1}{5} = \left(\frac{5}{6} + \frac{1}{4}\right) + \frac{1}{5}$$

$$= \left(\frac{20 + 6}{24}\right) + \frac{1}{5} = \frac{26}{24} + \frac{1}{5}$$

$$= \frac{26 \times 5 + 24}{24 \times 5} = \frac{130 + 24}{120} = \frac{154}{120}$$

	1 / 3			1 / 4			1 / 5		
1	+	3	5	+	20	26	+	130	154
2	2	6	6	6	24	24	24	120	120

(d)-(f)   Similar

2.

	c / d		
a	+	a × d	(a × d) + (b × c)
b	b × c	b × d	(b × d)

3.   Some of the disadvantages are:
     Method 1: Writing representatives is time-consuming (process shortened in Exercise 1)
     Method 2: Answer is not in reduced form.
     Method 3: Boxes are cumbersome and the answer is not in reduced form.

     Some advantages are:
     Method 1: No guesswork or memory work.
     Method 2: Formula available.
     Method 3: Fun and attractive display.

4.   (a) 60   (b) 3600   (c) 1764   (d) 9576

Pages
149 - 150

1. (a) $1/4 - 1/20 = 1/5$

(b) $43/60 - 5/12 = 3/10$

(c) $2/3 + 3/5 = 19/15$ or $19/15 - 3/5 = 2/3$

(d) $17/16 - 5/16 = 3/4$

2. (a) $1/2 = 1/3 + 1/6$

(b)-(d) Similar

3. $\dfrac{1}{n} + \dfrac{1}{n+1} = \dfrac{1}{n(n+1)}$, $\dfrac{1}{n} + \dfrac{1}{n+1} = \dfrac{(n+1) - n}{n(n+1)}$

$= \dfrac{1}{n(n+1)}$

Pages
150 - 151

1. $\dfrac{a}{m} = \dfrac{b}{n} + \dfrac{an - mb}{mn}$

2. $\dfrac{an - mb}{mn} + \dfrac{mb}{mn}$

3. (a) Associative law

(b) Additive commutative law

(c) Multiplicative commutative law

(d) Additive associative law

4. $\dfrac{b}{n} + \dfrac{an - mb}{mn} = \dfrac{bm + (an - mb)}{mn} = \dfrac{(bm + an) - mb}{mn}$

$= \dfrac{(an + bm) - mb}{mn} = \dfrac{(an + bm) - bm}{mn}$

$= \dfrac{an + (bm - bm)}{mn} = \dfrac{an}{mn} = \dfrac{a}{m}$

See Exercise 3 for the reasons.

5. Let n be any cardinal number and consider $(n - c) + c$.
Now $n - c = d$ if $n = c + d$ for some d, so $(n - c) + c$
$= d + c = n$. Does $(a + b) - c = a + (b - c)$?

$\big((a + b) - c\big) + c = \big(a + (b - c)\big) + c$?

$(a + b) = a + \big((b - c) + c\big)$?

$(a + b) = a + b$ Yes

6. (a) $5/12$ (b) Impossible (c) $13/77$ (d) Impossible
(e) $15/2600$ (f) $52/231$

Page 151

1. Similar: Both defined in terms of a previous operation.
Dissimilar: $b \neq 0$ in product.

2. $3 - 2 = 3/1 - 2/1 = 1$ $6 \div 2 = 6/1 \div 2/1 = 3$

3. (a) $1/3$ (b) 1 (c) 7

Page 152   1. $\dfrac{a}{m} = \dfrac{b}{n} \times \dfrac{an}{bm}$

2. $\dfrac{b \times an}{n \times bm} = \dfrac{ban}{bnm} = \dfrac{bna}{bnm} = \dfrac{bn}{bn} \cdot \dfrac{a}{m} = \dfrac{a}{m}$

3. $\dfrac{a}{m} \div \dfrac{b}{n} = \dfrac{an}{bm}$ means $\dfrac{a}{m} = \dfrac{b}{n} \times \dfrac{an}{bm} = \dfrac{a}{m}$ by Exercise 2.

4. $\dfrac{\frac{a}{m}}{\frac{b}{n}} = \dfrac{a}{m} \div \dfrac{b}{n} = \dfrac{an}{bm}$ by Exercise 3.

5.   (a) $\dfrac{\frac{3}{4}}{\frac{4}{5}} = \dfrac{\frac{3}{1}}{\frac{4}{5}}$ (b) $\dfrac{\frac{3}{4}}{5} = \dfrac{\frac{3}{4}}{\frac{5}{1}}$

6.   (a) 4/3   (b) 9/8   (c) 6/2   (d) 12/49   (e) 81/8

7.   (a) 16/3   (b) 9/49   (c) 18/16   (d) 49/8   (e) 5/8
   (f) 3/2

Page 154   1.   (a) $\dfrac{20}{155} - \dfrac{12}{23} = \dfrac{20 \times 23 - 12 \times 155}{3565} = \dfrac{460 - 1860}{3565}$; $\dfrac{12}{23} > \dfrac{20}{155}$

(b) $\dfrac{3}{10} - \dfrac{11}{37} = \dfrac{111}{370} - \dfrac{110}{370} = \dfrac{1}{370}$; $\dfrac{3}{10} > \dfrac{11}{37}$

(c) $\dfrac{29}{2} - \dfrac{46}{6} = \dfrac{87}{6} - \dfrac{46}{6} = \dfrac{41}{6}$; $\dfrac{29}{2} > \dfrac{46}{6}$

(d) $\dfrac{45}{117} - \dfrac{30}{78} = \dfrac{90 - 90}{234} = 0$;   equal

(e) $\dfrac{5}{19} - \dfrac{6}{23} = \dfrac{115 - 114}{19 \times 23} = \dfrac{1}{19 \times 23}$; $\dfrac{5}{19} > \dfrac{6}{23}$

2.   (a) 2/3 > 2/4   (b) 2/4 > 2/5   (c) 2/5 > 2/6   (d)
$2/n > 2/(n + 1)$

(e) $\dfrac{2}{n} - \dfrac{2}{n + 1} = \dfrac{2(n + 1) - 2n}{n(n + 1)} = \dfrac{2}{n(n + 1)} > 0$; $\dfrac{2}{n} > \dfrac{2}{n + 1}$

3.   (a) $\dfrac{3}{4} - \dfrac{1}{x} = \dfrac{3x - 4}{4x}$; $3x - 4 > 0$ $x > \dfrac{4}{3}$

(b) $0 < x < 6$ (c) $x \le 6/4$ (d) $0 < x \le 2$ (e) $x > 8/3$

Page 155   1.   (a) .5   (b) 2.5   (c) .25   (d) .75   (e) 1.75   (f) .20
   (g) .4   (h) 4.6   (i) .125   (j) .375   (k) .625   (l)
   3.375

2.   (a) 125/1000 = 1/8   (b) 123/1000 = 1230/10,000
   (c) 275/100 = 11/4   (d) 4734/100 = 2367/50
   (e) 4/1000 = 1/250   (f) 10,007/10,000 = 100,070/100,000
   (g) 94,213/100 = 942,130/1000   (h) 123,456/1,000,000
   = 61,728/50,000

Page 156		$a/b = c/1 + r/b$

Page 156	1.	$7 \div 2 = (70 \div 2) \cdot 1/10$
		$16 \div 2 = (160 \div 2) \cdot 1/10$ etc.

2. $(10a \div b) \times \dfrac{1}{10} = \dfrac{10a}{b} \times \dfrac{1}{10} = \dfrac{10a}{b \cdot 10} = \dfrac{10a}{10b} = \dfrac{10}{10} \cdot \dfrac{a}{b} = \dfrac{a}{b}$

Page 159

1. (a) $.3\overline{3}$ (b) $.16\overline{6}$ (c) $.\overline{142857}$ (d) $.1\overline{1}$ (e) $.0\overline{909}$
(f) $.083\overline{3}$ (g) $3.\overline{142857}$ (h) $1.\overline{0}$ (i) $2.\overline{0}$ (j) $.5\overline{0}$
(k) $.75\overline{0}$

2. $.\overline{142857}$, $.\overline{285714}$, $.\overline{428571}$, $.\overline{571428}$, $.\overline{714285}$, $.\overline{857142}$;
$a/7 = a \cdot (1/7)$

3. a/b where $a \cdot 10^n \div b$ is an integer, n also an integer.

4. (a) 33% (b) 17% (c) 14% (d) 11% (e) 9% (f) 8%
(g) 314% (h) 100% (i) 200% (j) 50% (k) 75%

Page 160

1. Example 3 has three repeating digits, while Example 4 has only one repeating digit.

2. 100; 1,000,000

3. $10^n x - x$

Page 160

1. We must obtain a number with a repeating decimal immediately following the decimal point.

2. $1000x - 10x$

Page 162

1. (a) 6842/10,000 (b) 6842/9999 (c) 6836/9990
(d) 6774/9900 (e) 6158/9000 (f) 3553/100 (g) 3518/99
(h) 3198/90

2. (a) 1/10 (b) 9/90 = 1/10 (c) 8/90 (d) 1

3. Numbers which have repeating zeros or repeating nines.

4. (a) 12/100 (b) 1234/10,000 (c) 1111/9000
(d) 1222/9900

5. (a) $26/74 = .3\overline{51}$ (b) $242/303 = .7\overline{986}$ (c) $265/505 = .5\overline{247}$

6. Hints: $\dfrac{he}{she} = \dfrac{whe - wh}{900}$ (why?). Then $he(900) = she(whe - wh)$ (why?) What must e be? Then what must h be?

1.   (a)

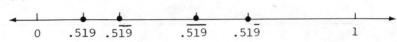

0   .519 .5$1\overline{9}$ .5$\overline{19}$.$\overline{519}$ 1

(b)

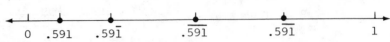

0   .591   .59$\overline{1}$ .5$\overline{91}$.$\overline{591}$ 1

2.

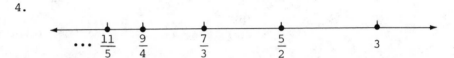

0   10%.160$\frac{1}{6}$ 20% $\frac{2}{5}$ 50%   70% $\frac{4}{5}$ $\frac{5}{6}$ 90% 1

3.   No, 0 $\neq$ 1/b for any b.
       No, if 1 = n/(n + 1), then n + 1 = n or 0 = 1.

4.

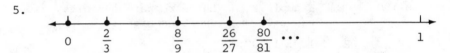

··· $\frac{11}{5}$ $\frac{9}{4}$ $\frac{7}{3}$ $\frac{5}{2}$ 3

5.

0          $\frac{2}{3}$ $\frac{8}{9}$ $\frac{26}{27}$ $\frac{80}{81}$ ···   1

6.

0 $\frac{1}{16}$ $\frac{1}{8}$ $\frac{3}{16}$ $\frac{1}{4}$ $\frac{5}{16}$ $\frac{3}{8}$ $\frac{7}{16}$ $\frac{1}{2}$ $\frac{9}{16}$ $\frac{5}{8}$ $\frac{11}{16}$ $\frac{3}{4}$ $\frac{13}{16}$ $\frac{6}{8}$ $\frac{15}{16}$ 1

NOTE: This is only a few of the points that are
included.

7.   (a) {0/1, 1/5, 1/4, 1/3, 2/5, 1/2, 3/5, 2/3, 3/4, 4/5,
           1/1}
           {0/1, 1/6, 1/5, 1/4, 1/3, 2/5, 1/2, 3/5, 2/3, 3/4,
           4/5, 5/6, 1}

       (b)

0 $\frac{1}{9}$ $\frac{1}{8}$ $\frac{1}{7}$ $\frac{1}{6}$ $\frac{1}{5}$ $\frac{2}{9}$ $\frac{1}{4}$ $\frac{3}{7}$ $\frac{1}{3}$ $\frac{3}{8}$ $\frac{2}{5}$ $\frac{3}{7}$ $\frac{4}{9}$ $\frac{1}{2}$ ···   1

8.   Impossible to name—between any two rational numbers
       there is another rational.

9.   (a)

$\frac{5}{324}$ $\frac{5}{36}$

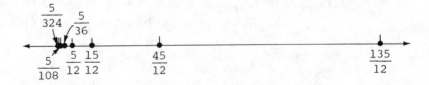

$\frac{5}{108}$ $\frac{5}{12}$ $\frac{15}{12}$ $\frac{45}{12}$ $\frac{135}{12}$

(b)

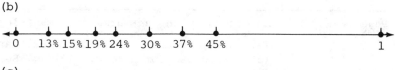

(c)

(d)

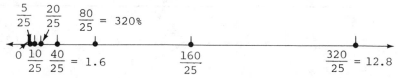

10. These depend upon their use and the personal views of the user.

Page 168   0

Page 169   1.   (a) 8/7 (b) 1 (c) 1/12 (d) 3/2 (e) Impossible
                   (f) 0 (g) 0 (h) 4/3

2.   Multiply by inverses
      Multiplicative association
      Multiplication tables
      Identity

3.   (a) $1/a$ if $a \neq 0$ (b) $(1/a)(ax) = (1/a)b$ (c) Associativity, identity, closure

---

Page 171   1.   2, 0, −8

3.   Consider sets and one-to-one correspondences.

4. $x = 1 - 2, 2 - 3, 3 - 4$, etc.

Page 173   1.   (a)   (b)   (c)

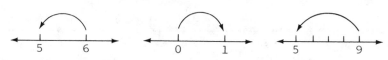

(d)-(g) Similar

2.   (a) $0 - 3, 1 - 4, 2 - 5, \ldots$

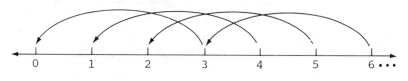

(b)-(d) Similar

Page 174   1. An octopus with many arms or a many-legged bug.

2. (a) Jump goes from 2 to 0.   (b) See part (c).
    (c) Jump goes from n to 0.   (d)-(g) See part (h).
    (h) Jump goes from 0 to n.

3. (a) 5 (b) ⁻5 (c) ⁻5 (d) ⁻6 (e) 6 (f) ⁻6 (g) ⁻12
    (h) 12 (i) 1 (j) 1 (k) ⁻2 (l) ⁻10 (m) ⁻1 (n) ⁻3
    (o) ⁻3

Page 175   1.

1   4   7   10   13   ···

2.

···⁻5 ⁻3 ⁻1 1 3 5 7 9 11 13 ···

3.

···⁻4 ⁻2 0 2 4 6 8 10 12 ···

4.

···⁻27 ⁻22 ⁻17 ⁻12 ⁻7 ⁻2 3 8 13 18 23 28 33 ···

5.

2/3

6.

··· ⁻9   ⁻4   1   6   11 ···

7.

··· ⁻6   ⁻2   2   6   10 ···

8.

··· ⁻10   ⁻5   0   5   10   15 ···

9.

··· ⁻6   ⁻4   ⁻2   0   2   4 ···

10.

⁻2   ⁻1   0   1   2   3 ···

11.

⁻1   0   3   8   ···

12.

···⁻1/2 ⁻2/5 ⁻1/4   0   1/2   2

13.

14.

15.

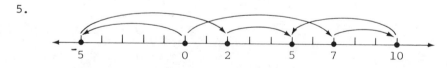

PAGE 179

1. Go to 6 and jump to 3. Since 4 − 6 is the same as
    1 − 3, we jump on to 1, so (3 − 6) + (4 − 6) = (1 − 6).

2. $(c + a) - (c + b) = (c - c) + (a - b)$ by definition

$$= 0 + (a - b)$$

$$= (a - b)$$

3. $(a - b) + (b - c) = (a + b) - (b + c)$ Definition of
    addition

$$= (a + b) - (c + b)$$

$$= a - c \text{ by Exercise 2.}$$

4. (a)

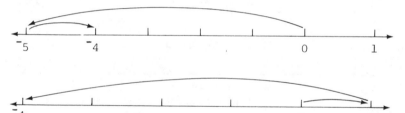

(b), (c) Similar

5.

(b) − (e) Similar

6. (a) (3 − 5) is the solution of $x + 5 = 3$. The equation
    is unchanged if we add or subtract any c. $x + 5$
    $+ c = 3 + c$: solution $(3 + c) - (5 + 3)$, or
    $x + 5 - c = 3 - c$: solution $(3 - c) - (5 - c)$.

    (b) Just replace 3 by a and 5 by b in part (a).

7. $(a - b) + (c - d) = (a + c) - (b + d)$

    and

$$(a-b) + \big((c+n) - (d+n)\big) = \big(a + (c+n)\big) - \big(b + (d+n)\big)$$
$$= \big((a+c) + n\big) - \big((b+d) + n\big)$$
$$= (a+c) - (b+d) \quad \text{by Exercise 2.}$$

8. The same

9. (a)

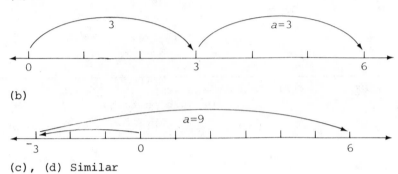

(b)

(c), (d) Similar

Page 180   1. See the examples if this is difficult.

2. Let A, B, and C be sets with $C \subset B$, where A, B, C represent a, b, c, respectively. Then

$A \otimes (B \sim C) = (A \otimes B) \sim (A \otimes C)$ (check this out),

so $a \times (b - c) = (a \times b) - (a \times c)$.

Similarly for 1.

Page 181   Distributive law
Commutativity and distributive law
Now $(ac - bc) - (ad - bd) = x$ if

$$x + (ad - bd) = (ac - bc)$$
$$x + (ad - bd) + bd = (ac - bc) + bd$$
$$x + ad = (ac + bd) - bc$$
Exercise 3 page 150 and commutativity
$$(x + ad) - ad = (ac + bd) - bc - ad$$
Exercise 3 page 150
$$x = (ac + bd) - (bc + ad)$$
addition

Page 182   1. Any integer belonging to the same class as $c - 0$, cardinal number.

2. The number whose class is $\{a - a\}$, a any cardinal number.

3. Any integer which is not positive or 0.

4. $(0 - a) \times (0 - b)$ defined in the hint is equal to $(0 + ab) - (0b + a0) = ab$, positive.

5. $(b - 0)$ positive, $(0 - a)$ negative, where a and b are positive whole numbers; then $(b - 0) \times (0 - a) = (b0 + 0a) - (ba + 00) = -ab$, negative.

Page 183   Be inventive!

Page 184   1. Additive commutativity
Additive associativity
Definition of integer addition
Definition of 0 and identity property

2. Let $(a - b)$ represent an arbitrary integer and $(0 - p)$ represent a negative, where a, b, and p are positive whole numbers. Then

$$a - b = (p - p) + (a - b)$$
$$= \big((0 - p) + (p - 0)\big) + (a - b)$$
$$= (0 - p) + \big((p - 0) + (a - b)\big)$$

Now subtract $(0 - p)$ from both sides of the equation:

$$(a - b) - (0 - p) = (a - b) + (p - 0)$$

3. (a) $^-3 + {}^-2$ (b) $5 + {}^-3$ (c) $^-7 + {}^-4$ (d) $^-9 + 3$
(e) $11 + {}^-6$

4. (a) $^-5$ (b) 2 (c) $^-11$ (d) $^-6$ (e) 5

5. We have assumed $^+1 = {}^-1$, which is what we wished to prove.

6. $-({}^-a) = (-1) \times (-a)$

Page 185   1. (a) 3   (b) 7   (c) 7   (d) 12   (e) 12   (f) 1   (g) 7
(h) 1   (i) 7   (j) 0

2. If $x \geq 0$, then $|x| = x$; if $x < 0$, then $-x > 0$, so $|(-x)|$ $= -x$, since $(-x) - (-1) \cdot (x)$ and $|(-1) \cdot (x)| = |-1| |x|$ $= |x|$ by Exercise 3. Thus if $x < 0$, then $|x| = -x$.

3. $|a \times b| = |a| |b|$

4. $|a + b| \leq |a| + |b|$

5. None

Page 187   1. x, origin

2. x, a

3. (a) $x = 3$ or -3 (b) Impossible   (c) $x = 0$ (d) $x = 5$ or $x = -5$ (e) $x = 5$ or -5 (f) $x = 5$ or -5 (g) $x = 5$

or 1   (h) $x = 7/3$ or -1 (i) $x = 7/3$ or -1 (j) $x = 1$
or 5   (k) $x = 1/3$ or $-1/15$ (l) $x = -2$ or -6
(m) $x = -1$ or -2 (n) $x = \pm3$ or -3 (o) $x = 2$ or -2
(p) Impossible   (q) Impossible   (r) $x = 0$

Page 189   1.   No solution

2. -3

3.   No solution

4.   No solution

5.   1, -1

6.   1

7.   Any whole number

8.   No solution

9.   3, -3

10.   No solution

Page 189   If this is difficult, review previous work on groups.

Pages   1.   Need not have inverses under $\ast$
190 - 191
2.   Consider clock arithmetic with only four digits and multiplication defined as continued addition.

3.   See above for clock arithmetic; polynomials easy.

4. $(a \ast a) \mathbin{\#} (a \ast 0) = a \ast (a \mathbin{\#} 0)$ Property (3)

    $= a \ast a$ Property (1)

    So $a \ast 0$ is the identity under #, and hence $a \ast 0 = 0$.

5.   0—bald heads!

6.   See property (d).

7.   If $(x - 1)(x + 2) = 0$, then either $(x - 1) = 0$ or $(x + 2) = 0$. Thus x is either 1 or -2.

8.   (a) 1, 2, 3   (b) -1, 1, -3 (c) 1, -1, -3 (d) 2, -2
(e) 1, -1 (f) No solution

Page 192   1.   (a) $\begin{pmatrix} 2 & 2 & 3 \\ 1 & -1 & 0 \end{pmatrix}$ (b) $\begin{pmatrix} 5 \\ -1 \\ 4 \end{pmatrix}$ (c) $\begin{pmatrix} 0 & 0 \\ 0 & 0 \end{pmatrix}$

2.   (a) $\begin{pmatrix} 3 & 1 & 2 \\ 0 & 2 & 1 \end{pmatrix}$ (b) $(8, -2, -7, 1)$

3.   (a) $\begin{pmatrix} 0 & 0 & 0 \\ 0 & 0 & 0 \end{pmatrix}$ (b) $\begin{pmatrix} 0 & 0 \\ 0 & 0 \\ 0 & 0 \end{pmatrix}$ (c) $\begin{pmatrix} 0 & 0 \\ 0 & 0 \end{pmatrix}$

4. (i) Closure $\begin{pmatrix} a_1 & b_1 \\ c_1 & d_1 \end{pmatrix} + \begin{pmatrix} a_2 & b_2 \\ c_2 & d_2 \end{pmatrix} = \begin{pmatrix} a_1 + a_2 & b_1 + b_2 \\ c_1 + c_2 & d_1 + d_2 \end{pmatrix}$

(ii) Identity $\begin{pmatrix} 0 & 0 \\ 0 & 0 \end{pmatrix} = e$ (iii) Associativity and commutativity—you check.

(iv) Inverses $\begin{pmatrix} a & b \\ c & d \end{pmatrix} + \begin{pmatrix} -a & -b \\ -c & -d \end{pmatrix} = e$

5. No—no inverses for, say,

$$\begin{pmatrix} 2 & 0 \\ 0 & 2 \end{pmatrix},$$

since

$$\begin{pmatrix} \tfrac{1}{2} & 0 \\ 0 & \tfrac{1}{2} \end{pmatrix}$$

does not have integer entries.

6. Yes—check properties as in Exercise 4.

Page 193 1. $\begin{pmatrix} 2 & 0 \\ 0 & 0 \end{pmatrix} \times \begin{pmatrix} 0 & 0 \\ 8 & 16 \end{pmatrix} = \begin{pmatrix} 0 & 0 \\ 0 & 0 \end{pmatrix}$

2. You try!

Page 196   Bruce

Page 196   . . . a/b, $b \neq 0$, a and b integers, which are equivalent according to the following rule:

a/b is equivalent to c/d $(d \neq 0)$ if and only if $ad = bc$.

Pages   1. A field has all inverses under the operation $*$ except
197 - 198   for the element 0.

2. See example if this is difficult.

3. Try clock arithmetic with five elements.

4. Yes. Suppose $a \neq 0 \neq b$ but $a * b = 0$. Let c be the inverse of a. Then $a * c = e$, where e is the identity under $*$. But then $0 = c * (a * b) = (c * a) * b = e * b = b$. Thus $b = 0$, a contradiction.

5. Suppose c is the inverse of 0. Then $c * 0 = 0$ since $a * 0 = 0$ for any a. But $c * 0 = e$, multiplicative identity. Again a contradiction, since $e \neq 0$.

Page 198   1.

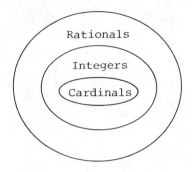

2.

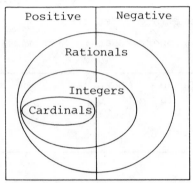

You try text diagram.

Pages   1.   (a) There are only two numerals and three positions to
200 - 201   fill, so 2 × 2 × 2 = 8.   (b) 6   (c) 0 * ($a + b$) = 0 and
                a * (0 + 0) = 0

           2.   Look at a multiplication table.

           3.   (a) Yes   (b) Yes   (c) No   (d) Yes   (e) No

           4.   Prime modulars

           5.   Impossible

           6.   Prime numbers

Pages   1.   2
206 - 208
           2.   -2/7

           3.   6/7

           4.   No solution

           5.   12/13

           6.   135/76

7. 39/76

8. 55/76

9. 23/110

10. No solution

11. No solution

12. -4/5

13. $x \equiv 4$ (mod 7)

14. No solution

15. $x \equiv -1$ (mod 6)

16. $x \equiv 4$ (mod 11)

17. $x \equiv 6$ (mod 12)

18. $x \equiv 12$ (mod 13)

19. No solution

20. $x \equiv 5$ (mod 8)

21. $x \equiv 2$ (mod 7)

22. No solution

23. Multiply first equation by 3
    Multiply
    Change $9y$ to $(27/3)y$
    Add equations—single arrow as it is no longer a system
    of equations but one equation.
    Multiply by 3/32
    Multiply

24. The y value found is the value at which both equations
    intersect or meet, thus x value must be the same in
    either equation.

25. 0 times any number is 0. We could alternately say x
    may be any number; then y is determined by x. This
    system is really just one equation.

26. (a) $x = 2$, $y = 0$ (b) No solution (c) $x = 2 + y/3$, y
    any number (d) $x = -3/40$, $y = -22/30$ (e) No solution
    (f) $x = -1/3$, $y = 1$, $z = -1/3$ (g) $x = y = z = 76/19$
    (h) $x = 2$, $y = 0$, $z = 2$ (i) $x = -3$, $y = -4$, $z = 12/5$
    (j) No solution

27. In equations (g) the constants on the right are all
    equal and the coefficients 1, -2, 3 are used in every
    equation. Thus $x = y = z$. In set (h), again the con-
    stants are all 8 but the y coefficient is always -2,
    hence $y = 0$.

28. Equations $\left. \begin{array}{l} 6a + 6b \qquad = 1 \\ \qquad 3b + 3c = 1 \\ 3a + 3b + 3c = 2 \end{array} \right\}$ $a = 1/3$,
    $b = -1/6$
    $c = 1/2$

Pages 210-211

1. Yes, see definition of accumulation point.

2. Each term has a different sign than its neighbors:

$$\left\{(-1)^n a_n\right\} = \{-a_1, a_2, -a_3, a_4, \ldots\}$$

3. Graphs are left to the student. Some points of the sets and accumulation points are listed below.

(a) $\{1/(\pm 1), 1/(\pm 2), 1/(\pm 3), 1/(\pm 4), \ldots\}$; 0

(b) $\{1/(\pm 1), 3/(\pm 1), 1/(\pm 2), 3/(\pm 2), 1/(\pm 3), 3/(\pm 3), \ldots\}$; 0

(c) $\{1/2, 1/4, 1/8, \ldots, 2/2, 2/4, 2/8, \ldots, 3/2, 3/4, 3/8, \ldots\}$; 0

(d) $\{n/3, n/9, n/27, n/81, \ldots\}$; 0; n any integer

(e) $\{n/(-3), n/9, n/(-27), n/81, \ldots\}$; 0; n any integer

(f) $\{-24/24, -23/24, -22/24, \ldots, -1/24, 0, 1/24, 2/24, \ldots, 48/24\}$; none

(g) $\{-1, -2, -3, \ldots, -1/2, -1/3, -2/3, -1/4, -3/4, -1/9, -2/9, -4/9, -5/9, -7/9, -1/18, -5/18, -7/18, -11/18, -13/18, -17/18, -1/36, -5/36, -7/36, -11/36, \ldots, -35/36\}$; none

(h) $\{\pm 1, \pm 2, \ldots, \pm n/2, \pm n/3, \pm n/6\}$; none

(i) $\{-1/2, 1/4, -1/8, 1/16, \ldots\}$; 0

(j) $\{2/2, 4/3, 6/4, 8/5, 10/6, \ldots\}$; 2

(k) $\{-8, 11/2, -14/3, \ldots\}$; 3, -3

(l) $\{-5, 5/2, -5/3, \ldots\}$; 0

(m) $\{-3/7, 5/10, -7/13, \ldots\}$; 2/3, -2/3

(n) $\{2/6, 7/10, 12/14, \ldots\}$; 5/4

(o) $\{3/2 + 3p, 9/4 + 3p, 25/8 + 3p, \ldots;$ $p = 0, 1, 2, 3, \ldots\}$; 0, 1, 2

(p) $\{-1, 1/2, -1/3, 1/4, -1/5, \ldots, 0, 3/2, 2/3, 5/4, 4/5, \ldots, 1, 5/2, 5/3, 9/4, \ldots, 2, 7/2, 8/3, 13/4, 14/15, \ldots\}$; 0, 1, 2, 3

(q) $\{\pm 1, \pm 2, \pm 3, \ldots, \pm 1/2, \pm 1, \pm 3/2, \pm 4/2, \ldots, \pm 1/3, \pm 2/3, \pm 1, \pm 4/3, \ldots, \pm 1/6, \pm 2/6, \pm 3/6, \ldots\}$; none

(r) $\{\pm 1/6, \pm 2/6, \pm 3/6, \ldots, \pm 1/12, \pm 2/12, \pm 3/12, \ldots\}$; every element in the set

(s) All rational numbers. Every point is an accumulation point.

Page 212

1. (a) $2n$ (b) $3n + 1$ (c) n^3 (d) $(1 + 2 + \cdots + n)6 + 1$ (e) $n/(n + 1)$ (f) $n/2$ (g) $(10n - 1)/2n$ (h) 2^{3-n} (i) $(n + 2)/3$

2. (e) 1 (g) 5 (h) 0

3. Left for the student

4. $(n - 1)(n - 2) \ldots (n - 5)$ is zero for $n = 1, 2,$
    $\ldots , 5$ but not for $n = 6, 7, 8, \ldots .$

5. See Exercise 4 for a hint.

Page 214 1. (a) $\Rightarrow$ (b) If every point on the number line is an ac-
    cumulation point, then between any two points there
    must be another, in fact infinitely more. (b) $\Rightarrow$ (a)
    If between any two points on the number line there is
    another point, then around any point there must be in-
    finitely many points. Note: This is not a proof, and
    you are not expected to prove this.

2. $(a/b + c/d)/2$ lies between a/b and c/d.

3. $\{\pm 1/2, \pm 2/2, \pm 3/2, \pm 4/2, \ldots \}$. You find three more.

4. $\{n - 1/n + 1; n = 1, 2, \ldots \}$. You find three more.

5. page 211 Exercise 3(r)

Page 218 1. $\sqrt{a/b} = \sqrt{a}/\sqrt{b}$ is only true if a and b are positive real
    numbers.

2. No. Consider the field mod 7: $3 + 4 = 7 \equiv 0$ (mod 7)
    but $\equiv 3 \not\equiv 0$ and $4 \not\equiv 0$ mod 7.

Pages   1. Good algebra review
219 - 220
2. (a) $-3/39 + (4/39)\sqrt{3}$

    (b) $-3/39 - (4/39)\sqrt{3}$

    (c) $3/39 + (4/39)\sqrt{3}$

    (d) $3/39 - (4/39)\sqrt{3}$

    (e) $-48/11 + (36/11)\sqrt{3}$

    (f) $-48/11 - (36/11)\sqrt{3}$

3. Review field properties if this is difficult.

4. (a) $R(\sqrt{2}) = \{x: x = a + b\sqrt{2},$ a and b rational$\}$

    (b) Yes; satisfies field properties

5. Yes; satisfies field properties

6. No; see page 222 Exercise 3.

Pages   1. Algebraic: (a), (b), (d), (e), (f), (g), (h), (j),
221 - 222   (k), (m), (n), (r), (s)

    (a) 4.12 (b) 4 (c) undefined (d) -2.57 (e) -2
    (f) 0 (g) .5 (h) -.667 (i) 1.77 (j) 1.15 (k) 2.15
    (l) 4.56 (m) 3.14 (n) 4.35 (o) 13.23 (p) 1
    (q) -.04 (r) -.04 (s) 2.87 (t) undefined

3. $(b\pi)(d\pi) = (0 + b\pi)(0 + d\pi) = bd\pi^2 \notin R(\pi)$

4. (a) If $i < 0$ and $-i < 0$, then $i + (-i) < 0$. But $i + (-i) = 0$.

   (b) Negative times a positive is negative—See Chapter 5.

   (c) $-i(i) = (-\sqrt{-1})(\sqrt{-1}) = -(\sqrt{-1})^2 = -(-1) = 1$

   (d) Again, if $i > 0$ then $-i < 0$ and $-i(i) < 0$. But $-i(i) = 1 > 0$.

5. (a) 2 (b) 2 (c) -2 (d) 2 (e) 1/2 (f) 2/3

6. (a) 1 (b) -1, i, $-i$

7. No; $\sqrt{(-4)(-9)} \neq \sqrt{-4}\sqrt{-9}$

8. No; $\sqrt{-4}/-9 \neq \sqrt{-4}/\sqrt{-9}$

9. See page 218 Challenges

Page 223 1. Since $1^2 < 3 < 2^2$, we have $1 < \sqrt{3} < 2$, i.e., $\sqrt{3} < 3 = \sqrt{3}\sqrt{3}$. So $1 < \sqrt{3}$, and similarly $\sqrt{3} < 2$. Thus $\sqrt{3}$ is not an integer.

2. $3 = \sqrt{3}\sqrt{3}$

3. $3 \div a/b = 3/(a/b) = \big(3/(a/b)\big)(b/b) = 3b/(ab/b) = 3b/a = 3(b/a)$

4. Use the same approach as the proof that $\sqrt{3}$ is irrational in the text.

5. Suppose $\sqrt{2} = a/b$, where a and b are reduced representatives (i.e., share no common factors). Then $2b^2 = a^2$, so a^2 is even. But then a is even, say $a = 2n$. But this gives $2b^2 = a^2 = 4n^2$ or $b^2 = 2n^2$, which implies b is even; a contradiction of a and b being reduced representatives.

6. Again, see the proof that $\sqrt{3}$ is irrational in the text.

7. $b = 1$

8. Let $\sqrt[3]{2} = a/b$, where a and b are reduced representatives, then $2b^3 = a^3$, so a^3 is even. But then a is even, say $a = 2n$. Now $2b^3 = a^3 = 8n^3$, so $b^3 = 4n^3$. Thus b is even, again a contradiction.

9. Similar to Exercise 8.

Pages 224 - 225 1. Correspond 0 with 1. Then match $-n$ to $2n + 1$ (the $n + 1$st odd counting number) and n to $2n$ (the nth even counting number), where n is a counting number.

2. Check the section on countable sets in any analysis book.

3. 2, 2.25, 2.37, 2.44, 2.49

4. Between 2 and 3. As *n* gets large we are looking at
    powers of numbers only slightly larger than 1.

5. Try any book of mathematical tables.

6. (a) 1 (b) *i* (c) $(e^{\pi i} + 1)^2 = e^{2\pi i} + 2e^{\pi i} + 1 = 0^2$
    $= 0$ or $e^{2\pi i} = 1$ and $e^{\pi i} = -1$

Page 226   1.   (a) $-i$ (b) $2/13 - (3/13)i$ (c) $2/37 - (12/37)i$ (d)
                 $(50 - 60i)/61$ (e) $(50 + 60i)/61$

           2.   This should be easy now.

           3.

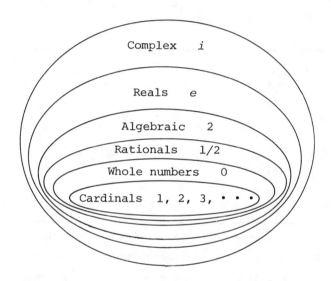

NOTE: Only a few examples of the numbers
in each set are given.

Pages   1. $\overline{.285714}$, $-.1\overline{35}$, $.\overline{263157894736842105}$
226 - 227
           2.   Eventually a set of digits will repeat indefinitely.

           3.   Consider n/m. There are only $m - 1$ possible remainders
                when performing the division. Hence at some step the
                remainder will repeat, and from that point on the dig-
                its in the expansion will repeat.

           4. $-23454/9999$, $559/990$, $296/90$

           5.   It has a common fraction representation, i.e., is
                rational.

           6.   Consider $a.\overline{bcd}$. Let $x = a.\overline{bcd}$. Then $10x = ab.\overline{cd}$,
                $1000x = abcd.\overline{cd}$, so $990x = abcd.\overline{cd} - ab.\overline{cd}$ or

$x = (abcd - ab)/990$, a fraction. This proves only a very special case but is sufficient for our purposes. You prove $.a\overline{b}$ is rational.

7. No. By Exercise 6 it would have a fractional representation and thus be a rational number.

8. Rational decimal expansions repeat, irrational decimal expansions do not.

Page 230 1. (a) 1.41 (b) 5.83 (c) .93 (d) 27.06 (e) 47. (f) 99.51

2. The algorithm deals with only two digits each step. Hence we are looking at a number less than 100 of the form ab. When we expand and square ab, we get $(10a + b)^2 = 100a^2 + 20ab + b^2$. The algorithm ignores b^2 and has used $100a^2$.

Page 230 (a) 1.73

(b) 6.56

(c) .82

(d) 15.41

(e) 83.00

(f) 99.43

(g) 1.96

Page 232 1. See page 230 and answers to (a)-(g) above.

2. How do you feel about them as classroom tools?

3. Check old arithmetic books and journals.

Page 233 1. Suppose $a > 0$. Then by definition $a - 0$ is positive, but $a - 0 = a$.
Suppose $a - 0$ is positive. Then by definition $a > 0$.

2. Similar to Exercise 1

3. Let $x = a - b$. Then x is either positive, zero, or negative. If $a - b$ is positive, then $a > b$; if $a - b$ is zero, then $a = b$; if $a - b$ is negative, then $b > a$.

4. If i is in the field, then either $i > 0$, $i = 0$, or $i < 0$. See Exercise 3, page 221.

5. It is, since $\sqrt{3}$ is a definite distance from the origin.

6. It is not; suppose $2/3 < 4/3$. But $2/3 \equiv (2 + 5)/3$ $= 7/3$ (mod 5) and $7/3 > 4/3$.

Page 234   1.   (a) 1 ft., 1½ ft., etc.

2.   Suppose $1/3 \in S$. Then $n/3n = a/2^m$ for some n and m. But $3n = 2^m$, since 3 does not divide 2.

3.   Change the words "least upper bound" to "greatest lower bound."

4.   It is the largest integer in B, a finite set.

5.   There are only a finite number of integers less than any integer n; $n - 1$, in fact.

6.,7.   Good luck!

Page 234   1.   Incompleteness. Consider the set.

$$\{x: x = 1 - \frac{1}{n}, \quad n \text{ a positive integer}\}$$

2.   A bounded subset where the least upper bound is not a member of the field.

3.   Lower bounds: negatives
Upper bounds: any number larger than 3.

4.   1/2, 1, 3/2, 3/4, 4/5

5. $\sqrt{3}$

6.   Look at problems 3, 4, and 5.

Page 236   These graphs are left to the student, who should be an old hand at this by now!

Page 240   Here are some possibilities, but certainly not the only ones:

$0 = 3(3 - 3)$; $1 = 3!/(3 + 3)$; $2 = 3 - (3/3)$;

$3 = \sqrt{3(\sqrt{3})(\sqrt{3})}$; $4 = 3 + (3/3)$; $5 = 3! - (3/3)$;

$6 = 3!(3/3)$; $7 = 3! + (3/3)$; $8 = 3(3) - [\sqrt{3}]$;

$9 = 3! + 3! - 3$; $10 = 3(3) + [\sqrt{3}]$;

$11 = 3! + 3! - [\sqrt{3}]$; $12 = 3 + 3(3)$;

$13 = 3! + 3! + [\sqrt{3}]$; $14 = 3! + 3! + [\sqrt{3!}]$;

$15 = 3(3) + 3!$; $16 = 3(3!) - [\sqrt{3!}]$; $17 = 3(3!) - [\sqrt{3}]$;

$18 = 3! + 3! + 3!$; $19 = 3(3!) + [\sqrt{3}]$;

$20 = 3(3!) + [\sqrt{3!}]$; $21 = 3(3! + [\sqrt{3}])$;

$22 = (3 + [\sqrt{3}])! - [\sqrt{3!}]$; $23 = (3 + [\sqrt{3}])! - [\sqrt{3}]$;

$24 = (3 + 3/3)!$; $25 = [\sqrt{3}] + (3 + [\sqrt{3}])!$;

$26 = 3^3 - [\sqrt{3}]$; $27 = (\sqrt{3}(\sqrt{3}))^3$; $28 = 3^3 + [\sqrt{3}]$;

$$29 = 3^3 + [\sqrt{3!}\,] ; \quad 30 = 3^3 + 3;$$
$$31 = (3!)(3!) - [\sqrt{\sqrt{(3!)!}}\,] ;$$
$$32 = (3!)[\sqrt{\sqrt{(3!)!}}\,] + [\sqrt{3!}\,] ; \quad 33 = (3!)(3!) - 3.$$

Page 244   1.   (a), (d), (f), (h), (i)

2.   (a) (i) 2   (ii) 0   (iii) 3/2   (iv) 5/2   (v) $2 - p$
      (vi) $2 - p - q$ (vii) $-p - q$

     (b) (i) 5   (ii) 11   (iii) 23/4   (iv) 19/4
      (v) $p^2 + p + 5$ (vi) $(p + q)^2 + (p + q) + 5$
      (vii) $(p + q + 2)^2 + (p + q + 2) + 5$

     (c) (i) 0   (ii) 2   (iii) 1/2   (iv) 1/2   (v) $|p|$
      (vi) $|p + q|$ (vii) $|p + q + 2|$

     (d) (i) 3   (ii) 5   (iii) 7/2   (iv) 5/2   (v) $|p + 3|$
      (vi) $|p + q + 3|$ (vii) $|p + q + 5|$

     (e) (i) Undefined   (ii) 1/2   (iii) 2   (iv) -2   (v) $1/p$
      (vi) $1/(p + q)$ (vii) $1/(p + q + 3)$

3.   No. $|3 + (-2)| = 1 \neq |3| + |(-2)|$ where $f(x) = |x|$.

4.   No. If $f(x) = x^2 + 2$ and $x \neq 0$, then $f(x^2) = x^4 + 2 \neq x^4 + 4x^2 + 4 = (x^2 + 2)^2 = \big(f(x)\big)^2.$

Page 246   1., 2., 3.   There are an infinite number of possible correct answers to these exercises. Remember that no relation that associates more than one element of the range to an element of the domain is a function.

Page 247   1. $\{(0,4), (1,1), (2,-2), (3,-5)\}$

2. $\{(1,1), (1/2,4), (1/3,9), (1/4,16)\}$

3. $\{(p,16), (i,9), (g,7), (s,19)\}$

Page 248   1.   Yes

2.   No; 1 is associated with both 1 and 2 (among others).

3.   Yes

4.   Yes

5.   No; we can't have both (2,3) and (2,1).

6.   Yes

7.   Yes

8.   No; b is associated with a, c, and d.

9.   No; essentially the same flaw as in Exercise 8.

10.   Yes

Page 249	1.	Onto: (a), (b), (d) One-to-one: (d), (e).

2. (a) $x = \pm \sqrt{y}$ (b) $x = y - 2$ (c) $x = (1/3)(y + 4)$
    (d) $\{(3,2), (4,3), (5,4), (6,5)\}$
    (e) $\{(3,2), (3,3), (3,4), (4,5), (4,6), (5,7)\}$

3. (b), (c), (d)

4. (c), (d), (e)

Page 251 1. $f(1) = g(1) = 1;\ f(2) = g(2) = 4;\ f(3) = g(3) = 9;$
    $f(4) = g(4) = 16;\ f(5) = g(5) = 25;\ f(6) = 36,$
    $g(6) = 156$

2. If one factor of a product is zero, then the whole
    product is zero: $(x - 1)(x - 2)(x - 3)(x - 4)(x - 5)$
    $= 0$ if we put $x = 1, 2, 3, 4,$ or 5 but not if we put
    $x = 6$, say.

4. (a) 364   (b) 4   (c) 7204   (d) $4 + 120\pi \doteq 380.9908$

5. Infinitely many possibilities. One, for example is
    $f(x) = (x + 1) + 17x(x^2 - 1)(x^2 - 4)$

6. (a) $f(x) = 3x - 2;\ f(x) = 3x - 2 + x(x - 1)(x - 2)$
       $(x - 3)(x - 4)$; or many other possibilities

    (b) $f(x) = x^3;\ f(x) = x^3 + (x - 1)(x - 2)(x - 3)$
       $(x - 4)$; etc.

    (c) $f(x) = x^2 + x;\ f(x) = x(x + 1)\big(1 + (x - 1)(x - 2)$
       $(x - 3)(x - 4)(x - 5)\big)$; etc.

    (d) $f(x) = x/2;\ f(x) = \tfrac{1}{2}\big(x + (x - 1)(x - 2)(x - 3)\big)$;
       etc.

    (e) $f(x) = x!$ (for $x = 0, 1, 2, 3, \ldots$);
       $f(x) = x! + x(x - 1) \ldots (x - 4)$; etc.

    (f) $f(x) =$ the greatest integer that is less than or
       equal to $\tfrac{1}{2}x$; etc.

    (g) $f(x) = 7x$; etc.

Pages   1.
256 - 257

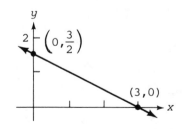

2.

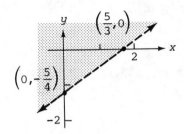

3.

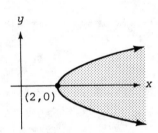

4.

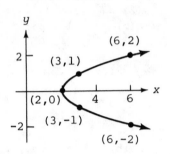

5.

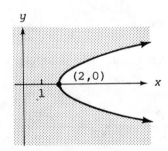

6.

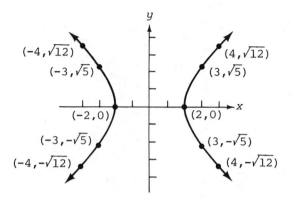

7.

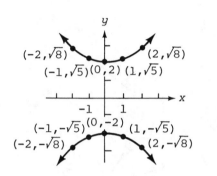

8.

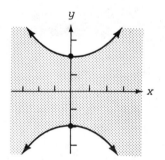

9.

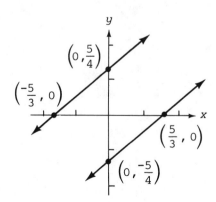

10.

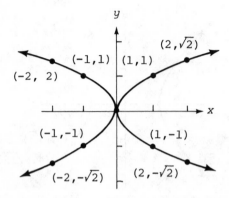

11.

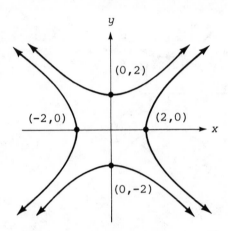

12.

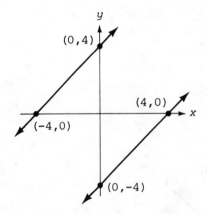

13.

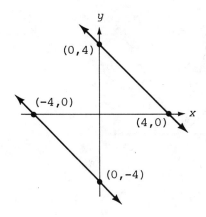

14. Yes. Above (or below) any point on the x-axis there is no more than one point of the graph.

Pages
258 - 259

1.

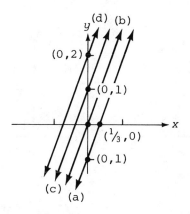

2. b determines where the straight line intercepts the y-axis.

3.

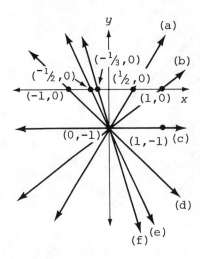

4. *m* determines how steeply the straight line slopes.

5. (a)   (b)

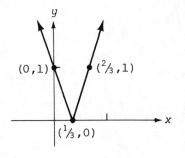   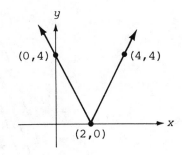

(c)   (d)

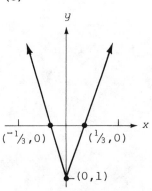   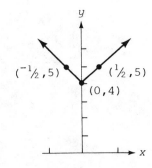

(e)

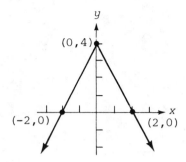

Page 260 1. (a)

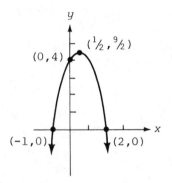

(b)

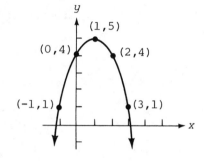

(c)

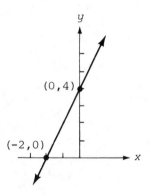

(d)

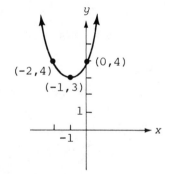

(e)

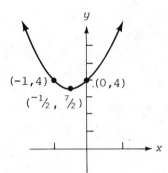

(f)

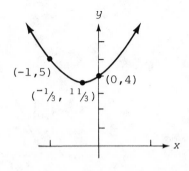

2. a determines whether the curve goes up or down and how
    steeply it goes up or down.

3. (a)

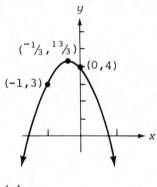

(b)

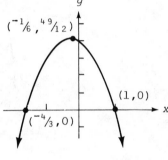

(c)

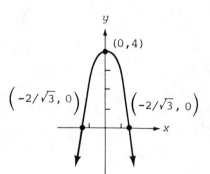

(d)

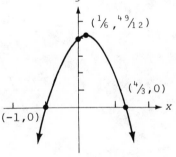

(e)

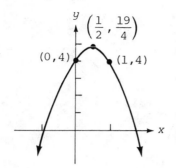

4. *b* determines where the horizontal "turning point" of the parabola occurs.

5. (a)

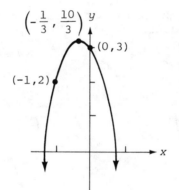

(b)

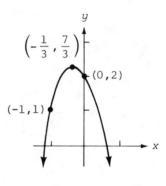

(c)

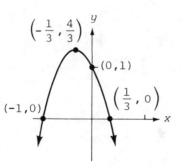

(d)

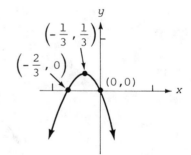

(e)

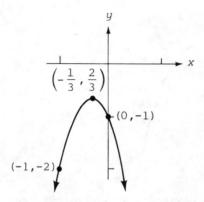

$\left(-\dfrac{1}{3}, \dfrac{2}{3}\right)$

$(0,-1)$

$(-1,-2)$

6. c determines the vertical position of the curve (and therefore where it intercepts the y-axis).

7. It depends on the professor whether or not it's "graft on the number line."

8. (a) 1   (b) $3x^2$ (c) $3x^2$ (d) $3x^2$ (e) $3x^2$ (f) $3x^2$
(g) $3x^2$ (h) $3x^2$ (i) $3x^2$

9. (a)

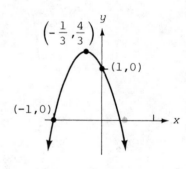

$(1,2)$

$(0,1)$

$\left(\dfrac{1}{3}, \dfrac{2}{3}\right)$

(b)

$\left(-\dfrac{1}{3}, \dfrac{4}{3}\right)$

$(1,0)$

$(-1,0)$

(c)

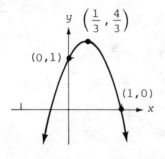

$\left(\dfrac{1}{3}, \dfrac{4}{3}\right)$

$(0,1)$

$(1,0)$

(d)

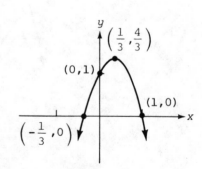

$\left(\dfrac{1}{3}, \dfrac{4}{3}\right)$

$(0,1)$

$(1,0)$

$\left(-\dfrac{1}{3}, 0\right)$

10. The first curves up; the second curves down.

1. (a)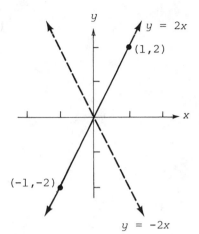

(b)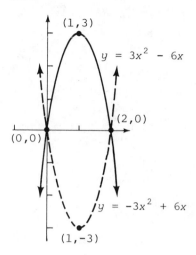

(c)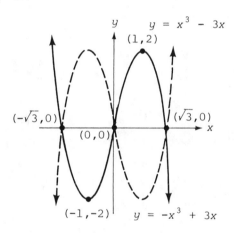

(d)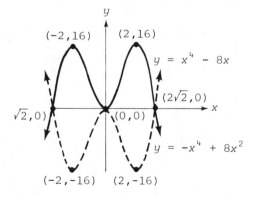

(e)

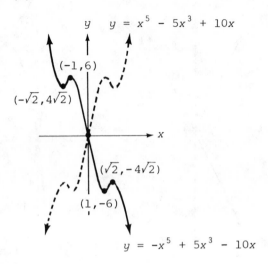

$$y \quad y = x^5 - 5x^3 + 10x$$

$(-1,6)$

$(-\sqrt{2}, 4\sqrt{2})$

x

$(\sqrt{2}, -4\sqrt{2})$

$(1,-6)$

$$y = -x^5 + 5x^3 - 10x$$

2. (a) S (b) W (c) M (d) N (e) N (f) M (g) S (h) W

3. (a)

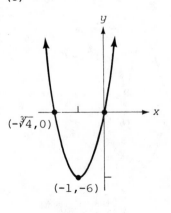

$y \quad \left(\dfrac{2}{\sqrt{3}}, 4\sqrt{3} \right)$

$(-2,0)$ $(2,0)$ x

$\left(\dfrac{-2}{\sqrt{3}}, -4\sqrt{3} \right)$

(b)

y

$(1,6)$

x

$(\sqrt[3]{4}, 0)$

(c)

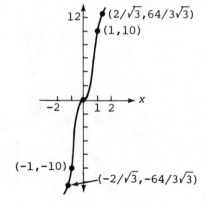

y

$(-\sqrt[3]{4}, 0)$ x

$(-1,-6)$

(d)

y

12 $(2/\sqrt{3}, 64/3\sqrt{3})$

$(1,10)$

-2 1 2 x

$(-1,-10)$

$(-2/\sqrt{3}, -64/3\sqrt{3})$

4. (a) $y = \left| \pm 2x \right|$

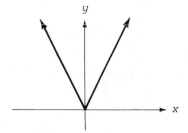

(b) $y = \left| \pm 3x^2 \mp 6x \right|$

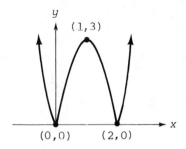

(c) $y = \left| \pm x^3 \pm 3x \right|$

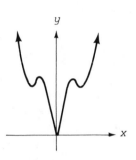

(d) $y = \left| \pm x^4 \mp 8x \right|$

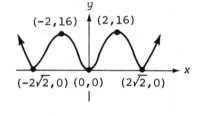

(e) $y = \left| \pm x^5 \mp 5x^3 \pm 10x \right|$

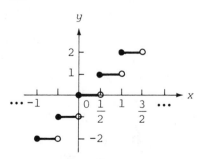

Page 264   (a)

(b)

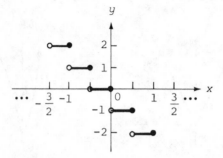

(c)

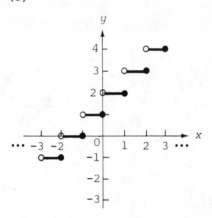

(d)

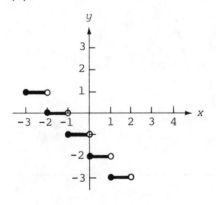

(e)

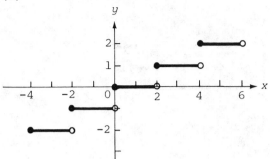

(f)

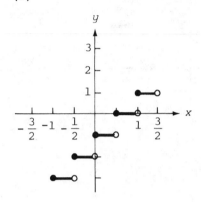

(g)

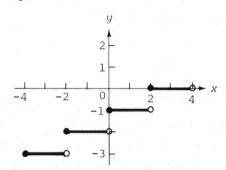

(h)

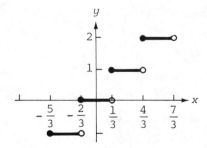

(i)

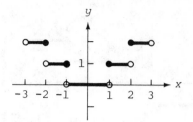

(j)

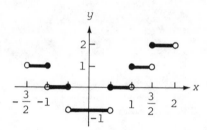

(k)

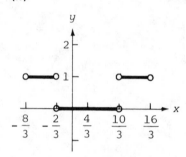

Page 265　　1.　See the answer for the Challenge on page 240.

　　　　　　2.　$0 = (4 - 4)(4 + 4)$; $1 = (4 + 4)/(4 + 4)$;

　　　　　　　　$2 = (4 \times 4)/(4 + 4)$; $3 = (4 + 4 + 4)/4$;

　　　　　　　　$4 = 4(\sqrt[4]{4} + \sqrt{4})/4)$; $5 = 4 + \sqrt{4 \times 4}/4$;

　　　　　　　　$6 = 4 + \sqrt{4}(4/4)$; $7 = 4 + 4 - 4/4$; $8 = 4 \times 4\sqrt{\sqrt{4 \times 4}}$;

　　　　　　　　$9 = 4 + 4 + 4/4$; $10 = (4 \times 4) - 4 - \sqrt{4}$;

　　　　　　　　$11 = 4 + 4 + \sqrt{4} + [\sqrt{\sqrt{4}}]$; $12 = 4 + 4 + \sqrt{4} + \sqrt{4}$;

　　　　　　　　$13 = (4 \times 4) - 4 + [\sqrt{\sqrt{4}}]$; $14 = 4 \times 4 - 4\sqrt{\sqrt{4}}$;

　　　　　　　　$15 = 4 \times 4 - 4/4$; $16 = (4 \times 4)(4/4)$; $17 = 4 \times 4 + 4/4$;

　　　　　　　　$18 = 4 \times 4 + 4\sqrt{\sqrt{4}}$; $19 = 4 \times 4 + \sqrt{4} + [\sqrt{\sqrt{4}}]$;

　　　　　　　　$20 = 4! - 4(4/4)$; $21 = 4! - \sqrt{4} - [\sqrt{\sqrt{4}}]$;

　　　　　　　　$22 = 4! - (\sqrt{4} + \sqrt{4})/\sqrt{4}$; $23 = 4! - 4/(\sqrt{4} + \sqrt{4})$;

　　　　　　　　$24 = 4!(\sqrt[4]{4} + \sqrt{4})/4$; $25 = 4! + 4^{4-4}$;

482　ANSWER SECTION

$26 = 4! + 4/4 + [\sqrt{\sqrt{4}}]$; $27 = 4! + \sqrt{4} + 4/4$;

$28 = 4! + 4 + 4 - 4$; $29 = 4! + 4 + 4/4$;

$30 = 4! + 4 + \sqrt{4}$; $31 = 4(4 + 4) - [\sqrt{\sqrt{4}}]$;

$32 = 4! + (4 + 4)[\sqrt{\sqrt{4}}]$; $33 = 4! + 4 + 4 + [\sqrt{\sqrt{4}}]$;

$34 = 4! + 4 + 4 + \sqrt{4}$; $35 = (4 + \sqrt{4})^{\sqrt{4}} - [\sqrt{\sqrt{4}}]$;

$36 = (\sqrt{4} + \sqrt{4} + \sqrt{4})^{\sqrt{4}}$; $37 = (4 + \sqrt{4})^{\sqrt{4}} + [\sqrt{\sqrt{4}}]$;

$38 = (4 + \sqrt{4})^{\sqrt{4}} + \sqrt{4}$; $39 = 44 - 4 - [\sqrt{\sqrt{4}}]$;

$40 = 44 - (\sqrt{4} + \sqrt{4})$; $41 = 44 - \sqrt{4} - [\sqrt{\sqrt{4}}]$;

$42 = 44 - 4/\sqrt{4}$; $43 = 44 - 4/4$; $44 = (44)4/4$. There are many other possibilities.

3. $0 = 2 - 2$; $1 = 2/2$; $2 = (\sqrt{2})^2$; $3 = 2 + [\sqrt{2}]$;

      $4 = 2^2$; $5 = \left[\sqrt{\sqrt{((2 + [\sqrt{2}])!)!}}\right]$; $6 = (2 + [\sqrt{2}])!$;

      $7 =$

etc.

4. $0 = 3 - 3 = (2 - 2)2 = (3 - 3)4$;

      $1 = 3/3 = \sqrt{2 \times 2}/2 = 4^{3-3}$;

      $2 = [\sqrt{3}] + [\sqrt{3}] = 2(2/2) = \sqrt{4}(3/3)$;

      $3 = \sqrt{3} \times \sqrt{3} = 2 + 2/2 = [3 + 3/4]$;

      $4 = 3 + [\sqrt{3}] = (\sqrt{2 + 2})^2 = 4(3/3)$;

      $5 = 3! - [\sqrt{3}] = 2^2 + [\sqrt{2}] = 4 + 3/3$;

      $6 = (\sqrt{3}\sqrt{3})! = 2 + 2 + 2 = 3^{\sqrt{4}} - 3$;

      $7 = 3! + [\sqrt{3}] = (2 + [\sqrt{2}])! + [\sqrt{2}] = 3 + 3 + [\sqrt{\sqrt{4}}]$;

      $8 = 3! + [\sqrt{3!}] = 2(2^2) = [33/4]$;

$9 = 3 \times 3 = 2 + \ldots = (3 \times 4) - 3$;

$$10 = \left[\sqrt{[3 + \sqrt{3!}]\,!}\,\right]! = \left[\sqrt{[2 + 2 + \sqrt{2}\,]}\,\right]! = (4 \times 3) - \left[\sqrt{3!}\,\right];$$

$$11 = \left[\sqrt{[\sqrt{\sqrt{(3!)!}}\,]\,!}\,\right] + \left[\sqrt{3}\,\right] = 22/2 = (4 \times 3) - \left[\sqrt{3}\,\right];$$

$$12 = 3! + 3! = (2 + 2)!/2 = 4 x \sqrt{3} \times \sqrt{3};$$

$$13 = \left(\left[\sqrt{[\sqrt{\sqrt{(3!)!}}\,]}\,\right]! \right] + 3 = \left[\sqrt{([2 + \sqrt{2}\,]\,!)!}\,\right]\Big/2$$
$$= 4 \times 3 + \left[\sqrt{3}\,\right];$$

$$14 = \left[\sqrt{\sqrt{[\sqrt{\sqrt{[3\sqrt{3!}\,]\,!}}\,]\,!}}\,\right] = \left[\sqrt{222}\,\right] = 4 \times 3 + \left[\sqrt{3!}\,\right];$$

$$15 = 3\left[\sqrt{\sqrt{(3!)!}}\,\right] = \left[\sqrt{\sqrt{\sqrt{\sqrt{(([\sqrt{22}\,]!)!)!}}}}\,\right] \div 2 = 4 \times 3 + 3.$$

There are other possibilities.

5.   If $n = 1$, $1 = \left[\sqrt{1}\,\right]$;

if $n = 2$, $1 = \left[\sqrt{2}\,\right]$;

if $n = 3$, $1 = \left[\sqrt{3}\,\right]$;

if $n = 4$, $1 = \left[\sqrt{\sqrt{4}}\,\right]$; if $n > 4$, $\sqrt{n} < n/2$ (since $n < n^2/4$, or $4n < n^2$, which follows from $4 < n$). Hence $\sqrt{\sqrt{n}} < \sqrt{n/2} < n/4$. Since n, $n/2$, $n/4$, $n/8$, etc. gets smaller and smaller, and since $\sqrt{\sqrt{\cdots \sqrt{n}}}$ is never less than 1, eventually $\sqrt{\sqrt{\cdots \sqrt{n}}}$ is just a little more than 1, so that $\left[\sqrt{\sqrt{\cdots \sqrt{n}}}\,\right] = 1$.

6.   The problems in this objective are puzzle problems which tend to catch children's interest. In the process of trying to solve these puzzles, the children get a lot of computational practice, as well as learning new operations (such as $\sqrt{}$, [ ], !, etc.).

Page 268   5.   Polk and Harding were both born on November 2.

6.,7. $$\frac{1 - (365 \cdot 364 \cdot 363 \cdot \ldots \cdot 336)}{365^{30}}$$

1. (a)

(i) Duration	Frequency	(ii) Duration	Frequency
45	••	45	2
44		44	
43		43	
42	•	42	1
41	•	41	1
40		40	
39		39	
38	••	38	2
37	•	37	1
36	••	36	2
35	••	35	2
34		34	
33		33	
32		32	
31	•	31	1
30	•	30	1
29	•	29	1
28		28	
27	•	27	1
26	••	26	2
25		25	
24		24	
23		23	
22		22	
21		21	
20	•	20	1
19		19	
18		18	
17	•	17	1
16		16	
15		15	
14		14	
13		13	
12		12	
11		11	
10	•	10	1

(b)

(i) Duration	Frequency	(ii) Duration	Frequency
41–45	••••	41–45	4
36–40	•••••	36–40	5
31–35	•••	31–35	3
26–30	•••••	26–30	5
21–25		21–25	
16–20	••	16–20	2
11–15		11–15	
6–10	•	6–10	1

(c)

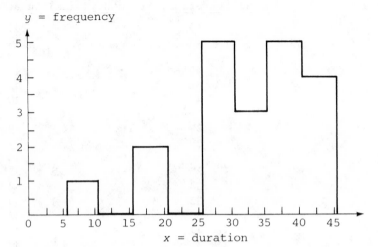

(d)

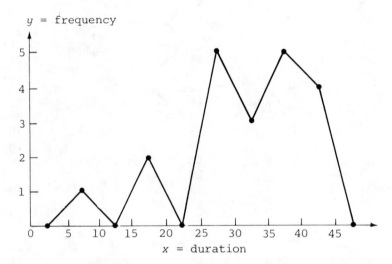

2. (a) (i)

No. Gripes	Frequency	No. Gripes	Frequency
98	•	51	
97		50	
96	•	49	
95		48	
94		47	•
93		46	
92		45	
91		44	
90		43	
89		42	
88	•	41	
87		40	
86		39	•
85		38	
84		37	
83	•	36	
82		35	
81		34	
80		33	
79		32	
78		31	• •
77		30	
76		29	
75	•	28	
74		27	
73		26	
72	•	25	•
71		24	
70		23	
69		22	
68	•	21	
67		20	
66		19	
65	•	18	
64		17	
63		16	
62		15	• •
61		14	
60	•	13	
59		12	•
58		11	
57		10	
56		9	
55	•	8	
54		7	
53	•	6	
52		5	
		4	•

(b) (i)

No. Gripes	Frequency	No. Gripes	Frequency
90–99	••	90–99	2
80–89	••	80–89	2
70–79	••	70–79	2
60–69	•••	60–69	3
50–59	••	50–59	2
40–49	•	40–49	1
30–39	•••	30–39	3
20–29	•	20–29	1
10–19	•••	10–19	3
0– 9	•	0– 9	1

(c)

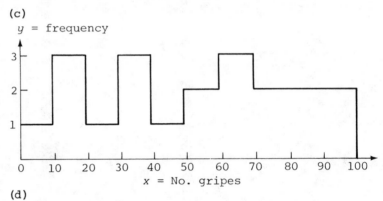

(d)

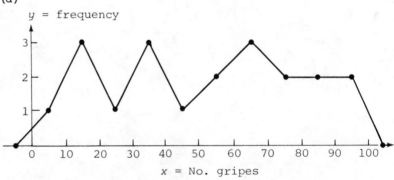

3.

(a)

Amount	Frequency
7	•
6	
5	••
4	••
3	•••
2	••••••
1	••
0	

(b)

Amount	Frequency
6–7	•
4–5	••••
2–3	•••••••••
0–1	••

(c)

y = frequency

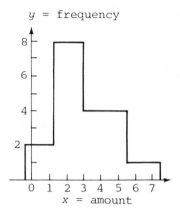

x = amount

(d)

y = frequency

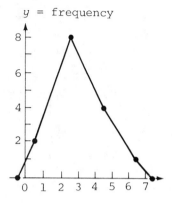

4. The areas are equal.

5. A histogram is not a graph of a function because each of its vertical edges contains infinitely many points corresponding to a single point on the x (horizontal) axis.

6. A frequency polygon is a graph of a function because above each point on the pertinent part of the x-axis there is a single point of the polygon.

Pages
284-286

1. (a) 3.33

    (b) 5.00, which is midway between 2 and 8

    (c) 3.20

    (d) 8.00, which is midway between both 2 and 14 and 5 and 11

    (e) 8.00

    (f) 18.00, which is 10 more than the mean in (e)

    (g) 20.00, 2 more than the mean in (f)

    (h) 40.00, twice as much as the mean in (g)

2. (a) 2 (b) 2,3 (c) 2, 3, 5 (d) 2, 3, 5, (e) 4
    (f) 2,4

3. (a) 3.00 (b) 3.00 (medians don't measure spread)
    (c) 4.00 (d) 7.50 (e) 9.00 (f) 9.00 (g) 3.75
    (h) 3.83 (i) 3.88 (j) 3.90 (k) $3.5 + (n - 1)/2n$

4. (a)

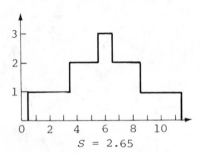

$S = 2.65$

(b)

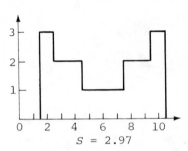

$S = 2.97$

(c)

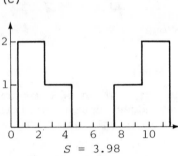

$S = 3.98$

(d)

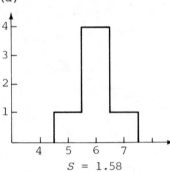

$S = 1.58$

(e)

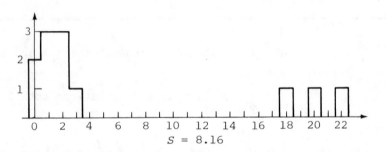

$S = 8.16$

(f)

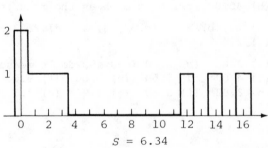

$S = 6.34$

(g)

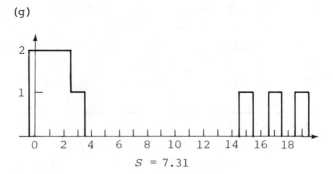

$S = 7.31$

(h)

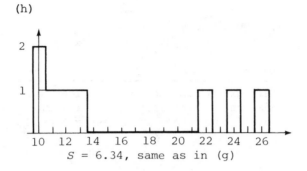

$S = 6.34$, same as in (g)

5. (a) Mn = 3. $S = 1.63$, both ways

    (b) Start with Mn = $(1/3)(a + b + c)$.

    (c) Essentially copy what you did for (b).

Page 287   1. (a) Toogy   (b) Tiggy's, thus upsetting Tiggy into erratic behavior on spelling tests.

2. (a) Tigville   (b) Tigville   (c) No; mathematics makes life rich, finances quite aside.

3. (a) Bo   (b) Moe (51 minutes is within one standard deviation of his mean, but not within one standard deviation of Bo's mean).

Pages   1. Results will vary with the experimenter.
293 - 296 2. (a) ½ (b) ¼ (c) ½ (d) 1/8 (e) 3/8 (f) 3/8
               (g) 1/2 (h) 1/3 (i) 1/6 (j) 1 (k) 0 (l) 1/6
               (m) 2/3 (n) 1/3 (o) 1/2 (p) 0 (q) 1/36 (r) 1/16
               (s) 1/18 (t) 5/9 (u) 3/13 (v) 1/4 (w) 1/2
               (x) 25/51 (y) 1/17 (z) 15/34

3. (a) 1/365 (b) 364/365 (c) 1

4. (a) $(1/365)^2 = 1/133,225$ (b) $3(1/365 \cdot 364/365) = 1092/133/225$ (c) $364/365 \cdot 363/365 = 132,132/133,225$ (d) 1

5. (g) 4/9 (h) 4/9 (i) 1/4 (j) 1 (k) 0 (l) 2/9
(m) 7/9 (n) 1/3 (o) 4/9

6. (g) 5/12 (h) 5/12 (i) 1/12 (j) 1 (k) 0 (l) 1/12
(m) 5/6 (n) 7/12 (o) 2/3

7. (a) 12/17 (b) 4/17 (c) 1/17 (d) 16/17 (e) 16/17

Page 299 1. (a) 1 to 100 (b) 1/101 (c) 100/101

2. (a) 5 to 8 (b) 8/13 (c) 5/13

3. (a) 40% = 2/5 (b) 3/5 (c) 3 to 2 (d) 2 to 3

4. 43 to 57

5. 7/8

6. (a) 1 to 1 (b) 1/2

Pages   7. This graph has its lowest values when the normal curve
302 - 303   has its highest values, and its highest values when the
normal curve has its lowest values.

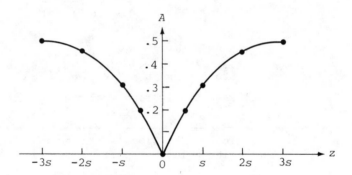

8.

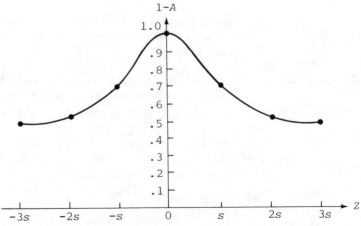

Looks like a normal curve floating .5 units above the
z-axis.

9. For baseball fans only

1. Because the histogram is symmetric about $x = 5$.

2. (a) -2.88 (b) -.63 (c) .63 (d) 2.88 (e) 5.00 (f) 12.50

3. A raw score that is as far below the mean as another raw score is above has the negative of the standard score of the higher raw score.

4. (a) -1.40 (b) -.20 (c) .40 (d) 2.20 (e) 3.00

5. Only in a punnitive (*sic*) situation.

6. (a) -2.00 (b) -1.00 (c) 0.00 (d) 1.00 (e) 2.00

1. (a) .68 (b) .95 (c) 1.00 (rounded off to the nearest hundredth) (d) .82 (e) .02 (f) .05 (g) .45 (h) .23 (i) 0.

2. (a) .68 (b) .07 (c) .01 (d) .87 (e) .05

3. (a) Approximately 430 to 570 (b) 630 to 800 (c) 0 to 430

4.

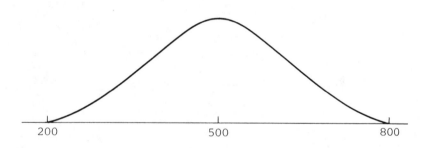

1. 1/2
2. 63/64
3. 57/64
4. .999 . . .
5. 1/2
6. 7/12
7. 149/216
8. 35/36
9. 3/4
10. 9/13
11. 10/13

12. 10/13

13. $1 - \dfrac{364 \times 363 \times 362 \times 361}{(365)^4} \doteq .023$

Page 314 1. Can start anywhere, and each drawing ends at the point at which it was started.

2. Can be drawn with a single stroke. Must start at either the upper side of the left-hand ear or at the left-hand base of the right-hand ear, and then end at either the right-hand ear or the left-hand ear, respectively.

Page 317 1. (a)

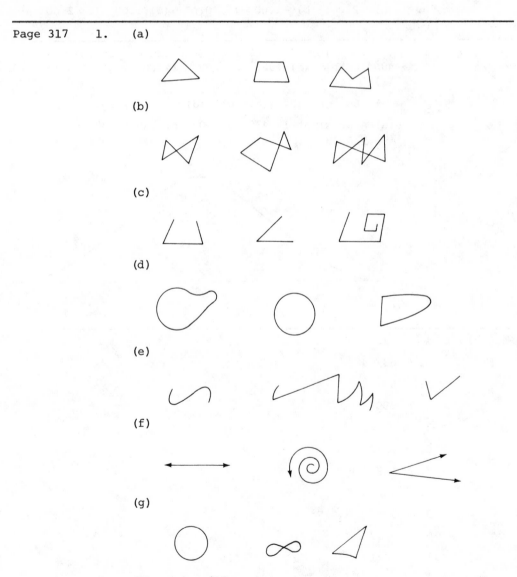

(b)

(c)

(d)

(e)

(f)

(g)

(h) Impossible

2. A: Not closed, not simple, linear
B: Closed, not simple, not linear
C: Not closed, simple, not linear
D: Closed, simple, not linear
E: Not closed, not simple, linear
F: Not closed, not simple, linear
G: Not closed, simple, not linear
H: Not closed, not simple, linear
I: Not closed, simple, linear
J: Not closed, simple, not linear
K: Not closed, not simple, linear
L: Not closed, simple, linear
M: Not closed, simple, linear
N: Not closed, simple, linear
O: Closed, simple, not linear
P: Not closed, not simple, not linear
Q: Not closed, not simple, not linear
R: Not closed, not simple, not linear
S: Not closed, simple, not linear
T: Not closed, not simple, linear
U: Not closed, simple, not linear
V: Not closed, simple, linear
W: Not closed, simple, linear
X: Not closed, not simple, linear
Y: Not closed, not simple, linear
Z: Not closed, simple, linear

Pages
319 - 320

1. (a) No (b) Yes (c) Yes (d) Yes (e) Yes (f) Yes
(g) No (h) Yes (i) Yes (j) Yes (k) Yes (l) Yes
(m) Yes (n) Yes (o) Yes (p) No (q) Yes (r) Yes
(s) Yes (t) Yes (u) Yes (v) No (w) No (x) No

2. (b) Any (c) Any (d) Lower left or right (e) Any
(f) Second from bottom at left or right (h) Top or
lower middle (i) Left or right (j) Any (k) Bottom
inner left or right (l) Any (m) Any (n) Any (o) Any
(q) Top or middle of right ear (r) Top of left or
right ear (s) Any (t) Either end of drooping eyelid
(u) Left or right

Pages
321 - 322

1. (a) 4 (b) 0 (c) 0 (d) 2 (e) 0 (f) 2 (g) 4 (h) 2
(i) 2 (j) 0 (k) 2 (l) 0 (m) 0 (n) 0 (o) 0 (p) 4
(q) 2 (r) 2 (s) 0 (t) 2 (u) 2 (v) 6 (w) 4 (x) 12

2. (a) Always (b) Never

3. (a) Never (remember that a vertex which is both a start
and a finish is called a through vertex).

(b) Always

4. (a) 2 (b) No maximum: as many as we please

5. (a) Any (b) At the same vertices at which we began
our stroke

6. Count the number of odd vertices; if it is 0 or 2, the network is traversable; otherwise, it is not.

7. Begin at the inner side of one ear and end at the inner side of the other ear.

8. We bet he or she does.

Pages 325 - 327

1. (a) 6 (b) 8 (c) 10 (d) $2(n + 2)$

2. (a) 2 (b) 4 (c) 6 (d) 8 (e) $2n$

3. (a) 3 (b) 6 (c) 10 (d) 15 (e) $1 + 2 + 3 + 4 + \cdots + (n - 1)$

4. (a) 2 (b) 2 (c) 4 (d) 6 (e) $2(n - 1)$

5. (a) 1 (b) 2 (c) 3 (d) 4 (e) n infinite edges

6. (a) 1 (b) 2 (c) 3 (d) 4 (e) n finite edges

7. (a) 1 (b) 2 (c) 3 (d) 4 (e) $(n - 1)$

8. (a) 1 (b) 2 (c) 3 (d) 4 (e) $(n - 2)$

9. $n - (m - 2) = n - m + 2$

11. (a) 1 (b) 3 (c) 6 (d) 10 (e) $1 + 2 + 3 + 4 + \cdots + (n - 1)$

Pages 330 - 331

1. (a) 15 cm (b) 1 m, 3 cm
   (c) 11 cm (d) 31 cm

2. (a) 82.4 cm

3. 32 cm

4. (a) 32, if we continue adding forever.
   (b) It's half.

Page 332

2.

English Unit	cm	m	km
1 in.	2.54	.0254	.0000254
1 ft.	30.48	.3048	.0003048
1 yd.	91.44	.9144	.0009144
1 mi.	160,934.40	1609.3440	1.609344

3.

Metric Unit	in.	ft.	yd.	mi.
1 cm	.39	.0328	.0109	.0000062
1 m	39.37	3.28	1.097	.0006212
1 km	39,370.	3281.0	1093.	.6212

4.   33 cm

5.   2 m 72 cm

6.   (a) 4,920 ft.   (b) 1,641 yd.   (c) .93 mi.

Pages
334 - 335

1.   (a)   (b)

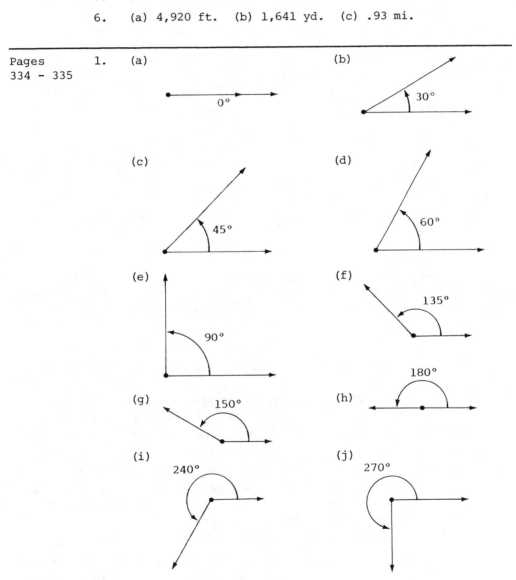

(c)

(d)

(e)

(f)

(g)

(h)

(i)

(j)

(k)

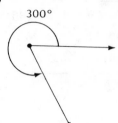

300°

(l)

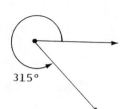

315°

(m)

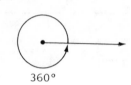

360°

(n)

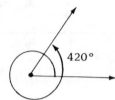

420°

(o)

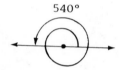

540°

(p)

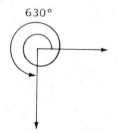

630°

(q)

750°

2. $128 = 2^7 = 2 \times 2 \times 2 \times 2 \times 2 \times 2 \times 2$. Therefore $128 \times (\frac{1}{2})^7 = 1$.

3. (a) No (b) No (c) Yes (d) No (e) No (f) Yes
    (g) No (h) Yes (i) Their measures are all powers of 2.

4. (a) Yes (b) No (c) No (d) No (e) Yes (f) No
    (g) If $n = 3 \times 2^k$, for some counting number k

5. (e) A line perpendicular to an angle bisector of two lines also bisects the supplementary angles formed by these two lines.

6. (a) 3 (b) 10 (c) 36 (d) 136 (e) $2^{n-1}(2^n + 1)$

7. (a) Rays emanating from the vertex of the angle forming three angles of one-third the measure of the original angle.

1. (a) Here's one:

    (b) (i) No

        (ii) No

        (iii) Yes

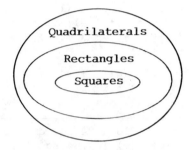

2.

3. (a)

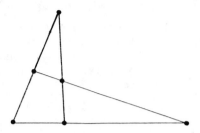

    (b) The set of parallelograms, say

4. (b), (c) If a rectangle is folded in two and forms
    a similar rectangle, then that similar rectangle when
    folded in two will form another similar rectangle.

5. $x/y = \sqrt{2}/1$.

6. (b) The lengths of the two diagonals are the same.

    (c) Here's one:

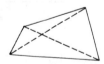

7. (b) The diagonals bisect each other.

    (c) For example:

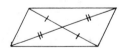

Pages
341 - 342

1. (a) 9 (b) 36 (c) 100 (d) $(1 + 2 + 3 + \cdots + n)^2$

2. (a) 68 (b) 136 (c) 208

3. $(3n - 2)n + (3n - 5)(n - 1) + (3n - 8)(n - 2) + \cdots$
    $+ (n - 2)3n + (n - 5)(3n - 1) + (n - 8)(3n - 2) +$
    $\cdots$, where no negative terms are counted (for exam-
    ple, for $n < 5$, no term beyond $(n - 2)3n$ would be
    counted).

4. $(3n - 2)(2n - 1) + (3n - 5)(2n - 3) + (3n - 8)(2n - 5)$
    $+ \cdots + (2n - 2)(3n - 1) + (2n - 5)(3n - 3) +$
    $(2n - 8)(3n - 5) + \cdots$, where no negative terms are
    counted.

5. $1^2 + 2^2 + 3^2 + \cdots + (3n)^2$

6. (a) 1 (b) $1 + 2 = 3$ (c) $1 + 2 + 3 = 6$
    (d) $1 + 2 + 3 + 4 = 10$ (e) $1 + 2 + 3 + 4 + 5 = 15$
    (f) $1 + 2 + 3 + \cdots + n$

7. If n is odd, $1 + (1 + 2 + 3) + (1 + 2 + 3 + 4 + 5) +$
    $\cdots + (1 + 2 + 3 + \cdots + n)$; if n is even, $(1 + 2)$
    $+ (1 + 2 + 3 + 4) + (1 + 2 + 3 + 4 + 5 + 6) + \cdots +$
    $(1 + 2 + 3 + \cdots + n)$

8. (a) 5 (b) 13 (c) 25 (d) $1 + 4(1 + 2 + 3 + \cdots +$
    $(n - 1))$

Pages
344 - 346

1. (a) 32.55 sq. in. (b) 1354.84 sq. cm (c) .1355 sq. m
    (d) 15499.97 sq. in. (e) 107.64 sq. ft. (f) 10.37
    acres (g) .96 acres (h) 15.54 sq. km (i) 2.32 sq. mi.

2.

English Unit	sq. cm	sq. m	sq km
1 sq. in.	6.45	.000645	.000000000645
1 sq. ft.	928.8	.09288	.0000000988
1 sq. yd.	8,359.2	.83592	.00000083592
1 sq. mi.	25,899,000,000.	2,589,900.	2.5899
1 acre	40,467,240.	4,046.7240	.0040467240

3.

Metric Unit	sq. in.	sq. ft.	sq. yd.	sq. mi.
1 sq. cm	.155	.0010764	.0001196	.0000000003861
1 sq. m	1,550.	10.764	1.196	.000003861
1 sq. km	1,550,000,000.	10,764,000.	1,196,000.	.3861
1 acre	6,272,640.	43,560.	4,840.	.00156

4. Chart 2; it has more metric entries and therefore more
    answers that can be got by merely moving the decimal
    point.

5. (a) 64 (b) 65 (c) We can't.

6.

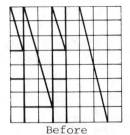

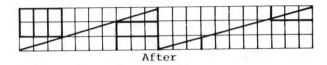

Before

After

7.　(a) 53 sq. cm　(b) 20 sq. cm　(c) 34 sq. cm

8.　(a) $2 = 1 \times 2$　(b) $\frac{1}{2}(1 \times 2)$　(c) $6 = 2 \times 3$
(d) $\frac{1}{2}(2 \times 3)$　(e) $12 = 3 \times 4$　(f) $\frac{1}{2}(3 \times 4)$
(g) $20 = 4 \times 5$　(h) $\frac{1}{2}(4 \times 5)$　(i) $1, 1 + 2, 1 + 2 + 3,$
$1 + 2 + 3 + 4$　(j) An n-by-$(n + 1)$ rectangle
(k) $\frac{1}{2}n(n + 1)$

Pages
348 - 349

1.　(a) False　(b) False　(c) True　(d) False　(e) True
(f) False　(g) False　(h) True　(i) False　(j) False
(k) True　(l) False　(m) False　(n) True　(o) True
(p) False　(q) False　(r) True

2.　Should be "right triangle" instead of "isosceles tri-angle."

3.

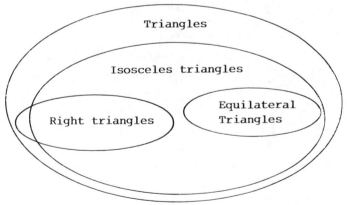

Pages
350 - 351

1.　(a) $1 + 2 + 3 + \cdots + n = \frac{1}{2}n(n + 1)$

(b) $1 + 2 + \cdots + (n - 1) = \frac{1}{2}n(n - 1)$

2. None

3.

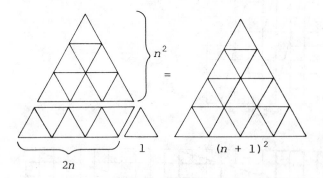

4. 48 triangles altogether

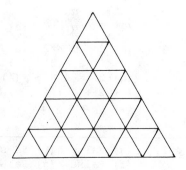

5. $1 + 2 + 3 + \cdot \cdot \cdot \cdot + (n + 1) = \frac{1}{2}(n + 1)(n + 2)$

6. (a)

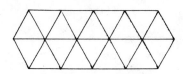

(b) $2 + 4n$ (c) $6n$ (d) $6n$ (e) $6n$ (f) 0 (g) $4 + 3n$

7. (a)

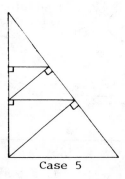
Case 5

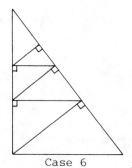
Case 6

(b) 3 (c) 5 (d) $2n - 1$ (e) $2n - 1$

8. (a)

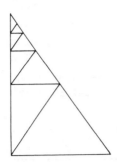

(b) 1 (c) 2 (d) n (e) n (f) If you don't take this as a joke, and consider "wrong" = "not right," then there are $2n$ wrong triangles.

Pages
352 - 353

1. 180° every time

2. (a) Same (b) Same (c) 180° (d) 180°

3. 180°

4. (a) Impossible—insufficient information (b) 45°, 45°, 90°, (c) 60°, 60°, 60°, (d) 30°, 60°, 90° (e) 30°, 30°, 120° (f) Impossible

5. 360°

6. (a)

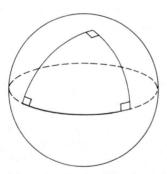

(b) There is no attainable minimum, but we can get as close to 180° as we desire (from above: 180.1° or 180.01°, etc.).

(c) The unattainable maximum is 540°.

Page 355

1. 60

2. 30

3. 5.

4. 21/2

5. 9/2

6. 9/2

Pages 356 - 357

1. 1: 5 II: 14 III: 21/2 IV: 21/2 V: 14 VI: 5

2. (a) Below (b) 24/5 cm (c) 24/5 sq. cm (d) 36/5 cm
   (e) 54/5 sq. cm (f) Add them and see if the sum is
   30 sq. cm.

3. (a) True (b) True (c) True (d) False

Pages 360 - 361

1. (a) 19 (b) 27/2 (c) 18

2. (a) Triangle (b) Yes: $h \times \frac{1}{2}(b + 0) = \frac{1}{2}bh$

3. The area of the rectangle = $h(b_1 + b_2)$ = twice the area
   of the trapezoid. Hence the area of the trapezoid is
   $\frac{1}{2}h(b_1 + b_2)$.

4. The area of the trapezoid = $\frac{1}{2}(h + y)b_2 - \frac{1}{2}yb_1 = \frac{1}{2}hb_2$
   $+ \frac{1}{2}y(b_2 - b_1)$. But $y = hb_1/(b_2 - b_1)$ (prove this!).
   Hence the area of the trapezoid = $\frac{1}{2}hb_2 + \frac{1}{2}hb_1 = $
   $\frac{1}{2}h(b_1 + b_2)$.

5. The area of triangle A_1 is $\frac{1}{2}hb_1$, and the area of
   triangle A_2 is $\frac{1}{2}hb_2$. So the total area is
   $\frac{1}{2}hb_1 + \frac{1}{2}hb_2 = \frac{1}{2}h(b_1 + b_2)$.

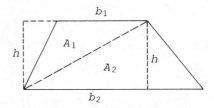

6. See the example in the text, Exercise 3, or even better, consult your own imagination.

Pages 361 - 362

1. (a) The sum of the measures of the angles of a triangle
   is 180°

   (b) We multiply both sides of the equation by 2.

(c) How about

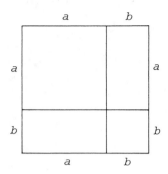

You could also just multiply out $(a + b)(a + b)$.

2. $c^2 = (x + y)(x + y) = (ab/h)(x + y)$, since $ab = hx + hy$ (why?). But $(ab/h)(x + y) = (ab/h)(ah/b + bh/a)$ (why?) $= a^2 + b^2$ (why?).

Pages
364 – 367

1. (a) $\sqrt{2}$ (b) $2\sqrt{2}$ (c) $3\sqrt{2}$ (d) $a\sqrt{2}$ (e) 3 (f) 6 (g) 15
    (h) $5a$ (i) $3a$ (j) 4, $2\sqrt{3}$ (k) 3 (l) $\sqrt{4/3}$

2. (a) $5 = 2^2 + 1$ (b) $10 = 3^2 + 1$ (c) $17 = 4^2 + 1$
    (d) $26 = 5^2 + 1$ (e) $x^2 + 1$ (f) $x^2 + 4$ (g) $x^2 + 9$
    (h) $x^2 + 16$ (i) $x^2 + y^2$

3. (a) $3\sqrt{2}/2$ (b) $\sqrt{5}$ (c) $3/2$ (d) $3\sqrt{3}/2$

4. 260 cm

5. (a) $\sqrt{2}$ (b) $\sqrt{5}$ (c) $2\sqrt{2} = \sqrt{8}$ (d) $\sqrt{13}$ (e) $3\sqrt{2} = \sqrt{18}$
    (f) $5 = \sqrt{25}$ (g) $4\sqrt{2} = \sqrt{32}$ (h) $(\frac{1}{2})(n + 1)\sqrt{2}$
    (i) $\sqrt{(n/2)^2 + (n/2 + 1)^2}$

6. (a) $(\frac{1}{2})(1 + 2 + 3 + \cdots + (n + 1)/2)$
    $= (1/16)(n + 1)(n + 3)$

    (b) $(\frac{1}{2})(1 + 2 + 3 + \cdots + n/2) = (1/16)n(n + 2)$

Pages
369 – 370

1. Here are the shapes:

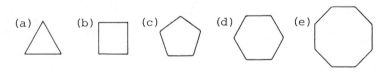

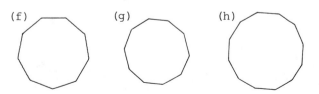

2. No; the angles are not all equal in measure, unless the rhombus happens to be a square.

3. (a) Impossible   (b)   (c)

    (d)   (e)

4. (a) Impossible   (b)   (c)

    (d)   (e)

   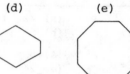

5. (a) 8/3 (b) 5 (c) 3 (d) 2.1 (e) 2.8 (f) 4.9
    (g) 2.1 (h) 4.2

6. (a)   (b)

    (c)   (d)

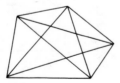   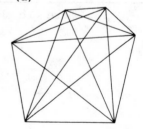

(e)

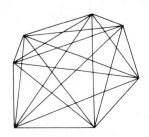

7. (a) 9 (b) 6 (c) 14 (d) 12 (e) 15

8. (a) Impossible   (b)

(c)   (d)

(e)

Pages   1. (a) $\frac{1}{2}(5)(5 + 1) = 15$ (b) $\frac{1}{2}(100)(101) = 5050$
372 - 373   (c) 499,500 (d) $\frac{1}{2}n(n + 1)$ (e) $n(n + 1) - 6 =$
                $(n + 3)(n - 2)$ (f) $\frac{1}{2}(3n + 6)(n - 1)$

2. "*Ligget se'.*"

3. At least 153

4. At least 101

5. (a) 1 (b) 5 (c) 13 (d) 35

6. (a) 180° (b) 360° (c) 540° (d) 720° (e) 900°
    (f) 180°$(n - 2)$

Pages   1. (a) Equilateral (b) Isosceles (c) Equilateral--only
377 - 378   one possibility (d) Impossible (e) Square (f) Regu-
                lar pentagon (g) Regular pentagon (h) Regular hexagon
                (i) Regular heptagon (j) Regular octagon (k) Square

(l) Square (m) Equilateral triangle (n) 10-by-2 rectangle—only possibility (o) 4-by-5-by-5-by-5-by-5 pentagon

2. (a) $\frac{1}{4}\sqrt{3}$ (b) .4

4. (a) $3\sqrt{3}/2$ (b) 2.6

6. (a) $2 + 2\sqrt{2}$ (b) 4.8

7. (a) $5/2\sqrt{2} + 2\sqrt{5}$ (b) 6.4

8. (a) 1.7 sq. in.   (b) 4.3 sq. cm   (c) 15.6 sq. cm
   (d) Impossible   (e) 25 sq. cm   (f) 27.5 sq. cm
   (g) 27.5 sq. cm   (h) 65.0 sq. cm   (i) 58.1 sq. cm
   (j) 120.7 sq. cm   (k) 100.0 sq. cm   (l) 100.0 sq. cm
   (m) 1.7 sq. cm   (n) 20.0 sq. cm   (o) 38.1 sq. cm

Pages 381 - 382

2. With the string drawn taut, the pencil is always the same distance from the tack.

3. (a) 2^{n-1} (b) 2^{n+1} (c) 2^{n+2} (d) $1/2^{n-1}$

   (e) $6.4/2^{n-1} = 1/(10(2^{n-7}))$

   (f) First, there is the whole circle; then there are twice the number of distinct pairs of vertices on the circle; that is, $2 \times (7 + 6 + 5 + 4 + 3 + 2 + 1) = 7 \times 8 = 56$ (where do the 7, 6, 5, etc. come from?).

   (g) $2^{n-2}(2^{n-1} - 1)$ (h) 2^{n+1} (all diameters)

   (i) $7(2^{n+2})$ (j) none

4. (a) n (b) $\frac{1}{2}n(n - 1) = 1 + 2 + \cdots + (n - 1)$

5. $\frac{1}{2}n(n - 1)$

6. And if the tenants hit several of these emissaries on the head, they'd be turning the knights into daze.

Pages 383 - 384

1. (c) Should get close to 3.14 each time

2. (a) 3.14286   (b) It's a little bit more.   (c) 3.14085
   (d) It's a little bit less.

4. $s^2 + s^2 = d^2$, by the Pythagorean Theorem.   Etc.

5. All of the triangles are equilateral.

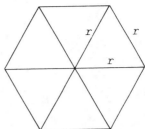

6. (a) $s/\sqrt{2} = s\sqrt{2}/2$ (b) $s + s\sqrt{2}$ (c) $s\sqrt{4 + 2\sqrt{2}}$

7. $\pi \doteq \dfrac{8s}{s\sqrt{4 + 2\sqrt{2}}} = \dfrac{8\sqrt{4 + 2\sqrt{2}}}{4 + 2\sqrt{2}} = \dfrac{8\sqrt{4 + 2\sqrt{2}}(4 - 2\sqrt{2})}{4^2 - (2\sqrt{2})^2}$

$= \sqrt{4 + 2\sqrt{2}}(4 - 2\sqrt{2}) \doteq 3.063$

8. (a) 36° (b) 36° (c) 72°

    (d) Because two angles of the smallest triangle both have measures 72°

    (e) Because α and β are both of measure 36°

    (f) Corresponding ratios of similar triangles

    (g) $r = \frac{1}{2}s(1 + \sqrt{5})$ (h) $\pi \doteq 10s/2r \doteq 3.0917$

Page 386 2. (a) 1.84 (b) 1.14 (c) .54 (d) .38

3. A is measured in sq. units (got from r^2) while C is measured in linear units (e.g., r cm).

Pages 388 - 389

1. (a) 28.27 sq. cm (b) 254.45 sq. cm (c) 2290.12 sq. cm (d) .35 sq. cm (e) .04 sq. cm

2. (a) 3.14 sq. in. (b) 12.57 sq. in. (c) 201.06 sq. in. (d) 51471.5 sq. in.

3. (a) $8\pi/3$ (b) 4π (c) 6π (d) 12π (e) $40\pi/3$

4. (a) $8\pi/3 - 4\sqrt{3}$ (b) $4\pi - 8$ (c) $6\pi - 4\sqrt{2}$ (d) $12\pi + 8$ (e) $40\pi/3 + 11\sqrt{3}$

5. (a) $\pi/12$ (b) $\pi/6$ (c) $\pi/4$ (d) $\pi n/12$ (mod π) (e) $\pi/12 - 1/4$ (f) $\pi/6 - \sqrt{3}/4$ (g) $\pi/2$ (h) $\pi/2$ if n is odd, π if n is even (i) $\pi - (5\pi/12 - 1/4) = 7\pi/12 + 1/4$ (j) $7\pi/12 + 1/4$ if n is odd, $\pi/12 - 1/4$ if n is even

6. (a) 1/4 (b) 1/16 (c) 1/64 (d) $(1/4)^k$

Pages
390 - 391

1.

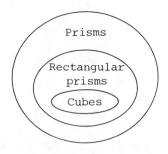

2.   (a)

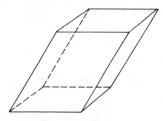

(b)

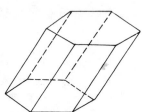

(c)

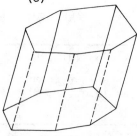

3.   (a) 6   (b) 12   (c) 20   (d) 30   (e) $n(n - 1)$

4.   (a) None   (b) 4   (c) 10   (d) 18   (e) $n(n - 3) + 2n$
      $= n(n - 1)$

5.   (a) Right   (b) $\sqrt{2}$ (c) $\sqrt{3}$ (d) $2 = \sqrt{4}$ (e) $\sqrt{n}$
      (f) Good luck!

6. 12.6 m^3

Pages
392 - 393

1.   (a) 400 cm^3 (b) 4700 cm^3 (c) $253,000 \text{ cm}^3$

2.   (a) $(98)^3 = 941,192$ (b) $6(98)^3 = 57,624$
      (c) $12 \times 98 = 1176$ (d) 8   (e) 0   (f) 0   (g) 0

3.   (a) 1   (b) 6   (c) 8   (d) 11   (e) 3   (f) 1   (g) 0

4.   (a) 1   (b) $1 + 4 = 5$ (c) $1 + 4 + 9 = 14$ (d) 30
      (e) 55   (f) $1^2 + 2^2 + 3^2 + \cdots + n^2$

5.   61.64 cubic cubits

Pages
396 - 397

1. Yes: (a)(c)—all faces bounded by a single polygon
   No: (b)—two "ring-shaped" faces;
       (d)—not all faces are planar.

10.

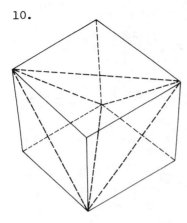

Page 398

2.

V	-e	+f	=
4	6	4	2
8	12	6	2
6	12	8	2
20	30	12	2
12	30	20	2

3. A convex polyhedron is a polyhedron such that if we select any two points on it or in its interior, then the line segment joining them lies entirely within the polyhedron.

4. The top two—the triangular pyramid and the truncated square pyramid.

5. Put in a tunnel or two.

Page 400

1.

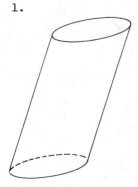

2.

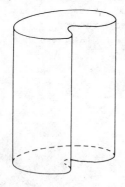

3.

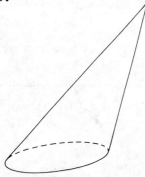

4.   (a)   (b)

         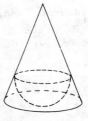

5.   (a)   (b)

         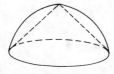

INDEX

*Italicized numbers indicate that the page includes the term definition.